Anthropology and Human Rights

Challenges and Opportunities in the New Millennium

Edited by

Buddhadeb Chaudhuri
Subir Biswas

RAWAT PUBLICATIONS
Jaipur • New Delhi • Bangalore • Guwahati • Kolkata

ISBN 978-81-316-0838-8

Published by
Prem Rawat for **Rawat Publications**
Satyam Apts, Sector 3, Jawahar Nagar, Jaipur 302 004 (India)
Phone: 0141 265 1748 / 7006 Fax: 0141 265 1748
E-mail: info@rawatbooks.com
Website: www.rawatbooks.com

New Delhi Office
4858/24, Ansari Road, Daryaganj, New Delhi 110 002
Phone: 011 2326 3290

Also at *Bangalore, Guwahati* and *Kolkata*

Typeset by Rawat Computers, Jaipur
Printed at Chaman Enterprises, New Delhi

Contents

Preface

Preface

The International Union of Anthropological and Ethnological Sciences (IUAES) is the highest body at the global level that concerns itself with all types of anthropological studies. There are several Commissions under IUAES that deal with the study, research, conferences and publications on different issues. The present edition is an outcome of an international conference organized by the Commission on Human Rights and Commission on Urban Anthropology and the Department of Anthropology, West Bengal State University in collaboration with the Anthropological Survey of India, the Indira Gandhi Rashtriya Manav Sangrahalaya, the Indian Council of Social Science Research, the Indian Council of Medical Research, Indian Museum and Centre for Alternative Research in Development. This successful international conference was held in Kolkata, India. We received 124 papers from our valued participants from Bangladesh, Chile, Canada, Greece, Mexico, Nepal, Turkey, UK, USA, and different parts of India. The theme of the conference was 'Mega Urbanization and Human Rights: Emerging Challenges and Opportunities'. Irrespective of geographical regions and political boundaries, the papers addressed many contemporary topical issues concerning the problems of mankind today and we are publishing a few of these papers in the field of Human Rights and Anthropology.

II

The editors record with appreciation, the support received from Indira Gandhi Rashtriya Manav Sangrahalaya, Anthropological Survey of India, Indian Council of Social Science Research, Indian Council of Medical Research, Indian Museum and Centre for Alternative Research in Development. It was possible to organize the conference successfully only through the active support of students and faculty members of Department of Anthropology, West Bengal State University and members of Centre for Alternative Research in Development. We are grateful to Professor Ashoke Ranjan Thakur, the then Honourable Vice-Chancellor of the University, for his keen interest, kind guidance, financial support, as well as active participation. We are also grateful to Professor Asis Kumar Banerjee, former Vice-Chancellor, Calcutta

University for delivering the valedictory address and his keen interest and kind guidance. We are thankful to all the delegates from various parts of the world for their active participation. Special thanks are due to Dr Sumita Chaudhuri, Co-Convener of the conference for her valuable help and contribution to organize the conference and editing the first volume, *Facets of Urbanization*, published from UK. The second volume, *Anthropology and Health Issues* has already been published by Rawat Publications. Finally we are also sincerely grateful to Rawat Publications for taking the responsibility to publish this volume, *Anthropology and Human Rights* containing twenty-five articles covering different issues and problems.

Buddhadeb Chaudhuri
Subir Biswas

Contributors

Abhijit Ghosal, Assistant Professor in Anthropology, Subarnarekha Mahavidyalaya, Gopiballavpur, District Paschim Medinipur, West Bengal. E-mail: anth.abhijit @gmail.com

Arunkumar, A.S., M.Phil Scholar, Department of Anthropology, Pondicherry University, Puducherry. E-mail: akred04@gmail.com

Binita Basu, Assistant Professor, Department of Anthropology, Govt. General Dagree College, Singur, West Bengal. E-mail: binita_2006@sify.com

Biswanath Gan, Cultural Research Officer, Cultural Research Institute, Kolkata, West Bengal. E-mail: biswanath_gan@rediffmail.com

Buddhadeb Chaudhuri is Chairperson of the IUAES Commission on Human Rights; Founder-Coordinator, Human Rights Programme of the Calcutta University and former Dr Ambedkar Chair Professor in Anthropology, University of Calcutta, Kolkata, India. He was also former Professor, S&S.E. Asian Studies, Calcutta University. E-mail: buddhadebc@gmail.com

Clarence J. Dias is President of the International Center for Law in Development, New York, Guest Visiting Professor to the Masters Degree Human Rights Program, Department of Anthropology, Calcutta University, Kolkata. E-mail: dias_clarence@yahoo.com

Dipak K. Midya, Professor in Anthropology, Vidyasagar University, Midnapore, West Bengal. E-mail: dipakmidya@rediffmail.com

Homprabha Biswas, Junior Research Fellow (UGC-NET), Department of Anthropology, University of Calcutta, Kolkata. E-mail: homprabha19@gmail.com

Jesurathnam Devarapalli, Assistant Professor, Department of Anthropology, Pondicherry University, Puducherry. E-mail: drjesudev@gmail.com

Jhilam Rudra De, Assistant Professor, NSHM College of Management and Technology, Kolkata. E-mail: rudrajhilam@rediffmail.com

José G. Vargas-Hernandez, University Centre for Economic and Managerial Sciences, Universidad de Guadalajara, México. E-mail: josevargas@cucea. udg.mx

Laura R. Valladares de la Cruz, Department of Anthropology, Universidad Autónoma Metropolitana-Iztapalapa, Uam-Iztapalapa, Mexico. E-mail: Lauravalladares.delacruz@gmail.com

Milka Castro Lucic, Director, Juridical Anthropology Program, Faculty of Law, University of Chile, Chile. E-mail: milka.castrolucic@gmail.com

Muhammed Shamsuddin, Human Rights Activist, Secretary General, Human Rights Lawyers Society-HRLS, Dhaka, Bangladesh. E-mail: advmsuddin@yahoo.com

Pinak Tarafdar, Assistant Professor, Department of Anthropology, University of North Bengal, Darjeeling, West Bengal. E-mail: pinak_anth@rediffmail.com

Rajesh Kumar Sharma, Head, Department of Sociology, Government P.G. College, Dholpur. E-mail: drrajeshdlp66@gmail.com

Samar Kumar Biswas, Associate Professor, Department of Anthropology, University of North Bengal, Darjeeling, West Bengal. E-mail: smrkbis@yahoo.co.in

Samik Roy, Researcher, West Bengal Legislative Assembly Secretariat, Assembly House, Kolkata. E-mail: samikking@yahoo.com

Sanjoy Roy, Associate Professor, Department of Social Work, University of Delhi, Delhi. E-mail: sanjoyroy30@gmail.com

Sarah Rogers, 9704 Tay Circle, Knoxville, TN 37922, USA. E-mail: sgrogers@memphis.edu

Saumitra Basu, Post Doctoral Research Associate, Indian National Science Academy, New Delhi. E-mail: bsoumitra2001@gmail.com

Somenath Bhattacharjee, Assistant Professor, Department of Anthropology, Assam University, Diphu, Assam. E-mail: bhattacharjee_somenath@rediffmail.com

Subha Ray, Professor, Department of Anthropology, University of Calcutta, Kolkata. E-mail: subharay@rediffmail.com

Subhankar Roy, Senior Research Fellow, Department of Anthropology, University of North Bengal, Darjeeling, West Bengal. E-mail: subhankar.anth@gmail.com

Swapna Bhattacharya (Chakraborti), Professor, Department of South & Southeast Asian Studies, University of Calcutta, Alipur Campus, Kolkata. E-mail: swapna.caluni@gmail.com

Swati Chakraborty, Consultant, National Human Rights Commission, New Delhi. E-mail: swatichakraborty02@gmail.com

Tilottam Paudel, Jagriti Child and Youth Concern Nepal, Kathmandu, Nepal. E-mail: jcycnepal@hotmail.com

Victoria Chenaut, CIESAS-Gulf, Mexico. E-mail: vchenaut@prodigy.net.mx

Introduction

Human Rights were evolved and developed mainly on the basis of certain European secular thoughts. It includes certain basic rights such as the right of free speech, right to a fair trial, right of an ordinary citizen against the arbitrariness of power and scope of individual participation in public decision-making and accountability of the state or authority to the public. Human rights are clearly defined and understood both at local and international level and have legal implications. It is clearly defined in the United Nation's Universal Declaration of Human Rights.

Human Rights concept is a dynamic one which will find expanded expression and constantly cover new areas as human society continues to evolve to higher levels of development. The original content of philosophy of fundamental freedom was limited in the main to civil and political rights of the individual, often referred to as "first generation" rights. The expansive nature of the concept of human rights clubbed with the realization that without guaranteeing economic, social and cultural rights, full enjoyment of civil and political rights was not possible led to the inclusion of economic, social and cultural rights, popularly described as "second generation" rights.

The concept of human rights in its expanding comprehension, has now travelled to encompass what are called "third generation" rights which include right to self determination, right regarded as belonging to peoples rather than individuals, right to sovereignty over natural wealth and resources of the country and right to development as well as rights of disadvantaged groups to special protection. Thus the road travelled by human rights movement has been historic and impressive.

The issue of Human Rights is inherent and universal, but we have been witnessing severe violation of human rights which take various expressions ranging from deprivation of basic needs and discrimination against women, children, Dalit, tribal, ethnic, linguistic and other minorities. These have resulted in conflict, insurgency and general resistiveness of the people resulting in their eviction, migration and untold sufferings.

Most of the countries in the world have experienced colonial rule, military, autocratic and chauvinistic majority regimes. In these systems, political repression takes the form of arbitrary arrest, detention, torture, disappearances, summary execution and extra judicial killings. In such setting, human rights issues and concerns have been too sensitive topics for public discourse.

On the other hand, global political and economic regimes and dominant development model in this era of globalization have resulted in the massive depletion of natural resources and exploitation of human labour leading to further marginalization and impoverishment of the people.

Recent changes in global politics, however, have ushered in changes creating more democratic space that makes favourable for people's movements, NGO's, civil society and people's alliances to engage in human rights protection and promotional work. Some of the governments have also established Human Rights Commission. These agencies are faced with numerous challenges that include changing the perception and attitudes; how to bring about reform in the bureaucracy and legal system; and democratization of institutions and governance through genuine people participation and empowerment. To meet these challenges there is a growing need to develop human resources for establishment of a truly democratic, just and peaceful society.

The place of Anthropology in the social science discipline is quite distinct and very relevant in the context of human rights. Anthropology is one of the few disciplines primarily based on empirical studies mainly at the micro-level. The methodology is more suitable for conducting studies among the peasants, indigenous population, rural societies or other small groups where human rights violation is more common. Since observation or participant observation is the main technique of data collection, the studies are made on the basis of intimate relation and understanding of the people.

Human rights are often examined only within the scope of law. It is true that legal provisions are essential to claim any right, including human rights, but perhaps mere legal provisions are not enough to understand, protect and promote human rights in most societies. Even though the general framework, philosophy and perception of human rights should be universal, the crucial point is, can we really understand the scope and dimensions of human rights without considering the concerned society and culture? Can it be society, culture and economy neutral? It brings to the issue of holistic understanding of human rights where anthropology with its holistic approach can contribute significantly in understanding the causes and factors of human rights violations and strengthening the forces of struggle for promoting and protecting human rights at different levels.

The papers in this volume reflect the declaration of Anthropology and Human Rights Committee for Human Rights adopted by the American Anthropological Association in June,1999. Anthropology as a profession is committed to the promotion and protection of the right of people. When any culture or society denies or permits the denial of such opportunity to any of its own members or others, there is an ethical responsibility to protest and oppose such deprivation. This implies starting from the base line of the Universal Declaration of Human Rights and associated implementing international legislation, but also expanding the definition of human rights to include areas not necessarily addressed by international law. These areas include collective as well as individual rights, cultural, social, and economic development, and a clean and safe environment.

Anthropology, with its holistic approach, is perhaps one of the most suitable disciplines to address these issues.

II

It has already been mentioned that there are twenty-five articles in the volume. The first three articles have examined cases of human rights violations in different parts of the world. Dr Dias has discussed major cases of human rights violations in India, Philippines, Timor, Cambodia and China and the lessons one can learn from them. In the next article, Paudel has discussed about the human rights violations during recent political struggle in Nepal when many persons were killed and even the children were not spared. In the next paper, Professor Midya has examined the situation at Jangalmahal, a tribal dominated area which has witnessed serious conflict in the recent past. It has been noted that the root cause behind the problem is not only socio-economic malaise, but it has considerable political bearing. The issue of human rights is practically a non-issue here as none of the conflicting groups has shown any concern over protection of the rights.

Next, there are four articles dealing with environment, resource, development and human rights. Dr Bhattacharjee has discussed about two migrant groups in India, one in West Bengal and the other in Assam and their struggle for survival. They are deprived in every aspect from the fundamental rights of livelihood and getting excluded from the common resources. Different situations were noted affecting their human rights. Dr Ghosal has presented a case of displacement due to development and how to address it in the context of a tribal community. Dr Biswas has conducted a study on an island where rate of suicide is very high. The area was affected by soil erosion and environmental degradation. The continuous pressure of insecurity and uncertainty seriously affected their mind. The responsibilities, duties, social burdens and the state of indebtedness made them psychologically ill and in most of the cases it turned into mental depression which ultimately promoted them to commit suicide. In the next article, Professor Chaudhuri has examined the issues of human rights and human security and the importance of democracy and sustainable development in protecting human security. In this context he has raised the question, what security means, security of the state or security of the people. He has further suggested that one cannot stop the exploitation of natural resources but what one is now looking for is how to achieve sustainable development. The traditional models of resource use may have an answer to this question.

There are three articles dealing with urbanization and human rights. Professor Vargas-Hernandez has pointed out that mining activities are perceived as the main economic factor of marginal regions and depressed zones in México. Mining concessions granted by Mexican government are centralized, brief and do not include public hearings. Affected groups and communities can not react immediately and mobilize against potential risks and dangers or to negotiate rights and interests. Mr Shamsuddin has discussed different types of problems and human rights violations faced by the urban poor in Bangladesh.

The demands and expectations of the urban poor are closely related to the problems they encounter. A review of their present condition shows that their demands and expectations primarily revolve around such aspects as housing, education, primary health, and social security. In the next article, Dr Roy has discussed the problems of slum dwellers and the nature of human rights violations. He has discussed the nature and trends of urbanization, national slum policy and strategy of slum development in this context.

After this, there are four articles dealing with different aspects of women. Dr De has examined the nature of domestic violence and human rights violations in the context of the females. It has been pointed out how education and women empowerment can solve this problem. In the next two articles, Ms Biswas and Professor Ray have discussed about decision making in family planning practices in the context of male dominated society and Dr Basu has examined the plight of the elderly females living in the old age homes. In the next article, Sharma has discussed the condition of Bengalee women in Vrindavan and about their human rights situation.

There are five articles on indigenous people, three on India and two on Latin America. Roy and Tarafdar have discussed on land alienation and indigenous rights of a small community in North Bengal, India. Dr Chakraborty has discussed the importance of education with reference to tribal women. Professor Bhattacharya has discussed about education of tribal girl with reference to Binapani Ashram, an institution established particularly for the development of the tribals. In the next article, Professor Lucic has discussed about citizenship, identity and human rights issue in the context of the indigenous population of Latin America. The next article is on Mexico, where Professor Laura Cruz has examined the rights of the indigenous people in Mexico City.

In the end of the volume, there are six articles dealing with the human rights situation of the migrants and workers. Dr Roy has discussed the situation of the bidi binders, who are mostly migrants and apart from socio-economic problems also face health problems because of their association with the particular profession. Dr Gan and Dr Biswas have discussed about the struggle for survival of a migrant group who survive crushing stones and living on the bed of a river. Arunkumar and Devarapalli have discussed about the sufferings of migrant construction workers in the context of Chennai city. Binita Basu has discussed issues relating to conflict among working and non-working mothers in an urban setting. In the next article, Sarah Rogers has examined the implications of mass migration in America. In the last article of the volume, Professor Chenaut has examined the legality, rights and identity problem of undocumented Mexican youth in a particular state of USA.

1

From Sites of Violent Struggle to Shrines of Learning

The Recovery of Truth and the Recovery of Justice

CLARENCE J. DIAS

I

Human Rights and Anthropology: A Powerful Duo for Accountability, Justice and Peace

Anthropology is the most humanistic of the sciences and the most scientific of the humanities.

—Alfred L. Kroeber

The purpose of anthropology is to make the world safe for human differences.

—Ruth Benedict

History is, strictly speaking, the study of questions; the study of answers belongs to anthropology and sociology.

—W.H. Auden

Anthropology

Anthropology is the study of human beings, past and present. Anthropology seeks to understand the full sweep and complexity of cultures across all of human history. Therefore, anthropology draws and builds upon knowledge from the social and biological sciences as well as the humanities and physical sciences. A central concern of anthropologists is the application of knowledge to the solution of human problems. Anthropologists often integrate the perspectives of several of these areas into their research, teaching, and professional lives.

Anthropology has penetrated most of the other Social Sciences:

Economic anthropology attempts to explain human economic behaviour in its widest historic, geographic and cultural scope. It has a complex relationship with the discipline of economics, of which it is highly critical.

Political anthropology concerns the structure of political systems, looked at from the basis of the structure of societies. Political themes are taken up at two main levels. First, anthropologists continue to study political organization and political phenomena that lie outside the state-regulated sphere (as in patron-client relations or tribal political organization). Second, anthropologists started to develop a disciplinary concern with states and their institutions (and of course on the relationship between formal and informal political institutions).

Political economy in anthropology is the application of the theories and methods of Historical Materialism to the traditional concerns of anthropology, including, but not limited to, non-capitalist societies. Political economy introduced questions of history and colonialism to ahistorical anthropological theories of social structure and culture. Three main areas of interest rapidly developed: pre-capitalist societies, the peasantry many of whom were involved in complex revolutionary wars such as in Vietnam; and colonialism, imperialism, and the creation of the capitalist world-system.

Ethnohistory is the study of ethnographic cultures and indigenous customs by examining historical records. It is also the study of the history of various ethnic groups that may or may not exist today.

Legal anthropology, also known as Anthropology of Law, specializes in 'the cross-cultural study of social ordering'. Earlier, legal anthropological research often focused more narrowly on conflict management, crime, sanctions, or formal regulation. More recent applications include issues such as Human Rights, Legal pluralism, Islamaphobia and political uprisings.

Anthropology of development tends to view development from a *critical* perspective. The kind of issues addressed and implications for the approach involve asking why, if a key development goal is to alleviate poverty, is poverty increasing? Why is there such a gap between plans and outcomes? Why are those working in development so willing to disregard history and the lessons it might offer? Why is development so externally driven rather than having an internal basis? In short, why does so much planned development fail?

Feminist anthropology is a four-field approach to anthropology (archeological, biological, cultural, linguistic) that seeks to reduce male bias in research findings, anthropological hiring practices, and the scholarly production of knowledge. Feminist anthropology engages often with feminists from non-Western traditions, whose perspectives and experiences can differ from those of White European and American feminists. Feminist anthropologists are centrally concerned with the construction of gender across societies.

Environmental anthropology is a sub-specialty within the field of anthropology that takes an active role in examining the relationships between humans and their environment across space and time.

The anthropology of religion involves the study of religious institutions in relation to other social institutions, and the comparison of religious beliefs and practices across cultures.

Urban anthropology is concerned with issues of urbanization, poverty, and neo-liberalism.

Applied anthropology refers to the application of the method and theory of anthropology to the analysis and solution of practical problems.

Anthropologists advocate for a *public anthropology* that is committed to bringing knowledge to broad audiences. Anthropologists collaborate closely with people whose cultural patterns and processes they seek to understand or whose living conditions require amelioration. An engaged anthropology is committed to supporting social change efforts that arise from the interaction between community goals and anthropological research. Because the study of people, past and present, requires respect for the diversity of individuals, cultures, societies, and knowledge systems, anthropologists are expected to adhere to a strong code of professional ethics.

Ethical Stances and Anthropology

Anthropologists urge, as part of their quest for scientific objectivity, *cultural relativism,* which has an influence on all the sub-fields of anthropology. This is the notion that particular cultures should not be judged by one culture's values or viewpoints, but that all cultures should be viewed as relative to each other. There should be no notions, in good anthropology, of one culture being better or worse than another culture.

Ethical commitments in anthropology include noticing and documenting genocide, infanticide, racism, mutilation, including circumcision and sub-incision, and torture. Topics like racism, slavery or human sacrifice, therefore, attract anthropological attention and theories ranging from nutritional deficiencies to genes to acculturation have been proposed, not to mention theories of colonialism and many others as root causes of man's inhumanity to man.

Anthropologists' involvement with the US government, in particular, has caused bitter controversy within the discipline. Franz Boas publicly objected to US participation in World War I, and after the war he published a brief expose and condemnation of the participation of several American archaeologists in espionage in Mexico under their cover as scientists. But by the 1940s, many of Boas' anthropologist contemporaries were active in the allied war effort against the 'Axis' (Nazi Germany, Fascist Italy, and Imperial Japan). Many served in the armed forces, while others worked in intelligence (for example, Office of Strategic Services and the Office of War Information). Attempts were made to accuse anthropologists of complicity with the CIA and government intelligence activities during the Vietnam War years.

Professional anthropological bodies often object to the use of anthropology for the benefit of the state. Their codes of ethics or statements may proscribe anthropologists from giving secret briefings. The Association of Social Anthropologists (ASA) of the UK and Commonwealth has called certain scholarship ethically dangerous. The AAA's current 'Statement of Professional Responsibility' clearly states that in relation with their own government and with host governments.

II

From Sites of Struggle to Sites of Learning: The Recovery of Truth and the Recovery of Justice

Amidst the Clash of Arms, the Laws are not Silent.

—Lord Atkin's dissenting judgment in *Liversidge v Anderson*

The Process of Transformation

The natural human reaction to sites of violent struggle, especially struggle which has taken human lives, is one of revulsion and horror. This is especially so if such site continues to be one where domination and exclusion continue unabated. However, often such sites become the focus and inspiration for broadening and deepening further struggle and as the saying goes, 'Say not the struggle, naught availeth'. Hence, when such sites, because of successful struggle become sites of liberation, a new reaction is called for, transforming such sites of struggle into sites of learning and remembrance. Such process of transformation involves learning and remembering about:

- What the struggle was about?
- Who were the different protagonists in the struggle?
- What role did force and violence play in the struggle: violence of the oppressor as well as the violence of defense and self-defense resorted to by the oppressed?
- What were the various stages (if any) of the struggle? Did failures become the stepping stones of success?
- What was the outcome of the struggle: a win-win situation; a lose-lose situation or a win-lose situation?
- At what price the struggle?

Transitional Justice

The five case examples below, very clearly demonstrate that if sites of struggle and massacre are to be transformed into sites of remembrance and learning, attention must be paid to transitional justice.[1]

The term 'transitional justice' refers to the set of judicial and non-judicial measures that have been implemented by different countries, in order to redress the legacies of massive Human Rights abuses. Transitional justice is not a 'special' kind of justice, but an approach to achieving justice in times of transition from conflict and/or state repression. By trying to achieve accountability and redressing victims, transitional justice provides recognition of the rights of victims, promotes civic trust and strengthens the democratic rule of law.

In periods of political transitions, from authoritarian, dictatorial regimes or from civil conflicts to democracy, transitional justice has often provided opportunities for such societies to address past human rights abuses, mass atrocities, or other forms of severe trauma in order to facilitate a smooth transition into a more democratic or peaceful future.

The different elements of a transitional justice policy are not parts of a random list, but rather, are related to one another practically and conceptually. The core elements are:

- Criminal prosecutions, particularly those that address perpetrators considered to be the most responsible.
- Reparations, through which governments recognize and take steps to address the harms suffered. Such initiatives often have material elements (such as cash payments or health services) as well as symbolic aspects (such as public apologies or day of remembrance).
- Institutional reform of abusive state institutions such as armed forces, police and courts, to dismantle – by appropriate means – the structural

machinery of abuses and prevent recurrence of serious Human Rights abuses and impunity.

- Truth commissions or other means to investigate and report on systematic patterns of abuse, recommend changes and help understand the underlying causes of serious human rights violations.

This is not a closed list. Different countries have added other measures. Memorialization, for example, the various efforts to keep the memory of the victims alive through, for example, the creation of museums, memorials, and other symbolic initiatives such as the renaming of public spaces, has become an important part of transitional justice in most parts of the world.

III

Five Case Histories of the Process of Transformation of Sites of Violent Struggle into Sites of Learning and Remembrance

India: From Jallianwala Bagh to Godhra and Beyond

Jallianwala Bagh

Jallianwala Bagh is a public garden in Amritsar in Punjab, India, and houses a memorial of national importance, established in 1951 to commemorate the massacre by British occupying forces of peaceful celebrators on the occasion of the Punjabi New Year on 13 April 1919, in the Jallianwala Bagh Massacre. Colonial British Raj sources identified 379 fatalities and estimated about 1,100 wounded. Civil Surgeon, Smith indicated that there were 1,526 casualties. The true figures of fatalities are unknown, but are likely to be many times higher than the official figure of 379. The 6.5 acre (26,000 m^2) garden site of the massacre is located in the vicinity of Harmandir Saheb, the holiest shrine of Sikhism.

World War I was about to conclude, and India was in ferment. In August 1917, E.S. Montagu, the Secretary of State for India, had declared on behalf of the British Government to grant responsible government to India within the British Empire. The war came to an end on 11 November 1918. On 6 February 1919, *Rowlatt Bills* were introduced by the British Government in the Imperial Legislative Council, and one of the bills was passed into an Act in March 1919. Under this Act, people suspected of so-called sedition could be imprisoned without trial. This resulted in frustration among Indians and there was great unrest. While people were expecting freedom, they suddenly discovered that chains were being strengthened. At that time, Punjab was governed by Lieutenant Governor Michael O'Dwyer, who had contempt for educated Indians. During the war, he had adopted unscrupulous methods for collecting war funds, press-gang techniques for raising recruits and had gagged the press. He truly ruled Punjab with an iron hand.

At this juncture, Mahatma Gandhi decided to launch a *satyagraha* campaign. This unique form of political struggle eschewed violence, was open, and relied on truth and righteousness. It emphasized that means were as important as the ends. The city of Amritsar responded to Mahatma's call by observing a strike on 6 April 1919. On April, during Ram Navami festival, a procession was taken out, in which Hindus and Muslims participated, giving proof of their unity, and the government ordered the arrest of the popular leaders of the people of Amritsar. They were deported to Dharamshala where they were interned. On 10 April, when people went to meet the Deputy Commissioner to demand the release of the two arrested leaders, they were fired upon. This event angered people and disorder broke out in Amritsar. Some bank buildings were sacked, telegraph and railway communications were snapped, three British people were murdered and one woman injured. On 11 April, Brigadier General R.E.H. Dyer arrived from Jalandhar Cantonment, and virtually occupied the town since civil administration under Miles Irving, the Deputy Commissioner, had come to standstill. On 13 April 1919, a public meeting was announced to be held in Jallianwala Bagh in the evening. Dyer came to Jallianwala Bagh with a force of 150 troops. They took up their positions on an elevated ground towards the main entrance, a narrow lane in which hardly two persons could walk abreast.

At six minutes to sunset they opened fire on a crowd of about 20,000 people without giving any warning. Arthur Swinson, thus, describes the massacre:

> Towards the exits on the either flank, the crowds converged in their frantic effort to get away, jostling, clambering, elbowing and trampling over each other. Seeing this movement, Brigs drew Dyer's attention to it, and Dyer mistakenly imagining that these sections of the crowd were getting ready to rush him, directed the fire of the troops straight at them. The result was horrifying. Men screamed and went down, to be trampled by those coming after. Some were hit again and again. In places the dead and wounded lay in heaps; men would go down wounded, to find themselves immediately buried beneath a dozen others. Some 1,600 rounds of bullets were fired by troops on 20,000 innocent people.

The firing still went on. Hundreds, abandoning all hope of getting away through the exits, tried the walls which in places were five feet high and at others seven or ten. Fighting for a position, they ran at the wall, clutching at the smooth surfaces, trying frantically to get a hold. Some people almost reached the top, only to be pulled down by those fighting behind them. Some, more agile than the rest, succeeded in getting away, but many more were shot as they clambered up. As many as 20,000 people were caught beneath the hail of bullets: all of them frantically trying to escape from the quiet meeting place which had suddenly become a screaming hell.

The flame lighted at Jallianwala Bagh ultimately set the whole of India aflame. It is a landmark in India's struggle for freedom. It gave great impetus to the *satyagraha* movement, which ultimately won freedom for India on 15 August 1947.

Dandi

The Salt March, also mainly known as the Salt Satyagraha, began with the Dandi March on 12 March 1930, and was an important part of the Indian Independence Movement. It was a direct action campaign of tax resistance and nonviolent protest against the British salt monopoly in colonial India, and triggered the wider Civil Disobedience Movement. This was the most significant organized challenge to British authority since the Non-Cooperation Movement of 1920–22, and directly followed the Purna Swaraj declaration of Independence by the Indian National Congress on 26 January 1930.

Mohandas Karamchand Gandhi (commonly called Mahatma Gandhi) led the Dandi March from his base, Sabarmati Ashram near Ahmedabad, to the coastal village of Dandi, located at a small town called Navsari, in the state of Gujarat. As he continued on this 24 day, 240 mile march to produce salt without paying the tax, growing numbers of Indians joined him along the way. When Gandhi broke the salt laws at 6:30 am on 5 April 1930, it sparked large scale acts of civil disobedience against the British Raj salt laws by millions of Indians. The campaign had a significant effect on the already changing world and on the British attitude towards Indian Independence and caused large number of Indians to join the fight for the first time.

The Salt Satyagraha campaign was based upon Gandhi's principles of nonviolent protest called *satyagraha,* which he loosely translated as 'truth-force'. Literally, it is formed from the Sanskrit words *satya*, 'truth', and *agraha*, 'force'. In early 1930, the Indian National Congress chose *satyagraha* as their main tactic for winning India's Independence from British rule and appointed Gandhi to organize the campaign. Gandhi chose the 1882 British Salt Act as the first target of *satyagraha.* The Salt March to Dandi, and the beating by British police of hundreds of nonviolent protesters in Dharasana, received worldwide news coverage and demonstrated the effective use of civil disobedience as a technique for fighting social and political injustice. The *satyagraha* teachings of Gandhi and the Dandi March had a significant influence on American civil rights activist Martin Luther King, Jr., and his fight for civil rights for Blacks and other minority groups in the 1960s.

The British used divide and rule tactics when leaving the Indian sub-continent creating two separate states: India, with a Hindu majority population and Pakistan, with a Muslim majority population. For both countries, independence proved to be the proverbial 'poisoned chalice' and has brought in its wake an interminable set of violent clashes between Hindus and Muslims with a combined death toll that is beyond estimation.

Ayodhya

The Ayodhya dispute is a political, historical and socio-religious debate in India, centred on a plot of land in the city of Ayodhya, located in Faizabad district, Uttar Pradesh. The main issues revolve around access to a site traditionally regarded as the birthplace of the Hindu deity Rama, the history and location of the Babri Mosque at the site, and whether a previous Hindu temple was demolished or modified to create the mosque. The Babri Mosque was destroyed by hardline Hindu activists during a political rally which turned into a riot on 6 December 1992. A subsequent land title case was lodged in the Allahabad High Court, the verdict of which was pronounced on 30 September 2010. In the landmark hearing, the three judges of the Allahabad High Court ruled that the 2.77 acres (1.12 ha) of Ayodhya land be divided into three parts, with one-third going to the Ram Lalla or Infant Lord Rama represented by the Hindu Maha Sabha for the construction of the Ram temple, one-third going to the Islamic Sunni Waqf Board and the remaining one-third going to a Hindu religious denomination Nirmohi Akhara. While the three-judge bench was not unanimous that the disputed structure was constructed after demolition of a temple, it did agree that a temple or a temple structure predated the mosque at the same site. The excavations by the Archaeological Survey of India were heavily used as evidence by the court that the predating structure was a massive Hindu religious building. In 2003, it was discovered that there are Buddhist ruins underlying both the Hindu and Muslim layers at Ayodhya.

On 9 May 2011, the Supreme Court of India stayed the High Court order splitting the disputed site in three parts and said that status quo will remain. The two judge bench of Supreme Court also remarked that the HC verdict was surprising as no party wanted a split of the site.

On 16 December 1992, the Liberhan Commission was set up by the Government of India to probe the circumstances that led to the demolition of the Babri Mosque. It was the longest running commission in India's history with several extensions granted by various governments. Many senior political leader were held responsible..

Many Muslim organizations have continued to express outrage at the destruction of the disputed structure. In July 2005, Islamic fighters attacked the makeshift temple at the site of the destroyed mosque. In 2007, M.N. Gopal Das, the then head of the Ram temple, received phone calls making threats against his life. Many terror attacks by banned *jihadi* outfits like IM cited demolition of Babri Mosque as an excuse for terrorist attacks.

Godhra

The Godhra Train Burning was an incident that occurred on the morning of 27 February 2002, in which 58 people, including 25 women and 15 children, died in a fire inside the Sabarmati Express train near the Godhra railway station in the Indian state of Gujarat. Many of the victims were Hindu pilgrims and activists who were returning from the holy city of Ayodhya. The official Commission set up to investigate the train-burning spent six years thoroughly going over the details of the case, and concluded that the fire was arson committed by a mob of 1000–2000 people, mainly Muslims. A court convicted 31 Muslims for the incident and the conspiracy for the crime although the actual causes of the fire have yet to be proven conclusively.

The Nanavati-Mehta Commission, the official Commission appointed to investigate the incident, concluded that Maulvi Husain Haji Ibrahim Umarji, an influential cleric and a social worker, planned the attack on the train. Umarji was arrested as the 'mastermind' of the train-burning, based on a statement made by Jabir Binyamin Behra, a criminal in custody. Later, during the trial he denied giving any such statement. Maulana Umarji was acquitted by the Nanavati-Mehta Commission of all the charges made against him in connection with the Godhra train-burning incident and was released for lack of evidence. The Commission held that a few Ghanchi Muslims, who used to stay around Godhra railway station, were the executors. Petrol was stored in seven or eight 20-litre cans and was kept in a nearby guest house.

The Prevention of Terrorism Ordinance (POTA) was invoked against all the accused, but was later suspended due to pressure from the Central government. In May 2003, the first chargesheet was filed against 54 accused. In November 2003, the Supreme Court of India put a stay on the trial. In 2004,

POTA was repealed after the United Progressive Alliance (UPA), with Manmohan Singh as the Prime Minister, came to power and it decided to review the invocation of POTA against the accused. In May 2005, the POTA Review Commission opined not to charge the accused under POTA. This was unsuccessfully challenged by a kin of the victim before the Gujarat High Court and later on appealed before the Supreme Court. In September 2008, the Nanavati Commission submitted its report on the incident. In 2009, after accepting the report of the Special Investigation Team (SIT) appointed by it, the court appointed a special fast-track court to try the case along with five other fast track courts established to try the post-incident riots. The bench hearing the case also said that public prosecutors should be appointed in consultation with the SIT chairman. More than 100 people were arrested in relation to the incident. The court was set up inside the Sabarmati Central Jail, where almost all of the accused were confined. The hearing began in May 2009. Additional Sessions Judge P.R. Patel was designated to hear the case. According to the chargesheet filed, 59 people were killed in the S–6 coach of Sabarmati Express when an unidentified mob of around 900 to 1,000 people attacked it near Godhra railway station. Initially, 107 people were charged, of which five died during the pendency of the case. Eight others were juveniles, who were tried by a separate court. As many as 253 witnesses were examined during the trial and more than 1,500 items of documentary evidence were presented in the court.

In May 2010, the Supreme Court restrained the trial courts from pronouncing judgment in nine sensitive riot cases, including the Godhra train incident. The trial was completed in September 2010; however, the verdict could not be delivered because of the Supreme Court stay. The stay was lifted in January 2011. In February 2011, the trial court convicted 31 people of murder and conspiracy and acquitted 63 others, saying the incident was a 'pre-planned conspiracy'. The death penalty was awarded to 11 convicts, particularly those the court believed were present at a meeting, held the previous night, where the conspiracy was formed, and those who, the court said, had actually entered the coach and poured petrol before setting it afire. Twenty were sentenced to life imprisonment. Maulvi Saeed Umarji, who was believed by the SIT to be the prime accused, was acquitted, along with 62 other accused for lack of evidence.

The process of recovery of truth was slow and measured in the case of Godhra. Despite controversy over the Supreme Court stay restraining the trial court from pronouncing judgment in nine sensitive cases, justice was done in the end. Several perpetrators were convicted. The festering sore was cauterized and the process of rebuilding peace was set in motion.

Gujarat 2002 Riot

The Godhra Train Burning is widely perceived to have triggered the violence that followed in Ahmedabad, Vadodara and some places near Godhra, from 28 February 2002, in the state of Gujarat. The day following the fire, coordinated attacks began. Men wearing saffron robes and khaki shorts arrived *en masse* in trucks. They had swords, explosives and gas cylinders which were used to destroy homes and places of business. Attacks were made in full view of police stations and police officers; however, the police did not intervene. The rioters used mobile phones to coordinate their attacks. By the day's end, on 28 February, a curfew was declared in 27 towns and cities.

Following the attack on the train, the Vishva Hindu Parishad (VHP) called for a statewide *bandh* (strike), even though these have been declared by the Supreme Court to be unconstitutional and illegal. It is common knowledge in India that these strikes are usually followed by violence. No action was taken by the state to prevent the strike, or stop the initial violence.

Dionne Bunsha, writing on the Gulbarg Society massacre and murder of Ehsan Jafri (member of the 6th Lok Sabha), has said that Jafri begged the crowd to spare the women, he was dragged into the street and forced to parade naked. He was then beheaded and thrown into a fire. The rioters returned and burned to death Jafri's family, including two small boys. After the massacre Gulbarg burned for a week. According to Siddharth Varadarajan (former editor of *The Hindu*), on 28 February in the districts of Morjari Chowk and Charodia Chowk, in Ahmedabad, of the 40 people killed by police shooting, all were Muslim. It is estimated that at least 250 girls and women had been gang raped and then burned to death. Children were killed by being burnt alive and those digging mass graves described the bodies as 'burned and butchered beyond recognition'. Children were force-fed petrol and then set on fire, pregnant women were gutted and their unborn child's body then shown to the women. In the Naroda Patiya mass grave, of the 96 bodies 46 were women. The murderers also flooded homes and electrocuted entire families inside. Violence against women included their being stripped naked, objects being forced into their bodies and then being killed. According to Kalpana Kannabiran (an Indian sociologist and lawyer), the rapes were part of a well-organized, deliberate and pre-planned strategy, and thus, the violence in the area constituted a political pogrom and genocide. Other acts of violence against women were acid attacks, beatings and the killing of women who were pregnant. Children were also killed in front of their parents. George Fernandes (the then Defence Minister, Government of India) during a discussion in Parliament on the violence, caused widespread furore in his defense of the state government, saying that this was not the first time that women had been violated and raped in India.

Children and infants were speared and held aloft before being thrown into fires. Describing the sexual violence perpetrated against Muslim women and girls. Renu Khanna (a feminist, women's health and rights activist) writes that the survivors reported 'that sexual violence consisted of forced nudity, mass rapes, gang rapes, mutilation, insertion of objects into bodies, cutting of breasts, slitting the stomach and reproductive organs, and carving of Hindu symbols on women's body parts. The Concerned Citizens' Tribunal characterized the use of rape 'as an instrument for the subjugation and humiliation of a community'. Testimony heard by the committee stated that: 'A chilling technique, absent in pogroms unleashed hitherto but very much in evidence this time in a large number of cases, was the deliberate destruction of evidence. Barring a few, in most instances of sexual violence, the women victims were stripped and paraded naked, then gang raped, and thereafter quartered and burnt beyond recognition. The leaders of the mobs even raped young girls, some as young as 11 years old, before burning them alive. Even a 20-day-old infant, or a foetus in the womb of its mother, was not spared'.

According to the official figures, the riots resulted in the deaths of 790 Muslims and 254 Hindus; 2,500 people were injured non-fatally, and 223 more were reported missing. There were instances of rape, children being burned alive, and widespread looting and destruction of property.

The Editors Guild of India, in its report on media ethics and coverage of the incidents, stated that the news coverage was exemplary, with only a few minor lapses. The local newspapers *Sandesh Gujarati* and *Gujarat Samachar,* however, were heavily criticized. The report states that *Sandesh* had headlines which would 'provoke, communalize and terrorize people'. The newspaper also used a quote from a VHP leader as a headline, 'Avenge with blood'. The report also stated that *Samachar* had played a role in increasing the tensions, but did not give all of its coverage over to 'hawkish and inflammatory reportage in the first few weeks'. The paper also carried reports to highlight communal harmony. *Gujarat Today* was given praise for showing restraint and for the balanced reportage of the violence.

Critical reporting on the Gujarat Government's handling of the situation helped bring about the Indian government's intervention in controlling the violence. The Editorial Guild of India rejected the charge that graphic news coverage aggravated the situation, saying that the coverage exposed the 'horrors' of the riots as well as the 'supine if not complicit' attitude of the state, helping propel remedial action.

The US Commission on International Religious Freedom Report in 2003 and 2004 called India a 'country of particular concern', and cited the violence in 2002 as one reason for this. It also stated that even though India has a tradition of democracy, minorities are subjected to mass killings and intense violence periodically. It also made a note that those who carry out these acts of violence are rarely held accountable for their actions.

An international fact finding committee formed of all women international experts from the US, UK, France, Germany and Sri Lanka reported, 'sexual violence was being used as a strategy for terrorizing women belonging to the minority community in the state.'

Organizations such as Human Rights Watch criticized the Indian Government as well as the Gujarat state administration for failure to address the resulting humanitarian condition of the people, the 'overwhelming majority of them Muslim,' who fled their homes for relief camps in the aftermath of the events, and for engaging in a cover-up of the state's role in the massacres.

Prosecution of those accused of criminal actions during the violence faced problems with witnesses being either bribed or intimidated, local judges were also biased. As of April 2013, 249 convictions had been secured, 184 Hindus and 65 Muslims; 31 of the Muslim convictions were for the train incident in Godhra.

The Indian Supreme Court has been strongly critical of the state government's investigation and prosecution of those accused of violence during the riots, directing police to review about 2,000 of the 4,000 riot-related cases that had been closed citing lack of evidence or leads. Following this direction, police identified nearly 1,600 cases for re-investigation, arrested 640 accused and launched investigations against 40 police officers for their failures.

Human Rights Watch alleged that state and law enforcement officials were harassing and intimidating key witnesses, NGOs, social activists and lawyers who were fighting to seek justice for riot victims. In its 2003 annual report,

Amnesty International stated, 'the same police force that was accused of colluding with the attackers was put in charge of the investigations into the massacres, undermining the process of delivery of justice to the victims.'

The Best Bakery murder trial received wide attention after witnesses retracted testimony in court and all of the accused were acquitted. The Indian Supreme Court, acting on a petition by social activist Teesta Setalvad, ordered a retrial outside Gujarat in which nine accused were found guilty in 2006. A key witness, Zaheera Sheikh, who repeatedly changed her testimony during the trials and the petition, was found guilty of perjury.

After a local court dismissed the case against her assailants, Bilkis Bano approached the National Human Rights Commission and petitioned the Supreme Court, seeking a retrial. The Supreme Court granted the motion, directing the Central Bureau of Investigation (CBI) to take over the investigation. The CBI appointed a team of experts from the Central Forensic Science Laboratory (CFSL) of the Central Bureau of Investigation, Delhi, and All-India Institute of Medical Sciences (AIIMS) under the guidance and leadership of T.D. Dogra of AIIMS to exhume the mass graves to establish the identity and cause of death of victims. The team successfully located and exhumed the remains of victims. The trial of the case was transferred out of Gujarat and the Central government appointed a public prosecutor. Charges were filed in a Mumbai court against 19 people as well as six police officials and a government doctor over their role in the initial investigations. In January 2008, 11 men were sentenced to life imprisonment for the rape and murders and a policeman was convicted of falsifying evidence.

In 2005, the Vadodara fast-track court acquitted 108 people accused of murdering two youths during a mob attack on a group of displaced Muslims returning under police escort to their homes in Avdhootnagar. The court passed strictures against the police for failing to protect the people under their escort and failing to identify the attackers they had witnessed.

Nine people were convicted of killing a Hindu man and injuring another during group clashes in Danilimda, Ahmedabad, on 12 April, while 25 others were acquitted.

A stringent anti-terror law, the POTA, was used by the Gujarat government to charge 131 people in connection to the Godhra train fire, but was not invoked in prosecuting any of the accused in the post-Godhra riots.

In 2012, Modi was cleared of complicity in the violence by a Special Investigation Team appointed by the Supreme Court of India. The Muslim community are reported to have reacted with 'anger and disbelief' and Teesta Setalvad, of the NGO, Citizen for Peace and Justice, has said that the legal process was not yet complete as there existed a right to appeal. In July 2013, allegations were made that the SIT had suppressed evidence.

On 29 July 2012, an Indian court gave the verdict in the Naroda Patiya massacre case and convicted 32 people, including former state minister Maya Kodnani and Hindu leader Babu Bajrangi of involvement in the attacks. The court case began in 2009, and over 300 people (including victims, witnesses, doctors, and journalists) testified before the court. For the first time, the verdict acknowledged the role of a politician in inciting Hindu mobs. Twenty-nine people were acquitted during the verdict. Teesta Setalvad, a Human Rights campaigner, said, 'For the first time, this judgment actually goes beyond neighbourhood perpetrators and goes up to the political conspiracy. The fact that convictions have gone that high means the conspiracy charge has been accepted and the political influencing of the mobs has been accepted by the judge. This is a huge victory for justice.'

More than 60 investigations by national and international bodies, many of which having investigated the incident, concluded there was support from state officials in the violence. The report from the National Human Rights Commission of India (NHRC) concluded that the attacks had been premeditated, that state government officials were complicit and that there was evidence of police not acting during the assaults on Muslims. The NHRC also stated that *res ipsa loquitur* applied since the state had comprehensively failed to protect and had not upheld the rights of the people as set out in the Constitution of India.

The Concerned Citizens Tribunal (CCT) report which was headed by Krishna Iyer, a retired justice of the Supreme Court, released its findings in 2003 and stated that contrary to the government allegation of a conspiracy in Godhra, this incident had not been pre-planned and there was no evidence to indicate otherwise. On the statewide riots, the CCT reported that several days before the Godhra incident, homes belonging to Hindus which were in Muslim areas had been marked with pictures of Hindu deities or saffron flags, this had been done to prevent any accidental assaults on Hindu homes or businesses. They also reported that 'the complicity of the state government is obvious. And, the support of the Central government to the state government in all that it did is also by now a matter of common knowledge'.

The state government commissioned J.G. Shah to conduct, what became, a controversial one-man inquiry into the Godhra incident. Its credibility was questioned and the NHRC and the National Minorities Commission requested that a sitting judge from the Supreme Court be appointed. The Supreme Court overturned the findings by Shah stating, 'this judgment is not based on the understanding of any evidence, but on imagination'. Early in 2003, the state government of Gujarat had set up the Shah-Nanavati Commission to investigate the entire incident, from the initial one at Godhra to the ensuing violence. The Commission was shrouded in controversy from the beginning. Activists and members of the opposition insisted that a judicial commission be set up and headed by a sitting judge rather than a retired one from the high court, but the state refused. Within a few months, the Commission, before hearing any testimony, declared that there was no evidence of lapses by either the police or government in their handling of the violence. In 2008, Shah died and was replaced by Justice Akshay Mehta, a retired high court judge. Mehta's appointment was controversial since he was the judge who allowed Babu Bajrangi to be bailed. Bajrangi is a leader of the Bajrang Dal and is a prime suspect in the massacre at Naroda Patiya. In July 2013, the Commission was given its 20th extension, and Mukul Sinha of the civil rights group *Jan Sangahrsh Manch* said of the delays, 'I think the Commission has lost its significance and it now seems to be awaiting the outcome of the 2014 Lok Sabha election.' In 2007, *Tehelka,* in an undercover operation, had said that the Shah-Nanavati Commission had relied on 'manufactured evidence'. *Tehelka* editor Tarun Tejpal had claimed that they had taped witnesses who stated they had given false testimony after they had been bribed by the Gujarati police force. *Tehelka* also recorded Ranjitsinh Patel as stating that he and Prabhatsinh Patel had been paid 50,000 rupees apiece to amend earlier statements and to identify as conspirators some Muslims.

While officially classified as a communal riot, the 2002 events have been described as a pogrom by many scholars and commentators. Other independent observers have stated that these events met the 'legal definition of genocide', and called it an instance of state terrorism. Still others have said the incidents were tantamount to ethnic cleansing. Instances of mass violence which occurred include the Naroda Patiya massacre that took place directly alongside a police training camp, the Gulbarg Society massacre where Ehsan Jafri, a former member of the Parliament, was among those killed, and several incidents in the city of Vadodara. Martha Nussbaum (a faculty at the University of Chicago) has said that 'there is by now a broad consensus that the Gujarat violence was a form of ethnic cleansing, that in many ways it was premeditated, and that it was carried out with the complicity of the state government and officers of the law'.

There was widespread destruction of property; 527 places of worship such as masjids, temples, cemeteries, dargahs and schools had been either destroyed or damaged. It is estimated that Muslim property losses were: '1,00,000 houses, 1,100 hotels, 15,000 businesses, 3,000 handcarts and 5,000 vehicles destroyed.' In total 27,780 persons were arrested, either for rioting or as a preventative measure. For criminal behaviour, 11,167 arrests were made of which 3,269 were Muslim and 7,896 Hindu. Preventive arrests were 16,615 of which 2,811 were Muslim and 13,804 were Hindu. It was reported by the Concerned Citizens Tribunal that 90 per cent of those arrested were almost immediately granted bail, even if they had been arrested on suspicion of murder or arson. There were also media reports that political leaders gave those being released public welcomes as they were given bail. This contradicts what the state government had been saying during the violence that 'bail applications of all accused persons are being strongly defended and rejected'.

Human Rights Watch has accused the state of orchestrating a cover-up over their role in the violence. Human Rights activists and Indian solicitors have urged that legislation be passed so that 'communal violence is treated as genocide'. Following the violence thousands of Muslims were fired from their places of work, and those who tried to return home had to endure an economic and social boycott.

In 2012, the Supreme Court-appointed Special Investigation Team (SIT) had asked for the death sentence for former state minister Maya Kodnani, who was convicted in one of the worst massacres of the 2002 riots. Kodnani was sentenced to 28 years in prison last year for the murder of 97 Muslims at Naroda Patiya village on the outskirts of Ahmedabad during the riots that raged through Gujarat in February 2002. Importantly, the trial court, while convicting Kodnani, termed her a prime conspirator. Kodnani, a doctor by profession, is the first MLA and the highest-ranking politician to be convicted in Gujarat riots case. The three-time MP from Naroda and despite the serious criminal charges against her in the riots case, she was made the state's Minister for Women and Child Development in 2007.

On 29 August 2012, a former state Education Minister and 31 others were convicted for their roles in the deaths of 94 people during one of the most savage attacks of the 2002 Gujarat riots.

Sixty-five years after Independence, India still finds itself unable to safeguard its minority populations. Recovery of truth has been incomplete. Recovery of justice has been inadequate and painfully slow.

The Gujarat riots have left an indelible imprint on the Indian psyche and both media and popular culture, especially films[2] ensure an ongoing process of remembrance and learning.

The Philippines: From Edsa to Mendiola and Beyond

The People Power Revolution (also known as the EDSA Revolution of 1986) was a series of popular demonstrations in the Philippines that began in 1983 and culminated in 1986. The methods used amounted to a sustained campaign of civil resistance against regime violence and electoral fraud. This case of nonviolent revolution led to the departure of President Ferdinand Marcos and the restoration of the country's democracy. It is also referred to as the Yellow Revolution due to the presence of yellow ribbons during the demonstrations following the assassination of Benigno Aquino, Jr. It was widely seen as a victory of the people against the 20-year running of an authoritarian and a repressive regime of the then president Ferdinand Marcos and made news headlines as 'the revolution that surprised the world'.

The majority of the demonstrations took place on a long stretch of Epifanio de los Santos Avenue, more commonly known by its acronym *EDSA,* in Metropolitan Manila from 22–25 February 1986 and involved over two million Filipino civilians as well as several political, military, and religious groups led by Cardinal Jaime Sin, the Archbishop of Manila. The protests, fueled by the resistance and opposition from years of corrupt governance by Marcos, culminated with the departure of the dictator from Malacañan Palace to the United States' state of Hawaii. Corazon Aquino was proclaimed as the legitimate President of the Philippines after the revolution.

Appalled by the many and flagrant election irregularities, the Reform of the Armed Forces Movement set into motion a coup attempt against Marcos. The initial plan was for a team to assault Malacañan Palace and arrest Ferdinand Marcos. Other military units would be taking over key strategic facilities, such as the airport, military bases, TV and radio stations, the GHQAFP in Camp Aguinaldo, and major highway junctions to restrict a counter-offensive by Marcos-loyal troops. Lt. Col. Gregorio Honasan was to lead the team that was going to assault Malacañan Palace. However, after Marcos learned about the plot, he ordered their leaders' arrest, and presented to the international and local press some of the captured plotters, Maj. Saulito Aromin and Maj. Edgardo Doromal.

Threatened with their impending imprisonment, Enrile and his fellow coup plotters decided to ask for help from then AFP Vice Chief of Staff Lt. Gen Fidel Ramos, who was also the chief of the Philippine Constabulary (now the Philippine National Police). Ramos agreed to resign from his position and support the plotters. Enrile also contacted the highly influential Cardinal Archbishop of Manila Jaime Sin for his support. At about 6:30 pm on 22

February, Enrile and Ramos held a press conference at Camp Aguinaldo, where they announced that they had resigned from their positions in Marcos's cabinet and were withdrawing support from his government. Marcos himself later conducted his own news conference calling on Enrile and Ramos to surrender, urging them to 'stop this stupidity.'

In a message aired over Radio Veritas at around 9 pm, Cardinal Sin exhorted Filipinos to aid rebel leaders by going to the section of EDSA between Camp Crame and Aguinaldo and giving emotional support, food and other supplies. For many, this seemed an unwise decision since civilians would not stand a chance against a dispersal by government troops. Many people, especially priests and nuns, still trooped to EDSA. Radio Veritas played a critical role during the mass uprising. Former University of the Philippines president Francisco Nemenzo stated: 'Without Radio Veritas, it would have been difficult, if not impossible, to mobilize millions of people in a matter of hours.' Similarly, a certain account in the event said: 'Radio Veritas, in fact, was our umbilical cord to whatever else was going on.'

During the height of the revolution, an estimated one to three million people filled EDSA from Ortigas Avenue all the way to Cubao.

At dawn, Sunday, government troops arrived to knock down the main transmitter of Radio Veritas, cutting off broadcasts to people in the provinces. The station switched to a standby transmitter with a limited range of broadcast. The station was targeted because it had proven to be a valuable communications tool for the people supporting the rebels, keeping them informed of government troop movements and relaying requests for food, medicine, and supplies.

Still, people came to EDSA until it swelled to hundreds of thousands of unarmed civilians. The mood in the street was actually very festive, with many bringing whole families. Performers entertained the crowds, nuns and priests led prayer vigils, and people set up barricades and makeshift sandbags, trees, and vehicles in several places along EDSA and intersecting streets such as Santolan and Ortigas Avenue. Everywhere, people listened to Radio Veritas on their radios. Several groups sang *Bayan Ko* (My Homeland), which, since 1980, had become a patriotic anthem of the opposition. People frequently flashed the *LABAN* (fight) sign, which is an 'L' formed with their thumb and index finger.

In the mid-afternoon, Radio Veritas relayed reports of Marines massing near the camps in the east and LVT–5 tanks approaching from the north and south. A contingent of Marines with tanks and armoured vans, led by Brigadier General Artemio Tadiar, was stopped along Ortigas Avenue, about two kilometres from the camps, by tens of thousands of people. Nuns holding rosaries knelt in front of the tanks and men and women linked arms together to block the troops. Tadiar asked the crowds to make a clearing for them, but they did not budge. In the end, the troops retreated with no shots fired.

By evening, the standby transmitter of Radio Veritas failed. Shortly after midnight, the staff were able to go to another station to begin broadcasting from a secret location under the name 'Radyo Bandido' (Bandit Radio) and the Radio Veritas' programme continued throughout the night and in the remaining days.

At dawn on Monday, February 24, the first serious encounter with government troops occurred. Marines marching from Libis, in the east, lobbed tear gas at the demonstrators, who quickly dispersed. Some 3,000 Marines then entered and held the east side of Camp Aguinaldo. Later, helicopters manned by the 15th Strike Wing of the Philippine Air Force, led by Colonel Antonio Sotelo, were ordered from Sangley Point in Cavite (South of Manila) to head to Camp Crame. Secretly, the squadron had already defected and instead of attacking Camp Crame, landed in it, with the crowds cheering and hugging the pilots and crew members. A Bell 214helicopter piloted by Major Deo Cruz of the 205th Helicopter Wing and Sikorsky S–76 gunships piloted by Colonel Charles Hotchkiss of the 20th Air Commando Squadron joined the rebel squadron earlier in the air. The presence of the helicopters boosted the morale of Enrile and Ramos who had been continually encouraging their fellow soldiers to join the opposition movement. In the afternoon, Aquino arrived at the base where Enrile, Ramos, RAM officers and a throng were waiting.

At around that time, reports were received that Marcos had left Malacañan Palace and this was broadcast to the people at EDSA. The crowd celebrated and even Ramos and Enrile came out from Crame to appear to the crowds. The jubilation was, however, short-lived as Marcos later appeared on television on the government-controlled Channel 4, (using the foreclosed ABS-CBN facilities, transmitter and compound) declaring that he would not step down. It was thereafter speculated that the false report was a calculated move against Marcos to encourage more defections. During this broadcast, Channel 4 suddenly went off the air. A contingent of rebels, under Colonel Mariano Santiago, had captured the station. Channel 4 was put back on line shortly after noon. By this time, the crowds at EDSA had swollen to over a million. (Some estimates placed them at two million.) This broadcast was considered the 'return' of ABS-CBN on air because this was the time when former employees of ABS-CBN were inside the complex after 14 years of closure since Marcos took it over during the Martial Law of 1972. In the late afternoon, rebel helicopters attacked Villamor Airbase, destroying presidential air assets. Another helicopter went to Malacañang, fired a rocket and caused minor damage. Later, most of the officers who had graduated from the Philippine Military Academy (PMA) defected. The majority of the Armed Forces had already changed sides.

Corazon Aquino was inaugurated as the 11th president of the Philippines on 25 February 1986, in a simple ceremony at Club Filipino in Greenhills, about a kilometre from Camp Crame, at Sampaguita Hall (Now Kalayaan Hall). She was sworn in as President by Senior Associate Justice Claudio Teehankee, and Laurel as Vice-President by Justice Vicente Abad Santos. The Bible on which Aquino swore her oath was held by Aurora Aquino, the mother of Ninoy Aquino. Attending the ceremonies were Ramos, who was then promoted to General, Enrile, and many politicians. Outside Club Filipino, all the way to EDSA, hundreds of people cheered and celebrated. *Bayan Ko* was sung after Aquino's oath-taking. Many people wore yellow, the colour of Aquino's campaign for presidency.

An hour later, Marcos conducted the inauguration at Malacañang. Loyalist civilians attended the ceremony, shouting '*Marcos, Marcos, Marcos pa rin!*(Marcos, Marcos, still Marcos!)'. On the Palace balcony, Marcos took his oath as the President of the Philippines, broadcast by IBC–13 and GMA–7.

None of the invited foreign dignitaries attended the ceremony for security reasons. The couple finally stepped out in the balcony of the palace in front of the 3000 KBL loyalists who were shouting to Marcos: *'Capture the snakes!'* First Lady Imelda Marcos sang one more rendition of *'Dahil Sa Iyo'* (Because of You), the couple's theme song, rather tearfully. After the inauguration, the Marcos family and their close associates hurriedly rushed to leave the Palace. The broadcast of the event was also cut off as rebel troops successfully captured the other stations. By this time, hundreds of people had amassed at the barricades along Mendiola, only a hundred metres away from Malacañang. They were prevented from storming the Palace by loyal government troops securing the area. The angry demonstrators were pacified by priests who warned them not to be violent.

At 3 pm, Monday, (EST) Marcos talked to United States Senator Paul Laxalt, asking for advice from the White House. Laxalt advised him to 'cut and cut cleanly', to which Marcos expressed his disappointment after a short pause. In the afternoon, Marcos talked to Enrile, asking for safe passage for him and his family including his close allies like General Ver. Finally, at Midnight, the Marcos family was transported by a US Airforce HH–3 Rescue helicopters to Clark Air Base in Angeles City, Pampanga, about 83 kilometres north of Manila, before boarding US Air Force DC–9 Medivac and C–141B planes bound for Andersen Air Force Base in Guam, and finally to Hickam Air Force Base in Hawaii where Marcos arrived on February 26.

When the news of Marcos' departure reached the people, many rejoiced and danced in the streets. Over at Mendiola, the demonstrators were finally able to enter Malacañan Palace, long denied to Filipinos in the past decade. Looting by overly angry protesters occurred, but mostly people wandered inside, looking at the place where all the decisions that changed the course of Philippine history had been made. Many people around the world rejoiced and congratulated Filipinos they knew. CBS anchorman Bob Simon reported: 'We Americans like to think we taught the Filipinos democracy. Well, tonight they are teaching the world.'

The revolution had an effect on democratization movements in countries such as Taiwan and South Korea; other effects included the restoration of the freedom of the press, adoption of a new constitution, and the subordination of the military to civilian rule, despite several coup attempts during the Aquino administration. The revolution provided for the restoration of democratic institutions after 13 years of authoritarian rule and these institutions have been used by various groups to challenge the entrenched political families and to strengthen Philippine democracy.

A statue was erected commemorating the revolution along EDSA near the entrance of Camp Aguinaldo. The EDSA Revolution Anniversary is a special public holiday in the Philippines.

One year later, the Mendiola massacre, also called Black Thursday by some Filipino journalists, took place in Mendiola Street, San Miguel, Manila, Philippines on 22 January 1987, in which state security forces violently dispersed a farmers' march to Malacañan Palace. Thirteen of the farmers were killed and many wounded when government anti-riot forces opened fire on them. The farmers were demanding fulfillment of the promises made regarding land reform during the Presidential campaign of Cory Aquino, and distribution of lands at no cost to beneficiaries.

By January 1987, the administration of Corazon C. Aquino had been in power less than a year since the ouster Ferdinand E. Marcos as President of the Philippines. The *Kilusang Magbubukid ng Pilipinas* (Filipino, 'Peasants' Movement of the Philippines'), a militant farmers' group led by Jaime Tadeo, demanded genuine agrarian reform from the Aquino government. On 15 January 1987, members of the *Kilusang Magbubukid ng Pilipinas* encamped at the Ministry of Agrarian Reform (now the Department of Agrarian Reform) in Diliman, Quezon City. The group presented their problems and demands, one of which was the free distribution of land to farmers. Dialogue between the farmers, represented by Jaime Tadeo, and the government, represented by then Agrarian Reform Minister Heherson Alvarez took place on 20 January 1987. Alvarez promised to bring the matter to the President's attention during the next day's cabinet meeting. The farmers barricaded the Ministry of Agrarian Reform offices on 21 January 1987 and prevented government employees from exiting the building. A negotiating panel was to be assembled the following day for further talks. On 22 January 1987, the farmers decided to march to Malacañan Palace in order to air their demands instead of negotiating with Heherson Alvarez. Marching from the Quezon Memorial Circle, Tadeo's group was joined by members of other militant groups: *Kilusang Mayo Uno* (May One Movement), *Bagong Alyansang Makabayan* (New Patriotic Alliance), League of Filipino Students and *Kongreso ng Pagkakaisa ng Maralitang Lungsod* (Unity Congress of the Urban Poor). At 1 in the afternoon, the marchers reached Liwasang Bonifacio and held a brief presentation. At around the same time, anti-riot personnel under the command of Capital Regional Command commander Gen. Ramon Montaño, Task Force Nazareno, under the command of Col. Cesar Nazareno and police forces under the command of Western Police District Chief Brig. Gen. Alfredo Lim were deployed around the vicinity of Malacañang.

The first line of civil disturbance control units consisted of policemen from the Western Police District. About ten yards behind the policemen were Integrated National Police Field Force units. The third line, a further ten yards from the second police line, consisted of a Philippine Marine Corps unit, the Marine Civil Disturbance Control Battalion. Positioned behind the Marines were army trucks, water cannons, fire trucks and two Mobile Dispersal Teams equipped with tear gas delivery gear.

The marchers numbered 10,000–15,000 by the time they reached Claro M. Recto Avenue. They clashed with the police, and the police lines were breached. At this point, gunshots were heard and the marchers disengaged from the melee, retreating towards Claro M. Recto Avenue. Sporadic gunfire could be heard amidst the withdrawal. Alfredo Lim, now Mayor of Manila, maintains that the Marines were responsible for the shooting.

In 1988, Philippine Congress finally enacted Comprehensive Agrarian Reform Law (Republic Act No. 6657), proving that the EDSA revolution was a reality, indeed.

Timor Leste: The Santa Cruz Massacre

The Santa Cruz Massacre (also known as the Dili massacre) was the shooting of at least 250 East Timorese pro-independence demonstrators in the Santa Cruz cemetery in the capital, Dili, on 12 November 1991, during the Indonesian occupation of East Timor.

In October 1991, a delegation to East Timor consisting of members from the Portuguese Parliament and 12 journalists was planned during a visit from UN Special Rapporteur for Human Rights on Torture, Pieter Kooijmans. The Indonesian Government objected to the inclusion in the delegation of Jill Jolliffe an Australian journalist who it regarded as supportive of the Fretilin independence movement, and Portugal subsequently cancelled the delegation. The cancellation demoralized independence activists in East Timor, who had hoped to use the visit to raise the international profile of their cause. Tensions between Indonesian authorities and East Timorese youth rose in the days after Portugal's cancellation. On 28 October, Indonesian troops had located a group of resistance members in Dili's Motael Church. A confrontation ensued between pro-integration activists and those in the church; when it was over, one man on each side was dead. Sebastião Gomes, a supporter of independence for East Timor, was taken out of the church and shot by Indonesian troops, and integration activist Afonso Henriques was stabbed and killed during the fight.

A number of foreigners had come to East Timor to observe the Portuguese delegation, including independent US journalists Amy Goodman and Allan Nairn, and British cameraman Max Stahl. They attended a memorial service for Gomes on 12 November, during which several thousand men, women and children walked from the Motael Church to the nearby Santa Cruz cemetery. Along the way, members of the group pulled out protest banners and East Timorese flags, chanted slogans, and taunted Indonesian soldiers and police officers. Organizers of the protest maintained order during the protest; although it was loud, the crowd was peaceful and orderly, by most accounts. It was the largest and most visible demonstration against the Indonesian occupation since 1975.

During a brief confrontation between Indonesian troops and protesters, a number of protesters and a Major, Gerhan Lantara, were stabbed. Stahl claimed Lantara had attacked a group of protesters, including a girl carrying the flag of East Timor, and FRETILIN activist Constâncio Pinto reported eyewitness accounts of beatings from Indonesian soldiers and police. When the procession reached the cemetery, the leading section of the procession entered the cemetery while many continued their protests before the cemetery wall, waving flags and chanting pro-independence slogans. Indonesian troops had been standing by during this time, then a new group of 200 Indonesian soldiers appeared and began shooting. Fleeing people ran through the main entrance and deeper into the cemetery and were pursued by the soldiers.

The massacre was witnessed by two American journalists – Amy Goodman and Allan Nairn (who were also attacked) – and caught on videotape by Max Stahl, who was filming undercover for Yorkshire Television. As Stahl filmed the massacre, Goodman and Nairn tried to 'serve as a shield for the Timorese' by standing between them and the Indonesian soldiers. The soldiers began beating Goodman, and when Nairn moved to protect her, they beat him with their weapons, fracturing his skull. The camera crew managed to smuggle the video footage to Australia. They gave it to Saskia Kouwenberg, a Dutch journalist, to prevent it being seized and confiscated by Australian authorities, who subjected the camera crew to a strip-search when they arrived in Darwin, having been tipped off by Indonesia. The video footage was used in the *First Tuesday* documentary *In Cold Blood: The Massacre of East Timor*, shown on ITV in the UK in January 1992, as well as numerous other, more recent documentaries. Stahl's footage, combined with the testimony of Nairn and Goodman and others, caused outrage around the world. The programme *In Cold Blood: The Massacre of East Timor* was the overall winner at the inaugural Amnesty International UK Media Awards in 1992.

At least 250 East Timorese were killed in the massacre. One of the dead was a New Zealander, Kamal Bamadhaj, a political science student and human rights activist based in Australia. Indonesian authorities described the incident as a spontaneous reaction to violence from the protesters or a 'misunderstanding'. Objectors cited two factors: the documented history of mass violence committed by Indonesian troops in places such as Quelicai, Lacluta, and Kraras, and a series of statements from politicians and officers in Indonesia, justifying the military's violence. Try Sutrisno, Commander-in-Chief of the Indonesian forces, said two days after the massacre: 'The army cannot be underestimated. Finally we had to shoot them. Delinquents like these agitators must be shot, and they will be'.

In response to the massacre, activists around the world organized in solidarity with the East Timorese. Although a small network of individuals and groups had been working for human rights and self-determination in East Timor since the occupation began, their activity took on a new urgency after the 1991 massacre. TAPOL, a British organization formed in 1973 to advocate for democracy in Indonesia, increased its work around East Timor. In the United States, the East Timor Action Network was founded and soon had chapters in 10 cities around the country. Other solidarity groups appeared in Portugal, Australia, Japan, Germany, Malaysia, Ireland, and Brazil.

The television pictures of the massacre were shown worldwide, causing the Indonesian government considerable embarrassment. The coverage was a vivid example of how growth of new media in Indonesia was making it increasingly difficult for the 'New Order' to control information flow in and out of Indonesia, and that in the post-Cold War 1990s, the government was coming under increasing international scrutiny. Copies of the Santa Cruz footage were distributed back into Indonesia allowing more Indonesians to see the actions of their government uncensored. A number of pro-democracy student groups and their magazines began to openly and critically discuss not just East Timor, but also the 'New Order' and the broader history and future of Indonesia.

The US Congress voted to cut off funding for IMET training of Indonesian military personnel although arms sales continued from the US to the Indonesian National Armed Forces. President Clinton cut off all US military ties with the Indonesian military in 1999. By 2005, the US had resumed training and cooperation and by 2012, President Obama had increased military financial aid to US $1.56 billion and approved the resumption of direct US military training of Indonesian special forces.

The massacre prompted the Portuguese government to increase its diplomatic campaign. Portugal unsuccessfully tried to apply international pressure by raising the issue with its fellow European Union members in their dealings with Indonesia. However, other EU countries like the UK had close economic relations with Indonesia, including arms sales, and were reluctant to jeopardize these.

In Australia, there was criticism of the federal government's recognition of Jakarta's sovereignty over East Timor. The government had been promoting increased ties with the Indonesian military at the time of the massacre, but in 1999 had temporarily cut off military ties in response to the violence after that year's independence referendum. Australian foreign minister Gareth Evans, described the killings as 'an aberration, not an act of state policy'.

Commemorated as a public holiday in now independent East Timor, 12 November is remembered by the East Timorese as one of the bloodiest days in their history, one which drew international attention to their fight for independence.

When film footage of the massacre at Santa Cruz. was broadcast to audiences around the world it provoked a significant international outcry against the practices of the Indonesian military in Timor-Leste. However, even in the face of strong international demands to bring those who had killed unarmed demonstrators to account, the institutional practices of ABRI/TNI provided the majority of perpetrators who were most responsible with effective impunity.

On the 20th anniversary of the massacre, ETAN (the East Timor and Indonesia Action Network) observed: 'While Timor-Leste is now independent, its people will not be able to overcome their tragic past without knowing what was done with their relatives' and friends' bodies. Ongoing impunity for decades of systematic Indonesian military and police atrocities keeps the East Timorese and Indonesian people from consolidating their democracies and moving on with their lives.'

Much remains to be done. A year ago, ETAN noted: 'Impunity for decades of systematic Indonesian military and police atrocities prevents both countries from consolidating the rule of law as they transition from military dictatorship to democracy.'

ETAN continued to urge the US Congress and the Obama administration to respond to the recommendations of Timor-Leste's Commission for Truth, Reception and Reconciliation, especially 'its calls for an international tribunal to try perpetrators of crimes against humanity during the Indonesian occupation, reparations from Indonesia and other countries that supported the occupation, and restrictions on foreign assistance to the Indonesian military.'

ETAN also urged the US and others to press Indonesia 'to immediately release all information that can help identify and locate those who were killed or disappeared during the occupation,.'

ANTI (Aliansa Nasional Timor-Leste Ba Tribunal Internasional) issued a Declaration in *Commemoration of the Santa Cruz Massacre, 12 November 1991–2013* which stresses: 'Truth and Justice are the foundations for developing democracy in Timor-Leste'.

ANTI delivered the following demands on the anniversary of the Santa Cruz massacre:

1. ANTI continues to demand that the international community not abandon their responsibility to prosecute serious crimes committed by the

Indonesian military during the illegal occupation because the impacts of impunity continue to haunt the Indonesian and Timorese people.

2. ANTI asks the international community to help the people of Indonesia and Timor-Leste create a credible justice mechanism so that we can end the prevalent culture of impunity.
3. ANTI calls attention to key nations, such as the USA, UK, France and Australia, which supported the military regime of Soeharto, and its illegal occupation of Timor-Leste from 1975 to 1999. In particular, through donor programmes, we ask that they give priority to the victims and their families as a special category which needs supports and especially deserves to share in the benefits of Timor-Leste's development.
4. ANTI also requests that international corporations and agencies which benefitted from selling weapons to Indonesia during the occupation in Timor-Leste, particularly those that provided materials which were used in Timor-Leste, must compensate through humanitarian funding for reparations for victims of human rights violations.
5. ANTI demands that all Member States of the UN refuse to issue visas to current and former Indonesian military officials whose names are mentioned in the *Chega* report, because they committed crimes or had commanded responsibility for such crimes. In this way, we also request that they be sanctioned, such as removing access to their bank accounts until such time as independent confirmation of their credibility and innocence is established. We are especially disappointed that accused criminal Wiranto is free to travel to certain nations, including speaking at a seminar in China at the beginning of 2013.
6. ANTI requests that the State of Timor-Leste ratify the International Convention on the Protection of all Persons from Enforced Disappearances because ANTI believes that Timor-Leste and Indonesia can use this mechanism to search for those people who disappeared during the war, including the many civilians which the Indonesian military are accused of being responsible for their deaths during the 1991 Santa Cruz Massacre.
7. ANTI also asks Timor-Leste State institutions, particularly the State Secretariat for Veterans Affairs and the Ministry of Social Solidarity, to support and facilitate families who are currently searching for the remains of their loved ones so they can bury them in an appropriate place, such as the Ossuaries that the State of Timor-Leste has already prepared.
8. Finally, ANTI also asks that all entities (religious institutions, NGOs, academics and the entire community) coordinate efforts to build a movement to search for those who disappeared to encourage the government and the National Parliament to realize this absolutely fundamental problem continues to be a concern of families and violates their right to truth.

Through this we can achieve peace and reconciliation for the present and the future.

Cambodia: The Pol Pot Genocide

Cambodia is a small country in South-East Asia, less than half the size of California. Following independence from France in 1953, Cambodia elected a Prime Minister who was subsequently overthrown by General Lon Nol in a coup. The population was 7 million at the time.

The genocide began in 1975 when the Khmer Rouge overthrew Lon Nol and lasted until the Vietnamese invaded in 1978. The Khmer Rouge began as a guerilla movement in the 1960s, led by Pol Pot. Pol Pot sought to deconstruct Cambodia back to a primitive and classless 'Year Zero', where all citizens would participate in rural work projects and all Western innovations would be removed.

In order to achieve the 'ideal' communist model, the Khmer Rouge believed that all Cambodians must be made to work as labourers in a huge federation of collective farms and all opposition was to be eliminated. Potential 'opposition' included intellectuals, doctors, teachers, professionals, monks, Buddhists, Muslims, Christians, ethnic Chinese, Vietnamese, Thai, and Cambodians with Chinese, Vietnamese, or Thai ancestry. The Khmer Rouge vigorously interrogated its members and frequently executed members on suspicions of treachery or sabotage. Survival in Khmer Rouge Cambodia was determined by one's ability to work.

During the Vietnam War, the United States backed South Vietnamese forces and Cambodia became a battlefield, despite its neutrality. High Cambodian civilian casualties resulted in opposition to western democracy, driving new recruits to the Khmer Rouge guerilla movement. Pol Pot's communism brought images of new hope, promise, and national tranquillity. Within days of the Khmer Rouge takeover in 1975, Pol Pot implemented his extremist policies of collectivization and communal labour.

Cambodians nationwide were forced out from their hometowns and villages. The ill, disabled, old, and young who were incapable of making the journey to collective farms and labour camps perished. Entire cities were forcibly evacuated to the countryside; all political and civil rights were abolished. Children were taken from their parents and placed in separate forced labour camps. Factories, schools, universities, hospitals, and all other private institutions were shut down and their former owners and employees were murdered, along with their extended families. Religion was banned: leading Buddhist monks and Christian missionaries were killed, and temples and churches were burned. It was common for people to be shot for speaking a foreign language, wearing glasses, smiling, or crying.

In an effort to create a society without competition, in which people worked for the common good, the Khmer Rouge placed people in collective living arrangements – or communes – and enacted 're-education' programmes to encourage the commune lifestyle. People were divided into categories that reflected the trust that the Khmer Rouge had for them; the most trustworthy were called 'old citizens'. The pro-West and city dwellers began as 'new citizens' and could move up to 'deportees', then 'candidates' and finally 'full rights citizens'; however, most citizens never moved up. Those who refused re-education were killed in the fields surrounding the commune or at the infamous prison camp Tuol Sleng Centre, known as S–21.

Cambodians who survived the purges and marches became unpaid labourers, working on minimum rations for endless hours. They were forced to live in public communes, similar to military barracks, with constant food shortages and rampant disease. These conditions of genocide continued for three years until Vietnam invaded Cambodia in 1978 and overthrew the Khmer Rouge government.

Ethnic groups were attacked including the three largest minorities; the Vietnamese, Chinese, and Cham Muslims, along with twenty other smaller groups. Fifty per cent of the estimated 4,25,000 Chinese living in Cambodia in 1975 perished. Khmer Rouge also forced Muslims to eat pork and shot those who refused.

Over two million were killed – more than 25 per cent of the total population. Cambodia lay in ruin under the newly-established Vietnamese regime. The economy failed under Pol Pot, as all professionals, engineers, technicians, and planners who could potentially reorganize Cambodia had been killed or fled during the genocide. Guerilla forces continued fighting between 1978 and 1989, and a peace agreement was reached in 1991. The nation's first democratic election was held in 1993.

After 1993, most of the Killing Fields have become museums or places of sad memory. The Killing Fields near Phnom Penh and Tuol Sleng are such places. From this perspective, the Cambodian society hasn't yet recovered and it still has a long way to go.

The Tuol Sleng Genocide Museum is a museum in Phnom Penh, the capital of Cambodia. The site is a former high school which was used as the notorious Security Prison 21 (S–21) by the Khmer Rouge regime from its rise to power in 1975 to its fall in 1979 (Khmer Toul Sleng) means 'Hill of the Poisonous Trees' or 'Strychnine Hill'). Tuol Sleng was only one of at least 150 execution centres in the country, and as many as 20,000 prisoners were killed there.

Out of an estimated 17,000 people imprisoned at Tuol Sleng, there were only 12 known survivors. As of September 2011, only three of them are thought to be still alive: Chum Mey, Bou Meng and Chim Math. All three were kept alive because they had skills their captors judged to be useful. Bou Meng, whose wife was killed in the prison, is an artist. Chum Mey was kept alive because of his skills in repairing machinery. Chim Math was held in S–21 for two weeks and transferred to the nearby Prey Sar prison. She may have been spared because she was from Stoeung district in Kampong Thom where Comrade Duch was born. She intentionally distinguished herself by emphasizing her provincial accent during her interrogations. Vann Nath, who was spared because of his ability to paint, died on 5 September 2011.

The prison had a staff of 1,720 people. Of those, approximately 300 were office staff, internal workforce and interrogators. The other 1,400 were general workers, including people who grew food for the prison. Several of these workers were children taken from the prisoner families. The chief of the prison was Khang Khek Ieu (also known as Comrade Duch), a former mathematics teacher who worked closely with Khmer Rouge leader Pol Pot. Other leading figures of S–21 were Khim Vat aka Hor (deputy chief of S–21), Peng (chief of guards), Chan (chief of the Interrogation Unit), and Pon (interrogator). Pon was the person who interrogated important people such as Keo Meas, Nay Sarann, Ho Nim, Tiv Ol, and Phok Chhay.

The documentation unit was responsible for transcribing tape-recorded confessions, typing the handwritten notes from prisoners' confessions, preparing summaries of confessions, and maintaining files. In the photography sub-unit, workers took mug shots of prisoners when they arrived, pictures of prisoners who had died while in detention, and pictures of important prisoners after they were executed. Thousands of photographs have survived, but thousands are still missing.

The defense unit was the largest unit in S–21. The guards in this unit were mostly teenagers. Many guards found the unit's strict rules hard to obey. Guards were not allowed to talk to prisoners, to learn their names, or to beat them. They were also forbidden to observe or eavesdrop on interrogations, and they were expected to obey 30 regulations, which barred them from such things as taking naps, sitting down or leaning against a wall while on duty. They had to walk, guard, and examine everything carefully. Guards who made serious mistakes were arrested, interrogated, jailed and put to death. Most of the people employed at S–21 were terrified of making mistakes and feared being tortured and killed.

The interrogation unit was split into three separate groups: Krom Noyobai or political unit, Krom Kdao or 'hot' unit and Krom Angkiem or 'chewing' unit. The hot unit (sometimes called the cruel unit) was allowed to use torture. In contrast, the cold unit (sometimes called the gentle unit) was prohibited from using torture to obtain confessions. If they could not make prisoners confess, they would transfer them to the hot unit. The chewing unit dealt with tough and important cases. Those who worked as interrogators were literate and usually in their 20s.

Some of the staff who worked in Tuol Sleng also ended up as prisoners. They confessed to being lazy in preparing documents, to having damaged machines and various equipment, and to having beaten prisoners to death without permission when assisting with interrogations.

Concentration Camp Rules

When prisoners were first brought to Tuol Sleng, they were made aware of 10 rules that they were to follow during their incarceration. What follows is what is posted today at the Tuol Sleng Museum; the imperfect grammar is a result of faulty translation from the original Khmer:

1. You must answer accordingly to my question. Don't turn them away.
2. Don't try to hide the facts by making pretexts this and that, you are strictly prohibited to contest me.
3. Don't be a fool for you are a chap who dare to thwart the revolution.
4. You must immediately answer my questions without wasting time to reflect.
5. Don't tell me either about your immoralities or the essence of the revolution.
6. While getting lashes or electrification you must not cry at all.
7. Do nothing, sit still and wait for my orders. If there is no order, keep quiet. When I ask you to do something, you must do it right away without protesting.

8. Don't make pretext about Kampuchea Krom in order to hide your secret or traitor.
9. If you don't follow all the above rules, you shall get many lashes of electric wire.
10. If you disobey any point of my regulations you shall get either 10 lashes or five shocks of electric discharge.

During testimony at the Khmer Rouge Tribunal on 27 April 2009, Duch claimed the 10 security regulations were a fabrication of the Vietnamese officials that first set up the Tuol Sleng Genocide Museum.

In 1979, Ho Van Tay, a Vietnamese combat photographer, was the first journalist to document Tuol Sleng to the world. Van Tay and his colleagues followed the stench of rotting corpses to the gates of Tuol Sleng. The photos of Ho Van Tay documenting what he saw when he entered the site are exhibited in Tuol Sleng today.

The Khmer Rouge required that the prison staff make a detailed dossier for each prisoner. Included in the documentation was a photograph. Since the original negatives and photographs were separated from the dossiers in the 1979–1980 period, most of the photographs remain anonymous today.

The buildings at Tuol Sleng are preserved as they were left when the Khmer Rouge were driven out in 1979. The regime kept extensive records, including thousands of photographs. Several rooms of the museum are now lined, floor to ceiling, with black-and-white photographs of some of the estimated 17,000 prisoners who passed through the prison.

The site has four main buildings, known as Building A, B, C, and D. Building A holds the large cells in which the bodies of the last victims were discovered. Building B holds galleries of photographs. Building C holds the rooms sub-divided into small cells for prisoners. Building D holds other memorabilia, including instruments of torture.

Other rooms contain only a rusting iron bedframe, beneath a black-and-white photograph showing the room as it was found by the Vietnamese. In each photograph, the mutilated body of a prisoner is chained to the bed, killed by his fleeing captors only hours before the prison was captured. Other rooms preserve leg-irons and instruments of torture. They are accompanied by paintings by former inmate Vann Nath showing people being tortured, which were added by the post-Khmer Rouge regime installed by the Vietnamese in 1979.

Today, the museum is open to the public and, along with the Choeung Ek Memorial (The Killing Fields), is included as a point of interest for those visiting Cambodia. Tuol Sleng also remains an important educational site as well as memorial for Cambodians.

The ECCC is the Cambodia Tribunal officially known as the Extraordinary Chambers in the Courts of Cambodia. ECCC is a court established to try the most senior and most responsible members of the Khmer Rouge. Since 2010, ECCC brings Cambodians on a 'study tour' to the Tuol Sleng, Choeung Ek and finishing at the ECCC complex. During 2010, around 27,000 Cambodians visited the museum through this tour. Some believed that ghosts of the victims continue to haunt the place.

The Khmer Rouge Killing Machine is a 2003 film by Rithy Panh, a Cambodian-born, French-trained filmmaker who lost his family when he was 11. The film features two Tuol Sleng survivors, Vann Nath and Chum Mey, confronting their former Khmer Rouge captors, including guards, interrogators, a doctor and a photographer. The focus of the film is the difference between the feelings of the survivors, who want to understand what happened at Tuol Sleng to warn future generations, and the former jailers, who cannot escape the horror of the genocide they helped create.

China: The Tiananmen Square Protests of 1989

The Tiananmen Square protests of 1989 were student-led popular demonstrations in Beijing which took place in the spring of 1989 and received broad support from city residents, exposing deep splits within China's political leadership. The protests were forcibly suppressed by hard line leaders who ordered the military to enforce martial law in the country's capital. The crackdown that was initiated on 3–4 June became known as the Tiananmen Square Massacre as troops with assault rifles and tanks inflicted thousands of casualties on unarmed civilians trying to block the military's advance on Tiananmen Square in the heart of Beijing, which student demonstrators had occupied for seven weeks. The scale of military mobilization and the resulting bloodshed were unprecedented in the history of Beijing, a city with a rich tradition of popular protests in the 20th century.

The protests were triggered in April 1989 by the death of the former Communist Party General Secretary, Hu Yaobang, a liberal reformer, who was deposed after losing a power struggle with hardliners over the direction of political and economic reform. University students who marched and gathered in Tiananmen Square to mourn Hu also voiced grievances against inflation, limited career prospects, and corruption of the party elite. They called for government accountability, freedom of the press, freedom of speech, and the restoration of workers' control over industry. At the height of the protests, about a million people assembled in the Square.

Starting on the night of 17 April 3,000 PKU students marched from the campus towards Tiananmen Square, and soon nearly a thousand students from Tsinghua joined. Upon arrival, they soon joined forces with those already gathered at the Square. As its size grew, the gathering gradually evolved into a protest, as students began to draft a list of pleas and suggestions (*Seven Demands*) for the government:

- Affirm as correct, Hu Yaobang's views on democracy and freedom.
- Admit that the campaigns against spiritual pollution and bourgeois liberalization had been wrong.
- Publish information on the income of state leaders and their family members.
- End the ban on privately run newspapers and stop press censorship.
- Increase funding for education and raise the pay of intellectuals.
- End restrictions on demonstrations in Beijing.
- Provide objective coverage of students in official media.

On the morning of 18 April, students remained in the Square. Some gathered around the Monument to the People's Heroes singing patriotic songs and listening to impromptu speeches by student organizers, others gathered at the Great Hall. Meanwhile, a few thousand students gathered at Xinhua Gate, the entrance to Zhongnanhai, the seat of the party leadership, where they demanded dialogue with the leadership. Police restrained the students from entering the compound. Students then staged a sit-in.

On 20 April, most students had been persuaded to leave Xinhua Gate. To disperse about 200 students that remained, police employed batons; minor clashes were reported. Many students felt they were abused by the police, and rumours about police brutality spread quickly. The Xinhua Gate incident angered students on campus, where those who were not hitherto politically active decided to join the protests. Also on this date, a group of workers calling themselves the 'Beijing Workers' Autonomous Federation' issued two handbills challenging the central leadership.

Hu's state funeral took place on 22 April. On the evening of 21 April, some 1,00,000 students marched on Tiananmen Square, ignoring orders from Beijing municipal authorities that the Square was to be closed off for the funeral. The funeral, which took place inside the Great Hall and attended by the leadership, was broadcast live to the students. General Secretary Zhao Ziyang delivered the eulogy. The funeral seemed rushed, and only lasted 40 minutes, as emotions ran high in the Square. Students wept.

From 21 to 23 April, students began organizing under the banners of formal organizations. On 23 April, the 'Beijing Autonomous University Students Union' ('the Union') was formed. It elected CUPL student Zhou Yongjun as chair; Wang Dan and Wu'erkaixi also emerged as leaders. From this vantage point, the Union called for a general class boycott at all Beijing universities. Such an independent organization operating outside of party jurisdiction alarmed the leadership.

On 22 April, near dusk, serious rioting broke out in Changsha and Xi'an. In Xi'an, arson from rioters destroyed cars and houses, and looting occurred in shops near the city's Xihua Gate. In Changsha, 38 stores were ransacked by looters. Over 350 people were arrested in both cities. In Wuhan, university students organized protests against the provincial government. As the situation became more volatile nationally, Zhao Ziyang called numerous meetings of the Politburo Standing Committee (PSC). Zhao stressed three points: discourage students from further protests and ask them to go back to class, use all measures necessary to combat rioting, and open forms of dialogue with students at different levels of government. Premier Li Peng called upon Zhao to condemn protesters and recognize the need to take more serious action. Zhao dismissed Li's views. Despite calls for him to remain in Beijing, Zhao left for a scheduled state visit to North Korea on 23 April.

Zhao's departure to North Korea left Li Peng as the acting executive authority in Beijing. On 24 April, Li Peng and the PSC met with Beijing Party Secretary Li Ximing and mayor Chen Xitong to gauge the situation at the Square. The municipal officials wanted a quick resolution to the crisis, and framed the protests as a conspiracy to overthrow China's political system and major party leaders, including Deng Xiaoping. In Zhao's absence, the PSC agreed that firm action against protesters must be taken. On the morning of 25 April, President Yang Shangkun and Premier Li Peng met with Deng at the latter's residence. Deng endorsed a hardline stance and said an appropriate 'warning' must be disseminated via mass media to curb further demonstrations. The meeting firmly established the first official evaluation of the protests from the leadership, and highlighted Deng's having 'final say' on important issues. Li Peng subsequently ordered Deng's views to be drafted as a communique and issued to all high-level Communist Party officials in an effort to mobilize the party apparatus against protesters.

On 26 April, the party's official newspaper *People's Daily* issued a front-page editorial titled 'It is necessary to take a clear-cut stand against disturbances'. It accused 'extremely small segments of opportunists' of plotting to overthrow the Communist Party and the political system. The statement enraged students, who interpreted it as a direct indictment on the protests and its cause. The editorial backfired. Instead of scaring students into submission, it antagonized the students against the state. The editorial proved to be a major sticking point for the remainder of the protests. It evoked memories of the 1976 Tiananmen Incident: an event that was initially branded as an anti-government conspiracy with much the same language as the 26 April editorial but was later rehabilitated as 'patriotic' under Deng's leadership.

Organized by the Union, on 27 April some 50,000–1,00,000 students from all Beijing universities marched through the streets of the capital to Tiananmen Square, breaking through lines set up by police, and receiving widespread public support along the way, particularly from factory workers. The student leaders, eager to show the patriotic nature of the movement, also toned down anti-Communist slogans, choosing to present a message of 'anti-corruption, anti-cronyism' but 'pro-party'. In a twist of irony, student factions who genuinely called for the overthrow of the Communist Party gained traction as a result of the 26 April editorial.

The stunning success of the March protests forced the government into making concessions and meeting with student representatives. On 29 April, State Council spokesman Yuan Mu met with appointed representatives of government-sanctioned student associations. While the talks discussed a wide range of issues, including the editorial, the Xinhua Gate incident, and freedom of the press, they achieved few substantive results. Independent student leaders such as Wuer Kaixi refused to attend.

The government's tone grew increasingly conciliatory as Zhao Ziyang returned from Pyongyang on 30 April and resumed his executive authority. In Zhao's view, the hardliner approach had proven to be useless, and concession was the only alternative. Zhao asked that the press be opened to report the movement positively, and delivered two sympathetic speeches on 3–4 May. In the speeches, Zhao said that the student's concerns about corruption were legitimate, and that the student movement was patriotic in nature. The speeches essentially negated the message presented by 26 April editorial. While some 1,00,000 students marched on the streets of Beijing on 4 May to commemorate the May Fourth Movement and repeat demands from earlier marches, many students were satisfied with the government's concessions. On 4 May, all Beijing universities, except PKU and BNU, announced the end of the class boycott. Subsequently, the majority of students began to lose interest in the movement.

Students began a hunger strike on 13 May, two days prior to the highly publicized state visit by Soviet leader Mikhail Gorbachev. Knowing that the welcoming ceremony for Gorbachev was scheduled to be held in the Square, student leaders wanted to use the hunger strike there as a bargaining chip to force the government into meeting their demands. Moreover, the hunger strike gained widespread sympathy from the population at large and earned the student movement the moral high ground that it sought. By the afternoon of 13 May, some 3,00,000 gathered at the Square.

Inspired by the course of events in Beijing, protests and strikes began at universities in other cities, with many students traveling to Beijing to join the demonstration. Generally, the demonstration at Tiananmen Square was well-ordered, with daily marches of students from various Beijing-area colleges displaying their solidarity with the class boycott and with the demands of the protest. The students sang *The Internationale*, the world socialist anthem, on their way to, and within, the Square.

Afraid that the movement would now spin out of control, Deng Xiaoping asked that the Square be cleared for the Gorbachev visit. Executing Deng's request, Zhao used a soft approach, and directed his subordinates to coordinate negotiations with students immediately. Zhao believed he could appeal to the students' patriotism, and that the students understood signs of internal turmoil during the Sino-Soviet summit would embarrass the nation (not just the government). Press restrictions were loosened significantly during early to mid-May. State media began broadcasting footage sympathetic to protesters and the movement, including the hunger strikers.

The students remained in the Square during the Gorbachev visit; his welcoming ceremony was held at the airport. The Sino-Soviet summit, the first of its kind in some 30 years, marked the normalization of Sino-Soviet relations, and was seen as a breakthrough of tremendous historical significance for China's leaders. That the smooth proceedings of this event had been derailed by the student movement embarrassed the leadership and drove many moderates onto a more 'hardliner' path. The summit between Deng and Gorbachev took place at the Great Hall amidst the backdrop of commotion and protest in the Square. When Gorbachev met with Zhao on 16 May, Zhao told the Soviet leader, and by extension the international press, that Deng was still the 'paramount authority' in China. Deng felt that this remark was Zhao's attempt to shift blame for mishandling the movement to him. The statement marked a decisive split between the country's two most senior leaders.

The hunger strike galvanized support for the students and aroused sympathy across the country. Around a million Beijing residents from all walks of life demonstrated in solidarity on 17–18 May. These included PLA personnel, police officers, and lower party officials. Many grassroot Party and Youth League organizations, as well as government-sponsored labour unions, encouraged their membership to demonstrate. In addition, several of China's non-Communist parties sent a letter to Li Peng in support of students. The Chinese Red Cross issued a special notice and sent in a large number of personnel to provide medical services to the hunger strikers in the Square. After the departure of Mikhail Gorbachev, many foreign journalists remained in the Chinese capital to cover the protests, giving the movement international spotlight. Western governments urged Beijing to exercise restraint.

Since the situation seemed intractable, the weight of taking decisive action fell on paramount leader Deng Xiaoping. On 17 May, a PSC meeting was called at Deng's residence. At the meeting, Zhao Ziyang's concessions-based strategy was criticized. Li Peng and Deng asserted that by making a conciliatory speech on 4 May, Zhao exposed divisions within the top leadership and emboldened the students. Deng warned that if Beijing is not pacified quickly, the country risked civil war and another Cultural Revolution; his views were echoed by the party elders. Deng then moved to declare martial law as a show of the government's no-tolerance stance. To justify martial law, the demonstrators were described as tools of 'bourgeois liberalism' advocates who were pulling the strings behind the scenes, as well as tools of elements within the party who wished to further their personal ambitions.

The Chinese government declared martial law on 20 May, and mobilized at least 30 divisions from five of the country's seven military regions. At least 14 of PLA's 24 Army corps contributed troops. As many as 2,50,000 troops were eventually sent to the capital, some arriving by air and others by rail. Guangzhou's civil aviation authorities put regular airline tickets on hold to prepare for transporting military units.

The Army's entry into the city was blocked at its suburbs by throngs of protesters. Tens of thousands of demonstrators surrounded military vehicles, preventing them from either advancing or retreating. Protesters lectured soldiers and appealed to them to join their cause; they also provided soldiers with food, water, and shelter. Seeing no way forward, the authorities ordered the army to withdraw on 24 May. All government forces retreated to bases outside the city. While the Army's retreat was initially seen as 'turning the tide' in favour of protesters, in reality mobilization took place across the country for a final assault.

Conservative party elders such as former President Li Xiannian supported the enforcement of martial law by force. On June 1, Li Peng issued a report titled 'On the True Nature of the Turmoil', which was circulated to every member of the Politburo. The report aimed to persuade the Politburo of the necessity and legality of clearing Tiananmen Square by referring to the protesters as terrorists and counter-revolutionaries. The report stated that turmoil was continuing to grow, the students had no plans to leave, and they were gaining popular support. Further justification for martial law came in the form of a report submitted by the Ministry of State Security (MSS) to the party leadership, which emphasized the infiltration of bourgeois liberalism into China and the negative effect that the West – particularly the United States – had on the students. The MSS expressed its belief that American forces had intervened in the student movement in hopes of overthrowing the Communist Party. The report created a sense of urgency within the party, and provided justification for military action.

At 4:30 pm on 3 June, the three Politburo standing committee members met with military leaders, Beijing Party Secretary Li Ximing, mayor Chen Xitong, and State Council secretariat Luo Gan, and finalized the order for the enforcement of martial law:

- The operation to quell the counter-revolutionary riot was to begin at 9 pm

- Military units should converge in the Square by 1 am on 4 June 4 and the Square must be cleared by 6 am.
- No delays would be tolerated.
- No person may impede the advance of the troops enforcing martial law. The troops may act in self-defense and use any means to clear impediments.
- State media will broadcast warnings to citizens.

The order did not explicitly contain a shoot-to-kill directive but permission to 'use any means' was understood by some units as authorization to use lethal force.

On the evening of 3 June state-run television warned residents to stay indoors but crowds of people took to the streets, as they had two weeks before, to block the incoming army. PLA units advanced on Beijing from every cardinal direction – the 38th, 63rd and 28th Armies from the west, 15th Airborne Corps, 20th, 26th and 54th Armies from the south, the 39th Army and the 1st Armoured Division from the east and the 40th and 64th armies from the north.

Unlike in the 1976 Tiananmen Incident when the authorities sent police and worker vigilantes with billy clubs to clear the Square of demonstrators, the soldiers in 1989 were armed with the Type 56 assault rifle, a variant of the AKS–47, and fired live ammunition at civilians. At about 10 pm, the 38th Army opened fire on protesters at the Wukesong intersection on Chang'an Avenue, about 10 km west of Square. The crowds were stunned that the army was using live ammunition and reacted by hurling insults and projectiles. The troops used expanding bullets, which expand upon entering the body and create larger wounds.

Pressure mounted on the student leadership to abandon non-violence and retaliate against the killings. At one point, Chai Ling picked up the megaphone and called on fellow students to prepare to 'defend themselves' against the 'shameless government'. But she and Li Lu agreed to adhere to peaceful means and had the students' sticks, rocks and glass bottles confiscated.

At about 1:30 am, the vanguard of the 38th Army and paratroopers from the 15th Airborne Corps, arrived at the north and south ends of the Square, respectively. They began to seal off the Square from reinforcements of students and residents, killing more demonstrators. Meanwhile, the 27th and 65th Armies poured out of the Great Hall of the People to the west and the 24th Army emerged from behind the History Museum to the east. The remaining students, numbering several thousand, were completely surrounded at the Monument to the People's Heroes in the center of the Square. At 2 am, the troops fired shots over the heads of the students at the Monument. The students broadcast pleadings back toward the troops: 'We entreat you in peace, for democracy and freedom of the motherland, for strength and prosperity of the Chinese nation, please comply with the will of the people and refrain from using force against peaceful student demonstrators.'

At 4 am, the lights on the Square suddenly turned off, and the government's loudspeaker announced: 'Clearance of the Square begins now. We agree with students' request to clear the Square.' The students sang *The Internationale* and braced for a last stand. Hou returned and informed student leaders of his agreement with the troops. At 4:30 am, the lights relit and the troops began to advance on the Monument from all sides. At about 4:32 am, Hou Dejian took the student's loudspeaker and recounted his meeting with the military. Many students, who learned of the talks for the first time, reacted angrily and accused him of cowardice. The soldiers initially stopped about 10 metres from the students. The first row of troops took aim with machine guns in the prone position. Behind them squatted and stood soldiers with assault rifles. Mixed among them were anti-riot police with clubs. Further back were tanks and APCs. Other troops beat and kicked dozens of students at the Monument, seizing and smashing their cameras and recording equipment. An officer with a loudspeaker called out 'you better leave or this won't end well.'

Some of the students and professors persuaded others still sitting on the lower tiers of the Monument to get up and leave, while soldiers beat them with clubs and gunbutts and prodded them with bayonets. Witnesses heard bursts of gunfire. At about 5:10 am, the students began to leave the Monument. They linked hands and marched through a corridor to the southeast, though some departed through the north. Those who refused to leave were beaten by soldiers and ordered to join the departing procession. After securing the Square, the military sent in helicopters to pick up large plastic bags piled by soldiers.

Just past 6 am on 4 June, as a convoy of students who had vacated the Square were walking westward in the bicycle lane along Chang'an Avenue back to campus, three tanks pursued them from the Square, firing tear gas and one drove through the crowd, killing 11 students, injuring scores.

Later in the morning, thousands of civilians tried to re-enter the Square from the northeast on East Chang'an Avenue, which was blocked by rows of infantry. Many in the crowd were parents of the demonstrators who had been in the Square. As the crowd approached the troops, an officer sounded a warning, and the troops opened fire.

On 5 June, suppression of the protest was immortalized in Western media by the famous video footage and photographs of a lone man standing in front of a column of tanks driving out of Tiananmen Square. The iconic photo that would eventually make its way around the world was taken on 5 June on Chang'an Avenue. As the tank driver attempted to go around him, the 'Tank Man' moved into the tank's path. He continued to stand defiantly in front of the tanks for some time, then climbed up onto the turret of the lead tank to speak to the soldiers inside. After returning to his position in front of the tanks, the man was pulled aside by a group of people.

By and large, the government regained control in the week following the military's seizure of the Square. A political purge followed in which officials responsible for organizing or condoning the protests were removed, and protest leaders jailed.

On 9 June, Deng Xiaoping, appearing in public for the first time since the protests began, delivered a speech praising the 'martyrs' (PLA soldiers who had died). Deng stated that the goal of the movement was to overthrow the Party and the state. 'Their goal is to establish a totally Western-dependent bourgeois republic,' Deng said of the protesters. Deng argued that protesters had complained about corruption to cover their real motive, which was to replace the socialist system. He said that 'the entire imperialist Western world plans to make all socialist countries discard the socialist road and then bring them under the monopoly of international capital and onto the capitalist road'.

The civilians killed in Beijing, according to the city police, 'included university professors, technical people, officials, workers, owners of small private enterprises, retired workers, high school students and grade school students, of whom the youngest was nine years old.' The number of deaths and whether there was bloodshed in the Square have been in dispute ever since the government's press conference of 6 June 1989. The number of dead and wounded remains unclear because the Chinese government has since suppressed the release of any information regarding the incident and prohibited any research of the subject matter in China. Hence, large discrepancies exist among various casualty estimates, which range from several hundred to several thousand.

Some of the early estimates were based on reports of a casualty figure of 2,600 from the Chinese Red Cross, which was quickly retracted.

On 6 June, State Council spokesperson Yuan Mu claimed that preliminary tallies by the government showed that about 300 civilians and soldiers died, including 23 students from universities in Beijing, along with a number of people he described as 'ruffians'. Some 5,000 soldiers and police along with 2,000 civilians were wounded.

On 19 June, Beijing Party Secretary Li Ximing reported to the Politburo that the government's confirmed death toll was 241, including 218 civilians (including 36 students), 10 PLA soldiers and 13 People's Armed Police, along with 7,000 wounded.

On 1 July, Chen Xitong, then Beijing mayor, reported that about 200 civilians and several dozen soldiers died.

Over 3,700 killed, excluding disappearance or secret deaths and those denied medical treatment – PLA defector citing a document circulating among officers; 2,600 had officially died by the morning of 4 June (later denied) – *Time* Magazine.

An unnamed Chinese Red Cross official estimated that, in total, 5,000 people were killed and 30,000 injured.

Since much of the shooting took place outside of the Square, a count of deaths within the Square is not reflective of the scale of violence that took place. In addition, the Army reportedly fired on students after they left the Square, especially in the area near the Beijing concert hall.

The authorities arrested tens if not hundreds of thousands of people across the country. Some were seized in broad daylight while they walked in the street; others were arrested at night. Many were jailed or sent to labour camps. They were often denied access to see their families and often put in cells so crowded that not everyone had space to sleep. Dissidents shared cells with murderers and rapists, and torture was not uncommon. Many workers were summarily tried and executed. In contrast, the students – many of whom came from relatively affluent backgrounds and were well-connected – received much lighter sentences.

The suppression on 4 June marked the end of a period of relative press freedom in China, and media workers – both foreign and domestic – faced heightened restrictions and punishment in the aftermath of the crackdown. State media mostly gave reports sympathetic to the students in the immediate aftermath. As a result, those responsible were all later removed.

All international networks were eventually ordered to cease broadcasts from the city during the military action, with the government shutting down satellite transmissions. Broadcasters attempted to defy these orders by reporting via telephone. Footage was quickly smuggled out of the country. The only network which was able to record shots during the night of 4 June was Televisión Española of Spain (TVE). During the military action, some foreign journalists faced harassment from the authorities.

The Chinese government's response was denounced, particularly by Western governments and media. Criticism came from both Western and Eastern Europe, North America, Australia and some west Asian and Latin American countries. Notably, many Asian countries remained silent throughout the protests; the government of India responded to the massacre by ordering the state television to pare down the coverage to the barest minimum, so as not to jeopardize a thawing in relations with China, and to offer political empathy for the events. Cuba, Czechoslovakia, and East Germany, among others, supported the Chinese government and denounced the protests. Overseas Chinese students demonstrated in many cities in Europe, America, the Middle East and Asia.

There was a significant impact on the Chinese economy after the incident. Foreign loans to China were suspended by the World Bank, Asian Development Bank, and foreign governments; tourism revenue decreased from US $2.2 billion to US $1.8 billion; foreign direct investment commitments were cancelled and there was a rise in defense spending from 8.6 per cent in 1986 to 15.5 per cent in 1990, reversing a previous 10 year decline. Chinese Premier Li Peng visited the United Nations Security Council on 31 January 1992, and argued that the economic and arms embargoes on China were a violation of national sovereignty.

The government prepared a white paper explaining the government's viewpoint on the protests. An anonymous source within the PRC government smuggled the document out of China, and Public Affairs published it in January 2001 as the *Tiananmen Papers*. Deng Xiaoping died in 1997.

Before his death in 1998, Yang Shangkun told army doctor Jiang Yanyong that 'June 4' was the most serious mistake committed by the Communist Party in its history, a mistake that Yang himself could not correct but one that certainly will eventually be corrected. Zhao Ziyang remained under house arrest until his death in 2005.

Images of the protests would strongly shape Western views and policy toward China in the next two decades.

The European Union and United States embargo on armament sales to the PRC, put in place as a result of the violent suppression of the Tiananmen Square protests, remains in place today. The PRC has been calling for a lift of the ban for years and has had a varying amount of support from EU members. Since 2004, China has portrayed the ban as 'outdated', and damaging to China-EU relations.

The Communist Party of China (CPC) forbids discussion of the Tiananmen Square protests, and has taken measures to block or censor information. Textbooks have little, if any, information related to the protests. Following the protests, officials banned controversial films and books, and shut down a large number of newspapers. Within a year, 12 per cent of all newspapers, 8 per cent of publishing companies, 13 per cent of social science periodicals and more than 150 films were banned or shut down. In addition, the government also announced it had seized 32 million contraband books and 2.4 million video and audio cassettes. Access to media and internet resources on the subject are restricted or blocked by censors. Public memory of the Tiananmen Square protests has been suppressed by the authorities since 1989. Print media containing reference to the protests must be consistent with the government's version of events. Presently, many Chinese citizens are reluctant to speak about the protests due to potential repercussions. Many young people born after 1980 are completely unfamiliar with the events and are apolitical while older intellectuals no longer aspire for political change and instead focus on economic reform. The Chinese government condemned the protests as a 'counter-revolutionary riot', and has prohibited all forms of discussion or remembrance of the events since. Due to the lack of information from China, many aspects of the events remain unknown or unconfirmed.

Leading up to and during the event's 20th anniversary on 4 June 2009, party authorities increased security around the Square. Members of the Public Security Bureau and the People's Armed Police were present at the Square in uniform along with several hundred plain-clothes officers. Journalists were denied entry in the Square. Those who attempted to film at the Square or interview dissidents were briefly detained. The anniversary also saw the shut down of global social-networking sites in China, as well as increased policing of dissidents. No protests were to be tolerated on this occasion.

Conclusion

Emma Bonino[3] offers us a profound epigram: 'There really can be no peace without justice. There can be no justice without truth. And there can be no truth, unless someone rises up to tell you the truth'. Therein lie the tasks of transitional justice:

- Recovery of truth
- Recovery of History
- Healing-relief-rehabilitation (trauma)
- Redress-remedies-rights
- Prevention
- Rebuilding constitutional orders
- Reconstruction of the justice system
- Human implications: lustration; capacity; mindset

Post-conflict processes involve moving from demoralization and phobia to understanding and appreciating differences and diversity. It is not wrong to be different. It is wrong to be treated differently, because you are different.

In the words of Milan Kundera: 'The struggle of Man over Power is the struggle of Memory over Forgetting'. As we move from struggle, to remembering and learning, key values drawn from the universal paradigm of human rights are vital: dignity; identity: both individual and collective; respect and compassion. 'I used to complain because I had no shoes. Until I met a child who had no limbs'.

After all, the greatest tragedy of all is the tragedy of not learning from tragedy.

Notes

1. This section draws upon experiences in 23 countries: Lebanon, Iran, Iraq, Timor, Bougainville, Bosnia, Afghanistan, Cambodia, Laos, Vietnam, Liberia, Nigeria, Ethiopia, Eritrea, Philippines, Nepal, Bangladesh, Sri Lanka, Uzbekistan, Kazakhstan, Moldova, Nicaragua, Haiti.
2. *Final Solution* is a 2003 documentary directed by Rakesh Sharma about the 2002 Gujarat violence. The film was denied entry to Mumbai International Film Festival in 2004 due to objections by the Censor Board of India, but won two awards at the 54th Berlin International Film Festival 2004. The ban was later lifted in October 2004. T.V. Chandran made a trilogy of Malayalam films based on the aftermaths of Gujarat riots. The narrative of all these films begin on the same day, 28 February 2002, that is, on the day after the Godhra Train Burning. The 2007 film *Parzania* was inspired by the true story of a 10-year-old Parsi boy, who disappeared after the Gulbarg Society massacre. The film traces the journey of the Pithawala family while trying to locate their missing son. *Firaaq* is a 2008 political thriller film set one month after the violence and looks at the aftermath in its effects on the lives of everyday people. The 2011 film *Mausam* ends amidst riots in Ahmedabad. The 2013 film *Kai Po Che* has the backdrop of the 2002 Gujarat violence. The film is based on the novel *The Three Mistakes of My Life* written by Chetan Bhagat.
3. Emma Bonino is an Italian politician, who has been Minister of Foreign Affairs since 28 April 2013. Previously she was a member of the European Parliament and a member of the Italian Senate.

2

Unrest, Conflict and the Issue of Human Rights in Nepal

TILOTTAM PAUDEL

Unrest and Conflict: These are two terms that impact society and affect the human rights in social terms. Here 'unrest' implies discomfort, disturbance, turbulence, etc. and the most direct and simple meaning of 'conflict' is confusion between two views. The dictionary meaning (*Longman Dictionary*, 1998: 1577) of unrest is 'a social and political situation in which people protest and tend to behave violently' and conflict means 'a situation in which you have to choose between two or more opposite needs or influences, or confusion on two ideas, beliefs, opinions, etc', (*Longman Dictionary*, 1998: 281) The word 'conflict' in itself does not have a negative implication. As an important part of the evolution of a society, conflicts are there continually in every society. Generally, conflicts contribute towards the progress of a society but, nonetheless, conflicts could end up in destruction and also lead to violence, if these are not identified properly and on time and also not given a proper outlet, given an opportunity. In reality the common practice is that conflicts are not recognized or taken on a serious note unless there is eruption of violence and it is quite late. As such, 'conflict' and 'violence' are often talked about synonymously. Violence and war, however, are negative outcomes of conflicts. By the time conflict transforms into violence, much of its constructive potential is lost.

The term 'Human Rights' refers to 'the basic rights and freedoms to which all humans are entitled'. The Right to Life and Liberty, Freedom of Thought and Expression, Right to Equality and Dignity are included within the purview of Human Rights alongside the Right to Food, Right to Life, Right to Education, Right to Freedom of Speech, Right to Adequate Standard of Living, Right to A3 – Accessibility, Affordability, Acceptability, Respect and so on. This leads us to say that Human Rights and armed conflict are interrelated to each other, because where there is armed conflict essentially there is some violation of Human Rights and we have raised our voices against the Human Rights violation.

Short History of the Armed Conflict in Nepal

The meaning of 'Unrest' and 'Conflict' having been explained earlier it may be mentioned here that in the present world situation the two terms directly impact issues related to the Human Rights of people. In Nepal, armed conflicts started on 13 February 1996 in the wake of the Maoist insurgency. The escalation of the Maoist insurgency and the State's counter-insurgency in the aftermath of the Maoists' 'People's War' have accelerated political violence and terror, an everyday reality of Nepali society, to the degree and scale never experienced before. The start of the Maoists' 'People's War' in 1996 which had led to the armed conflict in Nepal is described as the 'gravest internal crisis' in the recent political history of Nepal. The heavy loss of human lives killed in this 'war', the damage to physical infrastructures and disruptions of livelihoods of common peoples, the gross violations of Human Rights by the Maoists and the State, the displacements and dislocations of people and their social relations, the re-emergence of the oppressive monarchical government regime and the continuous militarization of society have altered the social landscape of the Nepali society (Dahal, 2007: 59). In Nepal, the Maoist armed conflict continued for 10 years from 1996 to 2006. During this one decade, some 13,000 people lost their lives and on a massive scale, people were victimized by both the parties in conflict.

Second Peoples Movement of Nepal

After 10 years of Maoist armed conflict and 237 years of absolute monarchy under which the King ruled over the people of Nepal, the latter were a dissatisfied lot and wanted to come out from the turmoil that prevailed in the country. The establishment of peace by resolving the 10-years-long armed conflict through a forward-looking political outlet became the need of the hour. In view of this, the implementation of the concept of full democracy through a forward-looking restructuring of the state to resolve the problems related to gender, class-ism and caste-ism and so on, of all sectors, including the political, economic, social and cultural, by bringing the autocratic monarchy to an end and establishing a full democracy became an inevitable need. For that, it is well known, a historic 12-point understanding regarding democracy, peace, prosperity and progress was reached between the seven political parties fighting for the end of absolute monarchy and the establishment of full democracy on 22 November 2005 (Peace Negotiation of Nepal 2008: 6). After the 12-point understanding, all of Nepal's people came out on the streets and started the nationwide people movement. This movement was started on 6 April 2006 by all political parties and civil societies of Nepal (INSEC, 2006: 15). At that time 'the king is making merry, while people are being killed. The king wants war while the people want peace,' the appeal said, calling on the people to free the nation from the autocratic rule. The second peoples' movement continued for 19 days in the form of nationwide general strikes even during the curfew hours announced by the government. It may be mentioned in this context that during that 25 people were killed by bullet injuries inflicted on them after the government-deployed police fired. Many more people who were willing to fight for the cause of the nation were injured and victimized. Finally, on 21 April 2006, King Gyanendra declared a memorandum letter in the name of the people. Thanks to this letter from the king, the Nepalese people would be getting their victory after

237 years of monarchial rule as the king had to leave all powers in the hands of the people for establishing full democracy. After this achievement, the Maoist also returned to the peace process on the basis of the 12-point understanding of the eight political parties. These points were made the Code of Conduct for ceasefire between the Government of Nepal and the CPN (Maoist) on 25 May 2006 (Peace Negotiation of Nepal, 2008: 15)

Post Conflict Situation of Nepal and Human Rights

After 25 May 2006, the situation in Nepal has rolled into the post conflict situation and transitional phase. In this transitional period many small armed groups came into existence, the numbers increasing day by day. Many a time they have announced their demands and to achieve their end, they cause major disruptions in public life. There have also been many instances of their violating human rights. We know that Nepal is the multi-cultural country with more than hundred ethnic groups living together in peace and harmony. But, unfortunately, once the peace process and the transitional period started, all the people began demanding their rights and their own state. The new government failed to address the demands. Worst is that there is not even a proper government. The present Prime Minister had given his resignation before 7 month ago and it was on 5 February 2011 that Nepal got a new Prime Minister at the end of a long political process. The new Prime Minister is here in power due to the coordination of the Maoists and the UML. Mentionable here is that in Nepal there are three major and big political parties, i.e. the Maoist, the UML and the Nepali Congress. This time the Maoists and the UML have joined hands to form a new government, while the Nepali Congress chose not to support the government. Despite everything, the peace process is in a critical situation. The UNMIN came in Nepal for the peace negotiation but then before the restoration of peace and the Cantonment Maoist soldiers' management, it had to backtrack. The ongoing debate between the political parties is still on. Hence, the Maoist soldiers' problems are not addressed yet and peace negotiations are yet to be completed. Consequently, crimes and inhuman activities are increasing everyday in this transitional period.

Many Human Rights violence cases occurred frequently in this transitional phase. The implementation of the related laws and rules has apparently become more difficult. Incidentally, after the second peoples' movement, Nepal came to be known as Federal Democratic Republic Nepal. Seven political parties joined hands and were committed to make Nepal a peaceful, prosperous and modern new country by involving the entire Nepali people, including the indigenous/nationalities, Madhesis, the oppressed and the women in the national mainstream by establishing a federal democratic republic state (Peace Negotiation of Nepal 2008: 175). After 237 years of Kingship and 10 years of the Maoists' armed conflicts, the Nepali people got a new government for ruling them well. The Nepal government successfully completed the Constitutional Assembly election from 2006 to 2010. The elections went quite well except for some minor skirmishes events. After the CA elections, 601 CA members were elected to make the new Constitution but the political parties did not believe in its strength and hence were not keen to achieve this end, the reason why they were lax about its completion on time even though they have crossed the deadline by more than a year. As per the above information it seems that all armed conflicts will finally end up in war. War is, therefore, positively correlated with any person's civil and political rights and marks the gross violation of Human Rights.

How to Protect Human Rights

A growing number of countries experience internal armed conflicts inflicting major sufferings on the population and raising distinctive issues for Human Rights defenders who are trying to curb Human Rights violations. The majority of violent and deadly conflicts in the world take place within states. Armed groups that are not under government control are a key figure of these conflicts and are responsible for many, sometimes extreme, abuses of Human Rights. These conflicts are of immediate concern to civilians affected by them; at the same time, they also bring to the fore issues for the national and international organizations that protect Human Rights and work for peace by providing humanitarian relief. In Nepal, more than 13,000 people have been killed in violence since insurgency that began 10 years ago; many of the victims were civilians caught in cross-fires between the armed groups and the security forces. Both parties engaged in the conflict are accused of instigating Human Rights abuses. Under the circumstance, it is the Human Rights defender who brings to the fore the plight of the sufferers and pressurizes the offending group not to engage in such kind of violence.

Common outcomes of Human Rights violation during armed conflicts and in the transitional phase:

- Death
- Injury
- Abduction
- Arrest
- Imprisonment
- Constant fear and threat
- Deprivation
- Torture
- Displacement
- Rape
- Disappearance
- Violation of food rights
- Violation of education rights
- Impact on health
- Damages and impediments to development infrastructure
- Most importantly, lack of security for humans and civil society lives in fear

These are the main points of Human Rights violation and, inside of those points, there have been so many instances of Human Rights violation by all the conflicting parties in the nation. Certainly, armed conflicts always leave a negative impact on the issue of Human Rights, which again influences the natural environment around in a negative way due to bomb blasts, gun firing and smoke from the explosive devices. So we could safely conclude that armed conflicts are never desirable.

Possible Interventions from Human Rights Defenders

- Human Rights activists can work as a pressure group to build peace.
- They can lead peace campaigns, building on them to create awareness in the country.
- They can monitor the situation through regular field visits and learn the actual facts. They may then present the fact finding report and pressurize the stakeholders.
- They may conduct interactions with all the stakeholders and hold peace rallies to put pressure on the government.
- They can work out a peace plan.
- The Human Rights defenders may meet among themselves to share and exchange ideas on how the Human Rights activists can work for peace.

Conclusion

Nepal, once known as a peaceful country, the birthplace of Lord Buddha, also known as the 'Light of Asia', has been facing many unrests and conflicts owing to 237 years of monarchical rule and 10 years of Maoist armed conflicts. These internal conflicts have affected the people of the country adversely. More than 13,000 people lost their lives, thousands of people were injured, many have migrated or were displaced and many Human Rights violations were committed. Human Rights should have been treated as special rights of individuals as these include under its purview most of the Fundamental Rights a nation grants its citizens through the Constitution, namely the Right to Survival, Freedom of Expression, Freedom of Participation and Freedom of Movement. This is according to the Geneva Convention. Unfortunately, these rights seem to exist only in words and slogans; they are not paid any attention during conflicts and unrests. Just as conflicts do not spare any single social element, its impact on issues of human rights is also negative as a result of which cases of Human Rights violation are on the increase. The State may have committed itself to the cause of Human Rights, yet it has, in reality, not yet taken any positive steps to promote the cause of Human Rights. To sum up, the armed conflict has had a negative impact on the development of the nation as well as its people, mainly owing to the gross violation of Human Rights. To quote Plato: 'Only the dead have seen the end of war'.

References

Dahal, K.B. 2007. Impact of Maoist Cantonment Camps on Life Situation: Livelihood Strategies and Health of Local People, Kathmandu: Nepal Forum of Environmental Journalists.

INSEC. 2006. *Jana Andolan–II: A Witness Account*. Kathmandu: Syuchatar.

Pyakuryal, K. 2007. Nepal in Conflict Theoretical Underpinnings, Conflict Resolution, Conflict Transformation, and Peace-Building. Sociological/Anthropological Society of Nepal (SASON), Kathmandu.

Peace Negotiation of Nepal. 2008. Government of Nepal Ministry of Peace and Reconstruction, Singhdurbar, Kathmandu, Nepal

Shrestha, Prakash. 2001. *Quest for Peace*, SAP-Nepal, Kathmandu.

Understanding Peace and Conflict Transformation in Asia 2005. Religious Perspective and Approaches, Asian Resource Foundation and Asian Muslim Action Network, Bangkok.

3

Who Cares for Human Rights when Social Unrest Turns Violent?

The Context of Junglemahal

DIPAK K. MIDYA

Violation of Human Rights is rampant all over the world, even in the most democratic civil society. The protection of Human Rights is, therefore, an urgent international issue. Human Rights, however, practically becomes a non-issue in a volatile social situation. We have numerous insights from scholarly studies on Human Rights violation (Cassese, 1990; Minow, 1998; Veuthey, 1998; Hubert and Weiss et al., 2001; Kennedy, 2001; Maiese, 2003; etc.). But how do the victims react to Human Rights issues or to the violation of those? Taking the case of the Maoist movement and the counter-insurgency measures taken by the State in the so-called 'Junglemahal' area of West Bengal, the present study tries to understand the causes of the social unrest in this area and to substantiate how the people living in the area think about Human Rights issues in their day-to-day life.

Social Unrest and Junglemahal

Currently, social unrest is a rapidly growing problem that human society faces globally. The word 'unrest' refers to a state of trouble or discontent, especially among a group of people (*Chambers Universal Learners' Dictionary,* 1994: 830). When the discontent or contradiction is manifested in the collective life of a society it may be called social unrest. This major international issue has earned close attention from several exponents. Aristotle, the world's first political scientist, was perhaps the first person to refer to social unrest while discussing the causes of the political revolution. According to him, the universal and principal cause of the revolutionary feeling is the desire for equality or the varying desires of sections of people for equality and the perception of inequality. In his own words:

> Inferiors revolt in order that they may be equal, and equals that may be superior. (Aristotle, N.D.: 212)

Social unrest is intrinsic to everyday social life. It is an important dimension of socio-cultural order, which exists beyond the habitual, orderly or routine way of life. Its manifestation may be seen as a departure from order, as un-order, dis-order and out-of-order (Stanage, 1974: 229). One of the earliest references to the problem appears in Ralph Linton's (1943) work where he talked about 'nativistic movements'. In this context, it is noteworthy to mention Linton's observations:

> The impact of European culture upon the small primitive societies of the world during the past centuries has frequently led to the appearance of what have come to be known as 'nativistic movements' wherein the primitive societies have reacted, sometimes violently against dominations of the European and engaged in organised attempts to revive or perpetuate certain aspects of their native cultures in the face of this pressure to change. Since the religious systems of the primitive societies typically embodied the central values of their culture, these nativistic movements almost always involved some type of religious or magical procedure as their essential elements and hence have provided us with crucial data of dynamics in religion. (Linton, 1943)

In this connection, Sunanda K. Datta Ray's (1980) observation on various socio-political movements that occurred in the post-Independence India deserves special mention. He questions whether the concentration of power in the hands of one set of people represented by a single political philosophy and a particular class and culture could actually serve a heterogeneous society like India. The Constitution of India is, he understands, unitary in nature and scarcely represents the ethno-cultural diversities of our country. As a result, the minority communities apprehend a kind of threat to their identity as well as individualism. In his own words:

> Santals, Mundas, Oraons, Bhumijs, Rajbansis, Harijans, even some Sikhs, all the tribes of the tormented North-East, and other ethnic and religious communities feel isolated in the land in which power is concentrated in the hands of people who speak Hindi and worship Hindu Gods. (Datta Ray, 1980: 8)

Datta Ray is referring to ethnic unrests in particular. Giddens (1984: 158), Taylor (1984: 176), Kelly (1994), Haugaard (2002) and Swain (1997) also make significant contributions to this field of research. Unrest may be time-specific, geo-specific as well as ethno-specific (including age and gender specific) (Danda, 2006: xx). Unrest erupts when people are not free to take their own decisions and to protect and maintain their own *ethos* and culture. Development and expression of mind need a free space – a world free from any fear, pressure and oppression. In the words of Rabindranath Tagore:

> … Where the mind is without fear and the head is held high;
> Where knowledge is free. (Tagore, 1910: 27)

Ethnic unrest becomes manifested when an ethnic group apprehends a threat toward their identity, culture or even their very existence. In India, ethnic unrest poses one of the greatest threats to her integrity and sovereignty. Theoretical reflections in this dimension of social reality in the works of Malkani (1980), H. Rahman (1980), Datta Ray (1980), Sumit Sarkar (1983), R.D. Munda (1988), S. Krishna (1996), S.K. Chaube (1990, 2006), J. Sarkar (2006), Midya (2006), R.K. Das (2006) and S.R. Mondal (2006) are of immense importance.

With this in the background, it has been attempted to examine the situation in the Junglemahal area at present. The so-called 'Junglemahal' is not by any means an administrative unit. Its boundary is socio-politically conceptualized to include the region covered or assumed to be covered by jungle (or forest) and spreads over the districts of Paschim Medinipur, Puruliya and Bankura in the Indian State of West Bengal. The area is predominantly populated by the indigenous people (who are designated as Scheduled Tribes in India) belonging particularly to the Santal, Bhumij and Sabar (also called as Lodha interchangeably) as well as the Mahata, a self-proclaimed indigenous people who are recognized as an Other Backward Class (OBC) community and used to occupy the same terrain with the tribal people.

Study Area and Methodology

For the present study, fieldworks have been carried out in seven villages altogether: Bhimarjun under Banspahari Police Station, Nalboni (JL No. 944), Kushboni (JL No. 943) and Chuasuli (JL No. 942) under Binpur Police Station, and Sangram (JL No. 179), Amlatora (JL No. 177) and Chilki (JL No. 173) under Jamboni Police Station during 2008–10.

All the villages are located within the Maoist trouble-torn area of Jhargram Sub-Division of Paschim Medinipur District in West Bengal. Therefore, random sampling technique has not always been a suitable tool for the selection of the study area. Instead, the purposive sampling method has sometimes been employed, keeping in mind the accessibility to the villages as well as to the domain of discourse.

The main source of data for the present study has, of course, been fieldwork. The villages were selected in such a way that the overtly expressed variation in terms of ethnic composition, politico-economic situation, distance from the main town of Jhargram, etc. may be accounted for. However, political instability and violent movements and regular killings in the so-called Maoist attacks as well as in the counter-insurgency measures taken by the State in the area have been the inescapable impediments toward just staying in the field and completing the work as well. The study has, therefore, been a very stressful and time-consuming one.

This study certainly used a mixture of observational tools and interview methods. It was started with the collection of household census data at its initial stage. For the production of household census data, Family Survey Schedules (FSS) were used. The Family Survey Schedules were devised to elicit information on age, gender, caste/tribe, clan, marital status, age at marriage, marriage distance, number of offspring, educational status, occupation, occupational shift, income and expenditure pattern, dietary habits, leisure time activities, etc. The data provided with information about the population number as well as their socio-economic and ethnic profile. While in the field for household census data collection, the respondents, in most cases, were the Head of the Family (HoF) or, in his absence, his wife or any other elderly member(s). For understanding the working condition in the day-to-day life, the respondents were selected through simple random sampling.

Socio-economic Context and the Roots of Unrest

Six decades of our Independence and over three decades of uninterrupted 'Left' rule in this area have not been enough time to ensure the basic facilities like food, healthcare and education for all. It has been observed through our field studies that a large number of families in all the villages surveyed were not getting even two square meals per day. The procedure of listing under the Below Poverty Line (BPL) scheme shows great arbitrariness as many people who were actually poor have not been included in the list. Dependency ratios among the communities living in this area are much higher (even more than 50%) (Table 1).

The villages in Junglemahal are, on the whole, small in terms of the number of families as well as population. The population figures of the villages (Table 2) show that everywhere, except among the Santals in Kushboni, the males outnumber the females. Gender ratio is, therefore, not balanced. The distribution of the populations by age and gender in Bhimarjun, Sangram and Amlatora, for instance, illustrates a great disparity in the gender-wise distribution, particularly in the age group of below 15 years. This is reportedly owing to the fact that healthcare measures in cases of illness of girl children draw less importance. This leads to higher death rate at the after-birth stage and thereafter in case of the girl child.

Table 1

Distribution of Tribes/Communities by Family and their Dependency Ratios

Village (JL No.)	*Police Station*	*Tribe/Communities*	*Families No. (%)*	*Dependency Ratio*
Bhimarjun	Banspahari	Bhumij	114 (100.0)	57.00
Nalboni (944)	Binpur	Santal	24 (92.31)	
		Mahata	2 (07.69)	
		Total	24 (100.0)	75.34
Kushboni (943)	Binpur	Santal	8 (32.00)	
		Mahata	17 (68.00)	
		Total	25 (100.0)	55.55
Chuasuli (942)	Binpur	Santal	36 (67.92)	
		Mahata	17 (32.08)	
		Total	53 (100.0)	49.72
Sangram (179)	Jamboni	Sabar	59 (66.29)	
		Santal	2 (02.25)	
		Napit	5 (05.56)	
		Kulu	2 (02.25)	
		Kamar	2 (02.25)	
		Tanti	2 (02.25)	
		Baisnab	5 (05.62)	
		Dhopa	3 (03.37)	
		Others	9 (10.11)	
		Total	89 (100.0)	60.57
Amlatora (177)	Jamboni	Santal	54 (80.60)	
		Mahata	13 (19.40)	
		Total	67 (100.0)	48.55
Chilki (173)	Jamboni	Santal	18 (56.25)	
		Mahata	6 (18.75)	
		Kamar	3 (09.37)	
		Patar	5 (15.62)	
		Total	32 (100.0)	57.31

Source: Fieldwork data, 2008–2010.

The villages are basically agrarian in nature though cultivable land is not sufficiently available everywhere. Since Bhimarjun is located on the hilly terrain, agricultural land is almost negligible there. The Bhumij are basically dependent on gathering pursuit in the surrounding forests. In Chuasuli, there are plenty of agricultural lands and the Santals do have moderate landholding. It is reflected in their comparatively low dependency ratio (43.90% compared to 49.72% of the entire village community). In Nalboni and Kushboni, on the other hand, the available agricultural land is not sufficient and that, too, is of the barren type. In Nalboni the Santals, as also the Mahatas, work basically as day-labourers in the agricultural pursuits in the nearby villages. But in Kushboni the major share of agricultural land is in the hands of the Mahatas. Here, the dependency ratio for the Santals is 78.54 per cent in contrast to that among the Mahatas (55.55%). In Amlatora, both the Santals and the Mahatas possess some agricultural land. Here, the dependency ratio is as low as 49.75 per cent and 48.55 per cent for the Santals and the whole village population, respectively. In Chilki, on the contrary, the dependency ratio is very high among the Santals (78.12%) though it is as low as 57.31 per cent for the whole village community. This is because the agricultural land is in the hands of the communities other than the Santals. However, in Sangram, the dependency ratio among the Sabars as well as the other communities is low. This is due to the fact that the number of children in the age-group of 10–14 years and that of girl child in the age group of 5–9 are excessively low. It does not mean anyway that their economic condition is better off.

Table 2

Distribution of Population by Gender

Village	*Tribe/ Community*	*Population*			*Sex-Ratio*
		Male No. (%)	*Female No. (%)*	*Total No. (%)*	
Bhimarjun	Bhumij	300 (54.25)	253 (45.75)	553 (100.0)	83.3
Nalboni	Santal	66 (51.56)	51 (39.84)	117 (91.40)	
	Mahata	8 (06.25)	3 (02.34)	11 (08.59)	
	Total	74 (57.81)	54 (42.19)	128 (100.0)	72.9
Kushboni	Santal	10 (11.90)	15 (17.86)	25 (29.76)	
	Mahata	35 (41.67)	24 (28.57)	59 (70.24)	
	Total	45 (53.57)	39 (46.43)	84 (100.0)	86.6
Chuasuli	Santal	97 (36.60)	80 (30.19)	177 (66.79)	
	Mahata	47 (17.74)	41 (15.47)	88 (33.21)	
	Total	144 (54.34)	121 (45.66)	265 (100.0)	84.0
Sangram	Sabar	114 (34.13)	94 (28.14)	208 (62.27)	
	Santal	2 (00.60)	2 (00.60)	4 (01.20)	
	Napit	17 (05.09)	13 (03.89)	30 (08.98)	
	Kulu	2 (00.60)	1 (00.30)	3 (00.90)	
	Kamar	2 (00.60)	2 (00.60)	4 (01.20)	
	Tanti	3 (00.90)	1 (00.30)	4 (01.20)	
	Baisnab	16 (04.79)	14 (04.19)	30 (08.98)	
	Dhopa	9 (02.69)	6 (01.79)	15 (04.49)	
	Others	20 (05.99)	16 (04.79)	36 (10.78)	
	Total	185 (55.39)	160 (44.61)	334 (100.0)	86.4

Cont'd...

...Cont'd

Amlatora	Santal	153 (42.74)	142 (39.66)	295 (82.40)	
	Mahata	35 (09.77)	28 (07.82)	63 (17.60)	
	Total	188 (52.51)	170 (47.48)	359 (100.0)	90.4
Chilki	Santal	30 (23.25)	27 (20.93)	57 (44.18)	
	Mahata	17 (13.18)	14 (10.85)	31 (24.03)	
	Kamar	9 (06.98)	7 (05.43)	16 (12.40)	
	Patar	14 (10.85)	11 (08.53)	25 (19.38)	
	Total	70 (54.26)	59 (45.74)	129 (100.0)	84.2

Source: Fieldwork data, 2008–2010.

Birth registration system is almost lacking in these villages. The child-women ratio can therefore be taken as a rough measure of fertility. The child-women ratio at Amlatora village, for example, may be mentioned here (Table 3). It is moderately low.

Table 3

Child-Women Ratio in Amlatora

Tribe/ Community	*No. of Children upto 4 years (A)*			*Women with the Age-group 15–44 yrs (B)*	*Child-Women Ratio (A/B x 100)*
	M	*F*	*T*		
Santal	16	13	29	71	40.84
Mahato	03	02	05	18	27.78
Total	19	15	34	89	38.20

Source: Fieldwork data, 2009.

The percentages of illiteracy in all the villages, with the lone exception of Amlatora, are alarmingly very high. This is 61.12 per cent, 51.28 per cent, 57 per cent and 60 per cent among the village community of Bhimarjun, Nalboni, Chuasuli and Kushboni, respectively, compared to 42.28 per cent in West Bengal and 42.36 per cent in undivided Medinipur District (as per 1991 census). The illiteracy percentage is very high (65.86%) among the Sabars at Sangram and a majority of the literate persons here falls under the lower age groups. A similar pattern is observed in the other villages also. Chilki, for instance, exhibits the presence of more than 64 per cent illiterates in its population. Among the villages, only Amlatora could be singled out where the illiteracy rate among the Santals has come down below 50 per cent (42.71%). What is more alarming is the rate of illiteracy among the females as it stands as high as 68.03 per cent, 57 per cent, 73.33 per cent and 78.66 per cent in Nalboni, Chuasuli, Kushboni and Bhimarjun, respectively.

The indigenous people of this vast area are the greatly disadvantaged section of our society indeed, for they suffer from various disabilities. They are erstwhile forest dwellers and there are still some among them who continue to reside in the forest. In fact, those who continue to live in the forest are resistant to all or most of the changes that have impacted most people, and as a result of which, their traditional lifestyle continues to rule them. Ethnicity seems to play a major role in this sphere. The *Panchayat*s in this region are executing their programmes in their own way, often without considering the tribal peoples' socio-economic urgency, identity, value, culture and ethnic dimensions.

Quite expectedly therefore, the rate of early marriage is very high (69.01% to 81.27%) among all the village communities under this study. Without referring to the details of the prevalent community-wise marriage pattern here, it is worth mentioning that most of the girls (67.13%) have been given in marriage at an age between 11 and 15 years. Only 11 per cent of the girls were married off at 16–17 years and another 12 per cent at the age after 16–17 years. Early marriage for males was also very frequent among all the tribes. The tribes and other backward caste people of this region show no differential patterns with regard to early marriage. Early marriage results in pregnancy at a premature age which has been the common cause of teenage delivery deaths. Deaths from pregnancy as well as cases of pre-birth or after-birth death of babies are reportedly very common among the Bhumij and the Sabar in particular. The physical structure of the Sabar and Bhumij children and women itself speaks of severe malnutrition. Furthermore, they do not have proper housing facility.

Healthcare measures are not available to them for various reasons. In Bhimarjun, there is no healthcare centre in the nearby areas. And, though a PHC is situated at Andharia about 1 to 3 km. away from Chuasuli, Nalboni and Kushboni, the healthcare delivery system here is as good as near-to-absent. This is particularly because (i) the doctors and other para-medical staff are very irregular, (ii) there is a poor stock of medicine, (iii) the staff have a very casual approach, and (iv) the general lack of health awareness among the tribals themselves. The situation at Sangram, Amlatora or Chilki is not different anyway.

These villages hardly have proper facilities of safe drinking water and safe hygienic living condition, including hygienic sanitation. The people have, therefore, time and again placed demands for arrangements towards the provision of safe drinking water, hygienic food and shelter. But apparently it seems that the administration is not compliant and violates all democratic norms and suppresses the genuine demands of the people. Moreover, it has been noticed that once a political party finds a line of thought undesirable, all arrangements are made to ensure the suppression of that thought. As a result, the common people have lost their democratic rights along with their Human Rights and things move only at the political whims and fancies of the political person(s) concerned. Peoples' opinion is reportedly not taken into consideration since long.

The local governments, including the *Panchayats* and the *Panchayat Samitis,* are basically non-functioning entities. These institutions have failed to deliver because people's participation in the activities of the *Panchayat*s as well as the meetings of the *Gram Samsad*s is practically non-existent. Rather, these have become the leaders' den that remains busy reportedly over manipulating funds and submitting the pre-fixed utilization certificates. As many as 86.12 per cent of the respondents appear to be ignorant about the functioning of the *Panchayats* concerned. Meetings of the *Gram Samsads,* a statutory and mandatory provision under the Panchayati Raj Act in West Bengal, are not held desirably. In spite of that the required records of such meetings, as 90.12 per cent of the respondents believe, are kept ready in other ways. The process of selection of the beneficiaries under various schemes is grossly unfair and is based on the personal whims of the political leaders in power. Some informants have reported that although their names were enlisted in the official records of the beneficiaries, they neither knew anything about the scheme nor even received any benefit by any means. The benefits have, however, been received in the names of the persons whose names figure in the records. The respondents further confided that they did not dare to raise their voices over the malpractices due to political reasons as they feared that such a step would only lead to dire consequences for them, even to the extent of homelessness and/or physical punishment. People have, therefore, been very frustrated and feel alienated, disinterested and indifferent towards the so-called developmental programmes. They are of the view that the existing administrative-political order could not respect them and would not protect the indigenous people's rights and culture. They felt that this order could neither meet their daily basic needs nor even fulfill their expectations. They are in the midst of grave poverty in their day-to-day life, on the one hand, and are in the face of the threat of losing their culture as well as identity, on the other. So their life is always in a sea of discomfort and discontent.

The forest has been an inseparable part of tribal life. It is of immense importance in socio-cultural, symbolic and economic life of the Bhumij, Sabars and Santals as they depend on the forest for every sphere of their livelihood – from food to fuel, house-building materials, agricultural implements and for performing rituals, rites and ceremonies. Many families who depend basically on the Minor Forest Resources (MFR) are living at the mercy of the middlemen who buy MFR at a rate well below the market place. On the other hand, there are some people who are dominating in and controlling the service and trading sectors as well as the political meadow. They are basically outsiders who came to this region for jobs or for business purposes. Notwithstanding, they however reached the position to manoeuvre the political regime of the region. The economic control of the region is in their hands. However, the successive forest policies in pre- and post-Independence India, on the one hand, and the Wildlife Conservation Act, 1972 and the Forest Conservation Act, 1980 have imposed certain restrictions on them on the other, and as a result, their livelihood is at stake to a good extent. The tribal people who have no other avenues to make a living are now denied of their traditional rights over forests. The situation becomes more alarming with the forest coverage in its declining edge with the ever-increasing impetus toward industrialization and urbanization.

The draft forest policy contains many rights and privileges for the poorest people. But are these rights enjoyable at all? The Government of West Bengal is prioritizing the plantation of eucalyptus. To what extent would the rights and privileges of the forest dependent tribals be served by such plantation needs to be scrutinized, for the latter is of no value to them and the other marginalized people, as the latter perceive. People develop a symbolic relationship with nature in the form of forests with diverse varieties of plants and animals, including birds and insects, all of which a eucalyptus plantation lacks.

The Bhumij, Sabars and Santals under study are basically uneducated and unskilled people. They can hardly think of their rights to work and education, since they are suffering from severe malnutrition and starvation for decades. Even death due to starvation, an issue that has earned much political uproar in

West Bengal in the recent past, is not new to the Bhumij in Bhimarjun and its adjoining areas in particular. These poor people are suffering from extreme poverty and hunger resulting in untimely deaths.

The Bhumij, Sabar, Santals and the associated Mahatas have a strong sentiment that they are the earliest settlers or original inhabitants of this region. The forests and the natural resources of the area are theirs. So long they were used to living in their own world with their own values and culture. But they now apprehend challenges in their economic sustenance and maintenance of culture from the *diku* (the outsiders) or encroachers, as they understand, into their territory who comprise businessmen and servicemen, including the forest personnel. They have, therefore, created a sense of ethnic solidarity within themselves through a process that takes the shape of an ethnic unrest.

Under this circumstance, various political parties – national, regional and local – and ultra-violent groups are found to be playing their own games. All of them are pretending to be fighting for the causes of these disadvantaged tribal populations, often culminating into political militancy. All the seven villages included in this study as well as many others in the surrounding areas are under severe political disturbances and unrest that involve killings and counter-killings of poor tribal people by the rival groups.

Human Rights Issues

Given the above context, the issue of protecting Human Rights is nothing but exaggeration since food, shelter, healthcare and safety are extremely uncertain in the life of the indigenous people of Junglemahal. The presence of the Maoists (then MCC) was palpable even during our field visit around Banspahari in 1998. They were then trying to fetch a higher price for *babui* rope that the tribal people used to sell to the middlemen. The Maoists in the meantime have built up their guerilla bases in the forest and hilly areas of Junglemahal. They have already achieved in creating a positive impact in the minds of the poor indigenous people of this region through some popular activities, like confiscating and redistributing land of big land-holders who are dominant political leaders, eliminating the strongholds of landlords and contractors who are mostly the shadow-actors of political leaders, targeting food shop-owners who were appointed for public distribution of foodgrains and accused of siphoning off these for sale in black market, protecting local people from harassment by police as well as forest officials. Balagopal (2006) and Banerjee (2002, 2006) also observe similar phenomena. The Maoists seem to have gained support initially from the locals because the latter were also interested in eliminating political patronage in each and every sphere of life and police harassment as well as in regaining their democratic rights lost since long time. The incidences of the ruling party's alleged atrocities on the villagers of Nandigram and Singur further paved the way for the Maoists here. Furthermore, massive police atrocities on the tribals, including women, at Lalgarh and other areas of Junglemahal appear to have given the desired chance to the Maoists to have mass mobilization programmes against the police as well as the ruling party. However, the Maoists are found to be losing grounds in the event of forcible setting up of people's court to deliver justice, compelling the poor from each and every family within their strongholds to participate in night-marches, extortion of money and their indiscriminate killing of the rural poor in the name of 'annihilation of class enemies'. These acts are self-reflective and prove to the indigenous groups that the Maoists are not visibly concerned about the Human Rights of the victims.

The counter-insurgency measures adopted by the State through the deployment of the Joint Forces and the armed political cadres backed by the Joint Forces have also resorted to penal actions and killings of the local poor who are suspected to be Maoist cadres or supporters. Thus, the State machinery too dares to protect the Human Rights of the poor tribals. In this connection, some case studies may substantiate how the indigenous people of Junglemahal think of Human Rights or how far their Human Rights are protected. Fulmoni Singh (name changed), aged 41 years, of Bhimarjun assesses how the Maoist movement and the counter-insurgency programme have shattered their forest dependency and violated all Human Rights norms. In her own words (free translation):

> We have an innate relationship with the forest from times immemorial. Our forefathers used to live in the forest. They used to subsist on jungle tubers and mushrooms. Cultivation was not in practice then. The forest had been the source of our food for generations till date. But now we are dying in the midst of the Maoists and the police-guards. When we proceed towards the jungle for gathering, we usually wear the *saree* above our knees. This gives a bulging appearance around our waists since most part of our *saree*s are tucked around the waists.
>
> In such a situation, the police patrolling the forest suspect me as a Maoist carrying weapons hidden under my *saree* in the waist portion. I was forced to un-tuck my *saree* to show that no weapon was inside and the process got myself assaulted sexually. Today I am ready to avenge the offence committed on my honour any day I confront a police personnel.

Lakshmi Murmu (name changed), aged 35 years, of Chuasuli raises some questions on Human Rights issues. She states (free translation):

> Have I no dignity since I was born in a Santal family? Because I am a Santal woman I am regarded as a Maoist by the police and, at the same time, as a police-informer by the Maoist! We have settled in the forest. That is why we are supposed to be Maoists or sleeping with the Maoists. And at the same time the police used to raid our homes at night now and then. Who thinks of our rights? Who considers us as humans?

Sombari Baskey (name changed), aged 40 years, of Kushboni describes the present context (free translation):

> We are poor day-labourers. We are forced to take part in the *gana-adaalat* (people's court) and *michhil* (rally) organized at night by the Maoists and also to join the counter rallies organized by the ruling party at day time, day after day. In such a situation, how could we work and make our living? Nobody protects our rights. Both sides are involved in killing of our poor fellows. Both of them are ruthless enough to keep us under their control.

Thus, under such a violent situation, neither the Maoists nor the police and administration are in a position to think about protecting the Human Rights of the rural poor. The tribal people of Junglemahal are in a state of great resentment.

Conclusion

The tribal people of Junglemahal do not have a viable economy outside the forests. They have to walk down a very long distance to collect fuel woods from the forests and to sell them for a living. They do not have sufficient cultivable land and even if they possess some land, that is infertile in character and without any source of water for irrigation, for the Sub-Division is basically a dry area marked by low average rainfall. The demographic profile of the tribal population indicates a high illiteracy rate, high rates of infant mortality and death at child-birth, early marriage of girls and high rate of alcoholism, causing great deal of impoverishment. The medical facility is insufficient or completely lacking in some areas and the people are also reluctant to some extent towards modern medicines. Moreover, the people are not aware of the poverty-alleviating schemes supposed to be running under the local governments. Most of the government programmes, thus, prove to be ineffective in alleviating the miserable life conditions of the tribal people as most of them do not reach them. Early marriage results in teenage pregnancies and death of teenage mothers at the time of child birth. The girl children are married off very early owing to severe poverty, lack of proper education and lack of knowledge of reproductive health. Most of the children are either non-school-goers or dropouts in the early primary stage. More importantly, the economy of these tribal people is in the marginal level, which does not ensure even two square meals per day. The administrative machinery and the developmental programmes are obviously designed without keeping in mind the indigenous people's requirements, value and culture. So, there is very conspicuous inequality and disparity in resource accessibility and utilization between the indigenous people of the region on the one hand and the immigrants on the other. As a result, with the passing of time the indigenous people of this region have been alienated from the frontline polit-ico-economic scenario.

All these conditions probably lead the tribal population of the region to the domain of ethnic unrest and bring them under the clutches of one or another political or ultra-violent group for their mere survival. This ultimately leads them towards violent movements in one or other way.

The deprivation of the basic needs in essence of human existence, however, reinforces a section of these indigenous people to be indifferent to the mainstream socio-political order and, at the same time, to be attracted to the philosophy of ultra-violent movement led by the Maoists. The latter, on their part, appears to be making good use of the feeling of discontent of the poor masses in the pretext of bringing them out of extreme poverty and age-old deprivation. Unfortunately, there is neither any administrative initiative for reducing the feeling of deprivation nor any deliberate measure for achieving distributive justice.

Having no certainty about at least two square meals everyday coupled with the lack of proper healthcare mechanism, insufficient housing facility, irresistible threat to their culture and identity and values, their life is not much above an animal stage. The elders could not show the slightest rays of hope to the younger. Here the women are found to work hard throughout the day. Under such circumstances, the teenagers dream of bringing in change – a change that could make them free from all hardships. They are found to take up arms to ensure their minimal rights.

The administration has failed to deliver completely. It only resorted to police deployment and penal action, without giving any importance to the economic development of the communities here and the creation of a democratic atmosphere. Owing to this, the situation has been gradually worsening and going out of control.

Under this circumstance, the Maoists have been trying to unite the people against the administration, calling for boycotting the government initiatives, giving leadership in the movement against alleged police atrocities – which are partly true. They have floated a mass organization called People's Committee against Police Atrocities (PCPC) and pertaining training to the people, especially the teenagers, to fight the guerilla war. Initially many people got attached to the movement rationally as well as emotionally. The Maoist cadres took up the responsibility to let the people get their democratic rights and developmental resources. The local people, even the women, accepted them as friends who were fighting for the former's causes. The situation has, however, changed now as the Maoists acquired the desired control and have started controlling the area with the whims and guns. With the collapse of the administrative set up, the village people are in no position to resist the Maoists and today they have a few of their own young boys and girls involved in their activities.

Another interesting phenomenon that gets observed is that most of the leaders of the movement against police atrocities belong, however, to the Mahatas. They take decisions on behalf of the tribals as a result of which they (the tribals) are in a real complicated situation, a kind they never witnessed earlier. They may not always be accepting the decisions taken in the name of the PCPA, but then they are forced to follow the dictums before guns. They are not in a position to disown or resist any decision taken on their behalf. Here the issues of tribal culture, values or identity are in fact non-issues. The movement is, by any means, not a tribal movement or rebellion. It is a clash between the Maoists and the CPI (M) party as well as the State Government led by the party. Here the poor tribal people are used as means for resisting the opposing forces. So they become the most vulnerable entity. Protecting their human rights is practically a non-issue now.

Under the above background, a comprehensive development plan is the urgent need of the situation. The plan must ensure active participation of the stakeholders. The administration ought to have a soothing approach toward the tribal and other poor people of the region who have been facing age-old deprivation and violation of democratic rights to win over their confidence. The indigenous people of the region should no longer be considered as '*jungli*' or uncivilized by any means; rather they should be treated as our fellow citizens. A situation is to be created so that they can express their views and enjoy the freedom of speech. Ameliorative measures are to be taken to eradicate poverty and unemployment. The indigenous people should be provided with adequate facilities of food, shelter and education. The administrative set up has to come forward with the right mechanism for providing with justified and need-based distribution of resources and protecting the indigenous people's rights over natural resources. The people are to be motivated not to give their children in marriage at an early age, which would thereby help towards reducing the possibilities of teenage pregnancy. Their cultural and value-laden elements are to be cared for and preserved for the sake of human society. The entire Junglemahal may be declared as a Special Category Zone or could be brought under a master plan requiring urgent bulk fund, the cost of which would perhaps work out to be much less than that of the joint forces operation. A democratic atmosphere ought to be created as an urgent need. Democracy, Amlan Datta (2010:14) observes, is not just a peaceful method of political change, but a system representing the maximum possible opportunity for the individual to develop what is unique in him and to enrich society through the contribution of his creative uniqueness. Otherwise, the issue of Human Rights is meaningless. And, it is always meaningless in a volatile situation as in Junglemahal.

References

Aristotle. 1999. *Politics*. Translated by B. Lowett, Kitchener: Batoche Books.

Balagopal, K. 2006. 'Maoist Movement in Andhra Pradesh'. *Economic and Political Weekly*, 26: 3183–3187.

Banerjee, S. 2002. 'Naxalbari: Between Past and Future'. *Economic and Political Weekly*, 1: 2115–2116.

Banerjee, S. 2006. 'Beyond Naxalbari'. *Economic and Political Weekly*, 22: 3159–3163.

Cassese, Antonio. 1990. *Human Rights in a Changing World*. Philadelphia: Temple University Press.

Chaube, S.K. 1990. 'Violence, Crime and Labour Unrest in Calcutta: A Comparative Analysis of Social Tensions'. In Jean Racine (ed). *The City, Its Crisis and the Debate on Urban Planning and Development*. New Delhi: Concept Publishing Company.

———. 2006. 'Social Unrest in India'. In A.K. Danda, S. Chakrabory and A. Basu (eds) *Social Unrest*, Kolkata: INCAA, pp. xxxii–xliii.

Danda, A.K. 2006. 'Introductory Remarks'. In A.K. Danda, S. Chakrabory and A. Basu (Eds), *Social Unrest*, Kolkata: INCAA, pp. xv–xxv.

Das, R.K. 2006. 'The Resurgence of Nationalism in Manipur'. In A.K. Danda, S. Chakrabory and A. Basu (eds) *Social Unrest*, Kolkata: INCAA, pp. 217–227.

Datta, Ray, and Sunanda K.1980. 'Challenges of Diversity: Fringe Peoples Out in the Cold'. *The Statesman*. Calcutta, July 16.

Datta, Amlan. 2010. *For Democracy*. Kolkata: Radiance.

Giddens, A. 1984. *The Construction of Society*. Cambridge: Polity.

Haugaard, Mark. 2002. 'The Birth of the Subject and the Use of Truth: Foucault and Social Critique'. In Sinisa Malesevic and Iain MacKenzie (eds) *Ideology after Poststructuralism*. London: Pluto Press, pp. 157–170.

Hubert, Don and Thomas G. Weiss (and others). 2001. *The Responsibility to Protect: Research, Bibliography, Background.* Supplementary Volume to the Report of the International Commission on Intervention and State Sovereignty. Canada: International Development Research Centre.

Kelly, M. 1994. *Critique and Power: Recasting the Foucault/Habermas Debate*. Cambridge Mass.: MIT Press.

Kennedy, Helena. 2001. 'Conflict Resolution and Human Rights: Contradictory or Complementary?'. http://www.arrc-hre.com/publications/hrepack1/5_01.html.

Kirkpatrick, E.M. (ed.). 1980. *Chambers Universal Learners' Dictionary*. New Delhi: Allied Chambers (India) Limited.

Krishna, Sumi. 1996. *Environmental Politics: Peoples Lives and Developmental Choices*. New Delhi: Sage Publication.

Linton, Ralph. 1943. 'Nativistic Movements'. *American Anthropologist*. XLV: 230–240.

Maiese, Michelle. 2003. 'Human Rights Violations'. In Guy Burgess and Heidi Burgess (eds) *Beyond Intractability*. Conflict Research Consortium, Boulder: University of Colorado. <http://www.beyondintractability.org/essay/human_rights_violations/

Malkani, K.R. 1980. 'India: One and Indivisible – Hinduism's Resilience and Harmony'. *The Statesman*, Calcutta, 30 July.

Midya, D.K. 2006. 'Denial of Tribal Right to Livelihood and Emergence of Social Unrest: West Bengal Scenario'. In A.K. Danda, S. Chakrabory and A. Basu (eds) *Social Unrest*. Kolkata: INCAA, pp.135–142.

Minow, Martha L. 1998. *Between Vengeance and Forgiveness: Facing History After Genocide and Mass Violence*. Boston: Beacon Press.

Mondal, S.R. 2006. 'Social Movement, Social Unrest, Ethnicity and Development: Some Observations on Theoretical Issues and Empirical Realities. In A.K. Danda, S. Chakrabory and A. Basu (eds) *Social Unrest*, Kolkata: INCAA, pp.330–346.

Munda, Ram Dayal. 1988. 'The Jharkhand Movement: Retrospect and Prospect'. *Social Change*, 18: 2.

Rahman, Hosseinur. 1980. 'Being Muslim in India: Give and Take of Secular Harmony'. *The Statesman*. Calcutta, 9 September.

Sarkar, J. 2006. 'Emergence of Social Unrest to Restore Pride and Prestige of Ethnic Identity: A Case Study of the Bhainas of Chattishgarh'. In A.K. Danda, S. Chakrabory and A. Basu (eds) *Social Unrest*, Kolkata: INCAA, pp.114–122.

Sarkar, S. 1983. *Modern India 1885–1947*. Madras: Macmillan India Limited.

Stanage, S. 1974. 'Violatives: Modes and Themes of Violence'. In S. Stanage (ed.) *Reason and Violence*. Totowa, NJ: Littlefield/Adams.

Swain, A. 1997. 'Democratic Consolidation: Environmental Movements in India'. *Asian Survey (Berkeley)*, 37 (9): 818–832. University of California Press.

Tagore, Rabindranath. 1910. *Gitanjali*. London: MacMillan and Co. Ltd.

Taylor, C. 1984. 'Foucault on Freedom and Truth'. *Political Theory*. 12 (2): 152–183.

Veuthey, Michel. 1998. 'International Humanitarian Law and the Restoration and Maintenance of Peace'. *African Security Review*, 7:5. http://www.iss.co.za/Pubs/ASR/7No5/InternationalHumanitarian.html.

4

Depletion of Resources and Social Exclusion of the Displaced People

SOMENATH BHATTACHARJEE

I

Social exclusion is the deprivation or alienation of a person or persons in society, often as a result of poverty. Deprivation from poverty is more than material or physical deprivation; cultural alienation and lack of community as a result of one's economic situation create a feeling of helplessness and depression. Exclusion can be approached in three ways: liberal, social democratic, or republican. Liberalism, based on competition, describes social exclusion as the result of market failure. When markets or institutions discriminate through prices, quality, or supply, the gap between the rich and poor increases. Disparity of wealth then creates economic and social problems by changing social expectations and relationships between people, creating changed hierarchical relationships. The social democratic lens approaches exclusion through power dynamics. Exclusion is the exercise of social power through which those inside the in-group exclude the out-group in a fixed social system.

Social exclusion has been defined as 'a disadvantage in relation to certain norms of social, economic or political activity pertaining to individuals, household, special areas or population groups. It is a multiple and changing factors resulting in people being excluded from the normal exchanges, practices and rights of modern society' (Smith, 2000: 3). Here poverty is one of the most obvious factor and it also includes inadequate rights of housing, education, health and access to services.

Social exclusion is passive, active, or a combination of the two. Active exclusion integrates political action as a systematic denial of citizenship, while passive involves a societal development of alienation and separation. The difference lies in intent as well as manifestation of the exclusion. Active exclusion is legitimized through government action, while passive exclusion remains through discriminatory practices and everyday interactions.

In the creation of an identity, the 'self is reflexive in that it can take itself as an object and can categorize, classify, or name itself in particular ways in relation to other social categories or classification'. The self is determined as a 'unique entity, distinct from other individuals. The individual acts in terms of his or her own goals and desires.' People shape the world around them by imbuing it with meaning, while at the same time, meanings influence them from the surrounding social world:

- *Dimension in Social Exclusion:* The issue of social exclusion is correlated with a number of socio-economic as well as socio-cultural factors and it has multifarious dimensions.
- *Economic Dimension:* The fundamental aspect of social exclusion is abject poverty. It includes the less demand of labour force and an exclusion from the labour market of a particular individual and the concerned society. The issues of long-term unemployment and the continuous decrease of job security are the other major factors associated with the social exclusion from the socio-economic perspective.
- *Social Dimension:* The socio-cultural dimension of exclusion includes the breakdown of traditional household, joint family system and kinship-based social relation and interraction. On the other hand, it increases the maladies of teenage pregnancies, homelessness, and criminal activity.
- *Political Dimension:* The political dimension of social exclusion is primarily associated with the issue of disempowerment. Further, the issue of identity crisis, lack of electoral franchise and inadequate administrative support emerges out as a major problem related with a socially excluded sector.
- *Individual Dimension:* A socially excluded individual has an increased level of physical and mental ill health, educational underachievement, low self-esteem and lack of confidence. As a whole they gradually get segregated from the mainstream of the society and its modern means, along with the pace of the time.
- *Spatial Dimension:* In a socially excluded group, a large number of disadvantaged people are getting forced to live in a decaying area. The concerned individuals get scattered from the rest of the population in different areas and their kinship-based social solidarity has a very little prevalence.

Indicators of Social Exclusion

1. *Exclusion of Children:* In a socially excluded group, the number of uneducated children gets increased. There is the prevalence of the children with low birth weight. There occurs a continuous increase in the rate of dropout of the children particularly in the sector of formal education. The children concerned grow up in such households where acute economic insecurity is a common occurrence.
2. *Exclusion of Working Age People:* In a socially excluded group, the proportions of working age people gradually get decreased. The number of working age people get increased and their work force gets confined within the premises of workless household. The rate of unemployment is on a hike in the group concerned. The overall socio-economic insecurity and the hardship to accumulate the common minimum livelihood resources create

an acute psychological stress to the individual and it increases the death rate of the concerned society in the form of suicide and undetermined injury (Smith, 2000: 9–14).

II

Displaced People: Their Rights and Issue of Social Exclusion

The Universal Declaration of Human Rights spells out individual rights and freedom for everyone as well as *Magna Carta* for all humanity. The fundamental aspect of Human Right is to share a common vision and a common purpose to secure the freedom, well-being and dignity of all people throughout the entire world. The legislations of Human Rights states very clearly that all human beings are born free and are equal in dignity and rights. They are endowed with reason and conscience and should act towards one another in a spirit of brotherhood. It should secure the freedom from discrimination, freedom from fear, freedom from injustice, freedom of the thought and speech. The basic attributes of Human Rights clarifies that everyone has the:

- Right to life, liberty and security of a person.
- Right to a nationality, individual dignity.
- Right to culture and religious freedom.
- Right to justice.
- Right to social security and is entitled to realization through national effort and international co-operation and in accordance with the organization and resources of each state of the economic, social and cultural rights indispensable for his dignity and the free development of his personality. (Source: PDHRE, 2008)

However at present there are a number of factors which severely tell upon the fundamental human rights of a large number of people. Among these factors, the issues related to the displaced and refugee people deserve a special attention and in such cases mostly the political factors become the prime cause. Actually the refugees are extremely displaced people who have a well founded fear of persecution in their countries of origin and hence they are unwilling to return. The new human order is holistic in vision and operation and therefore, in the larger semantic sweep of Human Rights, humanitarian jurisprudence and refugee rights are also included. They have the fundamental right to:

- Equal protection of law.
- Right to a nationality.
- Right to life.
- Right to adequate standard of living, including adequate food, shelter and clothing.
- Right to work and to basic labour protection.
- Right to live in a healthy and safe environment.
- Basic right of education.
- Basic right to avail the highest possible standard of health. (Source: PDHRE, 2008)

It is to be mentioned here that displacement is one of the important factors that influence the socio-economic and other institutional changes in the society. The traditional culture, norms and values undergo change to cope up with the new physical and socio-cultural setting. Often in such case the fundamental Human Rights of the people concerned are being seriously violated and their survival faces a serious challenge. These issues have been observed among a section of people who were settled in Bangladesh earlier and due to displacement, they took refuge in India.

Ever since the Independence, India is facing the issue of migration and refugee problem. Since then nearly 35–40 million people have moved across the borders into the Indian subcontinent. During the political turmoil of Bangladesh in 1971, 10 million people fled from East Pakistan to India. Today, there are 2,50,000 refugees in India (Sreedevi, 2008: 53). In this context the present study has been done in North Bengal located in the Northern region of West Bengal and in the Karbi Anglong district of Assam. The phenomenon of migration has an immense importance in the context of the studied region.

Most of the migrants in this region have come from Bangladesh because hunger, poverty, security threat recognize no border (Datta, 2005: 147). Meanwhile, India shares 4,095 kilometres of border with Bangladesh while West Bengal has a border of 2,216 kilometre running with it. Again, Assam shares a highly porous 262 kilometre border with Bangladesh with portions of it left completely unchecked due to the difficult nature of the terrain. According to the estimate of the Border Police Department, about 1,000 migrants cross the border every day and they enter into West Bengal (Datta, 2005: 147). In this context the present study has been done among two different communities:

1. *The Rajbansi Stone Crushers of Balasan River Bed:* The Rajbansis are one of the early settlers of North Bengal and Bangladesh. They were primarily depended on agriculture. Their way of life and mode of behaviour were totally based on folk culture. Their existences were totally enmeshed with their land and neighbours. They shared their merriments commonly. But the dimension of time, place and situations are always changing. In 1971, there occurred a severe political unrest in Bangladesh. As a result, a huge number of people were forced to leave their early settlement; occupation and they become migrants. Question of daily existence was a prime factor for the migrated, landless and almost resourceless people who were devoid of any source of income. Thus, the land pressure due to continuous increase in population and the lack of purchasing capacity forced them to search for a permanent occupation to give a backbone regarding their establishment as early as possible. In this regard Siliguri is the most important place and it is the largest urban centre of North Bengal. Still it is a developing urban centre. Many rivers like Mahananda and Balasan pass through the heart of the Siliguri town and natural resources, like boulder, stone and sand come downward from the high hilly regions. These natural resources are used as raw materials for various urban constructions and it has emerged as the only earning source for a large number of people.

   The stone field of Balasan riverbed thus became unquestionably the best option for them because this work does not need any kind of capital investment. Moreover, the Balasan riverbed provided them the land to establish a new residence. For the past 35 years, the roofless, resource less migrated Rajbansis are living in the for the past Balasan riverbed. The study was done on 100 families of the said colony who were engaged in stone-based economy. The studied families had 503 population, with 252 males and 251 females; and the sex ratio was 996. The stone collection, stone crushing and the related socio-economic scenario had a direct impact on their livelihood, cultural aspects and particularly on the issues related to their Human Rights. These have been discussed here one after another.

2. *The Displaced People of Bangladesh in Karbi Anglong:* Illegal migration from Bangladesh into Assam has been a major political, economic, social and security issue for Assamese society. Though there is no documented data on the number of illegal migration, it is assumed that out of the 26 million people residing in Assam, around six million are illegal Bangladeshi migrants. The population of Assam was about 30 million (projected for 2009). The annual average rate of growth during 1991 and 2001 was 1.85 per cent. The natural rate of growth was 1.63 per cent in 1999 (and 1.59% in 2000). So there has been (inflow) net immigration to Assam, and the estimated rate of immigration has been 0.22 per cent per annum approximately. The population of Assam in 2001 was 26 million. So, the net immigration was 57,200 in 2001. In the years from 1969 to 2009, nearly 2.29 million people migrated into Assam from Bangladesh <http://www.idsa.in; http://www.satp.org>.

On the other hand, if we look at Bangladesh, the population in Bangladesh was 150 million (estimated) in 2008. The actual rate of growth of population was 2 per cent and the natural rate of growth of population was 2.2 per cent in 1995. So there is (outflow) net emigration from Bangladesh at the annual rate of 0.2 per cent. The population of Bangladesh in 1995 was 124 million. Therefore, we can estimate that 2,48,000 Bangladeshis emigrated in 1995. If we make the drastic assumption that emigration took place at that rate for 40 years (from 1969 to 2009), then we find that 9.9 million Bangladeshis left their country during this period of 40 years. We assume that most of the poor Bangladeshi families had entered into the North-East India. It is assumed that 80 per cent of the Bangladeshi migrants to the North-East were likely to come to Assam (*http://www.idsa.in; http://www.satp.org*). However, a number of emerging issues and challenges have become a great matter of concern in this regard.

The Bengali Hindus became the worst victim of partition in the North-Eastern states, particularly from socio-economic and political aspect. They were mostly treated as foreigners in the local context, although they were dwelling there since a prolonged period. During the period of partition, the then national leadership had promised to provide citizenship, rehabilitation and safeguards to the Hindu migrants coming from Bangladesh, but it was yet to be kept. In the past three years (2007–10) officially 5,175 people were traced as illegal Bangladeshi migrant in Assam. From 2007 to April 2010, 441 illegal Bangladeshi migrant were suspended from Indian citizenship. It is to be mentioned here that up till 2008, total 5,41,884 Bangladeshi migrants came to Assam. Among them government had unauthorized 12,625 individuals as citizenship of India; while 31,229 individuals were staying in India beyond their stipulated period. It revealed the fact that nearly 20,000 Bangladeshi migrants were either untraceable or residing illegally in India. Although the people authorized had no affiliation with Bangladesh since long, still they were recognized as foreigners. Even after dwelling in the studied area since last three generations, till date they have had no administrative provision to live with their own identity and fundamental rights. On the other hand, the Bangladeshi migrants who spread in other regions of India at least had a secured means for common minimum livelihood. However, in case of North-East India, the people concerned were yet to achieve any such security. While the people concerned were still struggling for their common minimum livelihood, the administration had been thinking to displace them once again. Meanwhile, in the year 2004, by issuing a special ordinance, Indian citizenship was given to the displaced and resettled people of Gujarat and Punjab. However, the Bangladeshi displaced people in North-East were debarred from this opportunity <http://www.idsa.in; http://www.satp.org>.

This issue was observed among 100 families settled in Panbari hamlet of Diphu sub-division in Karbi Anglong Assam. The studied families had 790 population, with 403 males and 387 females; and the sex ratio was 960. Displacement and insecurity of settlement had a direct impact on their livelihood, cultural aspects and particularly on the issues related to their Human Rights. These have been discussed here one after another.

Methodology Applied

The entire study has been done through intensive field work. In this regard Preliminary Census schedule was applied on 100 stone crushing families of Balasan colony and 100 families dwelling at the Panbari settlement of Diphu Karbi Anglong to collect data about their period of migration, cause of migration, occupational change, present occupational pursuits, daily working schedule, education, marital status, age at first marriage and first child, concept of health, disease and treatment and their daily food habit. Further, interviews were taken from the key informants to know about their early settlements, their previous socio-cultural practices and concerned changes of those issues due to migration. Interview was also taken about the formation of the studied settlement. The data collected through field work was analysed in detail to know about the various factors related to the daily livelihood of the people concerned.

Livelihood of the People Concerned before Migration

It is to be noted that the early settlement of the studied families were in Bangladesh. They were villagers and their prime occupational pursuit was settled agriculture. They were far from urban accessories and their livelihood was confined within the villages. Their daily existence had a deep correlation with the surrounding environment. They utilized the natural resources as raw materials to fulfil their requirements like food, dress and shelter in daily livelihood. Although they were not economically wealthy, but their livelihood was quite secured because they could easily accumulate their common minimum essentialities from the surrounding environment without any financial expenditure. Agriculture was their prime economic pursuit and in this regard the entire family was associated with this work. Their family type was joint in nature and strong kinship bondage prevailed among the family members. They always shared and participated in each others' joys and suffering. They had their own traditional cultural practices and it was enculturated through generation after generation. They had a number of religious festivals among which a few were related to their traditional agricultural occupation. All of those festivals were celebrated by all community members and those were primarily performed with a prayer for the betterment, safety and protection of the entire community. Their social life was very much peaceful and co-operative. Earlier, the social life and the associated cultural practices of the studied people were not merely confined to the community members rather it was very much associated with the surrounding nature and all other living objects as a whole. Ultimately, during their earlier settlement in Bangladesh, the studied people had their own social security and they had the scope to perform their traditional cultural performances. Earlier, their arrangements of activities were organized by keeping in view the broader in spite of the community in spite of any individual's vested desire. The productions from the land and the resources collected from the neighbourhood were equally distributed among the members of the family. All family members were collectively involved to fulfil the essential requirements for the purpose of their common minimum livelihood. In this regard the issues of individual betterment and personal sharing were strictly forbidden. Earlier, they had a strong community consensus and peace, harmony and co-operation always prevailed in their livelihood.

Displacement and Identity Crisis

The migration of people to the Balasan River bed started in 1970s and it is still going on. In case of Panbari, the people were forcefully displaced during the period of independence and it still prevails. Most of the migrated families were from Bangladesh. In case of Balasan colony, mostly the migration took place during 1970–1979 due to severe political unrest in Bangladesh. They started to build their settlement on the vested land of Balasan riverbed and at Panbari. Near about all of them were devoid of any claim to any sort of official records related with their resettlement and occupancy of the land, under the Panchayat, block or sub divisional administrative level. Even most of the inhabitants of the colony did not have their own ration card, although they were dwelling in the area for the last three decades. In Balasan colony, among the total studied population only 8.71 per cent male and 8.48 per cent female had their own ration cards, while most of them had become the beneficiary merely a year ago. In case of Panbari, only 5.35 per cent male and 5.29 per cent female had the ration card. They had repeatedly sought the appeal to higher administration for the provision of ration card but all their efforts went into vain. It is to be mentioned here that among the studied families those who had attained their age (as directed by Indian Constitution) to opine the electoral franchise, a number of them either had no voter identity card and if it was present, some major errors were there. From the overall circumstances, it can be stated that although the studied families were dwelling in the studied areas for more than three decades but they had no proper legal authorization. They were settled in the vested land without any sort of administrative authorization. On the contrary, it is also true that if the government wants to uproot the studied people from their settlement then the common mass had no way to highlight their authorization and claim over their land. The entire situation had resulted in an acute identity crisis for the people. They had no legal authenticity regarding their citizenship as an Indian. Moreover, as they had no adequate permission related to their settlement, so they were always under stress that any administrative action might tell upon their inhabitation and it would force them into roofless and resourceless in condition. Although they got the chance of resettlement after the political turmoil, but till date they have been treated as the roofless and resourceless refugees.

Present Occupation and Working Condition

Before migration they were settled agriculturists in most of the cases. Now they were not at all in any position to reinstate their traditional caste-based occupation of settled agriculture. On the contrary, they found the stone crushing occupation as the best way of survival and readily accepted it. The analysis of generation wise occupation from parental generation to the descendants revealed that there occurred a complete shift over in their occupational pursuit from agriculture to stone crushing either primarily or secondarily. Their parental generation was totally agriculturist but the present generations are mostly (90%) engaged in stone based economy. The dwellers of Balasan riverbed were engaged in collection and supply of those raw materials for urban constructions to the adjacent areas. The stone-based economy was the prime source of income for most of the studied families. Hard manual labour was the only requirement for the said occupation. This occupation was devoid of age and gender biasness. The working atmosphere on the Balasan riverbed was a dusty and polluted one. Simultaneously, the stone crushers always had to work in touch with the river water. They worked day long under scorching sunlight, shivering cold and under heavy showers. Mostly they used crude iron implements and they worked without any sort of protecting device for their eyes and hands.

Among the studied families, in most of the cases the entire family worked as a production unit. Excluding the children, 94.82 per cent male and 87.16 per cent female were either primarily or secondarily involved in the stone crushing work. The main interesting feature was that their daily requirements had forced most of the women to give prime importance to the work despite their household activities. It is to be mentioned here that the females and the children who were primarily engaged in household work and education respectively, were simultaneously involved in the stone crushing work secondarily either in the stone field or in their houses to fulfil their familial requirements. The work was conducted in any climatic condition and the people concerned went to the riverbed early in the morning and did their work throughout the day. Most of the working population had to work for more than 8 hours. The female who were mostly involved in the household work, also did the stone crushing work for 3–4 hours in a day. They worked under '*sardars*' and could get their payment once in a week (on Tuesday) according to their quantity or amount of work. Considering the family income, 13 per cent families could earn below ₹ 1,000 per month, 77 per cent families earned between ₹ 1,001 to ₹ 2,000 and only 10 per cent families had the monthly income between ₹ 2,001 to ₹ 3,000.

Again, at Panbari most Bangladeshi migrants were involved in the manual workforce like auto rickshaw pulling, house construction workers, house painters, gardeners, field workers, road construction workers, vegetable vendors, etc. Women immigrants mostly work as maids. They had to work very hard, at odd hours and in the most arduous activities to sustain their common minimum livelihood. Excluding the children, 97.83 per cent male and 96.28 per cent female were either primarily or secondarily involved in the stone crushing work. Their average monthly income is ₹ 1,500 to ₹ 2,000.

From the empirical field data it had been revealed that, per head per capita income of the studied occupational group was ₹ 292.85 per month and ₹ 9.76 per day. Again the average family income of the studied families was ₹ 380.48 per month and ₹ 12.68 per day. With this mere amount of income they had to maintain an average five membered family. So, every individual of the studied families had an average income of ₹ 2.54 per day. It is to be mentioned here that the per head per capita income of our country in the year 2008–2009 was ₹ 25,494 (*India 2010*: 133), while in case of West Bengal it was ₹ 25,223 (*Manorama Year Book 2000*: 667). Thus, it was ₹ 2,124 per month and ₹ 70.82 per day in India. Again, the Ministry of Labour, Government of West Bengal has fixed the daily wage of unskilled workers involved in the stone breaking and stone crushing occupation to ₹ 116.23 per day (Ministry of Labour, Government of West Bengal, 2009: 5, dated 5/1/2009). Thus, it could be easily revealed that in comparison with the national and state level their category of income was bizarre in condition. In the year 2000–2001, the per capita income of Assam state and India was ₹ 10.198 while in case of India it was ₹ 16,487 (Source: *Assam Human Development Report*, 2003: 52).

Thus, despite their hard manual labour the people concerned earned a very little amount. Earlier the people were mostly dependent on the agricultural crops and fishes of their own land, village ponds and nearer rivers but now this scenario has changed completely and they are primarily dependent on market-based products. Their average family member was five in number and with this mere source of income they had to face all sorts of inconveniences to fulfil their daily livelihood requirements.

Impact on Education

Education is the cradle of every society. Like others the stone crusher people are also interested to give higher education to their children and make them well established. In Balasan colony, the literacy rate of male and female was 75.06 per cent and 70.37 per cent, respectively. At Panbari, the literacy rate of male and female was 42.03 per cent and 37.30 per cent, respectively. But the parents and other elderly members were mostly illiterate and they were too much busy in their working schedule. In this regard the economic scarcity was a great hindrance for them to provide adequate educational requirements and basic infrastructure of study to their children. On the other hand, in the studied area there was only a primary school and the nearest high school was located at a distance of 2–3 km. It had turned out as a great hindrance for them to seek the secondary level of education because the parents concerned were quite reluctant to accompany their children to such a distance from their very crucial working schedule. Moreover, the children often went out from the classes and joined with their parents in the stone crushing work. Although the enrollment in primary education is cent per cent but as they gradually grown up the cases of dropout become a very common phenomenon, and it is more acute among females. After getting detached from formal education, the children were directly involved in stone-based work. In Balasan area, among the male, educational confinement was mostly (96.54%) up to class VIII level and among the female it was mostly (64.37%) up to class IV.

While at Panbari, among the male, educational confinement was mostly (98.23%) up to class VI level and among the female it was mostly (94.57%) up to class IV standard. They had a keen desire to educate their children. However, during such admissions, a number of documents related to their identity and citizenship were required to be submitted. Obviously they were lacking from such evidences and it had gradually reduced their scope to enroll their children in the educational domain. There was not a single female child in both the areas who had qualified secondary level of education. During the study it was noticed that the population of Balasan colony and Panbari increased manifold from its earlier population and it led to a definite competition among the families for survival. Despite that the people concerned were unable to look after any other sort of work, because they neither had the proper educational knowledge to acquire urban-based official jobs nor they were skilled enough to compete and find their own place among the skilled labour workers of urban Siliguri or Diphu and other suburban areas.

Socio-Cultural Factors and Livelihood Conditions

Before migration, the studied people were settled agriculturist and resided in the houses build on the open space in the middle of their own agricultural land. A poor cultivator had a simple family with his parents, wife and children. Adult members lived in separate rooms. Joint family or extended family was under the authority of one head. The elderly person of the family was the sole authority and everyone was bound to abide by his direction. The families were patrilineal and patrilocal with recognition of social relations with the kin members on both sides. Rarely a married son got separated from the family and lived elsewhere. The relatives and kin members participated altogether in their social, religious and other festivals. They had a number of religious festivals related with the agriculture and other purposes. Those festivals were mainly performed for the betterment of the entire community. Along with that, they had their own folk cultural performances which were practiced by them with utter enthusiasm during their leisure.

But due to displacement and migration, they were forced to leave their relatives and kin members and sometimes even their wives and children. Further, they settled in the studied areas with their family members and in some cases they got remarried and started a new family life. Here all the studied family members of Balasan riverbed were involved in the stone crushing work for most of the time, while in Panbari they were involved in hard manual labour works and they were no more related with agricultural works and allied practices. Most of the families were nuclear and their neighbourhood relationship was no more integrated, harmonious and affectionate as it was earlier. People were quite busy with their hard working schedule to accumulate a fold of rice in the context of their survival. In this regard they could hardly pay enough attention to their neighbourhood. It has been reported that now the young generations are getting separated from their parents after their marriage to live their own personal life and they barely accept any opinion of their guardians. Most of the families were far from their close kin members and they had little contact with them. Their familial integration had broken very rapidly in these circumstances. Often, neighbourhood quarrels could be seen among them. Their social integration was no more peaceful and harmonious as it had been earlier. As a result, social structure and social organization based on familial and neighbourhood interaction level has changed a lot from their earlier feature. The contemporary social functions have confined to the circumference of nuclear familial level despite the entire societal level as it was prevalent earlier. Most importantly, a family is the prime source of socialization and personality formation for a child. Meanwhile, in the studied area most of the children were lacking the guidance and affection of their close kin members, particularly of their grandparents. From early childhood they could observe familial tension, quarrel with neighbours and acute poverty.

Further, the poor level of income had provided a very little chance to the stone crushing families to acquire better living conditions. Most of the families had only a couple of room to reside and in some cases they resided in a single room. Positions of kitchens were mostly outside the room and even in some cases they cooked inside the room. Most of the houses were devoid of proper drainage and sanitary means and for this purpose they often used the riverbed. The environment around most of the houses was not adequate from the perspective of health and hygiene. Particularly in rainy season their shanty lanes became waterlogged and muddy due to improper drainage system. Lack of proper household infrastructure had created psychological stress among the family members and it specially affected the children very much. Despite their hard work they had a very mere chance to enjoy mental recreation and in the evening most of them got involved in a number of addictions. Most of the adult male members were alcoholic and were involved in gambling. They almost spent their entire earning in it. Even teenage children were addicted to alcohol, tobacco use and sometime gambling. Ultimately a very little amount of money was left for the women to fulfil their familial needs and in this regard they had to face all sorts of inconveniences. The continuous pressure of need and lack of its fulfillment ultimately turned out into familial tension among the married couples and often the wives were maltreated by their husbands. Those intricacies created a problem among their children and in this regard their simple tender mind had to face all sorts of complexities. These ultimately hampered their education as well as socialization and personality formation as a whole. Meanwhile, it is to be mentioned here that poverty had created an acute hindrance for the guardians to organize the marriage ceremony of their daughters. The studied people mostly practiced the community endogamy but during the study it was reported that the demand of dowry was quite high from the family members of the groom. In this regard, the parents of the bride had to face all sorts of inconveniences to meet up with the demand of the dowry. It had forced them to conduct the marriage even by taking debt from the local money lenders at a quite high interest because they were seldom reluctant to turn down the chance of their daughters' marriage with a suitable mate. Poverty, addiction and familial tensions were a great hindrance for them to lead a joyful life. Further, in the present settlement, a number of religious festivals were no more practiced by the people concerned, as those were related with their traditional agricultural occupation. On the other hand, now they no more had period of leisure to cherish their folk cultural performances. As a result these performances were almost being forgotten by them, particularly in the case of the younger generation. Moreover, it had taken a serious toll upon their united participation, common celebration and social consensus. Thus, it is to be noted here that the socio-economic and socio-cultural life of the studied people got altered a lot after their displacement and migration from early settlement.

III

General Observation

The idea behind the concept of social exclusion is not radically new, the evaluative research in the field has helped an in-depth understanding and empirical analysis of certain aspects of poverty and deprivation. No concept of poverty can be satisfactory if it does not take adequate note of the disadvantages that arise from being excluded from shared opportunities enjoyed by others. In this essay, an attempt of a critical examination of the idea of social exclusion, particularly in the context of deprivation and poverty, has been made. Here social exclusion has been placed within the broader perspective of poverty as capability deprivation, and this conceptual linkage both provides more theoretical understanding of the approach which helps us to extend the practical use of the same in the empirical field research. The perspective of social exclusion reinforces rather than competes with the understanding of poverty as capability deprivation.

Such a situation can be specifically noticed among the displaced people of Bangladesh during the partition of India. The contemporary political elites took the decision by thinking a limited vested achievement without properly predicting the long term adverse circumstances. The displaced non-Muslim people took India to be their motherland, but India was not ready to accept them as their citizens. Their rights to citizenship or to a nation are never granted and they find themselves located in the circumstance of statelessness, with no one to take care of their rights.

They are completely in the opposite domain of this progressive world and are gradually lagging far and far behind in the steady and faster rate of overall societal and techno-economic development. The displaced families of Bangladesh are in such a situation. In Bangladesh, they had their own land, settled means of livelihood and stable economic pursuit. They were not economically wealthy but their livelihood was quite protected in the lap of nature. In early settlement they had the right to nationality, individual dignity and pursuance of social and cultural practices. But the imposed political decisions left a major impact on their right to social security, individual dignity and right to life. The overall adverse circumstances forced them to leave the settlement and they were displaced as a roofless and resourceless migrant. Even after the resettlement they were enmeshed into a number of inconveniences and still now struggling for their survival. Although they were resettled since many decades but they had no identity as an Indian citizen and they had no authorized document of their present settlement. They were simply known as an unwanted refugee population but they were not known on the basis of their own individual social or cultural identity. Further, after the resettlement a strong economic backbone was their prime need. But the confinement of urban capital wealth had deprived them from their common minimum requirement. In most of the present settlement, they had no scope to accumulate the natural resources related with their daily livelihood. On the other hand, economic scarcity was a great hindrance for them to depend on expensive market based products. Thus, they had to face severe struggle for their survival. Further, their household infrastructure was mostly lacking sufficient rooms, scientific means of sanitation and proper drainage. Lack of purified drinking water is an added criterion to their misery. Moreover, the poverty and pressure of familial requirements had forced their children to get involved in diversified manual labour from an early age. It had severely affected their education. Along with that, the economic scarcity had caused hindrances for the parents in providing adequate educational requisites to their children. From the overall circumstances, it can be stated that due to displacement a severe socio-economic and socio-cultural crisis had emerged among the people concerned as well as it had exposed them to an insecure environmental circumstances. They were completely devoid of the basic attributes of fundamental Human Rights related to their settlement, nationality, standard of living, security of food and nutrition, basic right of education and highest possible standard of health which they should deserve simply by virtue of being a human being. In many cases they were dwelling in a close proximity to the different urban settlements but ironically they were far away from the modern urban facilities. Displacement had led them towards a poverty stricken life; on the other hand, due to poverty they had lost the minimum security related with daily livelihood. Further, it gradually made them excluded from the national mainstream and they were deprived of the basic Human Rights in every aspect of their livelihood. They had a feeble economic backbone and their individual identity as well as socio-cultural tradition was facing an acute crisis. Politically they were lagging far behind from any decisive role. Ever since partition and thereafter unwanted political decisions were imposed upon them by the national authorities. With the changing dimension of time the security of their stable life was totally disrupted and lost its balance in the last 50 years and even now they are facing the consequent result. If adequate steps are not taken immediately then the forthcoming period will tell us whether their society will exist or not; or they will leave this place again to move on the way of their uncertain future.

Note

* *Acknowledgement:* The author sincerely acknowledges to the Honourable Vice Chancellor of Assam University, Silchar; the Honourable Pro-Vice Chancellor of Assam University, Diphu Campus; Head, Department of Anthropology, Assam University, Diphu Campus; Honourable Ph.D. supervisor Dr Samar Kumar Biswas, Department of Anthropology, North Bengal University and all the people of the studied area, for their inspiration and support.

References

Ahuja, R. 1999. *Society in India*, Jaipur: Rawat Publications.

Assam Human Development Report. 2003. Planning & Development Department, Government of Assam, Guwahati.

Biswas, S.K. 2005. 'Asantosher Karon' (in Bengali). In G. Roy (ed.), *Bisay: Santras*, Siliguri: Baitanik Patrika Gosthi, pp. 81–93.

Biswas, S.K. and S. Bhattacharjee. 2006. 'Effect of Land Alienation: A Study Between a Scheduled Caste and a Primitive Tribal Group'. In S.H. Samel (ed.), *Rights of Dalits*, New Delhi: Serials Publication, pp. 89–114.

——. 2008. 'Misery of Displacement: A Study of the Rajbansis of Tarijot Colony'. *Voice of Dalits*, 1(2): 217–230, New Delhi: M.D. Publication. pp. 167–180.

Census of India. 2001. New Delhi: Government of India.

Datta, P. 2005. 'Undocumented Migration from Bangladesh to West Bengal'. In Vijoy S. Sahay, Pradip K. Singh and Gautam K. Bera (eds), *Dimension of Research in Indian Anthropology*. New Delhi: Serials Publication, pp. 147–159.

http://www.idsa.in/issuebrief/BangladeshiIllegalMigrationintoAssam_ngoswami_140110, accessed on 22.01.2010, 18:00 hrs.

http://www.satp.org/satporgtp/countries/india/states/assam/documents/papers/illegal_migration_in_assam.htm, accessed on 22.01.2010, 19:00 hrs.

Manorama Year Book. 2000. Kottayam: Malayala Manorama Press.

Ministry of Labour. 2009. Annual Report. Kolkata: Government of West Bengal.

Nanda, S. 1984. *Cultural Anthropology* (2nd ed). California: Wordsworth Publishing Company.

National Human Rights Commission, http://www.nhrc.nic.in, accessed on 3 November 2009.

National Sample Survey, 50th (1993–94) 55th (1999–2000). Rounds, Employment and Unemployment Situation Among Social Groups in India. New Delhi: Government of India.

Shah, G. (ed.). 2001. *Dalit Identity and Politics*, London: Sage Publications.

Smith, J.P. (ed.). 2000. *Policy Responses to Social Exclusion: Towards Inclusion*. Buckingham: Open University Press.

Sreedevi, P. 2008. 'The Refugee Definition and Link to Human Rights', In S.S. Krishna and A.K. Samudrala (eds) *Refuge and Human Rights*, New Delhi: Serials Publications, pp 53–58.

Vidyarthi, L.P. and B.K. Rai. 1977. *The Tribal Culture of India*, Delhi: Concept Publishing Company.

5

Minimizing Development-Induced Displacement

A Study Among the Santals of Raniganj

ABHIJIT GHOSAL

Tribals are the most vulnerable section of the population in India. They are exploited by the most age-old social and cultural handicaps coupled with environmental factors. The age old exploitation and repression of the tribals have considerably cut them off from the main stream of socio-economic development of the country as a whole. During the British rule in India, by passing the 'Crown's Control Over Forests Act' in 1865, they took away the autonomy of tribals over the forests making them 'encroachers' on land that had been theirs for ages. With one legislative change, they became trespassers in their own forests, victimized by externally motivated systems of forest management that directly violated various facets of their economic and cultural survival. Their forests and other resources in their areas were increasingly seen as commodities, their lands expropriated as private property and their growing dependence on ruthless money lenders linked with powerful feudal landlords and local politicians led to massive land alienation, and permanent or seasonal migration. Added to this environmental transition was the imposition of an alien judicial system and 'law and order' machinery that subjugated them further, compounding their vulnerability and subservience. Their own highly subtle and organically embedded systems of conflict resolution were undermined. As a result of all these changes the tribals lost their self-respect and dignity to a considerable amount, and are in an identity crisis at present. Before Independence the tribal areas were loosely administered with a very little or no accent on development. After Independence the central and state governments have given adequate thrust on developing the living standards of tribals in parity with that of other citizens. The Constitution of India has made definite provisions for the welfare and uplift of the tribal people.

In the mid-19th century, people in India's tribal areas organized protests and rebellions against British colonial laws such as the Forest Act of 1876, which prevented their use of the forest lands on which their way of life depended. Though India gained its Independence in 1950, the displacement once associated with colonialism continues in the name of development. Different developmental projects have been implemented under India's Five Year Plans and as a results of these projects near about 5,00,000 persons have been evicted from their lands by direct administrative actions of government. India's recent thrust to open itself to the global economy and rely more on market forces will surely accelerate the displacement. Hydroelectric and irrigation projects are the largest source of displacement and destruction of the habitat. Other major sources are mines, thermal and nuclear power plants, industrial complexes, weapon testing grounds, railways and roads expansion and the expansion of reserved areas, sanctuaries and national parks.

Coal has been mined intensively in eastern India since the mid–1800s. Since then mines have had an influence on the surrounding social fabric, stimulating migration, leading to urbanization and industrialization, and have modified the physical environment (Lahiri-Dutt 2001). Over 70 per cent of the Indian coal is used for power generation. Coal companies owned by the government operate both underground and open-cut collieries, and use an intricate network of distribution to supply coal to the consumers. Much of this coal, however, is transported by rail, and point-to-point deliveries are made by trucks. The sightings of coal cyclists, especially on the highways of Jharkhand, have become common in the past few years. This time period has also been one of intense changes in the coal mining industry; mines have become more mechanized, larger, and have led to more displacement of the local communities than ever before (Lahiri-Dutt 2003).

Displacement results in dismantling production system, severing trade and market links, scattering kinship groups and extended families and weakening cultural systems of self-management and control. They also lose access to the fuel, fodder and food they traditionally collected for their households from common land. They, thus, face increased pauperization and are thrust into the margins of the labour market. Though India's tribal people make up 8.2 per cent (2001 Census) of the total population, over 50 per cent of those displaced from 1950s to 2000 were from tribal communities. Planners and administrators invariably capitalize on and manipulate the relatively weaker socio-economic and political position of most of the people facing displacement. Their numbers are underestimated, they are treated indifferently and only minimal cash compensation, if at all, is paid. They are rarely granted security of tenure on alternative developed land sites. All too often, after a painful and traumatic period of establishing a new lifestyle, they are informed they must move again to make way for yet another project. Despite the scale of the displacement, the efforts continue to be substandard and disgustingly inadequate. What the industrialization process has brought to tribal peoples territories today for the development of their peoples raises a serious question. The development method in these territories, through the formal sector, to which the informal sector is tagged, has been an experience of unfaithfulness for the tribal people.

The present paper dealt with the displacement threat and the problems of the tribals in the Santal village, Diguli in Burdwan, Asansol. It also gives a general overview of the extractive industries and also its impact on the indigenous people in the frame of formal and informal sectors. In order to understand the situation of the Santals in the village surrounded by mines it is important to understand the coal mining project's background in detail.

Extractive Industries and its Implication on Indigenous Peoples: Formal and Informal Sector

The problem with extractive industries operating on indigenous people's areas and territories worldwide is that its impact is more indirect than direct. This impact staggers on indirectly to the extent that without a deep analysis, it would not be possible to understand and analyse the sensual link between the opening up of extractive industries and the degradation of the life of the indigenous peoples.

To understand this process we need to look into India's industrial policy. India has accorded great importance to mining in its industrial development and the overall growth of the country. Mining and a policy on the management of mineral resources were part of India's industrial policy and initial Five Years Plans, both in the non-scheduled or scheduled areas – the latter are areas specified by the India's Constitution having indigenous population. Land in the scheduled areas cannot be owned by non-indigenous persons unless it is for 'public purpose' and other such uses. In these areas, massive industrial programmes were carried out in the 1950s and 1960s enabling the industrial sectors to fuel development in other sectors. Huge amount were invested in large projects such as irrigation, power plants, steel plants and mines. The massive industrialization not only put tremendous pressure on the mineral resources of the country, but also on the traditional lands and resources of tribal communities in India. These large scale extractive industries in localized zones breed an informal cycle of economy. The formal cycle of economy, on the other hand, is known as the backward and forward linkage of capital. For the formal sectors to become viable and functional it is necessary to develop certain infrastructural nets which economist call overheads. Extractive industries like oil, gas and coal need a highly developed network of transportation which requires building up of networks, rail heads, linkages to ports amongst others, and all these means further erosion of tribal peoples' rights over land, forest and their livelihood resource base.

Extractive industries not only require capital in form of money but also sophisticated machines. The other important requirements in these industries are skilled labour, management and technical scientists. So briefly we can say that to run an extractive industry smoothly it is necessary that technical skilled population of non-indigenous people are brought to the area. Thus, by definition, setting up extractive industry implies, not only curbing of rights of indigenous people towards lands forest resources but also of putting them into radically subordinate position vis-à-vis a population of non-indigenous peoples with urban life orientation. This is so because indigenous people from the agrarian and traditional way of life, even if they are appointed in the extractive industries, perform only the manual and unskilled tasks. The non-indigenous population provides for the bulk of skilled and technical staff.

Even if we take the formal sector of economy, two things are certain: (1) there is a loss of rights of indigenous peoples towards the land, forest and water resources, (2) they are placed in a subordinate position to the skilled and manual task force.

As far as the loss of rights towards forest, water and land resources are concerned there is only limited understanding about what constitutes fair and just compensation for such serious losses which have a devastating impact on human welfare and cultural integrity. But, on the whole, the protection of the indigenous people from this subordination by the non-indigenous people who are technically qualified and understand the dynamics of the extractive industry, is a serious question. An improvement in the lives of those whom a project otherwise imposes severe costs in order to create benefits for others should be considered an entitlement, not an act of reluctant generosity – a basic test of project benefit. While the first goal should be to find alternatives that cause minimal displacement, in those instances where displacement is inevitable, it is imperative that the full costs of rehabilitation be internalized into the project cost. The present paper dealt with the displacement threat and the problems of the tribals in the Santal village Diguilin Burdwan, Asansol. In order to understand the situation of the Santals in the village surrounded by mines it is important to understand the coal mining project background in detail.

The Sarisatali Coal Mining Project

One of the most significant examples that can be cited as development at the cost of displacement is that of the coal mining activities being undertaken in the Burdwan district and the 'Rasunpur' Forest Area. All the tribal villages falling under this district have been displaced in this process. The Calcutta Electric Supply Corporation (CESC) and Integrated Coal Mining Limited (ICML) owned jointly the coal mining area. Since the year 2002, the ICML has started their 'Sarisatali Coal Mining Project' and the Government of West Bengal gives them permission to acquire 2,615 acres of land. The area comprises 1,715.79 of agricultural land and 154 acres of forest land of 'Rasunpur Reserve Forest', after uprooting near about 1,000 peasants from their land and rendering 1,500 share croppers and landless labourers devoid of any means of subsistence. Out of the total villages of 127 in this area, 121 villages are reeling under the eminent danger of subsistence. The coal from this area has been extracted in a very unscientific manner and, thus, the lives and property of so many villagers are hanging by a thread waiting for disaster to strike. Unfortunately the local political leader's leagued themselves with the land grabbers. The village Diguli fall under this area of ICML on account of faulty mining practices large mounds of stones and earth and large holes and crevices has been formed in the entire area, making the place unfit for human habitation. The displaced are being denied the minimum of Human Rights and the poor villagers mainly comprising the scheduled tribes are being forced to be merely onlookers to this greedy developmental destruction.

However, before starting the project, the administration and the ICML authority promised that they would provide the following facilities to the displaced people:

1. The land losers would be provided with photo identity card.
2. Persons affected would be granted subsistence allowances.
3. Persons holding identity card would be given preference in appointment.
4. By forming co-operative societies they will do their best to create green belt in the region by planting trees with the help of the forest department.
5. Technical support would be given to the land losers.

6. They will provide training to the villagers for rearing poultry farms, handicrafts, etc.
7. Construction of water reservoir for providing safe drinking water to the people of this region.
8. Better health facilities will be provided to them.

Neither the administration nor the ICML has fulfilled any of the promised and, on the other hand, coal mafias are taking advantage of these poor people and involving involve them in illegal selling and mining of coal.

Location of the Studied Area

The settlement of the Santals in the Diguli village is located in the west; Diguli is 12 km away from the Asansol station. The nearest village to Diguli is Rakhakura, at a distance of 3 km. In Diguli, there are 106 families out of which 43 families are Santal, consisting of 127 males and 118 females, respectively (Table 1).

Table 1

Distribution of Studied Population

No. of Santal Families	*Male*	*%*	*Female*	*%*	*Total*
43	127	51.84	118	48.16	245

Socio-Economic Background

Education

Education is considered as a key to the achievement of status and positions in a society. In India, tribal population due to isolation, poverty, primitive economy, etc. for a generation could not come up to the level of general population in different spheres of activities and as such due emphasis has been given for their social, economy and educational upliftment with an aim to integrate them with the general mass as early as possible. There is only one school called Churuliya Government High School in the studied area. The progress of secondary education among the Santals of this area has acquired very little momentum (Table 2).

Table 2

Literacy Rates Among the Studied Population

Category	*Male*	*%*	*Female*	*%*	*Total*	*%*
Illiterate	45	18.37	67	27.35	112	45.71
Pre-primary/Class I-IV	41	16.73	33	13.47	74	30.20
Class V – X	37	15.10	16	6.53	53	21.63
Class XI-XII	3	1.22	2	0.82	5	2.04
Graduation	1	0.41			1	0.41
Total	127	51.84	118	48.16	245	100.00

Table 2 shows that 33.47 per cent males are literate and 20.82 per cent females are literate. Out of 51.84 per cent males, only 18.37 per cent are illiterate and out of 48.16 per cent females, 27.35 per cent are illiterate. It shows that females are lagging behind males in educational standard.

Occupation

Table 3 shows that most of the Santal men were engaged as day labourers (40.48%); followed by agriculture (13.49%) and service holders (1.59%). There were 26.19 per cent of women engaged as day labourers 1.59 per cent in agricultural work, etc. The other categories include carpentry, crafts making, maidservants, etc.

Table 3

Occupational Status of the Population

Total Population		*Nature of Occupation*	*Male*	*%*	*Female*	*%*	*Total*	*%*
Male	*Female*							
		Agriculture	17	13.49	2	1.59	19	15.08
		Service	2	1.59	–	–	2	1.59
		Business	3	2.38	1	0.79	4	3.17
127	118	Day Labour	51	40.48	33	26.19	84	66.67
		Others	8	6.35	9	7.14	17	13.49
		Total	81	64.29	45	35.71	126	100.00

Average income of the studied villages was depending upon the number of people engaged in service. The average income of a villager was higher when a greater number of service holder was recorded. However, majority of the families belonged to lower income group (up to ₹ 1,500) (Table 4).

Table 4

Family-Wise Monthly Income of the Studied Population (previous years)

Monthly Income (in Rupees)	*No. of Families*	*%*
Up to 1500	19	44.19
1501–3000	13	30.23
3001–7000	8	18.60
7001 and above	3	6.98
Total	43	100.00

Hygiene Condition

The general condition of the houses was not satisfactory. People lived in rooms where proper ventilation was found to be absent as a result of which major portion of the room remains dark. The floor was made up of mud. There was no proper drainage system within the house as a result of which the whole courtyard was strewn with filth and mud. Sometimes the nearby cattle shed make the condition worse.

There is no fixed place for nature's call. No permanent structure like urinal or latrine is to be found within the houses. The nearby fields and bushes are used for nature's call. Indiscriminate spitting habit in and around also creates a deterrent effect on the health and hygiene of the people and locality. The people who are blessed with a better income have their own toilet facilities and they are the least in number.

There is no proper drinking water facility and out of three tubewells in Diguli only one is fit for drinking purpose and two wells which were also unsafe for drinking. The level of water goes down because of mining activities in the surrounding areas. Thus, there is a great problem of drinking water. During summer season they collect water from cracks and fissures appear in the rings and parapets which were unfit for drinking.

From Table 5 it is clear that most of the families use tubewell water for drinking (62.80%) and well water (37.20%). Pond water is also used for washing which is unhygienic, though nobody uses it for drinking.

For treatment of diseases they seek advice from the local quack doctor. For minor ailments they go to the traditional medicine man. There is only one government hospital called Kalla Hospital which is 20 km away from the locality. They have to face problems every time the need arises.

Table 5

Drinking Water Sources

Total Families	*Well*		*Tube well*	
	No	*%*	*No*	*%*
43	16	37.2	27	62.8

Environmental Consequences of Ranigunj Coal Mining Project

Before coal mining operation began in Ranigunj area, the environment was stable with abundant agricultural field and vast forest cover. It was gifted with plenty of natural resources. In the forest of Rasunpur, there were plants like mango, *pipal*, *kusum*, *kendu*, *harida*, *bhada* and *amla*. The region enjoyed good environment conditions before the ingress of coal mining. Coal mining and industrial activities have brought an adverse impact on environment and the region has now earned the uncertain distinction of being one of the most polluted zones of the country. The major impact on the environment comes from open cast mines. Although coal mining started in 1921, the real adverse effect on environment began with the coming up of open cast mining in 1960. In the case of underground mining, there is not much direct environmental impact as operations are confined to the underground and the nominal area of land is acquired. But in the case of open cast coal mining operations, which is carried out on the land surface and large scale acquisition of agricultural, homestead and forest land is required. Coal mining in Ranigunj has already resulted in the ecological imbalance, environmental pollution, water crisis and health hazards.

Ecological Imbalance

Open cast coal mining, which involved the acquisition of large agricultural tracts and forest, has disturbed the ecological imbalance. In the Ranigunj coal field area, the forest cover is depleting fast. Due to acquisition of vast agricultural, homestead and forest land, kitchen garden and cultivation have virtually come to an end. Green plants are gradually vanishing from the area. Coal dust made the remaining condition more adverse. The indiscriminate felling of trees and destruction of green plans brought about by the mining operation and absence of any measure of tree plantation has led to an abnormal rise in temperature in this area. There has also been a steady decline in rainfall in the region. Herbal medicines, fuel wood, fodder and other plants are no longer available in this area and the local poor people depending on forest produce have been affected adversely.

Environmental Pollution

An enormous quantity of coal dust is released into the air during mining and transportation of coal. During transportation heavy coal gets into the air. Constant plying of trucks, tippers and other vehicle pollutes the air around the roads. During blasting many toxic gases like sulfur dioxide, nitrogen oxide and carbon monoxide are also affecting the people. The atmosphere is perpetually filled with smoke and a layer of dust pollutes the water sources and vegetation. Hence, the plants in this area look black instead of green. The deposit of coal dust in the agricultural land has hardened the soil thereby reducing the fertility and productivity of land.

Tiwary and Dhar (1994) in their study showed that how the exploitation of Coal and related industries has exerted great impact on the environment. As a consequence of the underground mining, huge volume of polluted water flooded the mines and channelled into the stream or river which in turns chemically polluted. A large amount of water is released during coal mining and it is pumped out constantly in order to facilitate mining operation. The continuous draining out of such a huge amount of water has led to a progressive lowering of the ground water. Wells have dried up in villages in the close proximity of the mines. Villagers have to draw water from the deepest recesses. Toxic materials released from the coal washeries and the water released from both open cast and underground mines and surface run off carrying the waste into the stream.

Open cast coal mines at Ranigunj has led to the dumping on sites near the mines. They have covered up productive agricultural land. This causes loss of top soil, and land slides. The dumps have affected drainage, vegetation cover and water table. Waste products over this reduce the productivity of land. Also, noise pollution is one of the major problems in this area. The dynamite blasting in these mines area is the major part of the operation. The ground vibration has caused cracks and it damages their houses. Their occupants live in constant danger of being crushed under the roofs or walls of their cracked houses during the rainy season. Ground vibration has caused landslides, created fractures, fissures thereby altering ground water flow, drying up the existing and altering the quantity of ground water discharge elsewhere.

Health Hazards

Environmental pollution as a part of coal mining operation has led to deteriorating health conditions among the people of this area. The people are affected by diseases like gastro-enteritis, diarrhoea, bronchitis, eye irritation, tuberculosis, skin diseases, headache, dysentery, hearing problems, etc. (Table 6). Due to non availability of clean water for bathing, people are compelled to use the polluted mine water and get infected by it. As the old medicinal plants have been destroyed in the wake of the mining operation, herbal medicines are no longer available and the people are forced to spend a lot on other medicines for treatment.

Table 6

Pattern of Disease for Last One Year

Disease Pattern	*No*	*%*	*Male*	*%*	*Female*	*%*
Cough and Cold/Fever	39	27.08	19	13.19	20	13.89
Diarrhoea	22	15.28	13	9.03	9	6.25
Anaemia	22	15.28	3	2.08	19	13.19
Skin Problems	24	16.67	14	9.72	10	6.94
Asthma	6	4.17	6	4.17	—	—
Malaria	2	1.39	2	1.39	—	—
Pox	2	1.39	2	1.39	—	—
Tuberculosis	9	6.25	7	4.86	2	1.39
Eye Irritation	6	4.17	5	3.47	1	0.69
Hearing Problem	4	2.78	4	2.78	—	—
Jaundice	8	5.56	4	2.78	4	2.78
Total	144	100.00	79	54.86	65	45.14

Economic Problems and Cultural Scarcity

The Santals in Diguli are facing the problem of poverty and indebtedness. The main cause for the Santal poverty in Diguli is because of land alienation, illiteracy, unemployment, increase in population, lack of cultivable land, exploitation by moneylenders and middleman, lack of loan from banks for productive purpose, drinking habit and increase in health problems. These make them economically backward and marginalized in the society. The Santal workers are hired by the coal mafia primarily because they are tough and come cheap. The mafia fully exploit their poverty. Labour contractors approach a *sardar*, or the leader of a group of Santal workers, and have him bring a team of workers to an abandoned mine. In case of accidents the compensation paid to the Santal workers is far less than what local workers would have claimed. 'If a local man dies in an accident, his family would have to be paid at least ₹ 75,000 because of pressure from the local residents and politicians,' said a former labour contractor. 'In the case of a Santal the matter can be settled for ₹ 10,000 and the body can be disposed of. For a small payment, even the *sardar* will deny any knowledge of the deceased being part of his team.' (Chattopadhyay, 2001)

Their cultural heritage is in great danger. Their rituals and customs totally revolve around the natural environment. Here the land turns into a huge pit, forest no longer exists and most of it is continuously destroyed. Sacred grooves are patches of virgin forest that are left by these communities where they worship their ancestors. There are three such sacred groves in Ranigunj. One of those groves is now destroyed. In such a manner slightly they are just going far away from their own culture.

Present Scenario of Village Diguli and the Villagers

1. Houses of the people from the Diguli village are being brought down.

2. Thousands of mahua and other trees uprooted and the officials ignore the tribal relationship with these trees, which are also a source of livelihood.
3. Villagers lost acres of agricultural land to the Ranigunj mines and get a very meagre compensation in this regard.
4. Adults and children are suffering from various diseases like lung diseases, TB, jaundice, etc.
5. The sacred grove (*Jaherthan*) of the village no longer exists.

Case I

Bhola Hembrom, a 56-year-old man, has been living in this village for last three generations and before the advent of this mining project they have 4 acres of agricultural land which he cultivates with the help of his two sons. But now the scenario has changed, his family has lost 3 acres of land to the Ranigunj mine and though the government promised that his two sons will get jobs in this project area but they were not given to his sons. And as result of this, his family is now facing a crisis. A farmer by occupation, he had to be content with ₹ 50,000 as compensation for not choosing to go to the rehabilitation centre.

Case II

Lalmatti Murmu, a 37-years-old lady, was suffering from lung disease because of the methane gas from the mines and by inhaling coal dust from the open cast mining operation being carried beside her house. Her 45-year-old husband and younger son of 5 years of age died due to this problem. She was the only earning member of his family engaged in hand loading of trucks.

Case III

Raja Hembrom, aged 13 years, was suffering from tuberculosis which existed for six months. Due to economic crisis he did not receive a thorough treatment for this disease. The main reason the poverty and surrounding situation of this village.

Conclusion

There is a gross violation against the Scheduled Tribes of India. The main reason is the psychological make-up of the ruling groups which is that the tribals should be uprooted and finally exterminated. The people who are inducing the developmental projects in tribal areas are not the natural inhabitants of the region. Being aliens their disposition is to maintain their power over the region and also to extract the maximum benefits from the region. Thus, the result has been an illegal and unscientific exploitation of natural resources in these areas. The places inhabited by the tribals are very rich in minerals and natural resources which also happen to be their homes and means of livelihood. Any development work carried out in these areas is only bound to cause immense negative effect on the indigenous groups. And the hazards on physical and mental health as well as the harmful effect on the environment have been also proven. It can be said that the need for a new moral economy for mining regions need to be stressed, an economy in which local communities will play a powerful role. All illegal mining activities should be immediately stopped to check the further eviction of poor people. A successful resettlement with development should be a fundamental commitment and responsibility of the state. No development process should result in the complete alienation of the rights, customary and legal, of people through payment by one-time compensation or facilitated relocation and the process must result in the creation of new rights that will render people direct beneficiaries of the development project.

References

Chattopadhyay, S.S. 2001. 'The 'Ratholes' of Ranigunj', *Frontline*. 18(24), 24 November–7 December (http://www.frontline.in).

Lahiri-Dutt, K. 2001. *Mining and Urbanization in the Raniganj Coal Belt*. Kolkata: The World Press.

——. 2003. 'Informal Coal Mining in Eastern India: Evidences from the Raniganj Coal Belt. *Natural Resources Forum*. United Nations, 27(1), pp. 68–77.

Lahiri-Dutt, K and D.J. Williams. 2005. 'The Coal Cycle: Small Scale Illegal Coal Supply in Eastern India'. *Journal of Resource, Environment and Development*, 2(2), pp. 93–105.

Tiwary, R.K. and B.B. Dhar. 1994. 'Environmental Pollution from Coal Mining Activities in Damodar River Basin, India'. *Mine, Water and The Environment* 13(June–December), pp. 1–10.

6

Incessant Induced Suicide

SAMAR KUMAR BISWAS

I

The human beings wants to live forever but man is mortal and nobody can ignore such ever truth. We expect the natural death as it is the natural phenomenon whereas suicide is the tragic and ultimately a loss of human life, all the more devastating and perplexing because it is a conscious volitional act. Suicide is considered to be the commonest cause of unnatural death. In *Oxford Dictionary* suicide means 'the intentional killing of oneself'.

More than one million people commit suicide every year across the world. More people are dying by suicide than in all the armed conflicts around the world (Vijayakumar, 2003). According to WHO, estimates for the year 2020 and based on current trends, approximately 1.53 million will die from suicide, 10–20 times more people will attempt suicide worldwide. This represents, on an average, one death every 20 seconds and one attempt every 1–2 seconds.

The highest suicide rates for both men and women are found in Europe, more particularly in Eastern Europe, in a group of countries that share similar historical and socio-cultural characteristics, such as Estonia, Latvia, Lithuania and, to a lesser extent, Finland, Hungary and the CIS. Nevertheless, some similarly high rates are found in countries that are quite distinct in relation to these characteristics, such as Sri Lanka and Cuba (Bertolote and Fleischmann, 2003: 6).

It is true that suicide is increasing alarmingly. Presently 40–50 per cent of suicides occur in Asia. Over the last few years, there has been an alarming increase in the rate of suicide and attempted suicide in India. One person commits suicide every five minutes and one suicide is attempted every minute in India (Nambi, 2003: 86). 'There is an ugly rise of suicide among females and young people' (National Crime Research Bureau, 1996). It is estimated that 16 suicides took place every hour; and 1,35,585 persons in the country lost their lives by committing suicide during the year 2011 (NCRB, 2011: xviii). The suicide rate in India has been increasing steadily and has reached 11.2/1,00,000 population (total 1,35,585) in 2011 (NCRB, 2011: 190). India alone contributes to more than 10 per cent of suicides in the world. Further, majority of suicides occur among the men (75,702, i.e. 64.09%) and in younger age group. <http://www.maithrikochi.org/india_ suicide_statistics.htm, accessed on 27/1/2011>

There is no one reason why a person commits suicide. Normally nobody wants to commit suicide but sometimes several adverse situations may force a person to commit suicide to get relief from all the devastation as well as mental agony. Thus, there are so many reasons like loss of property, loss of life, social deprivation (poverty), unemployment, adjustment problems, marital disharmony, dowry, loss of prestige, influence of media, avoiding shame, influence of politics, mental illness, intractable physical pain (e.g. cancer), separation, social fragmentation (anomie), fear of punishment, hopelessness, helplessness, impulsive act or revenge for rejection, disorder thinking and so on.

Vijayakumar (2003) argues that it is very difficult to explain why certain people take this decision while others in similar or even worse situations do not. Suicide is the result of a complex interaction of biological, genetic, psychological, social, cultural and environmental factors.

A number of social scientists and doctors tried to examine the issues of depression, mental stress and suicide. Durkheim (1897) pointed out three categories of suicide namely, (i) egoistic suicide, which results from lack of integration of the individual into society; (ii) altruistic suicide, this kind of suicide results from the over-integration of the individual into his social group. Both kinds of suicide may be considered to be symptomatic of the way in which the individual is structured into the society; in the first case, inadequately, in the second case over-adequately; and (iii) anomic suicide which results from lack of regulation of the individual by society. Durkheim attributed anomic suicide to unlimited aspirations and the breakdown of regulatory norms (Durkheim, 1897; reprinted, 1975: 15).

No doubt, due to suicide and attempted suicide the concerned people, family, kins, friends and society are to carry a huge social, cultural and economic cost.

II

Case Study

Kinkar Sheet was an unmarried, class II, 22-years-old unemployed boy. By caste he was Dhoba (washer man) and resided at Bagpara village, Ghoramara Island. He died in July 1995 by consuming poison.

Family background: Kinkar Sheet was the son of Atul Chandra Sheet of 74 years old. There were 14 members in his family. They had to maintain their livelihood under severe poverty and utter constraints. They had 15 *bighas*[1] of land of which 7 *bighas* got eroded and another 3 *bighas* were outside of the river embankment and badly affected by saline water. As a result, for cultivation they had to depend only on 5 *bighas* of agricultural land. But due to continuous breaking up of embankment their crop cultivation was seriously affected consecutively for the last three years of the incidence. As a consequence, severe poverty afflicted their family. During the period of incidence, it was reported that they were going through almost starvation for more than a week.

Incidence: In this situation, once in an afternoon of the monsoon, Kinkar went to play football. After his coming back in the evening he was asked by his father about his whereabouts and further, his father expressed his anger that if

Kinkar would stay in house then he should get involved in some sort of work to earn a little bit. Those conversations were not appreciated by Kinkar and he refused to take any food. It is to be mentioned here that on the day of the incidence Kinkar went through starvation for the whole day. Ultimately at 10 o'clock in the night, he took poison (thymoid: a pesticide) and expired.

It was known that only at Sagar Island of Sagar Block, in the time span of nearly 10 years 8 months (1997 to 2007), 1,368 people committed suicide and attempted suicide. It was recorded that the majority of suicides and attempted suicides occurred among the female (61.99%). Apart from Sagar Island, to know the situation as well as the root cause of suicide and attempted suicide, a detail study was conducted only on the entire Ghoramara Island/mouza, covering six villages with a population of 5,236 (Census, 2001). The concerned study revealed that during the period of 1991 to March 2008, total 41 (100%) persons, among which 22 (53.66%) male and 19 (46.34%) female committed suicide and attempted suicide or similar type of death by several means.

The Studied Sagar Block

Administratively, two distinct populated islands namely Sagar Island and Ghoramara Island formed the Sagar Community Development Block in the district of South 24 Parganas, West Bengal. The Sagar Block lies between 21^0 37' – 57'N, 88^002' – 11'E. The geographical area of the islands was 219.26 km^2 (Bandyopadhyay, 1997b: 51). The deltaic Sagar and Ghoramara Islands of the Kakdweep sub-division situated at the mouth of the Hooghly River. This block, or the two islands were completely separated by a distance of 4 km. from each other and the mainland too and treated as merely remote regions in this country. It is to be mentioned that before 1904, these two islands were attached and then it was known as Sagar Island. It was bounded by the Hooghly river on the west and by the Baratala or Channel creek on the east, and on the south by the Bay of Bengal (O'Malley 1914, reprinted 1998: 325–326).

This area held an important position from the environmental and ecological point of view. Tidal flooding, river fluxes, waves, long-shore currents, sea-level changes, cyclones[2] and storms as well as the environmental hazards are dominant physical processes that continually modify the course in a short and long term basis (Das, 2006: 31–32). There are a number of factors such as salinity,[3] sandy soil, soil erosion,[4] the daily inter tidal flow or tidal waves, natural hazards, i.e. cyclones, storms, floods, etc. threaten the ecosystem as well as human life at Sagar and Ghoramara Islands.

Cyclones in West Bengal which were of oceanic in origin heat the coasts of South 24 Parganas four to five times a year. To such cyclones the area, Sagar and Ghoramara islands, were peculiarly exposed on account of its position at the head of the Bay of Bengal. The great atmospheric disturbance affected the whole delta and in this regard it was more serious particularly in case of Sagar and Ghoramara Islands. In June 1823, a storm destroyed the roads, embankments and tops on this Island. Only 10 years later again, in May 1833, the great gale and inundation occurred which destroyed the almost all progress of Sagar Island (Pargiter, 1934; reprinted, 2002: 338–341). Sagar Island was submerged to a depth of 10 feet, and the whole population of

3000–4000 souls is said to have perished (O'Malley, 1914; reprinted, 1998: 178). Storm occurred in June 1842, October 1848, and again in June 1852, which inflicted serious damage at Sagar Island (Pargiter, 1934; reprinted, 2002: 339). The serious cyclone took place on 5 October 1864, which swept over the Sagar Island with full force and wrought great havoc (Pargiter, 1934; reprinted, 2002: 341). Again on 1 and 2 November 1867 occurred another cyclone and high tide which caused great damage to the lives, crops and reduced the area under cultivation from 31,190 to 2,750 *bighas* (Pargiter 1934, reprinted 2002: 338–341). The cyclones of 1869 also affected the crop production very much (Mandal, 2004: 14). The most serious floods occurred in 1900, 1904, 1907 and 1909 (O'Malley 1914, reprinted 1998: 171–178).

The recent happening cyclonic storms and floods in 1942, 1971, 1973, 1976, 1981, 1988, 1996, 1997 and 1998 destroyed the crops, lives including man and cattle, houses and other properties to a great degree. The cyclonic storm that took place in November 1988 was caused by depression that blew over the area causing large scale devastation all around (Chakrabarty, 1995: 31). Three of the most destructive tropical storms that ever affected Sagar Island occurred on 21 May 1833 (near about 7,000 people died), 5 October 1864 (4,137, i.e. 73.6% people died) and 17 October 1942 (Bandyopadhyay, 1997a: 25).

In 1851–1855, the total area of the island was 284.55 km^2 which was reduced to 219.26 km^2 in 1997 (Bandyopadhyay, 1997b: 52–53). In fact, in the last 142 years (1855–1997) due to soil erosion 65.29 km^2 (23%) area of land was washed away and became a part of the river/sea. In this way the Ghoramara mouza was detached from main Sagar Island in 1904–05. Originally, the Sagar Block had 46 mouzas, but due to soil erosion three mouzas were eroded and its 23 mouzas were constantly being reduced due to soil erosion; among which nine mouzas had lost more than 25 per cent of their original extension (Bandyopadhyay, 1997a: 27–29; 1997b: 52–53; Bandyopadhyay et al., 2004: 253–254; and Maity, 2005: 25). Due to this fact it was noticed that 1,462 families were displaced only from Ghoramara Island which itself is a mouza.

Natural calamities and soil erosion mostly affected Ghoramara mouza where 55.01 per cent (1992) area of land was already eroded and became a part of the river. Due to continuous environmental degradation around 89 per cent studied families lost their main resource, the land, and it was in average 16.02 *bighas* per family and in total 5,412 *bighas* at Ghoramara Island. It is noteworthy to mention that the agricultural land ownership pattern was seriously affected and the land ownership got limited to only 193 (50.66%) families whereas in the past it was 342 (89.76%) families.

Considering the consequences of environmental degradation, the house erosion was well observed. Around 87 per cent of the families faced house erosion. Further, around 40 per cent families faced this disaster thrice and even more. Some of the studied families did not own homestead land.

Agriculture is the worst affected component of environmental degradation. It was noticed that all the agriculture practiced families at Ghoramara Island lost their crop production due to flood caused by breaking of embankment and natural calamities. The crop production was reduced due to soil erosion in case of 97.41 per cent families. Further, due to soil erosion, 195 (98%) families lost a large amount of agricultural land, in some cases total land was eroded and as a result both the amount of agricultural land and the agricultural productions were largely reduced. Due to environmental changes as an alternative economy the fishing was greatly affected. *Hilsa* and other marine fishing were already diminished. *Meen* (tiger prawn seed) collection was also on the wane. The boats of 20 fishing families were destroyed by storm and tidal wave.

Continuous soil erosion resulted in gradual degradation of cultivable land and thus the produced crop from their agricultural land and related earning were reduced. The labourers who were dependent on agricultural works could hardly manage their works and for a considerable period of time, they had no work and earning. Thus, the people were suffering from several problems to maintain their minimum livelihood. Moreover, owing to this recurring crop failure a famine-like situation happened. Thus, the agro-based economy was severely hit by soil erosion.

In spite of their hard struggle, per head average daily income was not more than ₹ 11.91. As a consequence of poor income they had no other alternatives than to face utter hardship to manage common minimum livelihood. Due to repeated environmental degradation, people lost their agricultural land and their houses several times. Consequently owing to the break up of embankment and influx of saline water their cultivated crops were damaged and their agricultural land lost its fertility. As a consequence, their agricultural productions and several related works suffered a major set-back. Ultimately it forced the people concerned to get enmeshed in the web of indebtedness in various ways. It was reported that they had to face difficulties to maintain their livelihood with such poor income and nearly 63 per cent families were compelled to be indebted. The amount of loan varied from ₹ 700 to ₹ 25,000.

Obviously, this situation had a direct reflection on food consumption. It was noticed that due to lack of natural resources and economic scarcity, most of the studied people had to face utter constraints to meet their hunger and sometimes they even had to remain on an empty stomach for the whole day. Considering the food taken by the people, it was noticed that 57.22 per cent families could manage food with utter hardship and they consumed it with delicacy of pulses and vegetables rarely. The protein-rich foods like fish, egg and meat were almost absent in their food. Further, nearly 17 per cent families could consume food for once or rarely twice a day with only rice, salt, chilli and infrequently pulses and vegetables. Animal protein was a mere dream to them.

Hence, soil erosion, other natural calamities and environmental changes adversely affected the backbone of the food and nutritional chain of the people concerned in both the situations.

III

Society has a direct relation with environment. The environment appears as a complex totality from many aspects. A man cannot separate the geographical environment as one order of things from the social environment as quite another and the social and physical aspects are blended in every concrete reality. The interaction between man and environment may be prevalent through its entire existence of life and ultimately it leads to the survival of human beings and preservation of their entire cultural heritages.

The environment is the prime source of several locally produced food and vegetation, which may provide the food and nutritional quality of the population concerned. Thus, any sort of environmental change ultimately determines the changes in livelihood condition; along with it, if the socio-economic conditions also get changed then the socio-cultural practices and the functions of social organization and social institutions must get altered which ultimately influences a lot the daily ways of living (Detels et al., 2002: 199).

The environmental situation like cyclone, destruction, breaking of embankment, soil erosion, flood and salinity, storm, etc. were very much responsible for poverty and loss which created continuous pressure of insecurity on them. For survival they had to take loans from the private sectors and money lenders for several times. But they failed to repay it and even in many cases nobody was ready to give them loan, as people knew that the poverty stricken people would not be in a position to repay it. As a result, they were forced to live in utter constraints and in several cases they became unable to steam their vessel. In each and every aspect insecurity and uncertainty were there and the severe pressure of poverty and the impact of adverse environment made their life miserably unsecured. The people concerned particularly the guardians or prime earners, were in the grab of a number of social, cultural, economic as well as other demands within and outside of the family. They repeatedly failed to provide the minimum requirements to their family members. Sometimes they had to face the problems of arranging the marriage of their bachelors and provide the materials and bear the expense of marriage. How they could accumulate a fold of rice? How he would be able to make a house which was eroded in the river? In this way continuously they had to face a lot of problems regarding the bearing of expenses for dress, treatment for ailment and pursue their education, performing other occasions and so on. Several uncertain questions were raised about their future settlement, livelihood or other safety and security and alike. In most of the cases, they failed to redress the constraint in each and every sector of their life and to provide the needs to their family members. As a result, the above all repeated situations created an acute mental and psychological pressure on them and sometimes it might have turned into a stage of depression. Besides all these uncertainties, particularly during storms and cyclone, the families related to fishing got the shivers of life in an acute fear about the security of their prime earning members or close kins who were fishing in the river or in the deep sea. It was reported in several cases that a number of people died or they were untraced under such situations.

Moreover, all the consequences created much of frustration which resulted in an acute mental depression and they were weakened and affected psychologically. These circumstances sometimes forced them to get involved in conflicts, criminal activities, illegal affairs, quarrels, gambling, addictions and alcoholism. For survival they attempted to exploit minimum available resources. But it could not fulfil their demand because most of the people concerned were in the same boat. The continuous scarcity compelled the people to get involved in a number of familial or inter-familial quarrel, conflict and clash. In several cases, they also made themselves involved in a number of offensive and criminal activities, often being undertaken out of the jealousy. The continuous increase of different illegal affairs might be due to their disturbances in the social, cultural as well as psychological life.

The continuous pressure of insecurity and uncertainty seriously affected their mind. The responsibilities, duties, social burdens and the state of indebtedness made them psychologically ill and in most of the cases it turned into mental depression which ultimately agonize them. In this regard, an individual could not find any sort of alternative to cope up with this situation or to redress their problem. Thus, to get rid of the situation, they often accepted the psychological defeat without having any sign to improve the situation in their life rather more deterioration possibly engulfed them and unnatural death was considered as the best possible alternative to redress these worldly problems.

The 41 (100%) case studies of Ghoramara Island proved that much devastation in their life was caused by the environmental degradation from which they could not get any relief and it had a continuous effect as the phenomena were recurring. There arose three sources of pressure – first, due to environmental degradation, earning sources were devastated and insecured; second, there was a continuous pressure of demand to fulfil the minimum requirements of the family members; and third, there was a pressure of repaying the loan. Thus, the continuous pressure from different aspects due to inability to fulfil the minimum demand or repay the loan caused by environmental degradation as well as uncertainty and insecured economy seriously affected their mind which resulted in mental disturbances in most of the cases. Disturbances pertained to how they would provide food to the hungry mouth, reconstruct the house and provide clothes to the family members? How they could fulfil the educational needs of their children? How the loan would be repaid? How they could arrange marriage of their younger daughter as their crops were damaged and working scopes were shrunk? All such anxiety had given them no escape and created some kind of inner conflict and tension within the mind of individuals. Its manifestation would affect all the persons within and surrounding family. The responsibilities, duties, social and economic burden made them psychologically ill and in most of the cases it turned into mental depression and conflict. The entire situation occupied with conflict and tension contributed to some kind of escapist attitude which ultimately made the individual bold enough to take such decisions like suicide. Thus, in the studied area, the repeated and recurring situations created acute mental and psychological pressure continuously on them that turned into a stage of depression. People often accept psychological defeat and without having any sign commit suicide which may be termed as incessant induced suicide.

Man is a social being and he needs social interactions to lead a normal life. But if continuous social, economic, psychological, political stress and scarcity happens to dominate one's life and if he has a mere scope of execution for social and kinship-based social interaction, then it tells upon his mind to think good or bad and under such a situation, he fails to understand what is to be done and what ought not to be done. Then human feelings would be lost and one gets puzzled and probably that is the time when any unhappy incident may occur. In such cases any sort of mishap can happen to him or his family members at any moment.

Notes

1. *Bigha:* A local unit for measuring land. It varies from one third of an acre to almost one acre. The standardized *bigha* in West Bengal is 14,400 square feet, which equals 1,333.33 square metres or roughly one third of an acre.
2. *Cyclone:* an atmospheric system characterized by the rapid inward circulation of air masses about a low-pressure centre, usually accompanied by stormy, often destructive weather. Cyclones circulate counter clockwise in the Northern Hemispheres and clockwise in the Southern Hemisphere.
3. *Salinity:* A measure of the quantity of dissolved solids in ocean water is salinity. The total salinity of sea water sample can be determined by measuring only the chloride ion concentration following the relationship – Salinity (ppt) = 1.80655×Chlorinity (ppt). The unit expressed of salinity is parts per thousand or ppt.
4. *Erosion:* The group of natural processes, including weathering, dissolution, abrasion, corrosion, and transportation by which material is worn away from the Earth's surface.

References

Bandyopadhyay, S. 1997a. 'Natural Environmental Hazards and Their Management: A Case Study of Sagar Island, India'. *Singapore Journal of Tropical Geography,* 18(1), pp. 21–45.

——. 1997b. 'Coastal Erosion and Its Management in Sagar Island, South 24-Parganas, West Bengal'. *Indian Journal of Earth Science*, 24(3–4), pp. 51–69.

Bandyopadhyay, S., D. Mukharjee, S. Bag, D.K. Pal, R.K. Das and K. Rudra. 2004. '20th Century Evolution of Banks and Islands of the Hugli Estuary, West Bengal, India: Evidences from Maps Images and GPS Survey'. In S. Singh, H.S. Sharma and S.K. De (eds) *Geomorphology and Environment*. Kolkata: ACB Publications, pp. 235–263.

Banthia, J.K. 2003. *District Census Handbook of 24-Parganas, West Bengal, 2001*. New Delhi: Government of India.

Bertolote, J.M. and A. Fleischmann. 2003. 'Cultural Perspective and WHO Suicide Initiative'. In L. Vijayakumar (ed.) *Suicide Prevention.* Chennai: Orient Longman, pp. 6–10.

Chakrabarti, S.P. 1995. *Twilight and Dark Life in a Sundarban Village*. Calcutta: Das-Gupta & Co. Pvt. Ltd.

Das, G.K. 2006. *Sunderbans Environment and Ecosystem,* Kolkata: Sarat Book Distributors.

Detels, R., J. McEwen, R. Beaglehole and H. Tanaka. 2002. *Oxford Textbook of Public Health* (4th edition), London: Oxford University Press.

Durkheim, E. 1897. *Suicide.* Translated 1930 and reprinted 1975. London: Routledge & Kegan Paul Ltd. http://www.maithrikochi.org/india_suicide_statistics.htm, accessed on 27/1/2011. Suicide in India.

Maity, J. 2005. *Sagardwip* (in Bengali), Kolkata: Standard Printing.

Nambi, S. (under the Chair of A.A. Leenaars). 2003. 'Ethical and Legal Issues: A Workshop', In L. Vijayakumar (ed.) *Suicide Prevention.* Chennai: Orient Longman, pp. 85–110.

National Crime Record Bureau. 1996. 'Accidental Deaths and Suicide in India 1996'. Ministry of Home Affairs. New Delhi: Government of India.

——. 2011. 'Accidental Deaths and Suicide in India 2011'. Ministry of Home Affairs. New Delhi: Government of India.

O'Malley, L.S.S. 1914 (reprinted 1998). *Bengal District Gazetteers,* Calcutta: Government of West Bengal.

Pargiter, F.E. 1934 (reprinted 2002). *A Revenue History of the Sundarbans,* Volume-I (From 1765 to 1870), Kolkata: Government of West Bengal.

Vijayakumar, L. (ed.). 2003. *Suicide Prevention,* Chennai: Orient Longman.

7

Human Rights, Human Security and Sustainable Development

BUDDHADEB CHAUDHURI

I

The Issue of Human Security

Let me start providing certain facts of the 20th century:

- In this period, some 100 million people were killed in armed conflicts and further 120 million dead as a result of politically related violence where religion or race or ethnicity or political background was the main factor.
- At the start of the century, during armed conflict, 5 per cent of the casualties were civilians, at the end of the century, 90 per cent of such casualties were civilians.
- Over 120 million land mines were deployed in more than 64 countries and most of the victims were civilians (Venkatachaliah, 2002).

The Universal Declaration of Human Rights adopted around 58 years back was a great step to eliminate conflict and establish equal and inalienable rights of all members of the human society, rich or poor, regardless of status, race, religion, colour, sex or political background. Nevertheless, the world has seen barbarous inhumanity during the two world wars. René Cassin, the noted French jurist, who was connected with this Declaration, was offered the Nobel Prize after 20 years in 1968. Once he said, 'Men are not always good'.

In the evolution of Human Rights, the western powers were more interested to give priority to the civil and political rights, often referred as 'First Generation Rights', while the Socialist countries were interested in the economic, social and cultural rights, often referred as 'Second Generation Rights'. The concept of 'Third Generation Rights' was introduced afterwards to refer the rights of the people or groups including right to Self-Determination, Development and Environment. The Vienna World Conference on Human Rights, 1993, reaffirmed that the civil, political, economic, social and cultural rights are 'universal, interdependent and indivisible'. It has been observed:

> Human Rights are best understood as part of law, part of philosophy and part of political movement. The values which drive the idea of human rights owe almost as much to poetry and music as they do to legal principles. They owe nearly as much to the spirituality of all the great religions and to the eternal quest for righteousness as they do to revolutions and the demand for freedom from state tyranny… . The idea of rights has changed over time because people have acted together to claim rights in different circumstances and with varying goals in mind… . In other words, in the history of humans, distinct periods arrive when new rights come into prominence as a force of change. That does not make economic, social and cultural rights and other rights any way less important than civil and political rights.
>
> It is really interesting to note the contribution of the International Human Rights regime in the last few decades. The development has profound impact on conceptual and practical issues. In international law, the sovereign states were the main subject and actors. The international human rights regime has projected on the centre-stage the individual. This has interesting implications in the context of the scope of Human Rights and human security.

The concept of 'human security' has initiated the debate – what 'security' means and how to achieve it. The concept has been defined and pursued in different ways by different nation-states as a means of reducing the human costs of violent conflicts, as a strategy to enable governments to address basic human needs and offset the inequities of globalization, and as a means to provide social safety nets to impoverished, marginalized people. The discussion on the disarmament-development nexus that took place in various UN forums in response to the Cold War arms race contributed to the understanding of human security. Besides, a number of commissions like the Brandt Commission, the Bruntland Commission and the Commission on Global Governance helped to change the focus of security analysis from national and state security to security of the people. In fact, subsequently there was a growing recognition of non-military threats in the global security debate. The *Human Development Report* of UNDP (1994) provided seven separate components of human security:

1. Economic security (assured basic income).
2. Food security (physical and economic access to food).
3. Health security (relative freedom from disease and infection).
4. Environmental security (access to safe water, clean air and a non degraded land system).
5. Personal security (security from physical violence and threats).
6. Community security (security of cultural identity), and
7. Political security (enjoyment of basic human rights and freedom).

Some have criticized the above scope and definition of human security as too broad. However, others feel that a broader definition is necessary and desirable considering the wider constituency of the UN. Some other definitions are more explicitly linked to Human Rights and humanitarian law. This marked a shift in the norms of state sovereignty with particular reference to Human Rights protection. Canada criticized the scope of human security as provided by UNDP for focussing more on underdevelopment and ignoring human security resulting from violent conflict (DFAIT, 1999). The varied notions and concepts of human security initiated an interesting debate in the context of national security and human security and 'freedom from want' and 'freedom from fear'. It is interesting to note that some Asian thinkers and governments see human security as yet another attempt by the West to impose its values and political institutions on non-Western societies. Others have pointed out the non-military threats to human security as a reality in many countries and emphasized the need of a collective human security agenda. Canada focussed human security as 'security of the people' which was also supported by Norway. The two countries have formed a Human Security Partnership identifying a nine-point agenda of human security covering:

> land-mines, formation of an International Criminal Court, human rights, international humanitarian law, women and children in armed conflict, small arms proliferation, child soldiers, child labour and northern cooperation.

The observation of Japan in the context of the perception of human security may be mentioned here:

> In Japan's view, however, human security is a much broader concept. We believe that freedom from want is no less critical than freedom from fear. So long as its objectives are to ensure the survival and dignity of individuals as human beings, it is necessary to go beyond thinking of human security solely in terms of protecting human life in conflict situations.

To understand human security, Astrid Suhrke (1999) emphasized the issue of 'vulnerability' with reference to three categories of victims: those of war and internal conflicts, those living at or below subsistence levels, and victims of natural disaster. Sverre Lodgaard (2000) of the Norwegian Institute of International Affairs advocated a narrower scope of human security which he felt should not be mixed up with human development. Thus, the debate of human security arises from varied perceptions: the western usage reflects the individualistic ethos of liberal democracy which conflicts with the Asian approach to human rights which, as felt by Asian thinkers should cover the different cultural contexts and historical experiences of Asia. Human security calls for a shift of security considering from state security to security of the people, which includes both individuals and communities considering the survival and well-being of all communities. The observation of Amartya Sen (1999), a Nobel Laureate and a Member of International Commission on Human Security, is worth mentioning here. He pointed out the crucial link between freedom from fear and freedom from want. Human security gives emphasis on human dignity without ignoring the rights of societies and non-political rights. Safety and dignity of individuals or people can not be compromised. In fact, in the human security paradigm, the tolerance of Human Rights violation for economic development or social stability is not acceptable.

Democracy and Human Security

In the last 20 years alone 81 more countries of the world have moved towards democratic practices, some 33 of them had their military regimes replaced by civil governments. Democratic governance and human development have an intimate interrelationship. Participatory decisions are at the heart of human development. Authoritarian regimes often argue that they have advantages in building strong states that can make tough decisions in the interests of people. They also argue that democratic processes create disorder and impede efficient management – 'that countries must choose between democracy and development, between extending political freedom and expanding incomes'. The *Human Development Report* 2002, however, provided the opposite picture:

> ... There are good reasons to believe that democracy and growth are compatible. With just two exceptions, all of the world's richest countries – those with per capita income of more than $20,000 (in 2000 purchasing power parity) – have the world's most democratic regimes. In addition, 42 of the 48 high human development countries are democracies... . A systematic study by Adam Prezeworski and others of 135 countries from 1950–90 discredits the notion of a trade off between democracy and development. (*Human Development Report*, 2002)

It has been further noted that democracies are better than authoritarian regimes in managing conflicts and catastrophes. Democracy provides for political space and institutional mechanisms for debate and change, particularly in managing sudden turn downs that threaten human survival. The *Human Development Report* says:

> ... In India famines were common under colonial rule – for example 2 to 3 million people died in 1943 Bengal famine. But since independence and democratic rule, there has been no recurrence of famine – despite severe crop failures and massive losses of purchasing power for large segments of population as in 1968, 1973, 1979 and 1987. Each time the government acted to avoid famine. Food production fell largely in 1973 during drought in Maharashtra, but famine was averted partly because 5 million people were put to work in public works projects. ... (*Human Development Report*, 2002)

Justice, equality and human dignity are the watch words of Human Rights discourse. But the inequity of the international economic order has produced unacceptable levels of inequality, both internally and internationally. In the USA (1994) itself the poorest quintile of the population had 1.5 per cent of income and consumption while the top quintile had 45.2 per cent. This reflects, in a non-trivial sense, the anomalies and inequities of the international economic order. Inequality between and amongst countries has also increased. The income gap between the fifth of the world's people living in the richest countries and the fifth in the poorest was 74 to 1 in 1997, up from 60 to 1 in 1990 and 30 to 1 in 1960 (*World Development Report*, 1999). Over the 30 years, from 1960 to 1990, the affluent 20 per cent of the world have enhanced their share of incomes and consumption from 70.1 per cent to 86 per cent while the poorest 20 per cent have had their share reduced to 1 per cent. This is the manifestation of a growth, which is ruthless, rootless, voiceless, jobless, and futureless.

By the late 1990s, the fifth of the world's people living in highest-income countries had:

- 86 per cent of world GDP – the bottom fifth just 1 per cent.
- 82 per cent of world export markets – the bottom fifth just 1 per cent.
- 68 per cent of foreign direct investment – the bottom fifth had just 1 per cent.
- 74 per cent of world telephone lines, today's basic means of communication – the bottom fifth just 1.5 per cent.
- Income of the richest 5 per cent of the world is 114 times that of the poorest 5 per cent.

- Richest 1 per cent has as much income as the poorest 57 per cent.
- In more personal terms, just three richest men, Bill Gates, Warren Buffet and Paul Allen, have wealth equal to the income of 48 poor countries, consisting of over a billion people.

Since Independence, India has made some impressive achievements. Particularly significant has been the increase in agricultural production. Between 1950 and 2000, the index of agricultural production increased more than four fold. Between 1960 and 2000, wheat production went up from 11 million tonnes to 75.6 million tonnes and the production of rice increased from 35 million tonnes to 89.5 million tonnes. This is no mean achievement for a country that relied on food aid until the middle of the 1960s. The rosy picture of the success of the green revolution is generally projected. It is true that the production has increased considerably, but it has also increased inequality. The rich have become richer and the poor poorer. Again, one may notice the many cases of suicide committed by the farmers in different parts of India. As 'modern' agriculture needs more investment, the farmers often are forced to take loan for agriculture and if they do not get the proper return, often they commit suicide, reflecting the increasing insecurity of human beings.

The most significant is population growth. Kerala has a fertility rate of 1.7, which is equal to that of Britain and France, is below 1.9 of China and 2 of the USA. This, according to Amartya Sen, has been achieved:

> with no coercion, but mainly through the emergence of new values – a process in which political and social dialogues have played a major part. The level of literacy in Kerala, especially the female literacy, is higher than that of every province in China. This has greatly contributed to making informed social and political dialogues possible.

In India, life expectancy was just 20.9 years in 1910. In 2000, the life expectancy of the urban female in Kerala went up to 80 years. There is abundant empirical evidence of the inter-link between the spread of education and economic achievement.

The lack of education is one of the major reasons for their unequal status of women in society. Denial of access to organized knowledge to women from ancient times has contributed to the increasing subordination of women.

Maternal anaemia in India is about 57 per cent. It is nearly 71 per cent for the Dalits and underprivileged sections. An international comparison of infant mortality and maternal mortality rates are given below:

Table 1

Health Situations in Different Countries

Country	*Maternal Mortality (per lakh birth)*	*Infant Mortality Rate (per 1,000 births)*	*Births attended by Skilled Health Staff*	*No. of Women getting Prenatal Care*
UK	7	6	98%	92%
USA	8	7	99%	94%
China	60	32	78%	79%
India	410	69	42%	60%

Within Indian society itself the intra-societal and inter-regional imbalances are significant. While the infant mortality rate in urban Kerala is about 12, it is still as high as 146 in Kishangunj in Bihar. One *Human Development Report* (UNDP) said that a child born in Kerala today can expect to live longer than one born in Washington. The percentage of child births under skilled health staff is 93 per cent in Kerala and 3 per cent in Uttar Pradesh.

The UNDP report of 1994 made a very interesting observation. In the developing countries, nearly 65 per cent of the diseases could have been eliminated if we could provide safe drinking water. Unfortunately, it is not happening.

The main issues of Human Rights in many countries are education, prevalence of maternal anaemia, low birth-weight related neurological deficiencies, children's education, particularly of the girl child. Poverty is of course, the worst and most crucial Human Rights deprivation.

Even in 1994, the *Human Development Report* of 1994, in its chapter 'New Dimensions of Human Security' had said:

> Fifty years ago, Albert Einstein summed up the discovery of atomic energy with characteristic simplicity: 'Everything changed'. He went on to predict: 'we shall require a substantially new manner of thinking if mankind is to survive. But five decades later we need another profound transition in thinking – from nuclear security to human security.

The report changed the concept of security from its earlier narrow connotation and attached it to the legitimate concerns of ordinary people who sought security in daily lives.

> For many of them, security symbolizes protection from the threat of disease, hunger, political repression and environmental hazards. With the dark shadows of the cold war receding, one can now see that conflicts are within nations rather than between nations. For most people, feeling of insecurity arises more from worries about daily life than from the dread of a cataclysmic world event. Will they and their families have enough to eat? Will they lose their jobs? Will their streets and neighbourhoods safe from crime? Will they be tortured by repressive state? Will they become victim of violence because of their gender? Will their religion or ethnic origin target them for persecution?

The UN Secretary General, in his *Millennium Report* said:

> The century just ended was disfigured, time and again, by ruthless conflict.... Grinding poverty and striking inequality persist within and among countries even amidst unprecedented wealth. Diseases, old and new, threaten to undo painstaking progress. Nature's life-sustaining services, on which our species depends for its survival, are being seriously disrupted and degraded by our own everyday activities.

II

The Case of the Indigenous People

Indigenous people can be regarded as those with a social or cultural identity distinct from the dominant or mainstream society which makes them vulnerable to being disadvantaged in the process of development.

Indigenous people can be regarded as one of the largest vulnerable segments of society. While differing significantly in terms of culture, identity, economic systems and social institutions, indigenous peoples as a whole most often reflect specific disadvantages in terms of social indicators, economic status and quality of life. Indigenous peoples often are not able to participate equally to development processes. It is neither desirable nor possible to insulate or exclude indigenous people from development. But indigenous people may not benefit from development programmes designed to meet the needs and aspirations of dominant or mainstream populations and may not get the opportunity to participate in the planning of such development. There is an increasing concern in the national/international development community that people be given the opportunities to participate to and benefit from development especially with other segments of society and have a role and be able to participate in the design of development interventions that affect them.

In India, the indigenous peoples are commonly referred to as tribals. The population of the tribal communities scheduled in the Constitution of India and known as Scheduled Tribes is 84.3 million as per 2001 Census and account for 8.2 per cent of the total population of India. They are found in all states and union territories except Punjab, Haryana, Delhi and union territories of Pondicherry and Chandigarh. The dilemma in preparing any policy for the Scheduled Tribes in India is how to strike the right balance between preservation of tribal identity, culture and values and at the same time increasing their access to education, healthcare and income generation so that there is an appreciable improvement in the quality of life. The implementation of this is rather difficult for two reasons, not only the number of individual tribes scheduled under the Constitution is quite large (nearly 700 state specific scheduled tribes), the heterogeneity is immense. Each tribe is quite distinct from the other having separate language and dialect, customs, cultural practices and lifestyles. To preserve this immense diversity is an enormously difficult task, particularly since in bringing benefits of development to them, a significant amount of mainstreaming and consequent loss of diversity is inevitable.

A number of development programmes have been initiated which have varied effect on population. In many places, the development programmes have benefitted some while created disruption and displacement for others. Displacement of a larger population mostly illiterate and unorganized weaker section in the context of development of the region or nation is very common in most of the countries in Asia, Africa and Latin America. Since there is displacement of a large section of population, the access and command over natural resources are affected, the survival and security of the people are also affected. One cannot stop exploitation of natural resources but what one is now looking for is how to achieve sustainable development. This may demand a new development strategy with a genuine participatory approach and creating a process of natural resource use which is open, accessible and accountable for the security of the larger population. In fact, development is expected to improve the quality of life which is not possible when security is affected for a sizable section of the population. Development may be considered as those changes which are required, but have minimum disruptive effects on the concerned population. The protest of the people in the context of different so-called development projects in different parts of the world or many forest development programmes raises a very fundamental question, the development does not start with goods, it starts with people. Again, globalization has created new opportunities and problems. Amartya Sen has noted that global participation is basically an enhancement of economic opportunity and its costs can be minimized through appropriate domestic policies, paying particular attention to the availability and distributional equity of economic and social opportunities. He also stressed the importance of certain positive social changes in this regard like land reforms, spread of education, better healthcare, freedom of work and freedom of fear, which are very much related to human security. He also observed, 'these are not much the social consequences of economic reforms, but the economic consequences of social reforms. The market economy flourishes on the foundations of social development – a lesson which India has yet to learn.'

The Commission on Global Governance distinguished between the security of state and security of people. Because of emerging socio-economic and political situation, the security of the people is very much affected. After the publication of the Commission Report in 1994, efforts have been made to define the security of people, the human security, more rigorously, along with practical ways of promoting it. Thus human security means the security of people: their physical safety, socio-economic well-being, protection of human rights and freedom. The fundamental components of human security are the security of people against threats to life, health, livelihood, personal safety and human dignity. Naturally, the concerned socio-economic and political systems play a very crucial role in the context of human security and its protection.

III

Environment, Development and Human Security

The world today is deeply concerned with ecological issues. Man for his ever-growing needs uses resources in nature. In this way, he promotes development. The use of natural resources and the initiation of development produce changes in ecology. The nature of changes in ecology manifests the character of development. The character of development, again, determines the use of resources. The pattern of use of resources reflects to a certain extent the path of development that a governing group has decided to follow. Although the issues have to be analysed from different points of view, the role of human being as an agent of change has to be taken as focal point. In the relationship between development and environment, adjustment is the need, but conflict is generally the outcome. Industrial, agricultural and infrastructural developments have created many environmental problems due to misunderstanding of the system in nature. In the planning model, the environmental issues were not adequately considered in the past. This is now regarded as too costly to be avoided. The process of planning and concomitant administrative decisions should attach top priority to the resolution of the contradiction between development and environment.

Immediately after the colonial rule in many countries there was an acute shortage of food for which the government of the country concerned desperately tried to increase food production at any cost. Maybe an increase or growth in production was the goal at that moment and maybe the objective was achieved in a given context, but is it possible to equate it with development? Any increase in production is growth but development is a broader and wider term and it has other connotations too. It not only includes growth, but an equitable distribution of facilities and resources and reduction, if not elimination, of exploitative practices are also implied. Of late, another very important and crucial indicator has also been added to it. It is the question of environment. Man, for his ever-growing needs, uses resources in nature. The use of natural resources and initiation of development produce changes in ecology. In the relationship between development and environment, adjustment is the need. Any activity is likely to produce some changes in ecology, but it is to be seen how these activities are affecting the ecology. Any activity adversely affecting the ecology cannot be considered as development. Thus, development includes both qualitative and quantitative changes – it improves the socio-economic condition and also quality of life of the majority population of the society concerned without adversely affecting the environment and, thus, not creating any problem for other groups or communities directly not involved in the activity. It, thus, helps to exploit the natural resources in a better way without any grave adverse environmental consequence.

Development of any region has three main dimensions, economic, social and environmental, and none of these dimensions can be neglected if the real development of a region is to be achieved. Of all the three, the environmental dimension is all pervasive, but it has been hitherto neglected. During the last couple of years, a wave to protect the environment is blowing everywhere. The potential environmental damage, the magnitude of the waste management problems are directly related to the growth of economic activities which demands some regions to reduce the rate of economic growth resulting in regional imbalances. On the other hand, a reduction of economic growth rate would lead to unemployment, poverty and several other social problems.

Economic activities always generate residuals and release them into the common property resources of air, water and land. They create external discomfort for the society, which resides there. However, there are strong moral and ethical justifications for not imposing such costs and injuries upon the region and the society. But, the internation of the externalities is virtually impossible in the case of large-scale production by the use of technology without proper policy to manage the environment. Though the principle of permitting optimal levels of emissions and environmental damages in every region for every economic activity sounds as a better rule to be followed in the regional development programme, it has to pay for the environmental damage in the long-run. Hence, the scale of regional development should be comprehensive enough to manage the environmental damage.

Other sets of social and political problems need to be examined. That what is regarded as an enormous ecological problem by one social group, may be regarded by another as an economic opportunity with negligible external costs. A sparsely populated region having large assimilative capacities in its air and water resources may appear to other regions or the nation as an ideal dumping ground of residuals which may be highly objectionable and unfair for the receiving region. It is also to be noted that the residents of well-developed region expects the residents of underdeveloped region to forego the benefit of regional economic development so that the residents of a well-developed region may have external economics of non-polluted vacation areas as second homes in the countryside.

Industrialized regions and nations have already started protecting their environment at the cost of other regions and environments by making heavy demands upon the existing limited stocks of non-renewable minerals, metals, fuels, and other natural resources. Some of the Third World countries find it difficult to take up costly protecting devices to save environment.

Development programmes initiated in tribal-dominated areas often adversely affected the tribal way of life, economy and habitat resulting in displacement. This was frequently followed by encroachment on traditional tribal areas by non-tribals and as the exploitation of natural resources became more intense, it generally affected the ecosystem of the tribal areas. There are inevitable difficulties of development policy in a situation where the component programmes are funded by international agencies and often supervised by them. Quite often greater emphasis and attention are given to the interests of the developed sectors of the country, such as the industrial sector or the dominant section of the country concerned. The rights and interests of the so-called backward tribals are often treated as being of secondary importance. Actually with the formation of new nation-states and increase in population, the exploitation of natural resources becomes more intense and there is tremendous competition to have access and command over natural resources and this often creates conflicts and tension at different levels. The developed countries or rather the multi-national organizations try to control the resources of the less-developed countries, while the dominant sections of the developing countries try to manipulate in such a way that they can enjoy the major share of the national natural resources often depriving the local population, mostly the tribals.

If we take the case of forest, there is no doubt that there is considerable degradation. Thus people, mostly the women, as they are primarily involved in the collection, are struggling more but getting less. This struggle is directly linked with the level of degradation of forest; where the forest is more degraded, people are forced to struggle more, where it is less degraded, the struggle is much less.

There has been significant land alienation, deforestation and mindless mining operations and other construction activities for the sake of defence establishments, all leading to displacement and great human misery. Unfortunately, many of these activities were undertaken in the name of development or 'national' interest. Quite often the project-affected people neither received adequate compensation nor resettlement support and little or no benefit out of these activities which greatly and adversely affected their life. The rationale of the 'national interest' to initiate these projects naturally needs thorough review and serious rethinking.

One cannot stop the exploitation of natural resources but what one is now looking for is how to achieve sustainable development. The traditional models of resource use may have an answer to this question. This may demand a new development strategy with a genuine participatory approach and creating a process of natural resource use, which is open, accessible and accountable by devolving power from the state to the local communities in the context of controlling the forest resources.

Conclusion

With increasing globalization, the exploitation of natural resources all over the world has become more intense often affecting the environment and the interests of the local people predominantly the indigenous people. Their access and command over natural resources are often denied affecting their life support systems. With the formation of new nation-states after the colonial rule, large-scale migration and movement of people have also been noted due to socio-political reasons. Now one may find a large number of displaced persons, the refugees or stateless population all over the world, many of whom are the indigenous people, where Human Rights violations are very common and human security is a major problem.

References

Acharya, Amitava. 2002. 'Debating Human Security: East Versus the West'. *Islamic Millennium*. 2(3–4), pp. 21–38.

Chapman, J.W.M. and I.T.M Gow. 1983. *Japan's Quest for Comprehensive Security*. London: Frances Printer.

Chaudhuri, Buddhadeb. 1991. 'Forest, Forest Development and Community Participation'. *Indian Anthropologist*. 21(1), pp. 9–19.

——. 1997. Development Environment and Forest – Conflict of Commercial and People's Interests: A Cross Cultural Study (A study on India and Malaysia). IDPAD Project Report. New Delhi: ICSSR.

——. 2007. 'Human Security, Human Rights and Development'. In B. Chaudhuri and S. Chaudhuri (eds), *Anthropology and Human Rights in Contemporary Era*. New Delhi: Inter India Publications.

Chaudhuri, Buddhadeb and A.K. Maiti (eds). 1989. *Forest and Forest Development in India*. New Delhi: Inter India Publications.

Dewitt, David B. and Amitava Acharya. 1996. 'Cooperative Security and Development Assistance: The Relationship Between Security and Development with Reference to Eastern Asia'. *Eastern Asia Policy Paper*, No. 16. Toronto: Joint Centre for Asia Pacific Studies.

Fernandes, Walter and E. Ganguly Thukral. 1989. *Development, Displacement and Rehabilitation*. New Delhi: Indian Social Institute.

Gadgil, Madhav and Ramachandra Guha. 1995. *Ecology and Equity*. London: Routledge.

Gadgil, Madhav, S. Narendra Prasad and Rauf Ali. 1983. 'Forest Management and Forest Policy in India: A Critical Review'. In Walter Fernandes (ed.) *Forest, Environment and People*, New Delhi: Indian Social Institute.

Ganguly, Thukral Enakshi. 1992. *Big Dams, Displaced Persons: Rivers of Sorrow, Rivers of Change*. New Delhi: Saga Publications.

Guha, Ramachandra (ed.). 1994. *Social Ecology*. New Delhi: Oxford University Press.

——. 1989. *The Unquiet Woods: Ecological Change and Peasant Resistance in the Himalaya*. New Delhi: Oxford University Press.

——. 1997. 'Social Ecological Research in India: A Status Report.' *Economic and Political Weekly,* 15 February.

Haq, Mahbubul. 1994. 'New Imperatives of Human Security'. RGICS Paper No. 17. New Delhi: Rajib Gandhi Institute of Contemporary Studies.

Hassan, M.J. 1996. 'The Concept of Comprehensive Security'. In M.J. Hassan and T. Ramnath (eds), *Conceptualising Asia-Pacific Security,* Kualalumpur: Institute of Strategic and International Studies.

Lodgaard, Sverre. 2000. 'Human Security: Concept and Operationalization'. Paper presented to the Seminar on Human Rights and Peace. Geneva, 8–9 December 2000.

Sen, Amartya. 1999. *Development as Freedom*. New York: Knopf.

Suhrke, Astrid. 1999. 'Human Security and Security Dialogue Interests of States'. *Security Dialogue*. 30 (3).

Tehranian, Majid. 2002. 'Cultural Security and Global Governance: International Migration and Negotiations of Identity'. *Islamic Millennium*. 2(3–4), pp. 1–20.

United Nations Development Programme. 1995. 'Redefining Security: The Human Dimensions'. *Current History*. 94(May), pp. 229–236.

Venkatachaliah, M.N. 2002. 'Democracy, Human Security and Development'. Special Lecture by Former Chief Justice of India and Chairperson, NHRC at West Bengal State Human Rights Commission on Human Rights Day. 10 December.

8

The Cerro de San Pedro Case

Grassroots Movements to Stop a Living Town from Disappearing

JOSÉ G. VARGAS-HERNANDEZ

Grassroots movements in relationships of co–operation and conflict between firms, communities and government have an important role to stop a living city from disappearing. This paper describes and analyses the implications of the collective action used by grassroots movements in the defense of an old mining town, Cerro de San Pedro of being disappeared due to the pollution of fresh watersheds by the operations of a mining company and the effects on the living city of San Luis Potosí, in the centre of Mexico.

The mining operations of the firm have been referred as an ecocide, contamination of watersheds, pollution of air and destruction of the historical heritage. The inhabitants of these communities supported by environmental groups and NGOs argue that the project will pollute sources of fresh water besides perturbing the environment and the ecology of the region.

According to the company Minera San Xavier (MSX), the 100 per cent-owned Cerro San Pedro gold and silver heap leach project is located in the historic Cerro San Pedro mining district in the State of San Luis Potosi, Mexico. The presence of MSX in Cerro de San Pedro has caused a severe social conflict among the inhabitants of San Pedro, Soledady San Luis and has called the attention of all who are concerned about historic heritage, cultural and environmental issues.

Geographical Localization

Cerro de San Pedro is a semi-abandoned historic mining town located in the centre of Mexico, the State of San Luis Potosi because it was an important mining town during the colonial period. However, when at the middle of the last century, the exploitation of silver and gold mines was abandoned, the town was also almost abandoned. Cerro de San Pedro is a small village 10 miles east of the City of San Luis Potosi, the Capital of the State of San Luis Potosi. Cerro de San Pedro is located in the mountains above the valley of San Luis Potosi and is part of the watershed area for the valley and its major cities. The valley is the source of 73 per cent of the water for the area.

It is a ghost town containing the ruins of shops, churches, estates and a hospital. Today, there are only about 100 people living in the Cerro. The Real hamlet covers the hills on both sides of the canyon; large and small houses flank the narrow streets (Cordero de Enciso, 1997). The remains of the 400-year-old town are still there, along with an active church and municipal office. Cerro de San Pedro sits in the high desert in the heart of Mexico, the kind of place with lots of road runners and big cacti. Four hundred years of mining did not alter the original appearance of Real, which is irregular and whose centre is the parish of San Pedro. The artistic and urban development that started in the 17th century is represented in Cerro de San Pedro. There are two structures particularly important from the historical heritage perspective. The Church of San Nicolas dates from 17th century and San Pedro Apostle which dates from the 18th century.

Tarascan Indians settled around the church and they adopted San Nicolás as their patron saint; the avenue in front of the church was used as an exchange and socializing place. Two churches were built in Cerro de San Pedro attended by the secular clergy helped by the Franciscan monks, and later by the Augustines who were able to speak Tarascan. The two churches built in the first half of the 17th century are identical, though the San Pedro church was later modified. The church of San Pedro is a rare example of a 17th century church; and its colouring is in aesthetic harmony with the hill behind it. The San Nicolás de Tolentino church is built on one side of the canyon and has become an urban area. The San Nicolás church kept its primitive appearance of only one nave and barrel vault. The section of town known as 'La Colonia de los Gringos' contains what once were company offices and living quarters of the American Smelting and Refining Co.

The purpose of this paper is to describe and analyse the relationships of cooperation and conflict between grassroots movements, a community and the role of government to stop the operations of a mining company which contaminate the watersheds, pollute the environment and destroy the living spaces of the town Cerro de San Pedro and affect the city of San Luis Potosi in México.

Historical Antecedents

The Guachichiles inhabited the area of Cerro de San Pedro hills before the Spanish came. The first original urban plan of Cerro de San Pedro dates from 1412. A couple of missionaries visited the area in the 1570s, but silver was found in the Cerro de San Pedro hills. Cerro de San Pedro used to be one of the biggest mining towns of the colonial New Spain 500 years ago, Spanish conquistadors carved up the earth as they plundered the town's riches, sending most of the treasure back to Europe. In March 1592, Don Miguel Caldera, a mestizo and commander of the Spanish army sent a group of miners to reconnoiter the land in the hills of the valley of San Luis Mexquitic and register the mines of the gold that called it Real de San Potosí.

Some 60 discoveries were registered with metals rich in lead. The richest minerals lay near the surface. After 40 years of struggle with the Guachichiles during the last decade of the 16th century, the Conquistadores convinced the Indians to plant crops and to have a sedentary life. Real de Minas de Cerro de

San Pedro was founded in 1583 after several mines in the vicinity began operations, although was established in 1592. Before that the capital of San Luis Potosi, discovered in the 16th century, due to its wealth, was baptized by the Spanish as the Potosi. Martín Pérez was one of the discoverers of the mines of el Cerro de San Pedro (SLP), on March 4, 1592 (Del Hoyo, 1979).

Cerro de San Pedro dates back to the 16th century and was the original location of the state capital of San Luis Potosi. But at the San Pedro Hill there wasn't enough water to support the town and for washing the metals, so they ended up moving. The Spaniards founded the village San Luis Potosi in the valley. The San Luis Potosi city's Coat-of-Arms had the Cerro de San Pedro on a blue and gold background with two silver and two gold cross bands, over which is lying Saint Louis King of France, testimony to its mining origins. The mountain is the symbol of their heritage.

Some Spanish families mestizos, mulattos and Indians founded Real de Cerro de San Pedro further up in the sierra which had their own governors and unions. Tlaxcalans, Tarascans and Otomies were brought in to work in the mines and the cattle ranches. The mining district Cerro de San Pedro has supported various periods of significant mining activity and has seen many production mining campaigns since its discovery over the past 500 years. There are no records of production during the period (1575 to 1660) of mining activity in the Cerro de San Pedro. The mines produced wealth in the first 30 years and the equivalent of some $ 62 million were paid in rights alone during its first 60 years of existence; that is, some $ 1 million per year (Cordero de Enciso, 1999).

In 1613, the Mayor, Pedro de Salazar had the famous Socavón del Rey built; a horizontal tunnel that gave access to deeper veins which produced around 30 tonnes of silver mixed with gold in a year. After 15 years of mining, the amount of precious metals reduced although there was a 'gold rush' that stirred greed among a group of men, who colluded in an enormous fraud and the owners of the Briones mine lost their property and finally in 1628 the houses in San Luis Potosí's main square were vacated. The last rich mine, the San Cristóbal, was closed down in 1656 although there were some bonanzas on El Cerro.

In 1690, the Mayor, Alonso Muñóz Castilblanque, opened the San Cristóbal mountain pass with the help of a loan made to him by the Viceroy, the Count of Galvez, and production increased to one-fifth of what it was in 1620. In 1740, 100 furnaces and 60 mineral crushers still existed in the region (Cordero de Enciso, 1997).

In the 18th century, the area had a reputation for maltreatment of indigenous people and anger. The poverty of the inhabitants of the Hill and its surroundings increased and became worst in 1767. The donations of silver given towards the reparation of the church were lost. The expulsion of the Jesuits resulted in an uprising in 1767. Cerro de San Pedro in 1767 was the focal point of a popular insurrection against the excess of Borbonic reforms. The serranos had demands and opposed the removal of the Jesuits but had to surrender. Viceroy Marquis de Croix sent Don José Galvez with 400 soldiers to punish the rebels and their families cruelly, but the serranos managed to have their taxes reduced and the church was repaired and improved.

By the mid-18th century, after 200 years of mining industry, Cerro de San Pedro was underdeveloped and the mines had low productivity due to lack of capital, technological insufficiency, limited capacity of the specialized workers, and shortage of supplies and labour, among other things (Villalba Bustamante, 2000). A few years later, Don Joseph de Castilla y Loaeza, a knight of Santiago, founded the Compañía Patriótica that invested 20,000 pesos and used old-fashioned techniques. In 1773, San Luis Potosí had around 20 mining communities in deplorable state of unproductiveness. By 1774, Cerro de San Pedro had to continue to struggle to restore exploitation of the local mines (López Miramontes and Urrutia, 1980).

In 1816, a horizontal tunnel was built in the Pópulo hill and the Socavón Aventurero de la Victoria, the tunnel of adventure and victory, restarted 60 years later. Compañía Metalúrgica Mexicana owned the railway that extended towards Río Verde to transport minerals from San Pedro to San Luis Potosi. A major period of mining activity began in 1870 and continued through the early 1950s. In 1930, American Smelting Company (ASARCO) worked the horizontal tunnel and the work continued until 1948 when the miners' strike broke out and the mine closed down.

By the late 1940s, gold, lead, iron, manganese and mercury deposits finally began to give out. By the early 1950s, it is estimated that approximately 2.5 million ounces of gold and 40 million ounces of silver had been produced from the Cerro San Pedro district. In 1993, the region of Cerro de San Pedro was declared an ecologically protected area. Local firms continue to extract limited quantities of minerals from the mines. Visitors can enter La Descubridora, the town's first mine.

Legal Background

Since the Prehispanic times in México, mining has played an important role in economic and political history. From 1986 to 1990, the World Bank granted credits to support structural adjustment economic policies. The credit 3359 supported structural adjustment of the mining sector categorized as B to eliminate environmental requirements and public hearings (Border Ecology Project 1994). Under a neoliberal economic policy, amendments to constitutional Article 27, a new Agrarian Law, a Mining Law (1993) and a Foreign Investment Law during the 1990s, allow the ejidatarios, originally limited owners of land rights, to change the ownership. Investors now could associate with ejidatarios, exploit land resources without buying it. The North American Free Trade Agreement (NAFTA) offer advantages and opportunities for investors.

The Mining Law (1993) and the Regulation to the Mining Law (1999) opened to foreign capital areas that were reserved for national investors and defined new rules for the development of national and foreign investments in exploration and exploitation of minerals as activities of public utility. The granting process of mining concessions does not require public hearings and most of the times the affected communities are the last ones to know about the project. There are some references about considering this and others 'competitive advantages that offer Mexico compared to their partners in NAFTA

(Bardacke, 1993). A mining concession cannot be cancelled for polluting the environment and only can be fined.

Minera San Xavier Project Development in Cerro de San Pedro

Renewed interest in the Cerro San Pedro district began in the 1970s with evaluations by various companies to determine the district's potential as a large tonnage, low-grade, bulk mineable deposit. In 1971, Las Cuevas mining company was unable to revitalize the mines. When the North American Free Trade Agreement (NAFTA) was enforced in 1994, the Canadian Company Metallica Resources Inc. started to explore the old mining town with the intentions to exploit its resources in gold and silver. In 1995, Metallica acquired an option to purchase Cerro San Pedro project and began an exploration programmes to expand the work of recent exploration programme conducted by other companies. Minera San Xavier (MSX) at Cerro de San Pedro is developing a gold mining project.

In February 2003, Metallica updated the Glamis' feasibility study run-of-mine development plan to provide for contract mining. The use of contract mining will reduce the project's capital cost to approximately $25 million, a result of eliminating the need to purchase the mining fleet. Metallica also updated the mineral reserve estimate using a higher gold price due to the strengthening of the gold market. Based on a $325 per ounce gold price and a $4.62 per ounce silver price, the mineral reserves stand at 61.1 million tonnes representing 1.8 million ounces of gold equivalent. The gold equivalent reserves increase to 2.1 million ounces at a $350 per ounce gold price and a $5 per ounce silver price (Metallica Resources, Inc. 2005).

In September 2003, an updated capital and operating cost study was completed for the Cerro San Pedro project. Metallica Resources (MR), promised to build what it announced as Wall Street, one of the greatest open pit mine of gold and silver of the world.

Actors Involved in the Conflict

(a) *The Mining Company:* Minera San Xavier (MSX) is the Mexican subsidiary of the Canadian company Metallica Resources involved in developing the San Xavier Mine in the municipality of Cerro San Pedro, San Luis Potosi, Mexico. The mining project of Minera San Xavier (MSX) is located 20 kilometres northeast of the city of San Luis Potosi, the state capital with a population of approximately one million people.

(b) *Community and Social Movements Involved:* The affected community is the small village of Cerro de San Pedro where it has formed an alliance with diverse civil groups, organizations and political parties in a coalition called Alianza Ciudadana Opositora a Minera San Xavier. Alliance in opposition to the San Xavier Mine is formed by social movements. Among the groups, the most involved are: Educación y Defensa Ambiental A.C., Environmental Education and Defense. Pro San Luis Ecológico A.C., Pro San Luis Ecology, Patronato Pro-Defensa del Patrimonio Cultural e Histórico de Cerro San Pedro, A.C., Patronato in Defense of the Cultural and Historical National Patrimony of Cerro San Pedro, and Asociación de Vecinos de Cerro San

Pedro, the Neighbours' Association of Cerro San Pedro. Other members that have joined the alliance are from more than 80 social movements. The alliance also counted on the support from the Catholic Church and its Archbishop. The citizen's group opposed to the project, the Ample Oppositional Front (Frente Amplio Opositor) is the citizens' movement that has a long-running struggle to prevent the destruction of the village of Cerro de San Pedro by a Canadian company that is planning to operate an open-pit gold mine. University of San Luis Potosi has conducted an independent review of the environmental impact study. Compas is one of the resistance movements of the San Luis Potosí civil society.

(c) *Government:* Municipal President of Cerro de San Pedro opposed the mining project and had not given his town's permission to the state government, the Governor of the State of San Luis Potosi and the President of Mexico. These three levels of government are actors on their own.

The Conflict

According to the company Minera San Xavier (MSX), the 100 per cent-owned Cerro San Pedro gold and silver heap leach project is located in the historic Cerro San Pedro mining district in the State of San Luis Potosi, Mexico. The presence of MSX in Cerro de San Pedro has caused a severe social conflict among the inhabitants of San Pedro, Soledad y San Luis and has called the attention of all who are concerned by historic heritage, cultural and environmental issues.

Minera San Xavier (MSX) argues that its operations would have some benefits: $4 million in taxes will be paid to the federation in eight years and would buy materials and provisions from local suppliers which would be the minimum because most of these suppliers would be foreign. Never the company referred the mining operations as an ecocide, contamination of watersheds, pollution of air and destruction of the historical heritage. The inhabitants of these communities supported by environmental groups and NGOs argue that the project will pollute sources of fresh water besides perturbing the environment and the ecology of the region.

At the centre of the controversy is the cheap and efficient technology. It is the use of cyanide and its impact on watersheds, the environment and human health. Lixiviation consists in pile-up mineral mixed with cyanide over a platform in such a way that gold will be residual. Cyanide is used for the extraction of metals since 1887 as a chemical reactive to solve gold in water (Logsdon, Hagelstein and Mudder, 2003). Twenty per cent of global production is used in a process of lixiviation to get gold. Almost 99 per cent of gold is separated from a rock and it is profitable to spend one ton of cyanide to extract 6 kilos of gold (Ronco, 2002).

Studies done by Minera San Xavier to evaluate pollution risk to the watershed of the valley of San Luis and to quantify the use of millions of cubic metres of water and its evaporation are insufficient and with a tendency. The hydrological card of INEGI the subterranean waters of San Luis Potosí and Cerro de San Pedro are the same in the geo hydrological zone. The daily use of 16 tonnes of cyanide and 32,000 tonnes of rock material that would require one million of cubic metres of water per year would have residuals of cyanide, heavy metals, toxic material and mercury stem can contaminate the watershed favoured by inclination of land and put at risk population

The process implies daily 16 tonnes of cyanide mixed with 32 millions of litres of water. According to the Environmental Impact Manifestation presented by MSX, erosion by deforestation, alteration of drainage patterns, cancellation of productive activities, pollution caused by deposits of toxic residuals are severe, irreversible and permanent damages. The Manifestation of the Environmental Impact of the company considers that 'the impact is significant and adverse for the extraction of water', 90 per cent of water consumption comes from the valley of San Luis which can be contaminated by the cyanide used in the lixiviation process (Martínez Ramos, 2004).

In the last 25 years, the major causes of cyanide spill over have been 76 per cent due to imperfections in the lixiviation yard, 18 per cent due to pipes and 6 per cent due to transportation accidents (State Environmental Resource Center 2004, 2004). Mining Companies have caused ecological catastrophes that have provoked reactions of civil society groups and governments around the World. Governments of many countries have prohibited open pit mining exploitation using cyanide (State Environmental Resource Center, 2004, also: Governor's office (2003); Friends of the Earth and Oxfam America, with support of Mineral Policy Center, 2003).

The company had constructed buildings in the village to be used for offices. The open-pit silver and gold mine planned for the area would have a dramatic effect and is being challenged in court by environmentalists. Environmentalists have a long battle against the company Minera San Xavier (MSX), a subsidiary of Canada's Metallica Resources that plans to build an open-pit silver and gold mine that would decapitate the mountain that looms behind the town Cerro de San Pedro. In a post-production model developed by the company, the area looks like a lunar landscape. The ore-processing plant, where the toxins would be used, sits just 20 minutes from San Luis Potosí, the capital of the state and home of about one million people.

Excavation for the mine will take place in an area where the mountain will be demolished and in its place will be large deep pits filled with the residue of the mining process. Soil cover will be lost in an area of approximately 500 hectares.

The pit is only about 600 metres from the town square and the tunnels from the old town go under the church and the square. If the mine project goes forward, a half-mile crater would be blasted at the top of mountain that sits behind the town of Cerro de San Pedro, Mexico. The proposed mine would destroy the historic remains of the old town and destroy the environment because of the cyanide leaching and potentially poison the water of San Luis Potosi. Greenpeace says cyanide high risk in mining plans by a Canadian firm in the Mexican district of Cerro de San Pedro. The firm Cambior has been involved in two most disastrous cyanide spills in mining history (Deza Arroyo, 2006. Also: Deza Arroyo, Nilton (2002) y Zenón, Iban/CEICOM (2006). Millions of litres of water were contaminated.

The project would entail moving part of the town and its historic buildings, but people did not want to move. To avoid damage of the buildings, the company plans would move the municipal buildings and the centuries old church another 600 metres away. The company would destroy the environment for a yield that would last only 6–8 years. MSX only vaguely outlined on the environmental-impact report. How it would restore the mountaintop, clean up the massive piles of bulldozed waste, protect rare plants and wildlife like the biznaga cactus and the desert tortoise, and safeguard the town's 16th century structures. It is estimated that profits from the exploitation would be low in comparison to the amount of destruction and permanent ecological damage that would result.

Most troubling was the company's unclear plan for the management and disposal of the toxins, including cyanide, that are used in gold mining. The daily use of 13 tonnes of explosives composed of nitrate 'Anful' will produce great quantities of dust which can cause irreversible ills. In fact, 640 million cubic metres of cyanide materials would be residuals covering a surface of 178 hectares which will not allow agricultural or cattle activities for generations. The potential poisoning of the watershed lands alone would have dramatic consequences for the inhabitants of San Luis Potosi (Campbell, 2004). However, MSX argues that it has clarified its plans and is implementing the 100 changes suggested by a group of Mexican academics who studied the environmental-impact report.

In spite of the fact that permits to exploit the mine in Cerro de San Pedro have been cancelled, the company has huge trucks, big tanks and workers on the site, and the land has been cleared for future use in an environmentally protected area, so the cleaning and clearing have been obviously illegal. A test drill resulted in a street collapsing because of the tunnels under the street and the company had 'repaired the damage' by dumping a load of gravel. If the project goes forward, MSX would add about 170 jobs to its existing staff of 34 to work on the mine, but the new jobs will require education and training that people from Cerro de San Pedro often lack. Some qualified residents would receive temporary housing a few miles from the town. Other villagers could choose to stay here and receive a monthly payment, based on the typical wage here, from MSX that could be used to strengthen their houses to protect them from the blasts.

The Company violated federal and state laws. Among the violated federal laws were:

> Presidential Decree of 2 June 1961. It forbids extraction of water in the valley of San Luis Potosi.
>
> Article 35 of Federal Law of fire arms and explosives. Store and consumption of explosives is only 50 metres from town instead of at least one kilometre.

The Agrarian Law establishes the obligation of the agrarian authority to staff and protect the ejidatarios or peasants possessing a small plot of communal property land. The Company leased ejidal lands from fake ejidatarios.

State Laws violated are:

> Article 7 of the Environmental Law of San Luis Potosí. It does not give faculty to the governor to authorize licences of land use. The Governor exceeded his authority to grant authorization of land use in may 2000.
>
> Article 15 of the State Constitution of San Luis establishes the right of citizens to enjoy a healthy environment and to prevent and combat environmental pollution.

Cooperation and Conflict Relationships between the Actors

A decree of September 1993 protects the area of the municipalities of Cerro de San Pedro, Soledad, and San Luis Potosi of any type of aggression against the natural environment. A Renewal Plan of San Luis Potosí and surroundings (Plan de Ordenación de San Luis Potosí y sus alrededores), launched by government in 1993, included Cerro de San Pedro and previewed ecological restoration during the following 20 years. On September 1993, the government of San Luis Potosi granted the plan, establishing that three-fourth of the municipality territory should be oriented toward development of wildlife, signalling the lack of water as a fundamental problem and the need to have recharging watersheds and giving priority to industries with low consumption of water and not polluted (*Periódico Oficial del Estado de San Luis Potosí*, 1993).

In 1994, MSX conceived the mining project to exploit Cerro de San Pedro in an open-pit process at only 50 metres from the town. Since 1995, information and letters have been sent to many officials. The citizen's group opposed to the project, the Frente Amplio Opositor (Broad Opposition Front), has won a number of legal battles. However, some people favour the project arguing that mining is part of this town's history and its economic legacy. On 5 May 1996 was founded the Patronato Pro Defensa del Patrimonio Cultural e Histórico del Municipio de Cerro de San Pedro, AC.

The mining project started in 1997, when MSX received authorizations from local authorities. The company argued that the Project Cerro de San Pedro would generate almost $ 200 million in investments, job positions for locals and 74 per cent of buying from local suppliers (Europa Press, 2004). With the announcement of the project was born also the opposition formed by environmental and architectonical conservation. MSX subscribed the leasing contract of land in March 1997 for a period of 15 years by fake ejidatarios that did not have land rights on the Ejido. The Environmental Impact Statement for the Cerro San Pedro project was submitted to the Mexican Federal authorities in October 1997.

Since then, the permit process has included a public hearing in March 1998 and a technical review of the permit documents by the University of San Luis Potosí as mandated by the state government. In 1998, a technical scientific opinion from the Commission to Review the Project Cerro de San Pedro and Minera San Javier from the Autonomous University of San Luis Potosi established over the environmental components that only prevents monitoring of water but not air and soil where the cyanide could harm (Comisión de la Universidad Autónoma de San Luis Potosí para la Revisión del Proyecto Cerro de San Pedro de Minera San Xavier, 1998). Researchers accepted the invitation under the condition that the results of the study should be published before shown to the Company and to Environmental and Natural Resources Secretary (SEMARNAT or Secretaría del Medio Ambiente y Recursos Naturales).

The researchers of the Autonomous University of San Luis Potosi had conducted the environmental study. However, this study has not been considered to be serious, complete and professional although it was considered as an instrument of expression of company's interests.

On 20 March 1998, the Municipal President was found dead by a bullet in his head. He was murdered after he requested an audit and wanted penal action against former municipal president that had sold illegally abandoned fincas to MSX. One day before he was murdered, an official of the company gave a presentation of the mining project at Hotel Westin in San Luis Potosí. After the lunch at El Saucito, the Municipal President argued with William Copeland Dodge, the manager of MSX. It was a lost case containing documents which proved the land, as communal property, that the murdered had with him. The Governor of the State of San Luis recommended the interested persons to review their motivations, to take care of themselves and warned that the officers of the company would do anything to get what they want.

An official from the International Council of Monuments and Sites (ICOMOS), an organization of UNESCO, declared that if the Minera de San Xavier project destroys the cultural heritage of Cerro de San Pedro, the Governor of San Luis Potosi will be remembered in history as responsible (La Jornada San Luis, 20 February 1999). Conservationist and environmentalist groups have asked stated government and federal government not to authorize the project. Government should find equilibrium between conservation of cultural values and exploitation of material resources in such a way that the solution should guarantee the integrity of historical monuments.

In 1999, the Secretary of the Environment and Natural Resources (SEMARNAT) authorized the project and its environmental impact in spite of serious violations to the General Law of Ecological equilibrium and Environmental Protection. In February 1999, the National Institute of Ecology (INE) granted environmental permit to operations of MSX against the existing plan of 1993 but establishing 100 conditions, among which, the number 12 established relocations of the communities Cerro de San Pedro and La Zapatilla. Condition 68 established that the company should consider a proposal for limiting the use of water through treatment and other alternatives (Instituto Nacional de Ecología 1999).

On the 26 February 1999, the National Institute of Ecology granted authorization at changed land use in Cerro de San Pedro. In the year 2000, the civic platform Pro San Luis Ecological presented an appeal against authorization of mining exploitation granted on 1999 to Minera San Xavier by the National Institute of Ecology. On 5 May 2000, the government of San Luis Potosi and the municipal of Cerro de San Pedro granted conditional authorization of land use for mining exploitation.

Since 2001, the Social Justice Committee of Montreal, Mining Watch Canada and the Mexican NGO FUNDAR Centre for analysis and research, funded by IDRC, are involved in a project to establish the impact of Canadian mining operations in Mexico, and to provide support to the affected Mexican communities. Field research was carried out in Cerro de San Pedro. Relationships between Canadian and Mexican partners are maintained, nurtured and deepened, linking communities and NGOs up with similar groups. A seminar on the impact of mining activities in Mexican communities was organized as well as case studies undertaken (Mining Watch Canada, 2002).

In April 2002, according to information from the company, the last of the amendments to the federal and state mining permits that had previously been issued was received by MSX. MSX acquired irregular form of water rights of ejidatarios and small land owners who have sued the company. The company obtained illegally and against conditioning 6,89,92,000 cubic metres of water from intermediaries of six concessions. An order of apprehension of MSX's officials was granted (*La Jornada San Luis*, 2002).

In August 2002, the Tribunal of the International Centre for Dispute Resolution on Investments established a laud in favour of the United States Enterprise Metalclad, imposing a fine of $16 million to the Mexican Government for discriminatory treatment after the authorities closed a land field for residuals and trash in Guadalcázar (San Luis Potosí, México). This was a dangerous antecedent that the commercial and business logic is above the health and welfare of communities.

In October 2003, Mexican state and federal agencies, and Catholic Archdioceses of San Luis Potosi, authorized the structural stabilization and installation of blast monitoring equipment at Cerro San Pedro Apostle Church. Metallica Resources Inc. was pleased to announce it on 23 October (OTC Bulletin Borrad, 20003). On 24 November 2003, the Agrarian Unitary Tribunal (Tribunal Unitario Agrario) emitted an agreement to stop operations of the transnational company, requested by the real ejidatarios to maintain the integrity of the land in conflict.

Approximately, $2 million was spent on initial project development during 2003. Construction of the mine began in the first quarter of 2004 with commissioning scheduled for the fourth quarter of 2004. The exploitation unit started to build in February 2004 with the withdrawal and reforestation of 21,000 protected cacti, while MSX affirmed being in possession of ISO 14001 certification. The topography report includes plans of geoposition of the National Institute of Geography and Statistics (Instituto Nacional de Estadística Geografía e Informática, INEGI) stating that the mining exploitation is on the area of the hill and in the town. On 11 February five years later, the company submitted the impact on health issues and the company has not given any information regarding the areas of conservation of five species of cactus to the SEMARNAT. Besides the historic architecture, there are five species of flora risking extinction.

Earlier, a group of nearly 20 environmental and civic groups charged Mexico's Ministry for Environment and Natural Resources of illegally rubberstamping in 1999 MSX's environmental-impact report. Cruz Camarena (2004) reports a confrontation early in March between 60 local environmental and community activists and representatives of the San Xavier Mine, the head of the State Unit of Civil Protection, Investigators from the Autonomous University of San Luis Potosí (UASLP) and the Secretary of Ecology and Environmental Organization.

On 17 March 2004, the Unitary Agrarian Tribunal rejected the rental contracts between the MSX and false ejidatarios. The Governor of the State of San Luis pressurized the President of Municipal Government of Cerro de San Pedro to grant the corresponding agrarian permits. He also pretended to cancel the decree that protects the ecological zone. The Secretary of the State Government also pressurized and wanted to bribe the Municipal President of Cerro de San Pedro to grant permits of land use and to give support for authorization of SEDENA'S permit to use explosives for bastings. The Secretary of

Economic Development of the State of San Luis has land properties neighbouring MSX and ceded 65 per cent of water rights. The President of the Mining Chamber of Mexico could raise the situation of conflict of interests; however he supported the blasting of MSX even though knowing that this was against judicial decisions

MSX has established programmes dedicated to the conservation of the environment. MSX has formed a non-profit foundation to supervise and administer the funds that Metallica donates to preserve the village of Cerro de San Pedro and assist the surrounding communities. On 12 April 2004, a protest mining at Cerro de San Pedro was organized by the National Liberation Zapatista Front (FZLN).

On 11 May 2004, Fred H. Lightner, General Director of Minera San Xavier, sent a letter to Herrera Muñoz insisting on the permit to use explosives, warning that Metallica Resources would announce publicly in United Status that the company is found without any possibilities to continue with the construction of the mine as it has no count with the general permit to use the corresponding explosives. He continued on saying that their investors and potential investors in other projects in Mexico would begin to question regarding the risks to invest in Mexico (Cruz Martínez, 2004).

On 18 May 2004, the Second District Court granted a suspension as part of the appeal 564/2004 promoted by inhabitants of Cerro de San Pedro to halt granting of construction and functioning of MSX. However, this permit was liberated on 7 August at Cabildo session.

In June 2004, the antimine coalition, Pro San Luis Ecológico won a federal court sided with environmentalists in effectively nullifying MSX's environmental permit, which halted the company's work. On 23 June, the Supreme Tribunal of Fiscal and Administrative Justice cancelled the environmental permit granted by the Secretary of Environment and Natural Resources (SEMARNAT) in February 1999. On 23 June, the 9th Collegiate Tribunal in Administrative Issues of the First Circuit of the nation Supreme Court of Justice (SCJN), declared that the licence of change of land use and open-pit mining project granted to MSX by the National Institute of Ecology violated the General Law of Ecological and Environmental Equilibrium and the Decree of Planning in the State of San Luis Potosi.

On 22 July, the Municipal Presidency was taken over by the Minera San Xavier (MSX), one week before an entrepreneur of the MSX intended to bribe the President. The Secretary of Economy of Mexico declared in August that MSX was a win-win project and authorized on 28 July a temporal occupancy of land against article 20 of the Mining Law that forbids a mining exploitation when there are population or an ecological reserve The environmental permit to operations of MSX was cancelled on 28 July 2004 the same that was granted by the National Institute of Ecology (INE). For more than one year, Fox visited the state once per month and promoted MNX. President Fox visiting Canada questioned the judicial decisions affecting operations of the mining company.

On 29 July, when visiting San Luis met the President Municipal of Cerro de San Pedro and recommended the approval of the municipal permits even against resolutions of the judicial power. According to Loredo, Fox told him that he was worried to achieve the mining project and that he (the President of Mexico) recommended its approval (Ramírez Cuevas, 2004). The argument used by government to support operation of the open-pit mining company is the generation of 300 low wages employments, for only 8 years. President Fox was criticized for having double standards. While he promotes disobedience to the law of the Municipal President of Cerro de San Pedro, he has accused the Mayor of Mexico City for the same fault. The Municipal President recognized that he authorized the operations of the open-pit mining because he was afraid of his life and the life of his family. In 1999, the Municipal President, the father of Loredo, was murdered because his opposition.

On 7 August, the Municipal President of Cerro de San Pedro approved the permits to build the mine and conformity regarding safety and location against a previous agreement of no approval done on 28 May, based on the appeal 564/2004 and agrarian and environmental resolutions had forbidden these permits. Loredo recognized that the permits were illegal; there was no other way to face the pressure. However, the session was tape recorded, where the Municipal President declares that he was under pressure by President Fox and the Governor of the State. The Municipal President declared that it was known beforehand that the federal government and the state government are in agreement and they are potent that one cannot be against them; they have the hand around their neck and there were some advertencies. When this decision was questioned, he responded asking if his life was not important.

On 9 August, the Second District Court admitted other appeal presented by ejidatarios and next day declared suspension in order that SEDENA could not authorize buying and using of explosives. On 10 August, the same court granted other suspension as part of the appeal 909/2004, to halt Sedena's actions to deliver to the company the permit to buy and use explosives, but licence was issued on the 12 October by the Secretary of Defense. On 18 August, a Congresswoman, Eliana García, presented to the Permanent Commission of Congress a point of agreement to request the Judicial Power to investigate federal and state officials involved in disobedience to the law.

On 21 August, opponents to the MSX's project closed the offices and demanded immediate exit of the company from Cerro de San Pedro. Among these opponents were Movimiento Pro-Cerro de San Pedro, Frente Cívico Potosino, Greenpeace, Frente Zapatista de Liberación Nacional y del Movimiento 'Ya Basta', inhabitants from Cerro de San Pedro, San Luis Potosí and Soledad, and a patrol of public security.

On 1 September 2004, a decision of the Mexican Federal Superior of Fiscal and Administrative Justice Court (TFJFA or Tribunal Federal de Justicia Fiscal y Administrativa) called for the mining company's permit granted in February 1999. The permit was granted to conditionally operate the mine. However, TFJFA revoked the permit because of its failure to comply with proper procedures with respect to their environmental impact study. The resolution states that because biodiversity is at danger, the project should not be authorized. Commencement of mine operations was anticipated to begin in the fourth quarter of 2004, subject to project financing.

In a resolution dated 1 September, TFJFA substantiated a case brought in 2000 by the civic union Pro San Luis Ecológico, opposing the authorization granted to the company the previous year by the National Institute of Ecology (INE). The delegates of the SEMARNAT in San Luis Potosí (2002–2004) created and managed Foundation of Potosi under the purpose declared by Minera San Xavier to fulfil the conditions established by the National Institute of Ecology to authorize the Manifest of Environmental Impact and to provide the compensations of ecological costs. The firm needed more than three years to fulfil only 32 of 100 conditions imposed by SEMARNAT while this Secretary only needed one month to accept them.

The court halted operations at the San Luis de Potosí Gold Project, owned by Minera San Xavier (MSX), a subsidiary of the Canadian company Metallica Resources. The Federal Court's resolution was based on the necessity of ecological preservation of San Pedro Hill, where some animal species are in danger of extinction, as well as risks derived from cyanide used in mining, which would put in danger the biodiversity of the area. In addition to this point, TFJFA recalls that the responsibility for preservation and regeneration of the environment lies with the federal authority. It concludes that the permit granted for the concession did not conform to 'applicable laws'.

The opponents to La Minera San Xavier consider that 'the project is dead', since any action that could undermine the federal justice decision 'would imply disrespect and transgression of the law'. The company has retorted that the decision lacks a scientific base and that it will harm Canadian investments in the country. Second District Judge of the Federal Judicial Power dictated suspension of plan as part of the appeal 909/2004, promoted by ejidatarios de Cerro de San Pedro, San Luis Potosí, to suspend permit of buying and using explosives by the company.

MSX appealed the ruling and, in September, lost again. Because the company's latest appeal was rejected, they are threatening to use NAFTA's Chapter 11 to sue the Mexican government for potential lost profits. On 27 September, the Broad Opposition Front asked the Sub Direction of Mining Rights to order cancellation of concession to Minera San Xavier.

On 7 October, personnel of the Secretary of Economy asked the ejidatarios to withdraw the land but a judge suspended the action. Against the owners of the land, during the first period of the project, more than 100 hectares of protected areas were illegally naked of protected species cutting the flora and expulsing the fauna. The Municipal President, who under pressure granted the permit, confronted a suit for not obeying the law because the municipal permit was suspended on 16 March 2004. On 6 February 2004, MSX did not acknowledge some of the environmental commitments acquired and underestimating obligations to fulfil conditionings.

The company also committed fraud against the three levels of government who granted respective permits for the mining project under the assumption that land tenure was not viscid. With a fake contract, MSX took possession of land causing destruction of old buildings and protected flora and fauna, a loss to the ecosystem.

The company also closed neighbourhood roads that had been used by inhabitants of La Zapatilla, Cuesta de Campa, Portezuelo y Cerro de San Pedro

(Montemayor, 2004a) without any permit, invaded land of national property where was the old track of the train Potosí-Rioverde was and installed a fence of several kilometres to avoid access to inhabitants to municipal land (Montemayor, 2004b).

On 26 October, the Federal Tribunal of Fiscal and Administrative Justice determined that authorization of conditioned land use granted in 1999 to the project of MSX was against federal norms and did not consider the existence of a protected area plan for the Cerro de San Pedro and surroundings. In a public speech on 28 October, the Minister of Environment and Natural Resources evaluated the resolutions of tribunals as the worst and spoke in favour of the company as having fulfilled all the requirements and considered as absurd the opposition of the inhabitants.

After SEDENA granted permits for use of explosives, on 18 November, an incident of violation of suspension granted to the appeal promoted by ejidatarios on 9 August was promoted. On 22 November, Semarnat promoted a revision against the resolution that cancels the permit of conditioned operation of the open-pit mining to MSX and SEDENA authorized to MSX the use of explosives.

On 29 November 2004, the Director of Mining in the State of San Luis Potosí declared that in the following days the Company would have the first blasts to prepare operations. On 30 November 2004, the Senate Chamber passed an 'obvious and urgent resolution' to stop programmed operations of MNX.

On 1 December, an Agrarian Unitary Tribunal defended its claim that MSX's lease excludes a group of land owners. The Agrarian Unitary Tribunal ordered to obey the sentence derived of an appeal 807/202 which determined the illegality of the leasing contract of land subscribed in March 1997 for a period of 15 years by fake ejidatarios, or false holders of land rights, who did not have land rights on the Ejido (Cruz Martínez, 2004). The Court cancelled rental contracts subscribed between the company and false ejidatarios. The ruling freezes MSX's land rights although the company constructed barbed wired fences around land that the company doesn't own (Cruz Martínez, 2004b).

The Agrarian Tribunal (Tribunal Unitario Agrario) has nullified the rental contracts for the land where important parts of the mine are located – on the grounds that the persons renting the ejidal (socially-owned) land to the company were not in fact members of the ejido, that is to say that their actions were fraudulent. About the land use, the company declared that the ejido leased of Cerro de San Pedro belongs to the municipality of Soledad de Graciano Sanchez. The intention is to avoid permits in area that is legally environmentally protected. Also, ejidatarios of Palma de la Cruz leased 136 hectares to Minera San Xavier to be used as shops but the company was using it for disposal of sulfurous material that is not lixiviable.

On 13 and 14 December, the company blasted the area of La Zapatilla incrementing tension among the inhabitants of the region. On 14 December, it began excavating the mountain. Inhabitants of the town La Zapatilla were relocated after the company initiated operations. When INAH knew about the blasting, requested the company to stop such activities arguing the defense of around 115 buildings dated from 17th to 19th centuries. Since 1998, INAH had warned about the danger to the heritage that would be the result of activating the mining. With the opposition of the National Institute of Anthropology and History (INAH), and the reluctant permission of the Secretary of Defense (SEDENA) for using explosives for blasting the mountain, the company has begun its operations. The company appealed but the judge did not grant suspension against INAH decision.

On 18 December, intellectuals, artists and around 50 civil, environmental and Human Rights organizations strongly requested President Fox to respect and enforce the law at Cerro de San Pedro and to order Minera San Xavier to suspend activities based on judicial resolutions and verdicts. The arguments of the organizations, among others, Frente Amplio Opositor, la Asociación Nacional de Abogados Democráticos, la Unión Nacional de Trabajadores Agrícolas y el Movimiento Agrario Indígena Zapatista (Maiz), were in favour to defend the environmental, cultural heritage and the imminent health of more than one million people. Ejidatarios continued with a safety line in front of the entrance to the mine although it was announced that the Secretary of Economy of Mexico will grant a permit of temporal land occupancy in the agrarian nucleus of Cerro de San Pedro in response to an application by MSX on 28 June 2004 (Cruz Martínez 2004a). Thus, the Company and government were looking for other options of land ownership such as expropriation or temporal occupancy. But expropriation is only by cause of public utility.

On 20 December, the Third District Court received the appeal presented by the company against the decision of the INAH. The Canadian firm Metallica Resources Incorporated suffered a second reduction in the year of 16 per cent in value of shares on 21 December, after informing shareholders over the resolutions of Unitary Agrarian Tribunal which nulls the contract of leasing of 300 hectares in Cerro de San Pedro. The first reduction in a year, of around 20 per cent, had occurred in mid-2004.Metallica Resources responded with an appeal and stating that it would look for other options of land tenancy to have access to mineral resources.

Members of Christian Science Monitor were the first Canadians to come and witness the damage that had already happened, and the potential for more harm. On 22 December 2004, under strategic action, Mexico citizen's group sought halt in the Canadian-owned mine, in respond to an urgent request for Canadian support to challenge legality and operations.

Sedena admitted participation in control and surveillance of blast that the company realized, confirming violation of suspension dictated by the judge in August 2004 ordaining not liberation of permit to use explosives (Cruz Martínez, 2004). Another round of blasting was scheduled for 31 December. On 18 December, the Municipal President of Cerro de San Pedro announced next detonation.

On 15 November 2003, the Commander of the 12 Militar Zone of San Luis Potosí considered that authorization of the permit could affect SEDENA negatively. The Secretary of National Defense, on 30 November 2003, agreed to suspend the permit to use explosives granted to the mining company, but on 12 October 2004, against resolutions of judge, signed and granted permits of use of explosives. The commander of the military zone that had opposed was removed from his position. On 22 November, SEDENA authorized MSX the use of explosives.

However, on 24 December, when authorizations were public already, the permits were suspended but not cancelled. The Secretaría de la Defensa Nacional (SEDENA) suspended the permit 3762-San Luis Potosí granted to MSX to buy and consume explosive material under the argument that the licence to the company was altering the peace, tranquility and public order among people living in the region of Cerro de San Pedro, although the inhabitants have denied alteration of public order (Cruz Martínez, y Balboa, 2004).

The National Institute of Anthropology and History (INAH) sued against directives of the Transnational for destruction and demolition of Finca Guadalupe that dated 18th century. The Broad Opposition Front sent a letter to the Canadian Embassy requesting intervention to halt operations of the Canadian company who is blackmailing and pressing inhabitants of Cerro de San Pedro using as arguments the NAFTA's framework (Román, 2004).

In the last two days of December 2004, the lawyer of the company MSX got signatures among fake ejidatarios from Cerro de San Pedro and La Zapatilla, who would agree to use TNT (Elizalde, *La Jornada*, Enero 2, 2005).

The Ministry of the Environment had taken legal steps to have the previous court rulings against the company overturned SEMARNAT had promoted an appeal of revision to the resolution of cancelled permit but had obtained in its favour a suspension to avoid cancellation of the permit. The Commission of Governance, Constitutional Issues and Justice of the Permanent Union Congress approved an agreement to request information to SEMARNAT about the legal status of Minera San Xavier and to accept the resolution of the Court that cancels the permit of operation of the open-pit mining. A plural commission travelled to Cerro de San Pedro (*La Jornada*, Enero 12).

The destruction of a historic building catalogued as a heritage monument of the 18th century in the town of Cerro de San Pedro by Minera San Xavier was reported by La Jornada San Luis and Triunfo Elizalde (2005). This historic building is the Finca o Casa de Guadalupe which is included in the National Catalog of Historical Monuments. Access to the Finca was denied to the Municipal authorities by the employees of the company when authorities went to take an affidavit because an inhabitant showed the titles of property. On 17 January, protesters of the Broad Opposition Front (Frente Amplio de Oposición, FAO) demanded information from the National Institute of Archaeology and History (Instituto Nacional de Arqueología e Historia, INAH) (Enciso, 2005f).

The inhabitants of Cerro de San Pedro only had obtained from Congress an agreement to request information from the SEMARNAT over the legal status of the company (Enciso, 2005f). On 18 January 2005, the INAH suited MNX for the intentional damages caused to real states that are heritage of Cerro de San Pedro and request suspension of actions to avoid damages against real states and the AOF accused the company to unfulfilled obligations. The suit was presented on 15 January because the Company did not request any authorization although on 18 November, the INAH had asked the Company for an immediate suspension of any activities and blast in the area. On 17 January, protesters of AOF (FAO) demanded INAH for information (Enciso, 2005e).

The owners of Casa Guadalupe, a historic real state demolished by MNX suited the company for dispossession and damages. The building is in the catalogue of historic constructions of the Instituto Nacional de Antropología e Historia (INAH). Personnel from INAH ordered to stop demolition on 15 January. The Patronato Pro Defensa del Patrimonio Histórico y Cultural del Municipio Cerro San Pedro demanded cancellation of concessions to MNX for non fulfillment of the Mining Law (Enciso, 2004d).

According to the Secretary of Environment and Natural Resources (SEMARNAT), Minera San Xavier fulfilled with 180 conditions established to favour sustainable development (Enciso, 2005c). On 20 January 2005, the Broad Opposition Front (AOF), Frente de Oposición Amplia (FOA), to the Minera San Xavier addressed an open letter to the Constitutional Governor of the State of San Luis to denounce damages caused by the blasts and the dangers and risks of planned mining operations (Governor's Office, 2003). The argument of the governor stating that it was 'an issue between particulars' is severely criticized (Cruz Martínez, 2005b).

Minera San Xavier sued for defamation members of the Broad Opposition Front, two ejidatarios of Cerro de San Pedro and the leader of a civil organization Pro Defensa de Cerro de San Pedro Cruz Martínez, 2005a) for the publication of an article in La Jornada (Ramírez Cuevas, 2005). The National Network of Civil Organizations of Human Rights, All the Rights for All (la Red Nacional de Organismos Civiles de Derechos Humanos Todos los Derechos Para Todos) started to circulate a letter of support to the three accused, as an Urgent Action. Minera San Xavier lost other judicial process when the Third Court of District from state denied an appeal against the National Institute of Anthropology and History (Instituto Nacional de Antropología e Historia, INAH), who requested last December suspension of blast explosions that damaged the historic heritage (Enciso, 2005b).

In a public message, AOF sustained that in a shameful act of cynicism and impunity, Cardenas Jimenez has recommended the Minera to go to the Tribunals without knowledge of the coursed legal process (La Jornada San Luis, 2005). The Broad Opposition Front to the MNX announced in mid-February 2005 that would promote a demand of political suit for negligence against the Minister of the Environment and Natural Resources who have supported the company in a public hearing on 11 February (Enciso, 2005g). The Senate approved an agreement requesting SEMARNAT and SEDENA to explain their involvement in the Minera San Xavier case (Cruz Martínez, 2005).

On 4 March 2005, a conference/forum Cuarto Concierto Cultural por la Defensa de Cerro de San Pedro took place for the defense of the environment, the village and the rights in Cerro de San Pedro, sponsored by Patronato Pro Defensa Cerro de San Pedro, marking the 413th anniversary of its foundation, on 4 March 1592.

On 17 March, a KAIROS delegation formed by seven Anglican, Lutheran, Presbyterian, and Roman Catholic and United church leaders went to Cerro de San Pedro to investigate a mining operation owned by Metallica Resources, a Canadian company based in Ottawa that stands accused of illegal gold mining in Mexico. The company threatens to destroy both the historic town and the surrounding fragile ecology. The Canadians met with KAIROS' Mexican partners and local people to bear witness to their struggle and brought details home to Canada, including video and other documentation. 'Foreign mining in Mexico is another by-product of NAFTA and the trade liberalization policies that affect the poor,' said Lutheran National Bishop Ray Schultz, a delegate with the KAIROS programme. 'When our Mexican partners raised concerns about this Canadian-owned mine, we felt we had to investigate.' (Kairos, 2004).

Representatives ants of Kairos, formed by a group of Canadian religious institutions, expressed concerns over the conflict of the Community of Cerro de San Pedro and the Canadian company considering that the practices of MNX violates Canadian Laws in Mexican territory (Muñoz, 2005). Previously, a member of the Broad Opposition Front had toured and campaigned in Canada lobbying leaders of opinion and legislators. On 18 March 2004, the Auxiliary Bishop Daniel Bohan of Toronto called on a Canadian company to abandon a Mexican gold and silver mining operation using cyanide that locals fear will poison their water. With a surge in gold prices, MSX executives want to move forward and are searching for a legal breakthrough that will allow MSX to begin excavation and resume operations by mid-2005 (Campbell, 2004).

Under an irregular procedure, the Canadian Company promoted two appeals, but was denounced by the Pro Ecology Group. On 6 April 2005, a tribunal in administrative matters of First Circuit informed to MNX that had lost the appeal. Canadian legislators and Human and Parliamentary Rights Canadian Organizations formed a follow-up and analysis committee to investigate actions of Metallica Resources, owner of the project Minera San Xavier. The Human Rights Canadian Organization had previously visited the community of Cerro de San Pedro (Enciso, 2005a).

The Canadian ambassador in Mexico met the Broad Opposition Front to the MSX on 4 May and expressed the concerns of the Canadian Government for the conflict between the company and the Community of Cerro de San Pedro. A group of 30 environmentalist organizations accused the Minister of the Environment and Natural Resources to benefit transnational corporations approving projects such as the open-pit mining at Cerro de San Pedro against the will of the community and demanded a change in the environmental policy (Enciso, 2005). The protesters also denounced that the Minister has prosecuted environmental activists.

Oppositional groups won the judicial controversy against MNX after the First Court of District (Juzgado Primero de Distrito) dismissed the appeal 503/2005, which was the last resource in the Company's defense (Hernández Lopez, 2005). The Governor of the State of San Luis Potosí ordered to highjack a complete edition of the newspaper La Jornada San Luis to avoid to be known through the publication of his official manoeuvering for pressure the decision to install the mining company Minera San Xavier (Hernández Lopez, 2005).

On 13 May 2005, it is reported that after Metallica Resources presented loses in its first report of the year, the owners of MNX planned to withdraw Cerro de San Pedro's project and will sue the NAFTA's panel for controversies (Cruz Martínez Ángeles, 2005a).

Final Remarks and Conclusion

Mining activities are perceived as the main economic factor for marginal regions and depressed zones in México. Mining concessions granted by Mexican government are centralized, brief and do not include public hearings. Affected groups and communities can not react immediately and mobilize against potential risks and dangers or to negotiate rights and interests.

The Canadian firm Metallica Resource Incorporated was at the point of destroying part of the environmental and cultural heritage of the country, although there were three judicial resolutions to halt operations granted by different authorities upon request of the ejidatarios, who have rights to own the land but had been dispossessed. It was assumed that operations of the firm were in complicity with the federal, state and local governments. The environmental and health risks would have side effects on more than one million people living in the localities of Cerro de San Pedro, la Soledad and San Luis Potosi. Norms were violated by the transnational Metallica Resource Incorporated when it started operations without obtaining legal permit of construction and operations and authorization to manage and to store explosives.

Exploitation of gold through open-pit mining and use of cyanide lead to destruction of natural environments and irreversible geomorphologic alterations, distortions of watersheds, reduction on the quality of available water, transport accidents of dangerous substances and spill over during the exploitation, irreversible destruction of natural scenic and generation of deposits highly risky pollutant materials which have social, cultural and environmental impacts on short, medium and long terms (Montenegro, 2004).

The negotiation agenda and international mobilization around the debate over the concept of sustainable development and defense of the environment is a paradigm presented as a model of cooperation and consensus where the needs of all are incorporated and the stronger have to compromise to support the weaker. Intervention of the international community to the benefit of the public interest, the common good, to control forces of the state and to achieve more equity among populations, together with the implementation of more sustainable production and consumer patterns, are common and always welcomed by the small local communities.

The lack of sensitivity of foreign mining companies toward the consequences and effects of their activities upon the local communities and damage to the surrounding environment is quite evident. To a certain extent, I disagree with Sánchez-Mejorada (2000) who argues that facts will not convince the fringe environmental activists. The best defense is to address all environmental concerns and to have an aggressive community relations programmes that will prevent the facts to the general population that will be affected by the project. Keeping a low profile will rarely work when being assaulted by activists on all fronts. But, an aggressive community relations programme will escalate the conflict.

This case also shows the lack of negotiation between firms, communities, new social movements and governments. Information about externalities and future costs of company activities is crucial but more crucial is formulation and implementation of more sensitive policies to avoid damage of the environment, biodiversity and health of population. Governmental institutions must be aware that their decisions may affect the quality of life of community's actual and future generations only for a small increment in economic growth and large increase in private benefits of a small group of investors.

More informed citizens tend to be more active protesters, such as the case of the students in San Luis. Contact between informed individuals of diverse groups and organizations help to exchange experiences and create public opinion in favour of mobilizations. Community participation and involvement in decision making of community development planning is quite limited by the lack of critical information. This fact is critical when the local government cannot provide the right information because there are other interests affecting the process.

References

Bardacke, Ted. 1993. 'The Mexican Gold Rush'. In *El Financiero Internacional,* September 27–October 3, pp. 14–15.

Border Ecology Project. 1994. 'Environmental Protection Within the Mexican Mining Sector and the Impact of World Bank Mining Loan #3359', Draft Report, April 1994.

Campbell, Monica. 2004. 'Mexican Town Curbs Mine Giant'. *The Christian Science Monitor*. 14 December.

Comisión de la Universidad Autónoma de San Luis Potosí para la Revisión del Proyecto Cerro de San Pedro de Minera San Xavier. 1998. *Opinión Técnico-Científica sobre los Componentes Ambientales del Proyecto Cerro de San Pedro de Minera San Xavier, San Luis Potosí,* December de 1998.

Cordero de Enciso, Alicia. 1997. 'San Pedro Hill it Still Worth a Potosi'. *México en el Tiempo* No. 19, July–August. Mexico desconocido Online. Retrieved from http://www.mexicodesconocido.com.mx/english/cultura_y_sociedad/actividades_economicas/detalle.cfm?idsec=17&idsub=83&idpag=689.

Cordero de Enciso, Alicia. 1999. *Real de Catorce, San Luis Potosí. Investigación y texto.* México: INAH: JGH.

Cruz Camarena, Beatriz. 2004. *Community, Environmentalists Fight Canadian Mine* Co. Mexican Labor News & Analysis, March 2004, Vol. 9, No. 3. Retrieved on 4 January 2012 from http://ueinternational.org/MLNA/mlna_articles.php?id=69#ttoc

Cruz Martínez, Ángeles. 2005. 'El Senado aprobó un punto de acuerdo en el que exhorta a las dependencias a informar. Semarnat y Sedena deben explicar su su participación con Minera San Xavier' *La Jornada*, Sunday 27 February.

——. 2005a. 'Dueños de Minera San Xavier planean retirar el proyecto, aseguran opositores' *La Jornada*, Friday 13 May.

——. 2005a. 'Dueños de Minera San Xavier planean retirar el proyecto, aseguran opositores' *La Jornada*, Viernes 13 de mayo del 2005.

——. 2005b. 'Minera San Xavier denuncia 'por difamación' a tres opositores a su proyecto de explotación', *La Jornada*, 23 January.

——. 2004. 'Admite Sedena que autorizó uso de explosivos a minera: ejidatarios', *La Jornada*, 24 December, 2004.

——. and Balboa, Juan. 2004.'Suspende Sedena permiso a Minera San Xavier para manejar explosivos' *La Jornada*, 26 December.

——. 2004a. 'Intelectuales y ONG exigen a Fox ordene a Minera San Xavier suspender actividades', *La Jornada*, 19 December.

——. 2004b. 'Tribunal emite ejecutoria que ratifica la ilegalidad de contrato de arrendamiento' *La Jornada*, Saturday 4 December.

Del Hoyo, Eugenio. 1979. *History of El Nuevo Reino de Leon (1577–1723)*. P.F.V. Col. Doc., I, Editorial Libros de Mexico, S.A., Mexico, D.F. p. 254.

Deza Arroyo, Nilton 2006. 'Oro, ciaburo y otras crónicas', Editorial Universitaria UNC, Cajamarca, Perú. Also: Deza Arroyo, Nilton (2002) Oro, cianuro y otras crónicas ambientales. Editorial Universitaria. Cajamarca, Peru. Zenón, Iban/CEICOM (2006). 'Minería de oro y plata en Sensuntepeque' Centro de Investigación sobre http://www.ceicomobservatoriodelsur.org/index.php?module=pagesetter&func =viewpub&tid=8&pid=4

Elizalde, Triunfo. 2005. 'Minera San Javier Recaba firmas de falsos ejidatarios para iniciar operaciones' *La Jornada*, 2 January.

Enciso, Angélica L. 2005. 'Ecologistas acusan a Alberto Cárdenas de beneficiar al sector Empresarial' *La Jornada*, 6 de Mayo.

——. 2005a. 'Legisladores y ONG de Canadá deciden investigar actos de Minera San Javier', *La Jornada*, 18 April 2005.

——. 2005b. 'Niegan amparo a Minera San Xavier' *La Jornada*, 3 February.

——. 2005c. 'Insiste Semarnat en defender a Minera San Xavier', *La Jornada*, 20 January.

——. 2005d. Dueños de la Casa Guadalupe denuncian a Minera San Xavier por daño y despojo', *La Jornada*, 19 January.

——. 2005e. 'Presenta el INAH demanda penal contra la Minera San Xavier', *La Jornada*, 18 January.

——. 2005f. 'Reculan legisladores en el caso de Minera San Xavier'. *La Jornada*. 17 January, 2005. Retrieved on 3rd. January, 2013 from http://www.jornada.unam.mx/2005/01/17/016n1pol.php

——. 2005g. 'promoverán juicio político contra el titular de la Semarnat' *La Jornada* February 14.

Europa Press. 2004. 'Tribunal mexicano paraliza el proyecto minero en San Luis de Potosí La empresa responde que ya tenía todos los permisos y que el Tribunal carece de conocimientos medioambientales' 2 November 2004.

Governor's Office. 2003. 'Governor Davis signs Legislation to stop proponed Gold Mine near 'Trail of Dreams' Sacred Site,' 7 April, 2003, Electronic document <http://resources.ca.gov/davis_agency_news.html> 30 November.

Hernández López, Julio. 2005. 'Astillero', *La Jornada*, Monday 9 of May 2005.

Instituto Nacional de Ecología. 1999. *Autorización DOO DGOEIA* 001130. México.

Kairos. 2004. *Delegation to Mexico looks at poverty, murder, Canadian mining practices and other free-trade by-products* MEDIA ADVISORY KAIROS–Canadian Ecumenical Justice Initiatives.

La Jornada 2005. Conflicto en Minera San Xavier, Cerro de San Pedro. La Jornada, 12 January.

La Jornada San Luis and Triunfo Elizalde. 2005. 'Minera San Xavier destruye un inmueble histórico del siglo XVIII', *La Jornada*, Sunday 16 January.

La Jornada San Luis. 2005. 'Le duela a quien le duela, es viable el proyecto de la Minera San Xavier'. La Jornada. 12 February.

——. 2002. 'La Minera San Xavier adquirió de manera irregular derechos de agua', 22 June, 2002.

——. 1999. 'Minera San Xavier podría afectar el patrimonio de SLP' February 20.

Logsdon, Mark J. MScKaren Hagelstein and Cihterry I. Mudder. 2003. *The Management of Cyanide in Gold Extraction,* In Mark J. Logsdon, Cihterry I. Mudder, published the Wendsday 3 of December, 2003, obtained on November 16, 2004 from http://www.ilustrados.com/publicaciones/EpZpVpEpkkjxcfwDzo.php

López Miramontes, Álvaro and Cristina Urrutia. 1980. *Las Minas de Nueva España in 1774*. Mexico: INAH.

Martínez Ramos, Mario. 2004. *Carta a Quien Corresponda*, San Luis Potosí S.L.P, México, September 23, 2004, Electronic document <http://www.esquelonline.com/~noalamina/Sanluispotosi.htm> 5 November, 2004

Metallica Resources, Inc. 2005. *Cerro San Pedro*. Electronic document retrieved from <http://www. metalres.com/main.asp? section=properties&page=cerro>

Mining Watch Canada. 2002. Mines Alerte. Newsletter, number 8, Winter/Spring 2002. Electronic document <http://www.miningwatch.ca/publications/newsletters/newsletter8.html>

Montemayor, Carlos. 2004a. 'Amenaza ambiental con Minera San Xavier', *La Jornada*, Monday 18 October, 2004.

Montemayor, Carlos. 2004b.' Minera San Xavier despojó de tierras a habitantes de Cerro de San Pedro', *La Jornada*, 20 October. III Parte.

Montenegro, Raúl A. 2004. *Estudio sobre el Impacto Ambiental y Sanitario de las minas de oro. El caso Cordón Esquel*, Electronic document <http://www.funam.org.ar/introduoro.htm> 4 November 2004.

Muñoz, Alma E. 2005. 'Destruye el TLCAN a las familias: grupos religiosos' *La Jornada*, 19 March, 2005.

OTC Bulletin Board. 2003. 'Metallica Resources Announces Authorization Proceed With Church Stabilization at the Cerro San Pedro Project, Mexico'. October 23.

Periódico Oficial del Estado de San Luis Potosí. 1993. 'Plan de Ordenación de San Luis Potosí y de su zona conurbada', published on 24 September, 1993.

Ramírez Cuevas, Jesús. 2004. 'De cómo el Presidente mide con dos varas. Fox promueve el desacato', published in the Suplement Masiosare, No. 349, from daily *La Jornada*, Sunday 29 August, 2004.

Ramírez Cuevas, Jesús. 2004. 'De cómo el Presidente mide con dos varas. Fox promueve el desacato', published on the Suplement Masiosare, No. 349, of the Daily La Jornada, Sunday 29 August.

Román, José Antonio. 2004. 'Piden a Canadá obligar a Minera San Xavier a respetar Ley mexicana', *La Jornada*, 28 December.

Ronco, Jorge. 2002. 'Fundamentos de la Campaña Esquel', *Eco sitio 2002–2004*, Electronic document <http://www.eco-sitio.com.ar/fundamentos_de_la_campana2. htm> 15 Nov, 2004.

Sánchez-Mejorada, Rodrigo. 2000. Mining law in Mexico. *Mineral Resources Engineering*, 9(1): 129–139.

State Environmental Resource Center 2004. Banning Cyanide Use in Mining, Electronic document <http://www.serconline.org/mining/talking.html> 21 July, 2004.

State Environmental Resource Center 2004. Banning Cyanide Use in Mining, Electronic document <http://www.serconline.org/mining/talking.html> 21 July, 2004. Also: Governor's office (2003). 'Governor Davis signs Legislation to stop proponed Gold Mine near 'Trail of Dreams' *Sacred Site*, 7 April, 2003, retrieved from http://resources.ca.gov/davis_agency_news.html, 30 de November del 2003. Friends of the Earth y Oxfam America, with the support from Mineral Policy Center (2003), *Glamis Gold: Estudio de caso de inversión en la destrucción*, noviembre del 2003, en http://www.oxfamamerica.org/newsandpublications/publications/research_reports/art6471.html

Villalba Bustamante, Margarita. 2000. *State and Business Initiative in the Formation of the Valenciana and Real de Catorce Mining Communities (Mexico), 1760–1790.* Colegio de San Luis. San Luis Potosí.

9

Urban Poor

A Vulnerable Issue of Human Rights in Bangladesh

MUHAMMED SHAMSUDDIN

Bangladesh, a densely populated country adjacent to India is being recognized now as an emerging tiger of Asia. Over a period of time, the capital city – Dhaka – turned to become a large overcrowded mega city in this world. The population of Dhaka is now presumed to be around 15 million whereas just 15 years ago, the total population of the city was only 5 million. The mega city accommodates around 4 million urban poor now, while Chittagong, the second largest city of Bangladesh, also has a population of around 1.5 million today. The population of the urban poor is increasing consistently everyday as the urban population itself is continuously growing. The population growth rate in other cities is nearly the same as in Dhaka. Interestingly, about half the world's population lives in the larger cities and urban areas. The mega-cities Dhaka and Chittagong are overloaded with people. Both the push and the pull factors bring the job-seekers, specially the poor people, to the city.

Urbanization, population growth and poverty are the key Human Rights issues of the urban poor in Bangladesh. This is not an analytical paper; the paper is based on the observation and experiences of a Human Rights activist like me working for the cause of Human Rights, particularly of the urban poor, for about 23 years.

Since its independence in the year 1971, Bangladesh has many achievements to its credit but then poverty has become an issue of serious concern. Unplanned urbanization and urban poverty are closely related in the context of Bangladesh and stand out as drawbacks to the phenomenon of urbanization. These could be considered as two contrary faces: prosperity and deprivation. While some have access to a high standard of living, implying a prosperous milieu, there are many who are outside the purview of the minimum basics of life, implying deprivation. This contradiction is clearly visible in urban Bangladesh.

The case for urban poverty merits attention on several grounds. The establishment of Human Rights is an important one among them and the recognition of the fundamental rights for the citizens, as mentioned in the pages of the Constitution, is another one. Among the rights, as laid down in the Constitution, the urban poor are mostly deprived of the rights to education, housing, health and others most significantly. One may take into consideration the following quotation to further understand the obligation of the Bangladesh government to the imperative of dealing with poverty, including urban poverty: 'Bangladesh's Constitution states that the Government of Bangladesh is responsible for creating an environment for its citizens that allows them to improve their quality of life to health, education and other basic services.' Besides the above there are other factors also that call for attention in the context of urban poverty.

There is a policy of distributing *khash* (unused government agricultural land) to the landless people. Few years ago, the government started a programme named *Ghorey Phera* (homecoming) for the urban poor which was jeopardized.

There are several reasons that led on to the spread of urban poverty. The establishment of Human Rights and the recognition of the basic needs as fundamental rights in the Constitution are two important factors. The right to education, housing and health and others are a few of the most important rights that the urban poor are mostly deprived.

The urban poor in Bangladesh commonly live in slum, under the open sky on streets, at railway stations, etc. A compared to the major cities in Bangladesh, Dhaka and Chittagong have the maximum number of the urban poor. The main occupations pursued by the urban poor are as garments workers, rickshaw pullers, domestic helps, hotel boys, taxi drivers, construction workers, hawkers, bus helpers, transport workers, workshop helpers, road cleaners, *tokai* (those who collect garbage to sell for recycling), cobblers, vegetable sellers, beggars, *koolie*/loaders in railway stations and bus stations.

A description of the core Human Rights issues that are viewed as most vulnerable is given hereafter:

Housing

Congestion is a major characteristic of the slums and it has multiple implications for those living in it. Slums automatically imply there is no space to stretch or breathe freely where the inmates live a crammed existence to the extent that any further inclusion is extremely difficult. For instance, on reviewing the extent of congestion, it is found that the size of a single room for a full family is from 70 to 250 square feet, even including the kitchen. The extent of congestion is reflected by the unusual number of people living in a single room, which varies from three to seven. In normal houses, the adults and the children can maintain a decent distance by living in separate rooms whereas in slums this minimum space is nearly absent.

The payment of rent is a common procedure for the dwellers in a slum. While it is compulsory for people in private slums to pay a rent, for those who dwell in public land, the procedure followed is slightly different – musclemen linked with the authorities are seen to be extracting rent in return for prevention of eviction. The rent amount payable in a slum may vary in different cities and even within the same cities. It has been noticed that depending on location, the rent amount varies from TK500 to TK1500.

Another prime characteristic of a slum is a minimum narrow thoroughfare. The types of house-building materials used for making slum houses also gives the slums a dismal picture and lends it a poor physical living condition. Bamboo, cane, mat (*chatai*) and polythene are the main building materials used for making the houses or huts. In few cases, tin is also used. A brick wall is rarely found in the slums here. Thousands of slums are gutted every year due to fire accidents owing to narrow thoroughfares.

Eviction

Disregarding the instructions in the verdict of the Hon'ble High Court and also going against the principles in the Housing Policy (no one can be evicted without appropriate rehabilitation), the slum dwellers are regularly evicted, both from public and private land by many means. They always feel threatened by the trends of eviction and encroachment. In different places the rent-seekers, having a close connection with the power structure have built slums on public land to rent them out. The threat of eviction has become a regular phenomenon in such slums. Again, there are times when the urban poor themselves raise low cost slums on empty public land. Interestingly, in suchlike situations, in very quick succession, the armed cadres take over the control and start extorting money from them. On the other hand, the private slum owners are constantly raising rent at an exorbitant rate. Quite naturally, due to situations like the above cited, the poor segments are denied the right to habitat.

Healthcare

The incidences of different diseases, that include water borne, air borne, contagious, gastro-intestinal, venereal and gynecological diseases, is high among the slum dwellers. The unhygienic condition in almost all slums only helps in worsening the health condition.

Self-medication, medication based on advice of the medicine shop attendants and quack treatment are common ways of medical treatment in these slums. The trend of visiting a nearby hospital or primary healthcare centre is relatively limited. Makeshift arrangements for child delivery is generally made in the house wherein the pregnant woman is living presently. This is also a common practice as, in the opinion of the slum dwellers, hospitalization is expensive. Besides, superstition and the lack of health awareness sometimes discourage the slum dwellers from visiting a hospital and seeking modern treatment.

As compared to the need, the number of public hospitals is inadequate and along with this, a long queue, lack of good services and treatment dissuade the slum dwellers from visiting a hospital when they are suffering. As most doctors these days are more interested in private practice, they pay little attention to the poor patients which impacts their health condition negatively.

Harassment Random Occurs

There are a few NGO operated health service outlets that provide medical services to the poor and needy. However, their services in the form of free diagnosis and treatment facilities and free delivery for the poor pregnant women and others as well as the distribution of free medicines like iron tablets, anti-worm drugs is very limited as compared to the demand for the same. However, these health service outlets can cover almost the entire population during the countrywide immunization programme for children in the 0–6 years age group.

Education

According to the law of the land, primary education is compulsory for all children and a child must be enrolled in any nearby primary school at the age of 6. Under the law, the parents are punishable if they disobey the law. The government is supposed to distribute books, free of cost, to the children who are enrolled for education in primary schools, up to class V. However, the supply of the provisions being inadequate to meet the demand, especially in the urban areas, it is not possible to provide every child with a complete set of books. Moreover, the number of schools is also not increasing according to the need of the urban poor. True that schools and colleges are coming up every other day, yet the access of the children of the urban poor to education is blocked for economic reasons. In fact, these upcoming schools are often out of the reach of the middle class too. Again, while in the rural areas, girls are provided a stipend, their counterparts here in the cities are not provided this benefit. Moreover, in the primary schools in urban areas, children from different economic classes take admission. The urban poor who have more of economic constraints are often discriminated against, resulting in their negligence by teachers and others in school, which gives them an inferiority complex.

Also it gets noticed that the quality of the teaching is not quite 'satisfactory' in such free primary schools where the children from the needy families are enrolled. It is difficult for the parents to afford private coaching fees for guidance through their children's education. Thus, in all respects, the education of the urban poor children is significantly affected and they are denied their rights to education.

The enrollment of the urban poor children is even lower at the secondary education level. This is mainly because, as a result of their family's poverty, these children have to engage their time in some work for earning a livelihood for themselves as well as their families. Economic constraints compel the parents and the affected children to give little or no importance to secondary education.

Utilities Services

Slums are generally constructed on public and private lands. Those which are located on the public land are deprived of the utilities provided by the city corporation and the service departments of the government. On the other hand, private owners are also little interested to invest for the improvement of the slum unless it brings additional profit. As a result, the utility services in the slums is extremely bad, which will be seen in the following areas.

Access to Water: There are insufficient sources of water supply points like hand tubewell, supply water, shallow tubewell, etc. in almost every slum. These are limited in terms of availability. Supply water is not only limited in the slums but it is also found dirty and foul smelling. Most of the slum dwellers need to buy water from NGO constructed community-based water supply sources, if these are available.

Sanitation: The sanitary facilities available in most slums in all the divisions are deplorable. In some areas there could be slabs and community latrines, but due to improper usage and maintenance, and insufficient numbers, the situation is worse. Open latrines and hanging latrines are common in most of the slums, except in Dhaka. Another common practice in every slum in all the cities is to use open drains as latrines.

Drainage and Sewerage: Drainage and sewerage facilities are significantly absent in almost all the slums of all the cities.

Access to Electricity: Most slums have a limited access to electricity and any government initiative in this regard is at present negligible. For example, in Dhaka, electricity is available in the private slums but each family needs to pay a monthly charge that is two to three hundred times higher than the rate fixed for normal consumers. So the slum dwellers restrict themselves to using only one–two points for using one bulb and one fan. Often the electric lines get snapped; load shedding is common and incidences of fire from short circuit have become frequent.

Access to Gas: Access to the supply of cooking gas is limited only to the slums of Dhaka and Chittagong; however, its availability is not only minimum but significantly inadequate compared to the need. Cylinder based cooking gas is expensive and almost unaffordable by the slum dwellers. Moreover, its availability is also difficult, the reason why in some places the slum dwellers depend on different organic wastes such as cow dung, resulting in severe pollution and chronic diseases, like asthma and bronchitis.

Gender Relations

Poor women are generally said to be the victims of two types of exploitation that stem from class and gender inequality. The women who live in the slum are subject to different types of exploitations, discussed below, and these vary by occupation and age.

Eve Teasing: Eve teasing and other kinds of incidents take place at the time the poor working women return from their place of work in the evening. There are cadres who indulge in such activities. At the extreme of such incidents, sexual harassments are also known to have taken place.

Sexual Harassment: This kind of risk at the workplace is most frequent among the household maids belonging to the slums. Often the law enforcing agencies refuse to provide the necessary assistance to the victims of sexual harassment by showing their unwillingness to register cases against the perpetrators. On the other hand, the complicity of political cadres in such incidents of sexual harassment only creates frustration among the slum dwellers. In Dhaka, for instance, since the political cadres are powerful, the urban poor women and adolescent girls are very vulnerable.

The fact is that the urban poor women, like the rest of the rural women in the country, are often hesitant to disclose incidents of sexual harassments. Victims of such sexual harassments are, on the other hand, lying face down to hide the incidents.

Trafficking: In some places women living in the slums have become vulnerable to trafficking across the borders and outside the country.

Wage Discrimination: Wage discrimination is another aspect of gender exploitation towards the women from slums almost everywhere. It has been noticed that for the same piece of work women workers are paid an amount that is 10 to 20 per cent lesser than that paid to their male counterparts.

Dowry and Child Marriage: The dowry system is very much existent in the slums, though in a different form in the sense that it is not demanded directly in the form of a dowry but rather as a help to the groom to support his career.

Security

Drug Addiction: Many young people in the slums are addicted to different types of drugs. In all divisions this phenomenon is reported and some idea is given about its magnitude. A good number of the young urban poor have taken to drug addiction and drug selling.

Involvement in Criminal Activities: A sizeable part of the slum dwellers are now engaged in criminal activities of different nature, including mugging, kidnapping, eve teasing and pick-pocketing. For example, 20 per cent slum dwellers in Sylhet are involved in mugging. Some slum dwellers are involved in drug business; 20 per cent of the slum dwellers in Dhaka are reported to have connection with drug business. Sometimes some powerful people from outside involve them in different criminal activities. Such a situation is an outcome of their poverty and it is mainly for economic gains that they get involved in such activities.

Extortion: Musclemen and cadres take extortion, by force, from the slum dwellers, particularly from those which are located in the government land. Normally it is on the ground of eviction that the extortionist demands an extortion.

Unattended Children: Since the parents of the children of the slums are engaged in work, many of them (children) remain unattended at home. No institutional support (e.g. day care centre) is available to take care of the unattended children. So, as reflected in some particular incidents, the consequence is obviously not desirable. In a few cases, a number of children, who were locked from outside, when fire broke out in the slum, were burnt alive. Again, the unattended children who play on the street fall victims to road accidents and while a few others get engaged in delinquent activities such as drug peddling and trafficking.

Inadequate and Poorly Managed Safety Net Programmes: Widows, disabled and the old people are more vulnerable among the urban poor. They are not in a position to get engaged in work, leading to their greater vulnerability. At present there are some special assistances, like pension facilities that are offered to these people; however, the amount is nominal and can hardly address the causes of their vulnerability. Unfortunately, this opportunity is not available to the urban poor. Similarly, the urban poor mothers are also deprived of from any maternity allowance

Garments: The wage structure in the garments sector has by now formalized to a large extent. Pay scales on different positions have also been fixed up. However, questions may be raised regarding its proper enforcement or whether it is properly followed, and adequacy, in the sense to what extent it can meet the needs of the garment workers or how regularly payment is made to the garment workers. The garments' workers have in a tripartite agreement recently made a demand for a minimum wage of TK 3,000.

Mobilization of Urban Poor

The demands and expectations of the urban poor are closely related to the problems they encounter occasionally or regularly. In other words, their deprivations mostly determine the form and nature of their expectations. It is also notable that the demands and expectations are multifaceted; sometimes it is about bringing changes in the existing policies and sometimes calling for a new one. Sometimes they demand for a direct transfer of resources/assistance to them. It also relates to effective services from public hospitals and the primary schools. The urban poor expect the service rendering organizations to effectively meet their demands. On a review of their present condition, it is observed that their demands and expectations primarily revolve around such aspects as housing, education, primary health, gender relation, utility and social security. However a more in-depth scrutiny can bring up other aspects also.

For the first time since 1998 after a devastating flood, the Coalition for the Urban Poor and, later on, the Centre for Urban Study mobilized the urban poor and provided facilities to build their capacity. Till date many groups were formed under one umbrella named BOSC – (Bostibashir Odhikar Surakha Committee). The leadership is now able to speak for its own rights in different national and international forum.

Perceived Challenges of the Urban Poor

To have a correct understanding of the demands of the urban poor is quite a challenge. Also the extent to which these demands can be met is a challenge. There is likely to be an unbridgeable gap between what the urban poor expects out of society and what best the society can offer to them. This may be attributed to the style of functioning of the different institutions working towards this end. Not to mention, these challenges are spread across the different aspects, housing, education, primary healthcare, gender relations, utilities and social security.

References

Banks, N. 2008a. 'Improving the urban poverty agenda: the need for realigned priorities and a better understanding of urban poverty', Paper presented at the conference on Understanding Urban Poverty, GTZ, Dhaka, 30 November.

——. 2008b. 'A Tale of Two Wards: Political Participation and the Urban Poor in Dhaka City'. *Environment and Urbanization*, Vol. 20, No. 2, October, pp. 361–376.

——. 2010. *'Employment and Mobility Among Low-income Households in Dhaka, Bangladesh'*, Unpublished PhD Thesis. UK: University of Manchester.

Centre for Urban Studies (CUS), NIPORT and Measure Evaluation. 2006. *Slums in Urban Bangladesh: Mapping and Census 2005*. Dhaka and Chapel Hill.

Hossain, N. 2005a. *Elite Perceptions of Poverty in Bangladesh*, Dhaka: University Press Limited.

Islam, N. 1995. *Dhaka Now: Contemporary Urban Development*. Dhaka: University Press Limited.

Islam, N., N. Huda, F.B. Narayan and P.B. Rana. 1997. *Addressing the Urban Poverty Agenda in Bangladesh: Critical Issues and the 1995 Survey Findings*. Dhaka: Asian Development Bank and University Press Limited.

Kamal, A. 2000. 'Accountable Governance and Poverty Alleviation' Paper for the Regional Workshops Democracy Forum 2000. Democracy and Poverty: A Missing Link?, 10–11 April 2000, Kathmandu.

Narayan, A., N. Yoshida and H, Zaman. 2007. 'Trends and Patterns in Poverty in Bangladesh in Recent Years'. World Bank. South Asia Region. Washington DC.

Rashid, S, and Y. Hossain, 2005. 'Constraints in Delivering Services to the Urban Poor Living in Slums in Dhaka, Bangladesh', Report Commissioned by the World Bank, Dhaka.

Ravallion, M., S. Chen and P. Sangraula. 2007. 'New Evidence on the Urbanization of Global Poverty'. World Bank Policy Research Working Paper Series No 4199. Washington DC: World Bank.

Sen, B. and D. Hulme. 2006. 'The State of the Poorest 2005/2006: Chronic Poverty in Bangladesh, Tales of Ascent, Descent, Marginality and Persistence', Bangladesh Institute of Development Studies and Chronic Poverty Research Centre, Dhaka and Manchester.

Wood, G. and S. Salway. 2000. 'Introduction: Securing Livelihoods in Dhaka Slums'. *Journal of International Development*. Vol. 12, pp. 669–688.

World Bank. 2009b. 'Dhaka: Improving Living Conditions for the Urban Poor'. *Bangladesh Development Series* No 17. Dhaka: World Bank.

WWF. 2009. 'Mega-Stress for Mega-Cities: A Climate Vulnerability Ranking of Major Coastal Cities in Asia'. Geneva: Worldwide Fund for Nature.

10

Urbanization and Problems of Slum Dwellers in India

Rights' Perspective

SANJOY ROY

Urbanization is an index of transformation from traditional rural economies to modern industrial ones. It is a long-term process. Number of urban agglomeration/town has grown from 1827 in 1901 to 5161 in 2001. Number of population residing in urban areas has increased from 2.58 crores in 1901 to 28.53 crores in 2001. Only 28 per cent of population was living in urban areas as per 2001 census. Over the years there has been continuous concentration of population in class I towns. On the contrary, the concentration of population in medium and small towns either fluctuated or declined. The graduation of number of urban centres from lower population size categories to class I cities has resulted top heavy structure of urban population in India. India's urbanization is often termed as *'over-urbanization'*, *'pseudo-urbanization'*. The big cities attained inordinately large population size leading to virtual collapse in the urban services and followed by basic problems in the field of housing, slum, water, infrastructure, quality of life, etc. Urbanization is a product of demographic explosion and poverty induced rural-urban migration. Urbanization is occurring not due to urban pull but due to rural push. Globalization, liberalization, privatization are addressing negative process for urbanization in India. Policy relates to proper urban planning where city planning will consist of operational, developmental and restorative planning. It was estimated that by the year 2008, more than half the human population, of 3.3 billion people will be living in urban areas. This number is expected to swell to 5 billion by 2030. The world's urban population has grown from 220 million to 2.8 billion over the 20th century. This scale of growth is expected to continue in the next couple of decades with Africa and Asia witnessing major growth.

India has a large network of cities and towns. In 1991, the network comprised 3,696 cities out of which 300 cities had a population of over one million. In 2001, the total number of cities had gone up to 4368 out of which 393 had a population of over one million (Kundu et al., 2007).

Indian Census Definition of Urban Area

In Census of India, 2001, two types of towns were identified (Census of India, 2001)

1. Statutory towns: All places with a municipality, corporation, cantonment board or notified town area committee, etc. so declared by state law.
2. Census towns: Places which satisfy following criteria:
   (i) A minimum population of 5,000.
   (ii) At least 75 per cent of male working population engaged in non agricultural pursuits.
   (iii) A density of population of at least 400 persons per sq km Urban Agglomeration: Urban agglomeration is a continuous urban spread constituting a town and its adjoining urban outgrowths (OGs) or two or more physical contiguous town together and any adjoining urban out growths of such towns. Examples of outgrowths are railway colonies, university campus, port area, military campuses, etc. that may come up near a statutory town or city. For Census of India, 2001, it was decided that the core town or at least one of the constituent towns of an urban agglomeration should necessarily be a statutory town and the total population of all the constituents should not be less than 20,000 (as per 1991 Census). With these two basic criteria (R.G 2001) having been met the following are the possible different situations in which urban agglomerations could be constituted. (i) A city or town with one or more contiguous outgrowths; (ii) two or more adjoining towns with or without their outgrowths; (iii) a city or one or more adjoining towns with their outgrowths all of which form a continuous spread.

Trend of Urbanization in India

India shares most characteristic features of urbanization in the developing countries. Number of urban agglomeration/town has grown from 1,827 in 1901 to 5,161 in 2001. Number of total population has increased from 23.84 crore in 1901 to 102.7 crore in 2001 whereas number of population residing in urban areas has increased from 2.58 crore in 1901 to 28.53 crore in 2001 (Table 1).

Table 1

Population of India by Residence

Census Year	*Number of Urban Agglomeration/Town*	*Total Population*	*Urban Population*	*Rural Population*
1901	1,827	23,83,96,327	2,58,51,873	21,25,44,454
1911	1,825	25,20,93,390	2,59,41,633	22,61,51,757
1921	1,949	25,13,21,213	2,80,86,167	22,32,35,046
1931	2,072	27,89,77,238	3,34,55,989	24,55,21,249
1941	2,250	31,86,60,580	4,41,53,297	27,45,07,283

Cont'd...

...Cont'd

1951	2,843	36,10,88,090	6,24,43,709	29,86,44,381
1961	2,363	43,92,34,771	7,89,36,603	36,02,98,168
1971	2,590	59,81,59,652	10,91,13,977	48,90,45,675
1981	3,378	68,33,29,097	15,94,62,547	52,38,66,550
1991	3,768	84,43,24,222	21,71,77,625	62,71,46,597
2001	5,161	1,02,70,15,247	28,53,54,954	74,16,60,293

Sources: Various Census reports 1901–2001.

Pace of Urbanization

Urbanization in India has been relatively slow compared to many developing countries. The percentage of annual exponential growth rate of urban population (Table 4) reveals that in India it grew at faster pace from the decade 1921–31 to until 1951. Thereafter it registered a sharp drop during the decade 1951–61. The decades 1961–71 and 1971–81 showed a significant improvement in the growth which has thereafter steadily dropped to the present level 2.73. The sharp drop in urban rate during 1951–61 was mainly due to declassification of a very large number of towns during that period. Rural growth has been fluctuating since 1901. The decline in rural population growth was within small range during 1981–91 and 1991–2001.

Table 2

Annual Growth Rate of Population by Residence

Census Year	*Annual Growth Rate (%) of Total Population*	*Annual Growth Rate (%) of Urban Population*	*Annual Growth Rate (%) of Rural Population*
1901–1911	0.51	0.03	0.62
1911–1921	–0.03	0.79	–0.13
1921–1931	1.04	1.75	.95
1931–1941	1.33	2.77	1.12
1941–1951	1.25	3.47	0.84
1951–1961	1.96	2.34	1.88
1961–1971	3.09	3.24	3.05
1971–1981	1.33	3.79	.69
1981–1991	2.12	3.09	1.80
1991–2001	1.96	2.73	1.68

Sources: Census of India 1901–2001.

Tempo of Urbanization

Tempo of urbanization refers to speed of urbanization and is measured as change registered in the level or degree of urbanization over the years. Table 3 following table states that tempo or speed of urbanization is not uniform over the years and it shows a fluctuating trend over the years 1901–1981 and a declining trend during 1981–91, 1991–2001.

Table 3

Tempo of Urbanisation 1901–2001

Census Year	*Growth Rate of (%) Urban Population-Tempo*	*Growth Rate of (%) Rural Population-Tempo*
1901–1911	–0.5240	0.6184
1911–1921	0.8250	–0.0099
1921–1931	0.7054	–0.0924
1931–1941	1.4444	–0.2139
1941–1951	2.2160	–0.4072
1951–1961	0.3846	–0.0823
1961–1971	0.1492	–0.0329
1971–1981	2.4629	–0.6434
1981–1991	0.9734	–0.3161
1991–2001	0.7714	–0.2815

Source: Census of India 1901–2001.

Table 4

Number of Towns and Percentage of Urban Population by Size Class

Census	*No. of Towns by Size Class*						*Percentage of Urban Population by Size Class*					
	I	*II*	*III*	*IV*	*V*	*VI*	*I*	*II*	*III*	*IV*	*V*	*VI*
1901	24	43	130	391	744	479	26.0	11.2	15.6	20.8	20.1	6.1
1911	23	40	135	364	707	485	27.4	10.5	16.4	19.7	19.3	6.5
1921	29	45	145	370	734	571	29.7	10.3	15.9	18.2	18.6	7.0
1931	35	45	183	434	800	509	31.2	11.6	16.8	18.0	17.1	5.2
1941	49	74	242	498	920	407	38.2	11.4	16.3	15.7	15.0	3.1
1951	76	91	327	608	1124	569	44.6	9.9	15.7	13.6	12.9	3.1
1961	102	129	437	719	711	172	51.4	11.2	16.9	12.7	6.8	0.7
1971	148	173	558	827	623	147	57.2	10.9	16.0	10.9	4.4	0.4
1981	218	270	743	1,059	758	253	60.3	11.6	14.3	9.5	3.5	0.5
1991	300	345	947	1,167	740	197	65.2	10.9	13.1	7.7	2.6	0.3
2001	393	401	1,151	1,344	888	191	68.6	9.67	12.2	6.8	2.3	0.2

Class I: Greater than 1,00,000 population Class II: 50,000–1,00,000 population, Class III: 20,000–50,000 population Class IV: 10,000–20,000 population, Class V: 5,000–10,000 population Class VI: less than 5,000 population.

Source: Various Census Reports 1901–2001.

Million-Plus Cities in India

Number of million plus cities (Table 5) have increased from 5 in 1951 to 23 in 1991 and to 35 in 2001. About 37 per cent of the total urban population lives in these million plus/UA cities. As per 2001 census, the newly added million plus cities are 12 in numbers, they are Agra, Meerut, Nashik, Jabalpur, Jamshedpur, Asansol, Dhanbad, Faridabad, Allahabad, Amritsar, Vijaywada and Rajkot.

Table 5
Million Plus Cities in India

Rank	*City*	*Population in Million*			
		1951	*1971*	*1991*	*2001*
1	Mumbai	2.97	5.97	12.57	16.37
2	Kolkata	4.67	7.42	10.92	13.22
3	Delhi	1.44	3.65	8.38	12.79
4	Madras	1.54	3.17	5.36	6.42
5	Hyderabad	1.13	1.80	4.28	5.53
6	Bangalore	0.79	1.66	4.09	5.69
7	Ahmedabad	0.88	1.75	3.30	4.52
8	Pune	0.61	1.14	2.49	3.75
9	Kanpur	0.71	1.28	2.11	2.69
10	Nagpur	0.48	0.93	1.66	2.12
11	Lucknow	0.50	0.81	1.64	2.27
12	Surat	0.24	0.49	1.52	2.81
13	Jaipur	0.30	0.64	1.52	2.32
14	Kochi	0.18	0.51	1.14	1.35
15	Coimbatore	0.29	0.74	1.14	1.45
16	Vadodara	0.21	0.47	1.12	1.49
17	Indore	0.31	0.56	1.10	1.64
18	Patna	0.32	0.56	1.10	1.71
19	Madurai	0.37	0.71	1.09	1.19
20	Bhopal	0.10	0.38	1.06	1.45
21	Vishakapatnam	0.11	0.36	1.05	1.33
22	Varanasi	0.37	0.64	1.03	1.21
23	Ludhiana	0.15	0.40	1.01	1.40

Source: Census of India 1951–2001.

Problem of Urbanization

Problem of urbanization is manifestation of lopsided urbanization, faulty urban planning, and urbanization with poor economic base and without having functional categories.

Hence India's urbanization is followed by some basic problems in the field of: (1) housing, (2) slums, (3) transport, (4) water supply and sanitation, (5) water pollution and air pollution, (6) inadequate provision for social infra-structure (school, hospital, etc.). Class I cities such as Calcutta, Bombay, Delhi, Madras, etc. have reached saturation level of employment generating capacity (Kundu, 1997). Since these cities are suffering from urban poverty, unemployment, housing shortage, crisis in urban infra-structural services, these large cities cannot absorb these distressed rural migrants, i.e. poor landless illit-erate and unskilled agricultural labourers. Hence, this migration to urban class I cities causes urban crisis more acute.

Most of these cities using capital intensive technologies can not generate employment for these distress rural poor. So there is transfer of rural poverty to urban poverty. Poverty induced migration of illiterate and unskilled labourer occurs in class I cities addressing urban involution and urban decay.

Indian urbanization involutes not evolutes (Mukherji, 1995). Poverty induced migration occurs due to rural push. Megacities grow in urban population not in urban prosperity and culture. Hence, it is urbanization without urban functional characteristics. These mega cities are subject to extreme filthy slum and very cruel mega city denying shelter, drinking water, electricity, sanitation (Kundu, Bagchi and Kundu, 1999) to the extreme poor and rural migrants.

Urbanization is degenerating social and economic inequalities (Kundu and Gupta, 1996) which warrants social conflicts, crimes and anti-social activities. Lopsided and uncontrolled urbanization led to environmental degradation and degradation in the quality of urban life – pollution in sound, air, water, created by disposal of hazardous waste. Illiterate, low-skill or no-skill migrants from rural areas are absorbed in poor low grade urban informal sector at a very low wage rate and urban informal sector becomes in-efficient and unproductive.

Urban Development: Changing Paradigms

Development paradigms have undergone significant changes over the years. In the last decade, in particular, approaches to development and projects have undergone considerable change with significant policy shifts in governance, gender, poverty eradication and environmental issues. This has been marked by a shift from sectoral interventions in urban development to more 'holistic' or 'integrated' approaches.

Development strategies implemented by multi-lateral and bi-lateral agencies over the years can broadly be classified as:

1. Trickle Down Approach – from the late 1940s to early 1970s
2. Basic Needs/Redistribution with Growth – from early 1970s to mid 1980s
3. Structural Adjustment – from 1990s

Trickle Down Approach

The modernization strategies of the late 1940s to the early 1970s used Keynesian economic models of demand-led growth and were influenced by the development theories of Harrod-Domar, Rostow and Lewis. Such strategies were characterized by the inclusion of import substitution, the creation of internal markets, eradication of pre-capitalist relations and modes of production and rapid industrialization. All this was carried out in the belief that the gains of industrialization in the north could be transferred to less developed countries, and that poverty, inequality and unemployment would disappear naturally with growth. This approach was commonly known as the 'trickle down' theory – the benefits of growth and development were expected to trickle down to the poor from growth-specific policies.

Basic Needs Provision/Redistribution with Growth

The limited financial resources of national governments in the south and their rapid pace of urbanization meant that modernization strategies were unable to meet the basic needs or to improve the lives of the urban poor. This led to a shift of policy from 'growth' to the World Bank's 'redistribution and employment' in aid programmes. Hoogvelt (1982) termed this shift to redistribution with growth as a change from 'global Keynesian to global social democracy'. At this time the orthodoxy in housing policy for low income population shifted, from conventional state housing, which had failed to meet need, on any meaningful scale, to site and service and upgrading initiatives. There was an acceptance of the arguments of the self-help housing, informal sector, and intermediate technology schools (Turner, 1976).

Typical site and services projects involved providing areas of land equipped with basic urban services for people to construct their own shelter. Although some case studies indicate that these types of projects have brought material benefits to the urban poor, many evaluations show that little impact has been made with regard to the overall socio-economic situation of the people living in the settlements. Frequently, these projects failed to reach the poorest groups, who would often be unable to afford the payment installments or even secure loan finance, for a serviced site.

Redistribution to Adjustment

Structural adjustment programmes precipitated a shift to urban management and urban productivity interventions, rather than channelling aid to specific projects or programmes. This approach entailed policies concerned with urban development, decentralization, privatization, private sector and NGOs involvement in service delivery, regulatory reforms and initiatives to encourage community groups to invest in their own development initiatives. The theory was that by freeing up the constraints on markets through privatization, institutional reform and capacity building, cities would become more productive and the opportunities of the poor would be improved. This was called the *'enabling approach'* in which there was a theoretical movement away from large scale government projects which are spatially-focused to an emphasis on policy and institutional environments. This approach encouraged the non-statist provision of urban services (Harris, 1992; Moser, 1993; UNDP, 1999).

Despite the rhetoric of the enabling approach, there was still a very strong focus on projects and sectoral programmes concentrating on shelter and basic infrastructure.

Policies and Programme Strategies of Urban Development in India

A review of the evolution of policy perspective on urban development indicates that until the Sixth Plan (1980–85), the policies addressed largely the problems of housing, slums and provision of civic amenities. The Seventh Plan explicitly recognized the problems of urban poor but the issues of employment generation, pro-poor growth strategy and infrastructural requirement did not figure in the strategy for this sector. The Eighth Plan (1992–97) for the first time talked of urban policies that could directly contribute to the goals of employment generation and poverty reduction by directing growth in certain directions. It envisaged a role for the local bodies in city development and stipulated cost recovery to be built into the municipal finance system. This perspective has further been reinforced in the Ninth Plan (1997–2002), which talks of 'cities as engines of growth'. It also puts forward a vision of market-oriented growth with substantial reduction in budgetary allocations for development of urban infrastructure. The Ninth Plan document explicitly recognizes 'although urban poverty is no less severe than rural poverty, the priority accorded to alleviation of urban poverty is low as the common perception is that urban poverty is a transfer of rural poverty into urban areas'.

With the passing of the 74th Amendment to the Indian Constitution and corresponding legislation, amendments at the state level, decentralization has been hailed as a panacea for the problems of urban management in the country. All these basically attempt to achieve two objectives:

1. Enabling/facilitating the local bodies to undertake management, planning and development responsibility; and
2. Transferring powers to these bodies for generating adequate tax and non-tax revenue for this purpose.

Urban planning in India has undergone significant changes in terms of both policy and strategy since its inception. There have been three distinct identifiable 'waves' of urban development in the Indian context.

Housing was the first wave, which started in the 1950s and still continues to be a priority. Some of the significant initiatives under the scheme have been:

> The Subsidized Industrial Housing Scheme (SIHS) was started in 1952 and provided subsidy on house construction to industrial workers with the co-operation of their employers who were also encouraged to build townships and construct houses for their workers. Since all the urban poor could not be covered by the SIHS, a separate housing scheme was started for the Economically Weaker Section (EWS) in the same year and Low Income Group Housing Scheme (LIGHS) was started in 1954. A separate Ministry of Works and Housing in 1954 was set up and it was responsible for carrying out public works and housing schemes. It went through many changes in its name, role and responsibilities and was until recently called Ministry of Urban Development and Poverty Alleviation. In 1956, the government introduced Slum Areas (Improvement and Clearance) Programme in six major cities. It was essentially a beautification programme for the cities where slums were cleared more than improved for the perception of slums and their inhabitants was that they bred unwanted elements. The government activated its power of eminent domain by introducing the Land Acquisition and Development Scheme (LADS) in 1959 to legitimize clearance of slums, among other reasons.
>
> In 1986, the government launched the Twenty Point Programme (20PP), which was primarily a rural programme with small urban components. This started a trend of merging housing schemes with other schemes like education, sanitation, and water supply in larger programmes.

1. *Nehru Rozgar Yojana* – A scheme for employment through Housing And Shelter Up-gradation (NRY-SHASU, 1989), Prime Minister's Integrated Urban Poverty Eradication Programme (PMI-UPEP, 1995), National Slum Development Programme (NSDP, 1996), Valmiki Ambedkar Awas Yojana (VAMBAY, 2001) followed this trend by having a housing component among other objectives.

The National Co-operative Housing Federation of India (NCHF) was set up in 1969 during the period when co-operatives were seen as an efficient method to gather scarce resources and minimize costs. NCHF is responsible for promoting state and primary co-operatives for the low-income category. Housing Development Finance Corporation (HDFC) and National Housing Bank (NHB) were set up in 1977 and 1988 respectively, though they have fewer programmes for financing the urban poor.

2. *Welfare*: Social welfare programmes constitute the second wave that started with the Urban Community Development Programme in 1958 and gained popularity in the 1960s and 1970s. The initiation of the Urban Basic Services (UBS) programme in 1986 was a major step towards change in the perception of urban poverty. From being viewed as a single sector problem of housing, urban poverty began to be perceived as a multi-sector problem. At the behest of the National Commission on Urbanization (NCU 1988), this programme was revised and launched as Urban Basic Services for the Poor (UBSP) with three main objectives: Effective achievement of social sector goals by introducing innovations to be cost effective; Community organization, mobilization and empowerment; Convergence of all urban poverty programmes like EIUS, Nehru Rozgar Yojana, and Low Cost Sanitation (LCS) through sustainable support systems.

   JNNURM, launched in November 2005, is the most comprehensive programme of urban reforms so far. The focus of urban reforms under this programme is to create equitable and self-sustaining cities, in a first of its kind acknowledgement that comprehensive urban governance reforms are required on a number of fronts – devolution of funds, functions and functionaries to local governments, basic services to the urban poor, urban planning, formalizing citizen participation, urban land reforms to name a few.

3. *Credit* and *Employment Schemes*: These started in 1977. RBI expanded the coverage of its Differential Rate of Interest (DRI) scheme to include the urban poor. As a part of this scheme, commercial banks were expected to advance 0.33 per cent of their total advances as subsidized credit on easy terms to the urban poor. Women were declared as beneficiaries for an income-generating scheme of the Urban Community Development Programme in 1958. After that women are beneficiaries in UPAPs in their role as a mother while they are pregnant or lactating. The economic contribution of women and their role as income generators was recognized only in 1986 in programmes like Support to Training and Employment Programme for Women (STEP) or Urban Basic Services Programme.

   The Infrastructure Leasing and Financial Services (ILFS), established in 1989, has emerged as an important financial institution in recent years. Its activities have more or less remained confined to development of industrial townships and roads and highways where risks are comparatively less. It basically undertakes project feasibility studies and provides a variety of financial as well as engineering services.

The 12th Schedule of the 74th Constitutional Amendment Act, or the Nagarpalika Act of India, defined new tasks in the functional domain of the Urban Local Bodies, as follows:

1. Urban Planning including town planning.
2. Regulation of land use and construction of building.
3. Planning for economic and social development.
4. Roads and bridges.
5. Water supply for domestic, industrial and commercial purposes.
6. Public health, sanitation conservancy and solid waste management.
7. Fire services.
8. Urban forestry, protection of the environment and promotion of ecological aspects.
9. Safeguarding the interests of weaker sections of society, including the handicapped and mentally retarded.
10. Slum improvement and up gradation.
11. Urban poverty alleviation.
12. Promotion of cultural, educational and aesthetic aspects.

Problems and Human Rights Violation of Slum Dwellers

Provisional data relating to slums in the 2001 Census throw some interesting light on the slum population. Nearly 28 million persons lived in the slums in 1981, accounting for 17.5 per cent of the urban population. The estimates for 1991 were 45.7 million slum dwellers accounting for 21.5 per cent of population. According to the 2001 Census, there are 40.6 million persons living in slums in 607 towns/cities, and they account for 22.8 per cent of the population of these cities. However, the latest Census data also reflect the problems inherent in not having an accepted definition of slums and absence of proper listing of slum settlements in the urban offices concerned with slum improvement and civic amenities. The practice of notifying slums under relevant laws is not being followed, especially where the land involved belongs to government or any of its agencies. As a result of these lacunae, these data are not definitive because towns with less than 50,000 population, and slum clusters which are not formally or informally recognized if the population was less than 300 are excluded. While demographic data on slum populations and on civic amenities to slum dwellers from the Census are still awaited, there appears to be no change in the basic level or improvement in the features of slum settlements despite several decades of programmes for the environmental improvement and upgradation of slums. There is cause to wonder whether 'Cities without Slums' is a slogan about an objective, which, however desirable, is believed to be unreachable, or whether it is a serious planning and urban development concern. Certainly the degree of effort to upgrade slums to a more habitable level does not indicate a serious effort in this direction.

The Draft National Slum Policy drawn up by the Department of Urban Employment and Poverty Alleviation in the Ministry of Urban Development in April 1999 had been widely debated and many comments received. It needs to finalize. A National Policy on Slums is of great significance given the degree of wrong perception regarding the nature and extent of the slum problem. Such a policy can help bring an attitudinal change among the authorities and the people at large, including the urban poor and the slum dwellers, regarding measures to improve their quality of life and make our cities free from the worst features of slums. Slums are generally treated as the inevitable outcome of continuing migration of unskilled labour, but, in fact, most slum-dwellers are permanent residents of the city. In many instances, families in slums span several generations. The main objectives of a slum policy would be:

1. To create awareness of the underlying principles that guide the process of slum development and improvement and the options that are available for bringing about the integration of these settlements and the communities residing there with the urban area as a whole.
2. To strengthen the legal and policy framework to facilitate the process of slum development and improvement on a sustainable basis; to ensure that the slum population is provided civic services, amenities, and economic opportunities so as to enable them to rise above the degrading conditions in which they live.
3. To arrive at a policy of affirming the legal and tenurial rights of the slum-dwellers.
4. To establish a framework for involving all stakeholders in the efficient and smooth implementation of policy objectives.

Focusing on slums enables planners to look beyond income levels to neighbourhood and environmental considerations and this result in a more multi-dimensional view of urban poverty. In view of the progress made in decentralized urban governance through the 74th Constitutional Amendment, it is necessary to ask how this has benefitted the slum dwellers and provided them an increased opportunity to articulate their needs, and obtain assistance from civic authorities and urban planners. It does appear that the effort has been more towards providing some amount of civic services in an un-coordinated fashion than towards devising all-embracing programmes with participation of the slum dwellers themselves, and finding solutions which provide not only a decent quality of life with prospects of further improvement, but also make slums redundant in our urban habitations. Slum dwellers need not perennially be at the receiving end of selected doles but must be made part of the urban economic and social processes with adequate opportunities for improving their lives, while contributing what is acknowledged to be a major share in the economic activities of the cities. Upgradation of living conditions of the urban poor has to be recognized as part of the national development process. Some of the obvious lapses in slum programmes are:

1. Non-listing of all habitations, big or small, which should be classified as slums.
2. Lack of basic information on the number of households in such habitations, and the status of basic amenities.
3. Absence of a master plan for a period of five years to gradually increase the level of civic amenities.
4. Adherence to outdated and totally inadequate standards of services to the slum dwellers, under the EIUS component.
5. Failure to provide specific provisions in municipal laws for dealing with issues relating to the urban poor, slums, and economic planning for poverty alleviation, etc. which flow from the 74th Constitutional Amendment; failure to build up capacity in municipal bodies to provide the required services to slum communities and the urban poor.

6. Uncertainty regarding agency arrangement for various slum improvement tasks between the municipal authority, development authority, slum board, housing board, parastatals, etc. and failure to provide a coordinating institutional arrangement;
7. Failure to implement provisions made in Comprehensive Development Plans for the housing, and economic needs (production and marketing activities) of the urban poor, especially provision of land, and facilities for street vendors and hawkers. In the absence of such planning, unplanned growth takes place leading to 'informal' or unauthorized low quality settlements, and unauthorized hawking which subjects the poor to harassment from petty officials. It is often said that 'there is no place for the poor in town planning process' and even existing provisions are not implemented for the benefit of the urban poor.
8. Failure on the part of land-owning agencies on which slums are located to take decisions on permission to make environmental improvement and in situ upgradation of slum clusters. Failure to converge available civic services in sanitation, paved access and drainage, streetlights, health-care, water supply, education, etc. by organizing responsibility cells and involving the beneficiaries in planning of services. Lack of a commitment to achieve a breakthrough in bringing slum dwellers out of the stigma and misery of living in slums, and instead, use funds such as National Slum Development Programme for tinkering with the symptoms.

National Slum Policy

All the six mega cities and 35 metros with a population of over one million will be made slum-free by 2010 under the National Slum Policy being evolved by the centre. First time such a policy was being framed since there was no integrated approach to the development of slums. States could announce their own policies keeping in view the framework of the national policy, but they would be required to specify a cut-off date for the rehabilitation of slum-dwellers. Broadly, the components of the policy would include rehabilitation of slum dwellers, re-location from hazardous places and upgradation of infrastructure.

Slum Improvement: The policy of the government lays emphasis on environmental improvement of urban slums rather than their massive clearance and relocation, the scheme envisages provision of seven basic amenities viz., water supply, sewerage, community baths, improved pathways, community latrines, street lighting and other community facilities to the slum dwellers. Slum improvement is rewarding theft. The programme is linked with the Urban Basic Services for poor and Nehru Rojgar Yojana by involvement of resident associations. Government action has focused on welfare and habitat improvements under various poverty alleviation programmes but has been unable to make linkages between these improvements and increase in productivity and income of the urban poor.

Resettlement Programme: The uprooted people not only went back to their original sites in the city, leaving the allotted plots that could not guarantee them employment but also disrupted their social life. Resettlement programmes that have moved the poor to fringe areas to provide them with improved shelter and environment have been antagonistic to the space economy of the poor households, which is typified by the need to be near a variety of income-earning opportunities and have resulted in loss of income of the poor. Also, many of the income earning opportunities exist among the poor themselves but require a minimum density of poverty to remain viable. Thus, scale and concentration of poverty provides its own level of agglomeration economies to provide income-earning opportunities where more dispersed patterns of living would not.

Strategy for Slum Development

Urban slums pose yet another problem to the development of the city owing to inadequate infrastructural facilities and environmental degradation resulting in crimes, gambling, distress among youth, and anti social activities. Improvement of slums and upliftment of the economically weaker sections should get priority as these may slowly spill over to the other areas too. With a boom in the construction industry the migratory population in search of employment had taken shelter in the slums, further worsening the living conditions. To curb this problem, rehabilitation, improvement and partial clearance, prevention measures and prohibition, etc. should be taken up in slums. For the regularization of *kutchi basties*, a holistic approach may be adopted by networking services and other infrastructure, which may benefit rest of the city also. Integration of slum settlements into urban areas as a whole, having a framework for involving all stakeholders in the slum development process and strengthen the legal and policy frameworks should be undertaken at the local level to fulfil these aims. Granting security of tenure and title of land for the squatters is an important issue. Security of land tenure would enhance the creditworthiness of the beneficiaries and encourage the individuals to invest in shelter upgrading.

Land adjustment mechanism is extensively used for urban extension programmes in Tokyo and has been successfully implemented in Hyderabad for development of slum areas located on private lands. Under the Hyderabad Slum Improvement Project (HSIP), the private owners retained part of the land while the slum households were assisted to build low cost houses, at a higher density, on a smaller area of land. The grant of additional Floor-Space Index (FSI) for slum occupied lands works as an inducement for developers to create extra space for sale in the open market. The shelter programme for the urban poor should be linked with provision of employment. Slum improvement and urban renewal programmes are significant from the point of view of ensuring economic growth in the urban areas. Government has adopted programmes to upgrade slums. Housing improvements have been left to individuals based on the assumption that the low-income households could and would mobilize personal resources for housing improvements if their neighbourhoods were improved. Amelioration of urban poverty should be accorded the same priority as that given to the rural poverty. A credit support programme would encourage self-employment of the urban poor. Production and market support should be given to the self-employed urban poor. The steps on improvement of slums and the policy in regard to the employment opportunities for the slum dwellers and urban poor and other related issues should also find their mention in the policy document. An appropriate blend of policies and institutions can improve urban living conditions at various levels of economic development. Quality of life, which is often measured by the availability and efficiency of public services, is also a major issue.

Strategies and Action Plans

The strategy in the Eleventh Plan should lay emphasis on faster, broad-based and inclusive growth. The policies and action plan in urban development should be in consonance with putting the economic development on a sustainable growth trajectory with a growth rate of about 10 per cent by the end of the plan period. In urban areas, apart from improving the urban infrastructure services, productive employment opportunities need to be created at a faster pace than before. It should reduce intra-city disparities by ensuring access to basic physical and social infrastructure services to all. The steps initiated as part of the National Common Minimum Programme during the Tenth Five Year Plan need to be strengthened and consolidated further in the Eleventh Plan. The key element of the strategy in urban development is inclusive growth by providing access to the basic facilities and services to all in urban areas. In the long run, good infrastructure in city/town determines the level of development of economic opportunities in the future. The private sector has a critical role in achieving the objectives of faster and more inclusive growth. The urban areas need to provide a conducive environment where all sectors and groups participate in an equitable manner for sustainable growth of towns and cities.

Development from Above

Keeping in view the national level policies and goals for economic and urban development, there is a need to follow the concept of integrated development planning linking the development plans from national to local levels in an hierarchical framework. At the national level, a National Urbanization Policy is overdue and the time is ripe to formulate a long term National Urbanization Policy indicating the emerging pattern of urbanization and measures to channelize the future urban growth in an equitable and sustainable manner. Within the broad framework of National Urbanization Policy, Regional Development Plan at the State level may be formulated as a broad policy and vision document for development of urban and rural growth centres in an integrated manner. At the district and metropolitan area levels, the District Development Plan and Metropolitan Development Plan, as envisaged under 74th Constitution Amendment Act, should be prepared by DPC and MPC indicating the potentials and growth perspective of various settlements as part of urban-rural continuum. At local level, City Development Plans, Ward and Local Area Plans indicating vision of the cities, priorities of development, investment requirements, resource mobilization, land use and location of facilities and services along with development promotion regulations may be prepared by Urban Local Bodies for achieving the objectives of planned development.

Then the legal institutions, mass-media, social welfare agencies/civil societies, social workers need to work towards developing and building force among slum dwellers for collective mobilization. This collective mobilization would integrate the understanding of substantive equality and intersectional discrimination regarding basic needs which are supposed to protect under the Constitution as a rights. Here, need is to take some directions, by the above parties especially social workers, to develop strategies on substantive equality through:

1. *Building Collective Consciousness:* An effecting way of building collective consciousness is by begging a dialogue among slum dwellers which will allow them to arrive at an understanding of their rights. Such dialogue could be initiated through workshops, social meeting in which they will be guided to reflect on them. Besides this, an affective methodology could be inculcated, such as writing, reading and enacting their own life stories based on daily life experiences which would encourage ventilation as well as the ability to articulate confidently in numeral formal and informal sessions. Their real life also could be developed and portrayed through using the media as an alternative tool.
2. *Collective Mobilization:* To develop an effective strategy, to develop leadership and create spaces for their voices are the collective experiences. When they will come together, they will make a social group and it will help them to articulate, clarify and understand oppression and violation of human rights in a more nuanced manner. Within this process, while they have been able to develop this consciousness, the immediate need is to build upon these experiences, connect them to others to build solidarity, replicate these and develop further leadership more specifically at the bottoms, both in the urban and rural context. Collective decision making helps them to have a safe space where they are able to discuss and express their concerns easily.
3. *Capacity Building:* Capacity building is essential for them and it can be enabled by the social workers through empowering them. Social worker can initiate income generating programmes for slum dwellers and for them whose rights have been violated and for this 'advocacy' could be an effective technique to develop their inner-self and make them self-reliant.
4. *Dealing with Issues:* Social worker could, with the help of NGOs, welfare agencies or civil societies, take those issues to the people to give them justice. This could be a good platform for them who could share their expectations.
5. *Providing Legal Aids and Secure Rehabilitation:* A social worker can provide legal aids to the victims who need support and for this social worker needs to work with advocate, with laws, court, etc. A social worker has to fight with the strong system where it is not easy to do that but they can try through social action mobilizing mass support from all corners of the society.

References

Beall, Jo. 2002. 'Globalization and Social Exclusion in Cities: Framing the Debate with Lessons from Africa and Asia'. *LSE WP*. Series No. 02–27, February.

Bhagat, R.B. 1992. 'Components of Urban Growth in India with Reference to Haryana'. Findings from Recent Census. *Nagarlok*. Vol. 25, No. 3, pp. 10–14.

Brockerhoff, M. 1999. Urban Growth in Developing Countries: A Review of Projections and Predictions. *Population and development Review*. Vol. 25. No. 4, pp. 757–778.

Bolay, Jean-Claude. 2006. Slums and Urban Development: Questions on Society and Globalization. *The European Journal of Development Research*, Vol. 18, No. 2, June, pp. 284–296.

Brockerhoff, M. and E. Brennam. 1998. 'The Poverty of Cities in Developing Regions'. *Populations and Development Review*. Vol. 24, No. 1, pp. 75–114.

Breese, G. 1969. *Urbanisation in Newly Developing Countries*. New Delhi: Prentice Hall.

Davis, Kingsley and H.H. Golden. 1954. 'Urbanisation and Development in pre-Industrial Areas'. *Economic Development and Cultural Change*. Vol. 3, No. 1.

Davis, Kingsley. 1962. 'Urbanisation in India: Past and Future'. In R. Turner (ed.) *India's Urban Future.* Berkeley: University of California Press.

Davis, K. 1965. 'The Urbanization of the Human Population'. *Scientific American*. 213(3), pp. 41–53.

Dubey, A., S. Gangopadhyay and W. Wadhwa. 2001. 'Occupational Structure and Incidence of Poverty in Indian Towns of Different Sizes'. *Review of Development Economics,* 5(1), pp. 49–59.

Friedmann, J. 1995. 'Where We Stand? A Decade of World City Research'. In P. Knox and P. Taylor (eds) *World Cities in a World System.* Cambridge: Cambridge University Press, pp. 21–47.

Gill, H.S. 2008. 'FDI in Housing and Integrated Township in India'. Policy Paper Developed for the Ministry of Housing and Urban Poverty Alleviation. Government of India.

Gill, H.S. and S. Varma. 2007. 'Development Strategies for Inclusive Cities'. Paper Presented at APROS 2007, New Delhi.

Guliani, Manraj. 2006. 'Urban Infrastructure and its Ecological Demands and Constraints – An Indian Perspective'. *TERI*, December.

Kumar, Aniruddha. 2006. 'Governing Emerging Mega-cities: Challenges and Perspectives'. JNNURM, December.

Kundu, Amitabh, Harbans Gill, D. Kundu and Niroop. 2007. 'Migration and Urbanisation in the Context of Development Dynamics'. Governmental Programmes and Evolving Institutional Structure in India, UNDF.

Kundu, A. and N. Sarangi. 2005. 'Employment Guarantee: Issue of Urban Exclusion'. *Economic and Political Weekly*. August 13, pp. 3242.

Kundu, A. 1983. 'Theories of City Size Distribution and Indian Urban Structure: A Reappraisal'. *Economic and Political Weekly*. 18(3): 345–347.

——. 1994. 'Pattern of Urbanisation with Special Reference to Small and Medium Towns in India'. In G.K. Chadha (ed.) *Sectoral Issues in the Indian Economy.* New Delhi: Har-Anand Publications.

Kundu, A., S. Bagchi and D. Kundu. 1999. 'Regional Distribution of Infrastructure and Basic Amenities in Urban India: Issues Concerning Empowerment of Local Bodies'. *Economic and Political Weekly*. 34(28), July 10: 787–789.

Kundu, A. and S. Gupta. 2000. 'Declining Population Mobility, Liberalization and Growing Regional Imbalances: The Indian Case'. In A. Kundu (ed.) *Inequality, Mobility and urbanization*. Indian Council of Social Science Research. New Delhi: Manak Publications.

Logan, J. and L. Molototch. 1987. *Urban Fortunes: The Political Economy of Place*. Berkeley: University of California Press.

Mahadevia, Darshini. 2004. *Inclusive Mega-cities in Asia in a Globalizing World*. Ahmedabad: Centre for Development Alternatives.

Marcuse, P. and R. van Kempen. 2000. 'Conclusion: A New Spatial Order'. In P. Marcuse and R. van Kempen (eds) *Globalizing Cities: A New Spatial Order.* London: Blackwell, pp. 249–275.

Mathur, Om Prakash. 2003. 'Impact of Globalisation on Cities and City-related Policies in India'. The Urban Partnerships Foundation. Occasional Paper No. 4, August.

Mathur, O.P. 1999. 'Fiscal Innovations and Urban Governance'. In O.P. Mathur (ed.) *India: The Challenge of Urban Governance.* New Delhi: National Institute of Public Finance and Policy.

Ministry of Urban Development. 1992. 'The Constitution Seventy-fourth Amendment Act 1992 on Municipalities'. New Delhi: Government of India.

Moser, C. 1993. 'Urban Social Policy and Poverty Reduction'. *TWURD,* Working Paper No. 10. Washington DC: World Bank.

——. 1997. 'Urban Social Policy and Poverty Reduction'. *The Challenge of Sustainable Cities.* London: ZED Press.

——. 1998. 'The Asset Vulnerability Framework: Re-addressing Urban Poverty Reduction Strategies'. *World Development*. Vol. 26 (1), pp. 1–19.

Moonis, Raza and A. Kundu. 1978. 'Some Aspects of Dis-functional Characteristics of Urbanisation'. *Socio-Economic Development Problems in South and South East Asia*. Bombay: Popular Prakashan.

Mukherji, Shekhar. 1993. 'Poverty Induced Migration and Urban Involution in India: Cause and Consequences'. International Institute for population Sciences. pp. 1–91.

——. 2001. 'Linkage between Migration, Urbanization and Regional Disparities in India: Required Planning Strategies'. *IIPS Research Monograph,* Bombay, pp. 1–226.

Nayak, P.R. 1962. 'The Challenge of Urban Growth to Indian Local Government'. In R. Turner (ed.) *India's Urban Future*. Berkeley: University of California Press.

Pathak, P. and D. Mehta. 1995. 'Recent Trend in Urbanisation and Rural-Urban Migration in India: Some Explanations and Projections'. *Urban India*, Vol. 15, No. 1, pp. 1–17.

Palnitkar, S. and D. Kundu. 2005. 'Achieving the Millennium Development Goals, Financing Housing, Water and Sanitation in the Cities of Middle-Income Countries: The Case of Delhi (mimeo)'. UNDP.

Premi, M.K. 1991. 'India's Urban Scene and Its Future Implications, *Demography India*, 20(1) pp. 324–329.

Registrar General. 1991. Census of India, Emerging Trends of Urbanisation in India, Occasional paper No. 1 of 1993, Registrar General, New Delhi.

Rao, P.S.N. 1999. 'Financing Urban Infrastructure: The Emerging Trends'. Papers of the International Seminar on Financing and Pricing of Urban Infrastructure, Human Settlement Management Institute, New Delhi.

Registrar General. 2001: Census of India 2001, Government of India.

Sen, A. and J. Ghosh. 1993. 'Trends in Rural Employment and Poverty Employment Linkage'. ILO-ARTEP Working Paper, New Delhi.

Sovani, N.V. 1966. *Urbanization and Urban India*. Bombay: Asia Publishing House.

UNDP. 1999. *Cities, People and Poverty: Urban Development Co-operation for the1990s*. UNDP Strategy Paper.

UN-HABITAT. 2003. *The Challenge of Slums: Global Report on Human Settlements*. UN- Habitat.

United Nations. 2003. *Cities of Today, Cities of Tomorrow*, United Nations, Geneva.

United Nations. 1992. *World Urbanization Prospects: The 1992 Revision.* New York: UN.

Varma, S. 2007. 'Development Strategies for Inclusive Cities'. *Shelter* 10(1), pp. 69–75.

11

Does Women Empowerment Ensure Mitigation of Domestic Violence in India?

JHILAM RUDRA DE

> You can tell the condition of a nation by looking at the status of its women.
>
> —Jawaharlal Nehru

The Indian Constitution grants women equal rights with men, but strong patriarchal traditions persist, with women's lives shaped by customs that are centuries old. Violence against women is the most pervasive Human Rights violation in the world today. Not necessarily do criminals live around rural thatched roofs only. They are found in sky scrapers and posh residential areas too. In 2009, rape cases in India had reached 2,497, domestic violence had crossed the 10,000 mark. In short, women are still treated as a lesser person. Much to their surprise, most Indian women are not even aware of their rights in a man's world. Women are principal providers of care and support to families. But in recent years, there has been an alarming rise in atrocities against women in India, in terms of rapes, assaults and dowry-related murders. Fear of violence suppresses the aspirations of women. Female infanticide and sex-selective abortions are additional forms of violence that reflect the devaluing of females in Indian society. While women are guaranteed equality under the Constitution, legal protection has little effect in the face of prevailing patriarchal traditions. Every social indicator shows a fundamental social bias and inequality. The latest Census (2001) data showing six point increase in sex ratio (number of females per 1,000 males) between the Census years 1991 and 2001 have come under cloud and doubts have been expressed whether women were under-enumerated in 1991 or they were over-enumerated in 2001. During the 10 year period between the two Censuses, considerable progress has been made in the domain of literacy. During the period under review overall literacy increased by 34.46 percentage points – that of males and females by 30.46 and 40.60 percentage points, respectively. Violence against women is a pandemic, one that transcends the bounds of geography, race, culture, class and religion. It touches virtually every community, in virtually every corner of the globe. Too often sanctified by custom and reinforced by institutions, it thrives on widespread impunity for perpetrators in what remains a patriarchal world that is reluctant to grant women equal rights and protection from gender-based violence.

Table 1

Sex-Ratio in India

Year	1901	1911	1921	1931	1941	1951	1961	1971	1981	1991	2001
Females per 1,000 males	972	964	955	950	945	946	941	930	934	927	933

Source: Government of India (2001). Census of India 2001.

Women receive far less education than men, due to both social norms and fears of violence. India has the largest population of non-school-going working girls.

India's Constitution guarantees free primary school education for both boys and girls up to age 14. This goal has been repeatedly reconfirmed, but primary education in India is not universal.

Sonalde Desai in *Gender Inequalities and Demographic Behaviour* (1994) asserts that parents' reluctance to educate daughters has its roots in the situation of women. Parents have several incentives for not educating their daughters. Foremost is the view that education of girls brings no returns to parents and that their future roles, being mainly reproductive and perhaps including agricultural labour, require no formal education. As more and more boys are engaged in education, there is a growing reliance on the labour of girls. Girls are increasingly replacing their brothers on the farm while carrying on their usual responsibilities in housework. A large proportion of the roughly 40 million 'nonworking' girls who are not in school are kept at home because of responsibilities in housework.'

Table 2

Literacy Rate in India

Year	*Male*	*Female*	*Total*
1991	42.85	52.74	32.17
2001	75.85	54.16	65.38

Source: Government of India (2001). Census of India 2001.

Chart 1

Increase in Sex Ratio

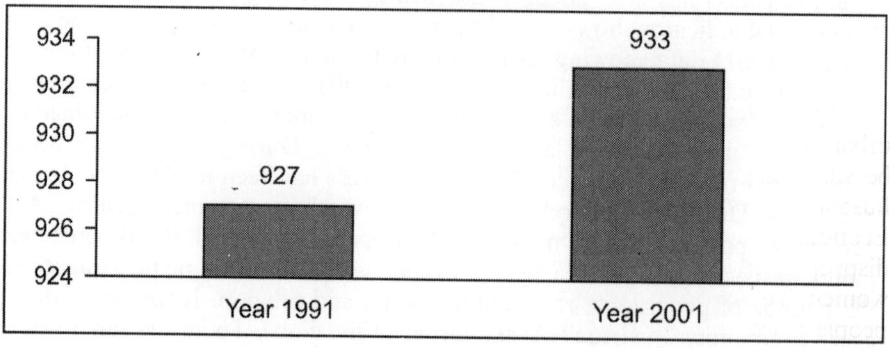

Chart 2

Literacy in Two Census Decades

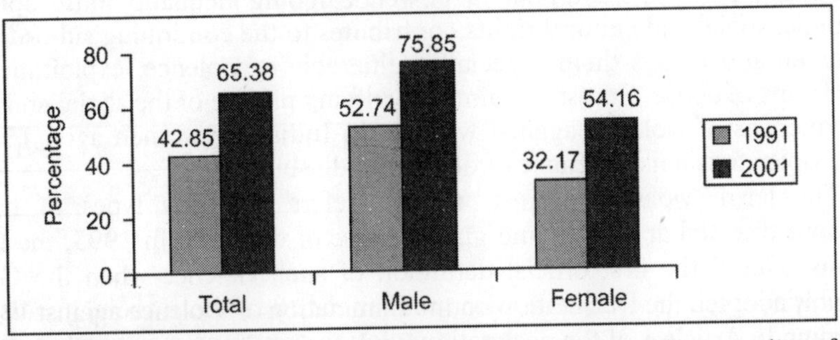

Though level of education and sex ratio have increased but, quality of life of women in this country is poor till now. The indexes show that, infant mortality rate per 1,000 live births is 70, total fertility rate (births per woman) is 3.2 and maternal mortality rate per 1,00,000 live births is 410. All these critical indicators contribute to the vulnerability of women, leading to all kinds of abuse and exploitation. The human development index identifies three basic parameters – literacy and education, expectation of life at birth and measures of material well-being. In this scenario, there is a vulnerability quotient, which is adverse to poverty reduction and sustainable development.

Figure 1

Vulnerability Nexus – Adverse to Poverty Reduction and Sustainable Human Development

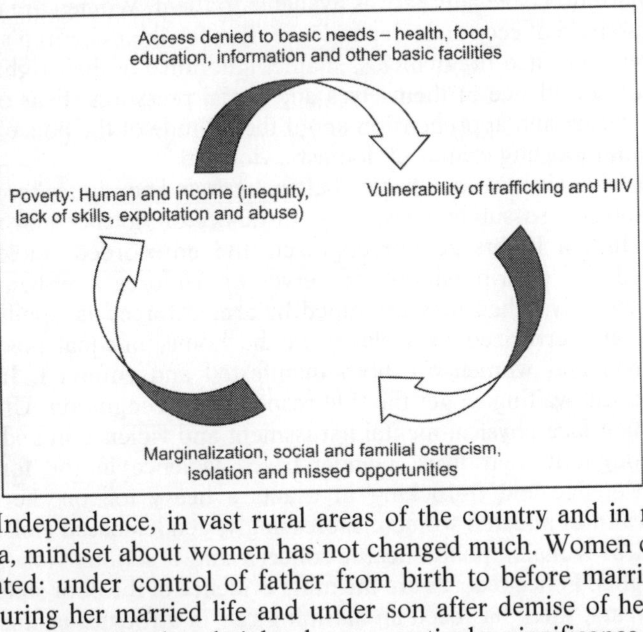

Post-Independence, in vast rural areas of the country and in majority of urban India, mindset about women has not changed much. Women continue to be subjugated: under control of father from birth to before marriage, under husband during her married life and under son after demise of her husband. Economic, social and cultural rights have a particular significance due to the disproportionate effect of poverty and social and cultural marginalization on women. Today, women represent approximately 70 per cent of the 1.2 billion people living in poverty throughout the world. Inequality with respect to the enjoyment of economic, social and cultural rights is a central fact of women's lives in every country in the world, and is a central manifestation of women's lesser social, economic and political power. Ongoing inequality in the sphere of economic, social and cultural rights contributes to the continuing subordination of women and makes them especially vulnerable to violence, exploitation and other forms of abuse. Statistics paint a horrifying picture of the social and health consequences of violence against women. In India, for women aged 15 to 44 years, violence is a major cause of death and disability.

The term 'violence against women' refers to many types of harmful behaviour directed at women and girls because of their sex. In 1993, the United Nations offered the first official definition of such violence when the General Assembly adopted the Declaration on the Elimination of Violence against Women. According to Article 1 of the declaration, violence against women includes:

> Any act of gender-based violence that results in, or is likely to result in, physical, sexual or psychological harm or suffering to women, including threats of such acts, coercion or arbitrary deprivations of liberty, whether occurring in public or private life.

Why Women are Abused?

It is a great tragedy that for most abused women, violence begins at home with husbands, fathers, brothers and uncles. In developed and developing countries alike, physical, sexual and psychological abuse within the family affects an astounding number of women. The reason why so many women 'put up with' abuse in the home is primarily due to their unequal status in society and the fact that they have no viable alternatives available to them. Women are often caught in a vicious circle of economic dependence, fear for their children's lives as well as their own, repeated pregnancies, shame, ignorance of their rights before the law, lack of confidence in themselves and social pressures. Fear of harming a husband's career and apprehension about the attitude of the police also prevent women from reporting crimes of domestic violence.

Violence against women begins before birth and continues throughout life, in subtle and not-so-subtle ways. Most instances of violence and violations of women's Human Rights go unrecognized and unrecorded. Violence against women feeds off discrimination and serves to reinforce it. When women are abused in custody, when they are raped by armed forces as 'spoils of war', or when they are terrorized by violence in the home, unequal power relations between men and women are both manifested and enforced. In India, the women are still waiting to get the due respect and recognition. Unlike ancient times, women face physical mental harassment and violence in and outside the family throughout their lives. Gender-based violence in the form of rape, domestic violence and trafficking in exacts a heavy toll on the mental and physical health of affected women. Increasingly, gender-based violence is being recognized as a major public health concern and a serious violation of basic Human Rights. Police records are the mute evidence of the poor state of woman. In recent years, there has been an alarming rise in atrocities against women in India. Statistical evidences show that in every 26 minutes, a woman is molested; every 34 minutes a rape takes place; every 42 minutes a sexual harassment incident occurs; every 43 minutes a woman is kidnapped and every 93 minutes a woman is burnt to death over dowry. One-quarter of the reported rapes involve girls under the age of 16, but the vast majority are not reported. Violence against women is compounded by discrimination on the grounds of race, ethnicity, sexual identity, social status, class, and age. Such multiple forms of discrimination further restrict women's choices, increase their vulnerability to violence and make it even harder for women to obtain justice.

For a country that registers two million cases of female infanticide and nearly 5,000 dowry deaths ever year, the less spoken on the status of its women, the better. The most devastating fact is that the nation of mothers still follows a culture where people idolizes son and mourns daughters. The UN figures out that about 7,50,000 girls are aborted every year in India. Abortion rates are increasing in almost 80 per cent of the Indian states, mainly Punjab and Haryana. These two states have the highest number of abortions every year. If the practice continues, then a day will come when Mother India will have no mothers, potentially, no life.

It is not the end of the whole story. The exploitation of women in India is not only limited to her childhood days, it remains constantly with her throughout the life though the nation nowadays is trying to prove that Indian women are more empowered than past, and as a healthy girl child, healthy adolescent, healthy mother, she will ensure a healthy nation.

Apart from childhood blues, the adolescent girls also face different economic, social and health related problems in this special period of life. Adolescence in girls has been recognized as a most vital period in their life cycle that requires specific and special attention. Unfortunately, the special needs of adolescents are rarely addressed by the educational, health, and family welfare programmes in India. Adolescence is a transition phase through which a child becomes an adult. It is the period during which rapid physical growth, physiological and psychosocial changes, the development of secondary sexual characteristics, and reproductive maturation occur. During adolescence, an intense sexual drive develops and adolescents typically start exploring relationships with the opposite sex. Adolescents start defining social relationships outside of the family. Their behaviour is guided by an intense desire for independence and identity. In the process, adolescents, specially the young women of India undergo intense psychological stress and personality change.

New studies on adolescent girls have found that one in four has been sexually or physically abused or forced by relatives to have sex against her will resulting in depression, teenage pregnancy, showing signs of risky health behaviours, including smoking, drinking and using drugs, eating disorders, etc. Sexual abuse of children as well as adolescent girls remain the most under-reported crime in the country. Child abuse is a crime that cuts across caste and class divides, and results in lifelong physical and psychological damage to the child. In the majority of cases, the offender is a member of the family. Since the abuser has relatively easy access to the child, abuse can be continual and can range from fondling and molestation to rape over a long period of time. In most cases, families are extremely reluctant to report the offence, since it involves 'family honour'. When they do gather the courage and resolve to take up the case, the child is exposed to a humiliating and traumatic process with no guarantee of justice at the end of it.

The traumatic journey of an Indian woman begins before birth and ends at the last day of her life, as at birth she is unwanted, she is not sent to school, and she is given less food to curtail her early growth. During childhood, her brother is loaded with new shoes, dresses and books to learn while she is gifted a broom, a wiper and lots of tears. She works in the home, looks after siblings, and assists her mother in the fields. In her teenage years, she misses tasty delicious food to eat and get only the crumbs. During her college days, she is forced to get married, a stage where illiteracy and lack of education has resulted in high fertility rate, aggravating the condition of females in the country. Again if this female gives birth to a girl child, the journey begins once again. She misses all roses of life and is finally fitted to a graveyard.

Around two-third of married women in India are victims of domestic violence and one incident of violence translates into women losing seven working days in the country, a United Nations report said domestic violence refers to violence, perpetrated within the home and the family.

'Domestic violence is not simply an argument. It is patterns of coercive control that one person exercises over another. Abusers use physical and sexual violence, threats, emotional insults and economic deprivation as a way to dominate their victims and get their way' (Susan Scheter, visionary leader in the movement to end family violence).

Far from being a heaven of safety and security, the family can be a 'cradle of violence'. Much of the violence within a home is directed against female members. Although the family is a source of love, sympathy and support, it is also the source of inequality, exploitation and violence. Mahatma Gandhi opines that violence includes exploitation – economic, social, and political – of an individual by an individual or of a nation by a nation and so on. Domestic violence includes all actions or behaviour of family members which causes either physical injury or emotional trauma or both to a woman. The expression of domestic violence can be seen in the form of wife battering, demand for more dowry, divorce, bride burning and conflicts in family life. The increased economic insecurity, unemployment and poverty in families may result in alcoholism, lack of status and sense of belongingness and fulfillment of basic needs, etc. Many affect women directly in the form of increased domestic violence. While science and technology are advancing, economic and social problems are worsening. Domestic violence is generally associated with very obvious physical, sexual and psychological abuse and torture of the woman. However, the scope of domestic violence extends further. It includes all such acts of intimidation and cruelty which force women to seek the help of outside agencies, other than the family or kin group.

Domestic violence includes not only inter-spousal violence, but also violence perpetrated by other family members. Generally, an important part of the power relationship between spouses and their families relates to dowry and its ramifications. Domestic violence can also be defined as 'anything that is experienced as fearful, controlling and threatening when used by those with power (invariably men) against those without power (mainly women and children)'. Domestic violence includes harassment, maltreatment, brutality or cruelty and even the threat of assault – intimidation. It includes physical injury, as well as 'willfully or knowingly placing or attempting to place a spouse in fear of injury and compelling the spouse by force or threat to engage in any conduct or act, sexual or otherwise, from which the spouse has a right to abstain'. Confining or detaining the spouse against one's will or damaging property are also considered as acts of violence. According to a survey in few states of India, illiterate women face more violence than literate women. Relationship between abusive behaviour and level of education has been found to be statistically significant. Illiterate women and those with education up to primary level tend to be more subjected to violence as compared to those who had received education beyond the primary level. It is also true that men, whose educational attainment is low, are more likely to beat their wife than men who are better educated.

Dowry is a social evil but continues to be a common practice in almost every part of India. Women at the time of marriage are expected to bring with them jewellery, cash and even consumer durables as a part of dowry to the in-laws and they are subsequently ill-treated, tortured or often violently burnt to death if they fail to do so. Every day, 50 cases of dowry related violence are reported and every third minute, a case of violence against woman is registered in India.

The forms of violence commonly found are slapping, kicking, tearing hair, pushing and pulling, hitting with an object, attempting to strangulate and threatening. Forms of psychological abuse were also found to exist, for instance, verbal abuse, sarcastic remarks in the presence of outsiders, imposing severe restrictions on freedom of movement, totally ignoring the wife in decision making processes, making frequent complaints against her to her parents, friends, neighbours, and kin much to the embarrassment of the wife. Some of the reasons given by the women were financial matters, behaviour with in-laws, back-biting, talking to any male without the liking of the husband, asking for money, preventing him from drinking and husbands' personality traits.

Types of Domestic Violence

1. *Physical Violence:* Which may lead to assault, serious injury or burns even if death of the victim.
2. *Sexual Violence:* Means robbing the dignity of women not only be indecent behaviour but also an esteem form of rape or ravishing her by use of force by family members and outsiders.
3. *Verbal Violence:* Which means indecency or use of abusive and filthy language against a woman or her near and dear ones.
4. *Social Violence:* Which includes demeaning, disparaging and humiliating a woman or her parental relatives and friends.
5. *Emotional Violence:* Leading to internal deprivation of love and affection, concern, sympathy and care and depriving her custody of children.
6. *Financial Violence:* Means depriving her of financial means and bare necessities of daily life and this also include taking away the assets which a woman possesses or earns.
7. *Intellectual Violence:* Means non-submission for confrontation or discussion for pressing issues, denial of rights to take part in decision making, etc.
8. *Other form of Violence:* May include not letting her avail the educational opportunities, denial of her reproductive rights, denial of access to health facilities or opportunities and to use her political rights, etc.
9. *State, Communal and Caste Instigated Violence:* Victims of state sponsored violence are mostly women. Caste and communal violence mostly target the women. 'Dishonouring' women is the most accepted norm of taking revenge on specified castes and communities.

Causes of Domestic Violence

Domestic violence against women is an age-old phenomenon. Women were always considered weak, vulnerable and in a position to be exploited. Violence has long been accepted as something that happens to women. Cultural mores, religious practices, economic and political conditions may set the precedence for initiating and perpetuating domestic violence, but ultimately committing an act of violence is a choice that the individual makes out of a range of options. Although one cannot underestimate the importance of macro system-level forces (such as cultural and social norms) in the etiology of gender-based violence within any country, including India, individual-level variables (such as observing violence between one's parents while growing up, absent or rejecting father, delinquent peer associations) also play important roles in the development of such violence. The gender imbalance in domestic violence is partly related to differences in physical strength and size. Moreover, women are socialized into their gender roles in different societies throughout the world. In societies with a patriarchal power structure and with rigid gender roles, women are often poorly equipped to protect themselves if their partners become violent. However, much of the disparity relates to how men-dependence and fearfulness amount to a cultural disarmament. Husbands who batter wives typically feel that they are exercising a right, maintaining good order in the family and punishing their wives' delinquency – especially the wives' failure to keep their proper place.

Table 3

Factors Perpetuating Domestic Violence

Cultural	• Gender-specific socialization • Cultural definitions of appropriate sex roles • Expectations of roles within relationships • Belief in the inherent superiority of males • Values that give men proprietary rights over women and girls • Notion of the family as the private sphere and under male control • Customs of marriage (bride price/dowry) • Acceptability of violence as a means to resolve conflict
Economic	• Women's economic dependence on men • Limited access to cash and credit • Discriminatory laws regarding inheritance, property rights, use of communal lands, and maintenance after divorce or widowhood • Limited access to employment in formal and informal sectors • Limited access to education and training for women
Legal	• Lesser legal status of women either by written law and/or by practice • Laws regarding divorce, child custody, maintenance and inheritance • Legal definitions of rape and domestic abuse • Low levels of legal literacy among women • Insensitive treatment of women and girls by police and judiciary
Political	• Under-representation of women in power, politics, the media and in the legal and medical professions • Domestic violence not taken seriously • Notions of family being private and beyond control of the state • Risk of challenge to status quo/religious laws • Limited organization of women as a political force • Limited participation of women in organized political system

Source: Heise, 1994.

Domestic violence is a global issue reaching across national boundaries as well as socio-economic, cultural, racial and class distinctions. This problem is not only widely dispersed geographically, but its incidence is also extensive, making it a typical and accepted behaviour. Domestic violence is widespread, deeply ingrained and has serious impacts on women's health and well-being. Its continued existence is morally indefensible. Its cost to individuals, to health systems and to society is enormous. Yet no other major problem of public health has been so widely ignored and so little understood.

According to a recent report of National Crimes Records Bureau (NCRB), violence against women is rampant in India, with southern Indian state of Andhra Pradesh having the worst record for crimes against women. For the year 2007–08, NCRB recorded 24,738 cases of crimes committed against women including 1,070 cases of rape, 1,564 cases of kidnapping and abduction, 7,613 cases of dowry deaths and 11,335 cases of domestic violence in Andhra Pradesh. Uttar Pradesh has also witnessed a stepping of crime against women with the state recording 21,215 cases of violence, including 2,066 cases of dowry death, 1,532 cases of rape and 3,819 cases of kidnapping. The NCRB also highlighted many incidents of rape of minor girls committed by the police personnel. Similarly, Haryana, a small state, has recorded 4,645 incidents of crime with as many as 269 cases of dowry deaths and 488 cases of rape. Bihar leads in cases of domestic violence with 59 per cent of married women suffering domestic violence. The NCRB recorded 7,548 cases of crime with 1,555 rape cases, 1,172 dowry death cases and 1,260 kidnapping and abduction cases in the state. These are the statistics of only the reported cases whereas several cases of violence against women goes unreported due to social stigmas attached to them and due to the fear of reprisals and threats from the culprits.

Health Effects

Health consequences can result directly from violent acts or from the long-term effects of violence.

- *Injuries:* Physical and sexual abuse by a partner is closely associated with injuries. Violence by an intimate partner is the leading cause of non-fatal injuries to women in India.
- *Death:* Deaths from violence against women includes honour killings (by families for cultural reasons); suicide; female infanticide (murder of infant girls); and maternal death from unsafe abortion.
- *Sexual and reproductive health:* Violence against women is associated with sexually transmitted infections such as HIV/AIDS, unintended pregnancies, gynaecological problems, induced abortions, and adverse pregnancy outcomes, including miscarriage, low birth weight and foetal death.
- *Risky behaviours:* Sexual abuse as a child is associated with higher rates of sexual risk-taking (such as first sex at an early age, multiple partners and unprotected sex), substance use, and additional victimization. Each of these behaviours increases risks of health problems.
- *Mental health:* Violence and abuse increase risk of depression, post-traumatic stress disorder, sleep difficulties, eating disorders and emotional distress.

- *Physical health:* Abuse can result in many health problems, including headaches, back pain, abdominal pain, fibromyalgia, gastrointestinal disorders, limited mobility, and poor overall health status.

Social and Economic Costs

Although most women in India work and contribute to the economy in one form or another, much of their work is not documented or accounted for in official statistics. Women plough fields and harvest crops while working on farms, women weave and make handicrafts while working in household industries, women sell food and gather wood while working in the informal sector. Additionally, women are traditionally responsible for the daily household chores (e.g. cooking, fetching water, and looking after children). More importantly, however, cultural practices vary from region to region. Though it is a broad generalization, north India tends to be more patriarchal and feudal than south India. Women in northern India have more restrictions placed on their behaviour, thereby restricting their access to work. Moreover, the social and economic costs of violence against women are enormous and have ripple effects throughout society. Women may suffer isolation, inability to work, loss of wages, lack of participation in regular activities, and limited ability to care for themselves and their children.

Yet these facts of domestic violence most probably represent only the tip of the iceberg, considering that only a fraction of all cases are ever reported. It is particularly ironic that, in spite of impressive economic, technological and social progress world-wide, millions of women around the world are routinely abused within their own homes – a tragic crime which needs to be urgently addressed and vigorously tackled.

Women Empowerment and Role of Education

To come out from this phase, educated society is of utmost importance. Education is the basic tool for empowering a woman. The comparison of the results obtained from the 1991 and 2001 censuses indicates that illiteracy has been declining among males and females in most states. However, the situation is still critical in states like Bihar, Rajasthan, Jammu and Kashmir, where female illiteracy is much higher than the national average. There are only three states – Kerala, Delhi, and Goa – where female illiteracy is 25 per cent or less.

There was a sharp decline in the proportion of female adolescents (ages 15–17) attending the school. Only 40.3 per cent attended school compared to 57.7 per cent of their male counterparts. Location had a significant influence on the schooling of females. In rural areas, only 32.7 per cent of female adolescents (ages 15–17) attended school compared with 60.5 per cent of female adolescents in urban areas. The attitude of adolescent girls towards population problem is poor among the rural as well as urban adolescent girls. However, urban adolescent girls are having relatively more awareness on the subject.

If we consider the number of female school dropouts, then the following question will definitely tickle like why did a fairly large number of adolescent girls not attend school? More than one-quarter of girls' lack of education was ascribed to their responsibilities for caring for siblings at home and other household responsibilities. In India, the minimum age for working in any factory or mine is 14 years and the minimum age for government jobs is 18 years, but use of young child labourers is quite prevalent.

The exploitation of the girl child as well as older woman in our society, can be nullified, if they are exposed to better education and can be empowered more, to work for their own benefit. They should be given chances to take active participation in decision making process, for herself, for her family and for the society as a whole.

Women empowerment is somehow too much dependent on the term women literacy. But according to last Census held in 2001, the percentage of female literacy in the country is 54.16 per cent. The literacy rate in the country has increased from 18.33 per cent in 1951 to 65.38 per cent as per 2001 Census. The female literacy rate has also increased from 8.86 per cent in 1951 to 54.16 per cent. It is noticed that the female literacy rate during the period 1991–2001 increased by 14.87 per cent whereas male literacy rate rose by 11.72 per cent. Hence, the female literacy rate actually increased by 3.15 per cent more compared to male literacy rate.

This is an encouraging fact for the country as a whole, but still Indian women have to go many a mile. Factors mainly responsible for poor female literacy rate are gender based inequality, social discrimination and economic exploitation, occupation of girl child in domestic chores, low enrollment of girls in schools, low retention rate and high dropout rate. The cause for the sad situation is the view of the parents that education of girls brings no returns to parents. This is the evidence that gender equity is a 'luxury good'; the demand for female schooling is more income elastic than that for male schooling. However, in urban India the view is changing as more and more families are taking up family planning and treating their daughters no less than their sons. But rural India, which constitutes around 70 per cent of the population, is still orthodox in their approach. The irony is that in spite of the fact that women contribute much to society, they work longer hours and their work is more arduous than men's. Yet men report that women, like children, are the non-productive part of the community.

It is assumed by social scientists, that, women's economic dependence on men impacts their power within the family. With increased participation in income-earning activities, not only will there be more income for the family, but gender inequality would be reduced. This issue is particularly salient in India because studies show a very low level of female participation in the active labour force. There are adequate provisions made in the Indian Constitution to empower woman and to ensure gender equity in various functionaries of government. Proposed Women Reservation Bill is one such attempt in this direction.

Constitutional Provisions for Indian Women

1. Equality before the law. Article 14
2. No discrimination by the State on the grounds only of religion, race, caste, sex, place of birth or any of these. Article 15(1)
3. Special provisions to be made by the State in favour of women and children. Article 15(3)
4. Equality of opportunity for all citizens in matters relating to employment or appointment to any office under the State. Article 16

5. State policy to be directed to securing for men and women equally, the right to an adequate means of livelihood. Article 39(a)
6. Equal pay for equal work for both men and women. Article 39(d)
7. Provisions to be made by the State for securing just and humane conditions of work and for maternity relief. Article 42
8. To promote harmony and to renounce practices derogatory to the dignity of women. Article 51(A)(e)

India, among few leading countries, had been a land where woman had been given the right to vote. There is no question of any less efficiency, ability and productivity in women than men. A country cannot realize its dream of becoming super power by ignoring the better half of the humanity. Researches have proved that a country where there are more employment opportunities for woman tend to provide better and honest governance.

But inequality and gender biasness is present throughout the society. To remove these misconceptions and empower a woman to think and decide for herself and help in the educational and mental development of her own children, a woman has to receive education first. To this end, after much deliberation, the adolescent age group was targeted and many schemes were thought of which would address the peculiar nature of the problems facing them. Most of the programmes were started on an experimental basis, to be followed-up and then, after making the necessary need-based alterations, these were implemented elsewhere in the country.

Education of women is always a critical input for improving nutrition levels, raising the age at marriage, acceptance of family planning, improvement in self-image, and their empowerment. The need of the hour is to improve female literacy. With the exception of Kerala where the female literacy is 86.9 per cent, in the states like Bihar, Rajasthan, Uttar Pradesh and Madhya Pradesh less than 30 per cent women are literate. The recent UNDP report placed India 103 out of 174 in the rank of 'gender-related development index'. Education is the key to development of women and at the same time development of the entire society. For educational development of women, a vigorous drive for universalization of elementary education, retention of girl child in school, reduction in drop out rate and promotion of adult literacy was taken up by government in the Five Year Plans. Some of the special initiatives were, review of school text books to remove gender bias, re-orientation of school teachers to present gender equality and setting up of Women's Development Centre in Universities and colleges to bring about social awareness on women's issues.

Education is the basic tool for empowering a woman. This is where the NGOs and Social Service Sector people need to work. There are phases of empowerment. The main strategies adopted by the government for increasing female literacy in the country include:

1. National Literacy Mission for imparting functional literacy
2. Universalisation for Elementary Education
3. Non-Formal Education

Once a girl undergoes the first phase of information, education and communication, she becomes aware of her surroundings. Then comes the phase of accountability, where she is given the ability to rationalize and take informed decisions for which she is accountable. Once she is educated and empowered, she is in a better position to take care of herself and this needs to be sustained. By these means may be it will be possible to mitigate the curse of domestic violence from our country.

On one side where there is a need to educate girls, it is also necessary that the other sex be sensitized towards her. It is important to usher in changes in societal attitudes and perceptions with regard to the role of women in different spheres of life. Adjustments have to be made in traditional gender specific performance of tasks. Mass media and inter-personal communication techniques should be utilized to achieve these ends.

The discrepancy in the ideology and practice of the empowerment policy of women in India constitutes its continued social, economic and cultural backwardness. As empowerment of women in a society is the most effective index of measuring modernization and development, it should be ensured therefore that at every phase of life, a woman needs to be given special inputs in terms of school education, higher education, health education, sex education, population education and education on self development, so that these may improve her status in the society and better the quality of her life, unless, the saying 'women empowerment may mitigate the occurrence of domestic violence' will certainly turn up to be a myth.

References

Chamaraj, K. 1997. 'The World of Working Children in Karnataka'. *Humanscape*. Vol. IV, Issue X.

Desai, Sonalde. 1994. *Gender Inequalities and Demographic Behaviour: India*. New York: The Population Council.

Kaur, R. and S. Garg. 2008. 'Addressing Domestic Violence Against Women: An Unfinished Agenda'. *Indian Journal of Community Medicine.* Vol. 33(2)

Sen, P. 1999. 'Enhancing Women's Choices in Responding to Domestic Violence in Calcutta: A Comparison of Employment and Education'. *The European Journal of Development Research*. Vol. 11, No. 2, December.

WHO. 1999. 'WHO Multi-country Study of Women's Health and Domestic Violence. Core Protocol'.

WHO. 1996. *Violence Against Women: WHO Consultation*. Geneva. WHO.

12

Decision Making in Family Planning Practices

A Human Rights Issue

HOMPRABHA BISWAS AND SUBHA RAY

The concept of reproductive health has recently emerged in response to the fragmentation of the existing services related to health in reproduction, and to their orientation. Reproductive health is not just a major health issue; it is also a development issue, and a Human Rights issue. Men can play a positive role in promoting women's reproductive health by sharing the responsibility of family planning using a male method, by supporting their partners in using female contraception and deciding on the appropriate family size, and by responsible sexual behaviour, including the use of condoms to protect their partners.

Reproductive health is an important component of health for both women and men, but is more critical, however for women. A major burden of diseases in females is related to their reproductive function and reproductive potential, and the way in which society treats or mistreats women because of their gender. Yet many people are denied their rights to sexual and reproductive health. Majority are poor women, men and young people in developing countries, where there is lack of access to sexual and reproductive health information and services.

In India, within the patriarchal set-up, women enjoy relatively lesser power. Young women are secluded and voiceless and have less control in matters relating to their lives. They are constrained from exercising choice in sexual and reproductive matters. National Family Health Survey–2 (NFHS–2) shows that only one in two ever-married women participated in decisions about their own healthcare. In several studies, the dominant role of husband in decision making related to the use of contraceptive, especially during the early years of marriage was noted. Most couples did not plan their child (ren) or discuss the use of contraceptive. Nationally, for example, less than one in five currently married women reported discussing matters related to family planning with their husbands. Research showed that family members (other than husband) also play significant role in deciding the reproductive health issue of a couple.

Women lack access to contraceptive to decide their family size which improves life expectancy of their children. Women die of complications from pregnancy, child birth, unwanted pregnancies, and due to abortion by unskilled personnel in unsafe places.

Communication and decision making are vital in assuring informed choice of family planning and reproductive health behaviour. Effective communication and decision making empower people to seek the best for their health and exercise their right to good healthcare (Rimal et al., 2002).

The importance of spousal communication is often emphasized in family planning programmes and research. Mott F.L. and Mott S. observed that spousal communication was the first step in rational fertility decision making. Numerous studies show that communication between partners was positively associated with contraceptive use (Kamal, 1999; Lozare 1976; Raju S., 1987).

Partner support is a significant predictor of the likelihood that women will attempt to use a contraceptive method (Green, 1994; Burwell, 1996). In this context, male involvement refers to any activity that seeks to enhance the provision of reproductive health services including information provided through activities targeted to males of all ages, either individually or as part of a sexually active couple (Danforth and Green, 1997). Studies using interpersonal communication strategies involving counselling sessions to provide men with relevant information can help them to be more supportive of contraceptive use and more aware of shared decision making. Tefere and Larson (1993) found that contraceptive use nearly doubled among couples that received husband–wife counselling.

Men may plan family as (a) decision makers along with their wives and (b) as users of male contraceptive method. In the latter case, few options are available (Atkins and Jezowski, 1983). Contraceptive methods that involve participation of men are condoms, vasectomy, withdrawal and periodic abstinence and amount to about one-third of all contraceptive use among married couples. Nevertheless, the two most effective male methods, condoms and vasectomy, are among the least used of all methods (United Nations, 1999).

Men play powerful and dominant role in reproductive decision making. They take decisions by themselves without considering the wish or the health consequences of their partner (David 2008). In contrast, couples who talk to each other about family planning and reproductive health reach healthier decisions. These couples are more likely to use contraception and use it wisely and effectively (Beckman, 2002; De-Silva, 2000; Lasee and Becker, 1997).

Most contraceptive methods are designed for use by women, and as a result target their information, counselling and services to women of reproductive age. Women often are not the sole decision makers about contraceptive use. Some make decision in collaboration with their husbands, others might have little autonomy in the home, husbands, in-laws or parents decide for them. This influence of husbands and other members was another topic explored by researchers in the Women's Studies Project (WSP). It was found that husbands play a critical role in women's family planning use and continuation. Women fearing disapproval, abandonment, divorce or severe consequences keep themselves away.

Reproductive decision making process of a couple is influenced by many factors (Hull, 1983; Hollerbach, 1983). Their perception towards fertility choices is not limited to individual families; rather they are influenced by other sources such as relatives, or extra-familial sources. Decision making of a couple is also affected by government programmes which not only make modern contraceptives available, but also actively encourage the acceptance of fertility limitation (Easterlin, 1978; Freedman, 1979; Lesthaeghe, 1980).

Community and culture affect a person's attitude towards family planning, desired sex of children, preferences about family size, family pressures to have children and whether family planning accords with customs and religious beliefs, Dixon-Meuller (1999); Greenwell (1999) and Vickers (1974). Community norms also prescribe how much autonomy individuals have in making family planning decisions. The larger the differences in reproductive intentions within a community, the more likely that community norms support individual choices Bosveld (1998) and Dixon-Mueller (1999).

Household and community influences can be so powerful that they can obscure the line between individual desires and community norms. For instance, in some culture, many women reject contraception because bearing and raising children is the path to respect and dignity in the society (International Planned Parenthood Federation, 1996; Cherkaovi, 2000; and Barnett, 2001).

A person's social environment usually has more influence on family planning decisions than do the attributes of specific contraceptives. People choose contraceptive methods that are commonly used in their community because they know that it is socially acceptable to do so, and they tend to know more about these methods (Rogers and Kincaid, 2004; Valente et al., 2000). Many women use the same family planning method that others in their social networks use (Godley, 2001). The role of social networks in the diffusion of new ideas about family planning has been recognized for several decades (Retherford and Palmore, 1999). As more and more people decide to use family planning, it has become increasingly acceptable for others to choose to do so as well (Cleland and Wilson, 2004).

In developing countries, however, the use and advocacy of birth control and abortion are more closely related to the issue of population control rather than as an expression of women's reproductive freedom. In general, family planning practice is believed to enhance women's status. Birdsall and Chester (1987) argues that accessibility to contraception enhances women's status by allowing women to control the timing and spacing of child bearing, which in turn increases women's educational and economic opportunities. However, with regard to the specific relationship between family planning practice and women's fertility decision making power, the existing literature presents inconsistent research findings. Kar and Tablot (1980) argue that in traditional societies women who use contraceptives tend to have greater autonomy in decisions and actions and greater freedom to discuss issues concerning family planning than those women who do not use contraceptives.

Literatures show that in South Asia, women of low socio-economic group possesses knowledge, practices and decision making power regarding family planning is less marked.

The objectives of the present study were to understand the existing family planning practices and decision making ability among the Muslim women of slums of Budge Budge, West Bengal, India.

Materials and Methods

The present study has been conducted in some of the slum areas located in Budge Budge in 24 Parganas South, West Bengal. The areas of the study have been selected on the basis of operational convenience.

A well-tested and structured schedule was canvassed in person to collect data on preliminary socio-economic condition which includes variables like age, occupation, educational level, monthly expenditure and so on. Data on reproductive history include the number of surviving and deceased children per couple, desire for children, knowledge and practice of various family planning methods, reason for selecting the particular type, and the role of women in taking decision in adopting family planning and its type(s). In addition to these, some detailed case studies have been made on both working and non-working women to gather certain insights about how couples choose and decide about their contraceptive types.

Data has been collected on 100 Bengali and Hindi speaking Muslim women (working 30 and non working 70), who are in wedlock and aged between 18 and 48 years, have at least one child, barring few who were newly married, had volunteered to participate. In the present study, women who are engaged in domestic works (homemakers) have been considered in the non working group and those who are working either outside or from home for earning money in addition to their own domestic work, have been recognized under working category.

Women who seemed to be articulate, rational and able to understand the subject matter and can respond accordingly by neither exaggerating nor downplaying the response have been selected as cases. While collecting the quantitative information on family planning practices, the authors observed each participant under study and tried to make an assessment on them for selecting as probable respondent based on the above criteria.

Prior to the collection of data, the nature of research was explained to all the participants and a verbal consent was taken from each of them. The entire data was collected during the period December 2008–April 2009.

Results

Socioeconomic Status

From Table 1 it shows that 51 per cent of the participants are masjid or religious text educated. While 17 per cent are secondary or below educated, only a, minimal of 2 per cent of the population were matriculate and above. Most women below the age of 25 years are studying beyond primary level. The monthly expenditure of the majority of the families is ₹ 4,000.

Table 1

Socio-Economic Characteristic of the Subjects

	Number	*Per cent*
Educational Status of the Subjects		
Non Literate	17	17.0
Masjid/Religious Texts	51	51.0
Primary and below	13	13.0
Secondary and below	17	17.0
Matriculate and above	2	2.0
Educational Status of the Husbands		
Non Literate	19	19.0
Masjid/Religious Texts	33	33.0
Primary and below	25	25.0
Secondary and below	16	16.0
Matriculate and above	7	7.0
Monthly expenditure (rupees)		
<4000	73	73.0
>4000	27	27.0
Family type		
Nuclear	80	80.0
Joint or extended	20	20.0
Household Size		
=5	57	57.0
>5	43	43.0
House type		
Own	64	64.0
Rented	36	36.0

Source: Field work.

Reproductive History

Table 2 shows that 65 per cent of the girls were married between 15–18 years. It was learnt that Muslims believe that girls should get married when they become fertile. The observations from reproductive history were serious and alarming. The 100 women had 322 surviving children at an average of more than three children per mother; 62 per cent of the woman had more than three whereas 26 per cent had five or more children. Lack of family planning services and desire for male heir is the main reason for more number of children.

Another important aspect was noticed. The sample population (100 women) had experienced four pregnancies per women. Every 1.33 women, there was a reproductive wastage. Death of the children accounted for 58 per cent of the wastage. Lack of medical care, delivery by untrained midwives and mal nutrition remains the factors.

Table 2

Reproductive History of the Subjects

No. of Surviving Children			
Category	*Frequency*	*Per cent*	*No. of Children*
One child	11	11	11
Two	27	27	54
Three	25	25	75
Four	11	11	44
Five and above	26	26	138
Total			322

No. of Child(ren) Dead		
	Frequency	*Per cent*
Deceased children	44	58.67
Spontaneous abortion	7	9.33
Induced abortion	21	28.00
Still birth	3	4.00
Total	75	100

Age at Marriage	
Age Category	*Frequency*
Below 10	4
11–14	14
15–18	65
19–22	11
23–26	3
27–30	2
31 and above	1
Total	100

Source: Field Work.

Family Planning Practices and Decision Making

Table 3 analyses the family planning practices of the women in the sample population. It was observed that women had adopted family planning. Of the 67 per cent using reversible method of family planning, it was seen that 65 per cent used oral contraceptives pills (OCP). The next preferred method was withdrawal (18%). In this regard it was worth mentioning that only 2 per cent used condom, in spite of the efforts of the government to create awareness as well as free availability. It was learnt that condom is not popular among their husbands.

In the study, it was noticed that all the available methods were used except male sterilization (vasectomy): 33 per cent of the population chose contraceptives on the basis of husbands liking, while 21 per cent on the basis of personal liking.

Only 4 per cent of the population had made their own decisions. In 64 per cent cases, the decision regarding the adoption of different methods of family planning was made by the husbands. The consent of women was never sought. It was noticed that with the increase in mother's age and family size, husband considered their wives in decision making (27%). They were deprived of their right to health and decision regarding child birth.

Table 3

Family Planning Practices and Decision Making

	Number	*Per cent*
Non adopters of family planning	17 (52%)	33
Having desire for more children	16 (48%)	
Adopters of family planning	67	67
Types of family planning method		
Irreversible (sterilization)	24	35.82
Reversible	43	64.18
Different types of reversible family planning method practiced (67 women)		
Pills only	28	65.12
Condom only	1	2.32
Withdrawal only	8	18.60
Pills and IUD	1	2.33
Pills and withdrawal	1	2.33
Safe period and withdrawal	4	9.30
Reason for adopting particular method (67 women)		
Personal liking	14	20.90
Husband's liking	22	32.83
Easy availability and cheap	2	2.98
No side effect	4	5.98
Joint liking	2	2.98
Family size obtained	14	20.90
Permanent solution	7	10.45
Others*	4	2.98
Decision makers for adopting family planning (100 women)		
Self	4	4
Husband	64	64
Husband and wife jointly	27	27
Others#	5	5

* Others: Include suggestion of doctors, friends, parents or in-laws.

\# Others: Mother-in-law, own mother, elder sister, sister-in-law and so on.

Source: Field Work.

Discussion

In the present study, an attempt has been made to understand the decision making roles of women and to know the differential situations in which women discontinue with or switch over to other contraceptive types than those already used. The cases stated in the text represent a cross-section of the study population.

Broadly, the findings of the present study can be discussed under the following heads (a) socio-economic condition, (b) reproductive history and (c) family planning practices and decision making.

Socio-economic Condition

The educational status of Muslim women is very poor. Among them 17 per cent of the populations are non literate and 13 per cent are primary educated; 75 per cent of the women had a monthly income of less than ₹ 4,000. Most women lived in nuclear family; 64 per cent resided in owned houses and 70 per cent of the women were homemakers.

The Muslim girls are deprived of the right to education due to socio-economic and cultural hindrances. Lack of education has forced the women to engage in unskilled works like embroidery (21%) and maid servant (4%). The study revealed that 65 per cent of the women got married before 18 years and became grandmother by the age of 35.

Reproductive History of Women

The study shows that each woman had four pregnancies on an average out of which 19 per cent resulted in death or abortion. 62 per cent of the women had more than three children while 26 per cent have five or more children. Lack of family planning and desire for male child are the main reason for the large family size. Death of children accounted for 58 per cent of the reproductive wastage which occurs due to lack of medical care, delivery by untrained midwives, mal nutrition, etc. Induced abortion (28 per cent) is the other reason for reproductive wastage.

Family Planning Practices and Decision Making

The use of specific contraceptive methods is determined by two related processes: the decision to adopt family planning method and to choose the contraceptive type. Again, choice of contraceptive type and family planning method in a community are likely to be related with factors such as the availability and knowledge of existing facilities, suitability of a method and the communities' perception about a specific method[1] (Hull, 1983; Hollerbach, 1983; Jain, 1989; Bulut et al., 1996; Lete et al., 2003). The provision of a wide range of contraceptives increases the opportunity for individual couples to select a method that suits their needs.

The study reveals that 67 per cent of participants were adopting family planning. Further, 64 per cent of them used reversible method of contraception while 36 per cent used non reversible method. This is in contrast to the findings of NFHS–3 where 52 per cent of the participants were not using any contraceptives. Women do not use contraceptive just after marriage, and not before the birth of the first issue some of them did not use any contraceptives till the attainment of the desired family size.

The participants of the present study have an exposure to contraceptive types like oral contraceptive pills, IUD and condoms and to some other family planning methods like withdrawal and sterilization. Within this existing range of knowledge regarding reversible birth control measures, use of oral contraceptive pills (28%) and withdrawal (8%) are more prevalent among these women, which conform to the general trend of the country (IIPS and ORC Macro, 2007). Although the use of former contraceptive type causes some health discomforts to the women, they still have to continue with these since the male contraceptive types are totally non-acceptable. It is worthwhile to mention only two per cent of the men used condoms while none of the women have ever used female condom. While the knowledge of family planning is nearly universal in India, only 36 per cent of married women aged 13 to 49 currently use modern contraception (IIPS, 1995). Female sterilization is the main form of contraception; over two thirds of the married women using contraception have been sterilized. Place of residence, education, and religion are strongly related to both fertility and contraceptive use. More than half of married women with a high school education or above use contraceptives, compared to only one-third of illiterate women. Not surprisingly, the total fertility rates for these two groups are insignificantly different: 4.0 children for illiterate women compared to 2.2 children for women with a high school education or above. Differentials among the religious groups also are pronounced: e.g. Muslims have the highest total fertility rate and the lowest contraceptive use (IIPS, 1995).

The NFHS–3 data shows that compared to the last three surveys (NFHS–1, and 2), the user of other reversible contraceptive types (like female condom) have increased. In general, studies on the women of the lower socio-economic group from Asia and Africa reflect the preference of use of oral contraceptive pills than the other contraceptive types (Bruce and Haberland, 1997; Roy et al., 2003; Schoemaker, 2005; Guillaume and Desgreis, 2002); the present study subscribes to this result. Moreover, it has been observed that in some developing countries like Bangladesh and Madagascar (Bruce and Haberland, 1997) as well as those in the present group, the working women generally procure oral contraceptive pills from the ICDS/voluntary health workers.

Thirty three per cent of the population chose contraceptives on the basis of husband's liking, while 21 per cent on the basis of personal liking.

The trends indicate that in 64 per cent cases, the decision regarding the adoption of different methods of family planning was made by the husbands. In most of the cases the husbands encouraged their wives to adopt oral contraceptive pills or forced her to abort the child. When these women find health discomfort using these contraceptive types, they pursue their husbands to practice withdrawal. Barring a few, all the husbands of these women prefer to practice withdrawal rather than using condom. Only four per cent women made their own decision. Most of the women go through forced pregnancy, i.e. without their will or conscience. Some women thought that it was their primary duty to provide the family a male child who would carry forward the generation. 21 per cent of women believed that it was not in their control. They were not even encouraged to discuss family planning with their husbands.

Of the various sources of acquiring knowledge on family planning, women of the present study group identified voluntary health workers and peer group members as the major ones, which corroborates with the findings from rural Kenya (Monica and Sain, 2003). The study revealed that 34 per cent of the women were unaware of IUD; 17 per cent, 16 per cent and 4 per cent of the women had not heard about condoms, withdrawal and sterilization, respectively.

Among the irreversible method of contraception, abortion was used very much – 21 cases of induced abortion were found in 15 women; 43 per cent of the women aborted to avoid birth of the unwanted child while 38 per cent adopted abortion to restrict the family size. It was noticed that the decisions of abortion were taken when the women already had few children. However, 58 per cent of the women did not know about the legalization of the abortion.

It is known that vasectomy is safer, less invasive, easier to perform and less expensive than the female-centred method of sterilization. In India, women still continue to be sterilized far more frequently than men (Puri et al., 2004; IIPS and ORC Macro, 2007) and the present study is not an exception. 35 per cent (24 women) of the participants were sterilized. The major reasons for adopting the method were to stabilize their family size and get rid of the inconvenience in the use of reversible contraceptives.

In the present study, one man used contraceptives that for a short spell of time but none underwent sterilization.

It is mentionable that there are a number of active organizations (like NGOs and ICDS) which work with this population of socio economically backward women and children by providing education and health awareness and services to these people. In addition to this, *Bharater Ganatantric Mahila Samiti* (Democratic Women Forum of India) provides contraceptives and awareness to the women.

Conclusion

The trend of the present research gives certain indications about the probable association between lack of education, economic backwardness of a woman and the autonomy to have a control over her own body. However, this needs to be explored and tested in differential socio-economic and socio-political situations across geographical diversification. The population relies on sterilization and OCP for family planning. Promotion of some other reversible contraceptive types like injections, IUD, female condoms and male sterilization can be tested for their effectiveness and acceptance. Recent national and regional levels data (NFHS–3) (IIPS and Macro, 2007) show that people have started accepting the use of other reversible contraceptive types (like female condom). The status of the women can only be improved through education. Efforts should be made to educate women so as to make her economically independent and enable her to take decisions. More researches need to be done to identify some culturally compatible ways by which men can be actively involved for accepting shared responsibility in improving reproductive health situation in general and that of women in particular.

References

Atkins, B.S. and T.W. Jezowski. 1983. 'Report on the First International Conference on Vasectomy'. *Studies in Family Planning*. 14(3), pp. 89–95.

Becker, S. 1996. 'Couples and Reproductive Health: A Review of Couple Studies'. *Studies in Family Planning*. 27(6), pp. 291–306.

Barnett, B. and Stein J. 1998. 'Women's Voices, Women's Lives: The Impact of Family Planning'. Family Health International. http://www.fhi.org/en/RH/Pubs/wsp/synthesis/ index.htm (acccessed 24 Sep 2010).

Bosveld, W. 1998. 'Explaining Between-Country Variation in Fertility: The Theoretical Link Between Individual Behaviour and Social Context. NETHUR – Demography, Paper no. 41.

Burwell, L.C., D.D. Hoover and D.K.A. Kouzis. 1996. 'Stages of Change for Condom Use: The Influence of Partner Type, Relationship and Pregnancy Factors'. *Family Planning Perspectives*. 28, pp. 101–109.

Beckman, L. 2002. 'Communication, Power and the Influence of Social Networks in Couples Decisions on Fertility'. In R.A. Bulatao, R.D. Lee, P.E. Hollerbach and J. Bongaarts (eds) *Determinants of Fertility in Developing Countries*. Vol. 2: Fertility Regulation and Institutional Influences. New York: Academic Press, pp. 415–443.

Chatterjee, Meera. 1990. 'Indian Women: Their Health and Economic Productivity'. *World Bank Discussion Papers*. 109. Washington, D.C.

Cleland, J. and Wilson. 2004. 'Demand Theories of the Fertility Transition: An Iconoclastic View'. *Population Studies*. 41(1), pp. 5–30.

Cochrane, Susan H. 1983. 'Effects of Education and Urbanization on Fertility'. Education and Training Series Discussion, Paper no. EDT 26, Washington D.C.: The World Bank.

Cherkaoui, M. 2000. Fertile Changes. ORGYN: 27–32.

De Silva, W.I. 1994. 'Husband-Wife Communication and Contraceptive Behavior in Sri Lanka'. *Journal of Family Welfare*. 40(2), pp. 1–13. June.

David, Oladeji Kamla-Raj. 2008. 'Communication and Decision-Making Factors Influencing Couples Interest in Family Planning and Reproductive Health Behaviours in Nigeria'. *Studies of Tribes and Tribals*. 6(2), pp. 99–103.

Desai, Sonalde, 1994, *Gender Inequalities and Demographic Behavior*, New York: The Population Council.

Dixon-Meuller, R. 1999. 'Gender Inequalities and Reproductive Health: Changing Priorities in an Era of Social Transformation and Globalisation'. Belgium, International Union for the Scientific Study of Population (Policy and Research Paper No.16), available: www.iussp.org/Publications_ on_site/PRP/prp16.htm

Easterlin, Richard A. 1978. 'The Economics and Sociology of Fertility: A Synthesis'. In C. Tilly (ed.) *Historical Studies of Changing Fertility*. Princeton: Princeton University Press.

Green, C.P. 1994. 'Male Involvement in Reproductive Health and Family Planning'. UNFPAMIRH, Programme Advisory Note. Technical Paper.

Greenwell, K.F. 1996. 'Contraceptive Method Mix Menu: Providing Healthy Choices for Women'. *World Health Statistics Quarterly*. 49(2), pp. 88–93.

Heise, L. M. Ellsberg and M. Gottemoeller. 1999. 'Ending Violence Against Women'. *Population Reports*. Series L, No. 11. Baltimore, Maryland: Population Information Program, Johns Hopkins University School of Public Health. Cited in WHO. 2002 *World Report on Violence and Health*. Geneva: WHO.

Kishwar, Madhu and Ruth Vanita (eds). 1984. *In Search of Answers: Indian Women's Voices from 'Manushi'*. London: Zed Press.

Hollerbach, P.E. 1983. 'Fertility Decision-making Processes: A Critical Essay'. In R.A. Bulatao and R. Lee (eds) *Determinants of Fertility in Developing Countries*. New York: Academic Press, pp. 340–380.

Hull, T.H. 1983. 'Cultural Influences on Fertility Decision Styles'. In R.A. Bulatao and R. Lee (eds) *Determinants of Fertility in Developing Countries*. New York: Academic Press, pp. 381–414

International Institute for Population Sciences (IIPS) and ORC Macro. 2000. National Family Health Survey (NFHS–2), 1998–99, Mumbai: IIPS.

International Institute for Population Sciences. 1995. National Family Health Survey, 1992–93, Mumbai: IIPS.

International Planned Parenthood Federation (IPPF). 1996. *IPPF Charter on Sexual and Reproductive Rights*. London: IPPF, p. 63

Jaconson, J.L. 2000. 'Transforming Family Planning Programmes: Towards a Framework for Advancing the Reproductive Rights Agenda'. *Reproductive Health Matters*. 8(15), pp. 21–32.

Kamal, N. 1999. 'Inter-spousal Communication on Family Planning as a Determinant of the Use of Modern Contraception in Bangladesh'. *Journal of Family Welfare*. 45(1), pp. 31–43.

Kim, Y.M., A. Kols and S. Mudieke. 1998. 'Informed Choice and Secision-making in Family Planning Counselling in Kenya'. *International Family Planning Perspectives*. 24(1), pp. 4–11, 42.

Lozare. B.V. 1976. 'Communication Between Couples and Decision-making in Relation to Family Planning'. In R.A. Bulatao (ed.) *Philippine Population Research*. Makati, Philippines: Population Center Foundation, 1976, pp. 307–322.

Lee, R., P. Hollerbach and J. Bongaarts. 1983. *Determinants of Fertility in Developing Countries*. Vol. 2. New York: Academic Press, pp. 295–339.

Lesthaeghe, Ron. 1980. 'On the Social Control of Human Reproduction'. *Population and Development Review*. 6(4), pp. 527–548.

Mason, K.O. 1997. 'Gender and Demographic Change: What Do We Know?'. In G.W. Jones, R.M. Douglas, J.C. Caldwell and R.M. D'Souza (eds) *The Continuing Demographic Transition*. Oxford: Clarendon Press, pp. 158–182.

Monica, A.M. and L.C. Sian. 2003. 'Trends and Determinants of Contraceptive Method Choice in Kenya'. *Studies in Family Planning*. 34, pp. 149–159.

Mott, F.L. and S. Mott. 1985. 'Household Fertility Decisions in West Africa: A Comparison of Male and Female Survey Results'. *Studies in Family Planning.* 16(2), pp. 88– 99.

Oni, G.A. and McCarthy J., 'Family planning knowledge, attitudes and practices of males in Ilorin, Nigeria', *International Family Planning Perspectives,* 1991, 17(2): pp. 50–54, p. 64.

Pachauri, S. and K.G. Santhya. 2002. 'Reproductive Choices for Asian Adolescents: A Focus on Contraceptive Behaviour'. *International Family Planning Perspectives* 28, pp. 186–195.

Population and Development Review. 1995. Program of Action of the 1994. *International Conference on Population and Development* (Chapters I-VIII). New York: Population Council. 21(1), pp. 187–213.

Raju, S. 1987. 'Husband-wife Communication and Contraceptive Behavior'. *Journal of Family Welfare*. 33(4), pp. 44–48 and S. Salway, 'How attitudes toward family planning and discussion between wives and husbands affect contraceptive use in Ghana', *International Family Planning Perspectives,* 1994, 20(2), pp. 40–47 and 74.

Retherford, R.D. and Palmore, J.A. 1983. *Diffusion Processes Affecting Fertility Regulation*. In R.A. Bulatao and R. Lee (eds.) *Determinants of Fertility in Developing Countries*. New York: Academic Press., Vol. 2, pp. 295–339.

Rimal, R.N., S.C. Ratzan, P. Arntson, Y.S. Freitmuth. 2002. 'Reconceptualizing the Patient: Health Care Promotion as Increasing Citizens' Decision-making Competencies'. *Communication*. 9(1), pp. 61–74.

Rogers, E.M. and D.L. Kincaid. 2000. *Communication Networks: Towards a New Paradigm for Research.* New York: Free Press, p. 386.

Shram, Shakti. 1988. Report of the National Commission on self employed women and women in the informal sector. United Nations 1995a. Report of the *International Conference on Population and Development*, Cairo, 5–13 September 1994. United Nations, New York.

Valente, T.W., S.C. Watkins, M.N. Jato, Van der, A. Straten and L.M. Tsitsol. 2000. 'Social Network Associations with Contraceptive Use Among Cameroonian Women in Voluntary Association. *Social Science and Medicine*. 45(5), pp. 677–687.

Vickers, C.A. 1974. 'Decision Making About Family Planning it Family Level'. In *American Home Economics and Family Planning*, Resource paper for curriculum development, Washington D.C. American Home Economic Association.

13

Plight of the Elderly Females in Old Age Homes of Kolkata

Human Rights Perspective

SAUMITRA BASU

Ageing as an Emergent Social Problem

Social position is the identification of a person in the social structure in relation to other members who too have distinct positions. Each position involves the performance of a set of socially specified tasks termed the role and carries certain privileges such as power, prestige and security which together may be termed as social status. Thus the position, role and status of a person are interrelated. However, from the point of view of a particular person social status may be regarded as the goal or end, and the position and role are the means. Therefore, normally a person would strive for a position, which would bring them the desired status (D'Souza, 1982).

As Simmons (1960: 66) has pointed out, older people all over the world are connected with the interests of 'Influence' and 'Security'. These interests broadly correspond with the category of 'States' in our conceptual framework of social structure. Now the same person occupies different positions and roles during his life course. The processes of growing and ageing themselves involve change in position and roles since any change in position and role also involves a change in status. A person would be always anxious to ensure that while changing his position and role he at least does not suffer any loss in status if he is unable to improve upon it.

With age, a person improves his skills and abilities for his efficient functioning. But with the onset of ageing, by virtue of continual deterioration in physical and mental capacities, become vulnerable to changes in position and roles. In their condition, role changes are likely to involve a diminution in status. Societies, however, are not always geared to the needs of efficiency and increasing production and so the status of position and roles is not always determined by these criteria. This is especially so in the pre-industrial and traditional societies. In such societies, the ageing process does not disqualify a person from filling positions of enhanced status. On the contrary, the older people are accorded higher privileges with advancing age. As a result, they are able to cope with the problems of old age with help of their own resources without feeling the necessity of approaching outside agencies.

The social scene in India is also changing fast because of rapid industrialization and urbanization. Effects of latter are felt among rural communities depending primarily on agrarian systems, urban living, family systems, and value systems and also in many other aspects of life. The social scientists often feel such a changing context, the condition of the aged in our society, and elsewhere, have worsened. The aged are compelled to expel their traditional role and status, and their adjustment to changing situation, or adherence to the traditional ways has become difficult, and has caused them stress. In short, aged is transformed into a marginal group.

The aged here have begun to face new problems, which are beyond their control under the changing social-cultural milieu. For example, security, status influence, power, etc. of the aged is declining. They have also begun to receive less attention from the family and they are faced with new problems of adjustment, e.g. economic, social and psychological under the impact of emerging industrial culture. The old is exposed to the hazards and uncertainties of old age loneliness and isolation. In such a situation old people are unable to stand their own.

Therefore, it is imperative that such a social category is understood clearly from different dimensions before effective and rehabilitators measures are adopted by the state. India stands at a crucial turning point for confronting the issues of ageing, since it has adopted modernization and globalization through effective social and economic development.

Need for Addressing the Concerns of Older Women

Gender governs the structure of relationships through the life cycle, from birth to old age. Gender differences in the ageing process reflect biological, economic, and social differences. It influences our access to resources and opportunities, and shapes our choices at every stage of life. While gendered experiences impact the health and well-being of both women and men in their later years, women who enter their older years with a past or continuing experience of discrimination, violence and abuse often suffer unrelenting poverty and persistent health problems including chronic pain, depression, and disability.

According to a United Nations publication, as assessed in 1980, the total population of the world in 1980 was 4432.1 million people, and that of 60 years and above was 375.8 million. In 2000, the total World Population was 6,118.9 million and people of 60 years and above will be 590.4 (United Nations, 1985). Within the elderly population, elderly females constitute a major segment. According to the UN estimations there are 208 million aged women in the world, and half of them live in rural areas of developing countries (United Nations, 1990).

Though women in India represent just about half of its general population, the story is different in the elderly (60+) population. It has been estimated that elderly women above 60+ would constitute 14.1 per cent of the total population of India by 2025 (United Nations, 1990). This speaks of the immensity of the problem. A significant feature of the third world population of elderly women is that most of them live below the subsistence level. Thus, the future projections shows that Indian population is ageing with increase in the member of aged women as against men.

In India, the proportion of the elderly females (aged 60–64 years) to the elderly population (aged 60 years and above) declined between 1961 and 1981. This declined trend will continue in 1991 and 2001. At the same time, the proportion of elderly females in the higher age group, 65–69 years and 70 years and above increased during the above period. This trend in the higher age groups which will continue during 1991 and 2001 is in conformity with the situation prevalent in most countries of the world.

If we distribute the aged women into three age groups namely, 60–64, 65–69 and 70+, slightly declining trend will be visible. At the same time an increasing trend is seen in the higher age groups. With the exception of two states, namely Kerala and Haryana, all other states follow a similar pattern. If we take female population only, the ageing process is distinctly more advanced in Kerala. In contrast to the all India picture, Kerala is exceptionally favourable to women. The average life expectancy at birth for women has been steadily increasing over recent decades. As a result, women survive longer and hence, at higher ages, outnumber men. This gender imbalance is much smaller in developing areas of the world, because the relative life expectancy of women in these regions is still significantly lower than in more developed areas. It is given in the Table 1.

Table 1

Expectation of Life (in years) at Birth in India

Year	*At Birth*	
	Male	*Female*
1961–71	46.4	44.7
1971–81	54.1	54.7
1981–91	58.1	59.1
1991–2001	62.8	64.2

Source: United Nations, 2000.

The life expectancy of women at 60 was 18.7 years, greater than that of men that was 16.4 years, in 2001 (Census of India, 2001). As a consequence, a majority of women may live right into a ripe old age but also mostly as widows with a greater proportion suffering from disability or other. Thus, the demographic scenario of elderly women is highly disconcerting.

However, there is another aspect which needs to be looked into from the social perspectives of ageing and widowhood. Widowhood is a possible event in the life cycle of every married person, which is of significance as it has several implications. It is reputedly experienced somewhat different by men than by women. Although there is a dearth of knowledge on this subject, in India, the religious and social stigma that is still attached to widowhood is so deeply rooted in Indian psyche that even talking about widowhood is considered inauspicious. (Jai Prakash, 1989). Widowhood is often considered as a major life event in later years that induces stress, lower status and affects the quality of life adversely.

Elderly females are subjected to various kinds of discrimination, oppression and exploitation, despite being central to the family and society. All these have an adverse impact on their well-being particularly in later life. There was a time in India when widow women were forced to throw themselves into the funeral pyre of their dead husbands and were termed as 'Sati'. Though it was banned in 1829 by the British as a 'barbarous act' but recently instances of revival of 'Sati' have been reported from various parts of India. And after the ban on Sati, widows were deemed in the pilgrim places like Kashi, Mathura, Brindavan and Navadwip by uncaring and ungrateful family members where their life is a pathetic spectacle of daily misery. Thus, most elderly women are terribly marginalized, first as women, second as aged women and third as widows.

Ageing and Human Rights

The world population is ageing at quite a spectacular rate. The total number of persons aged 60 and above rose from 200 million in 1950 to 400 million in 1982 and was 600 million in the year 2003 and will be 1.2 billion by the year 2025, of which over 70 per cent of them will be living in the developing countries (Bose, 2007). This is the fastest growing population group in the world, projected to increase 10 times between 1950 and 2025. These figures are illustrations of a quiet revolution, but one which has far reaching and unpredictable consequences and which is now affecting the social and economic structures of societies, both at the world level and the country level, and will affect them even more in future (Basu, 2000).

With more people living longer, the protection and promotion of older person's health and socio-economic security is a matter not only of public policy but of basic Human Rights. The constitution of World Health Organization confirms this view and defines health as 'a state of complete physical, mental and social well-being and not merely the absence of disease or infirmity'. It goes on to say explicitly that 'the enjoyment of the highest attainable standard of health is one of the fundamental rights of every human being'. (Bhatia, 1983).

The view of health as a basic Human Right is further strengthened by International Human Rights Law which, through international connections, specifically protects certain population groups, such as women and children, considered to be especially exposed to injustices. However, so far it has not been deemed necessary to extend such international Human Rights protection to older persons (Chaddha, 2000). The continuing ageing of the population will be one of the most significant changes in the social landscape for the remaining century and early decades of the next century. The impact of this phenomenon on health services, community services and families is receiving increasing attention.

Human Rights are rights inherent to all human beings, whatever our nationality, place of residence, sex, national or ethnic origin, colour, religion, language or any other status, All are equally entitled to Human Rights without discrimination. These rights are essential for all individuals, they are synonymous with the respect, dignity and freedom and are important for their mental, moral, social, physical welfare (Mahabal, 2004).

As Human Rights are a global issue, so are the rights for the ageing population. Never before in the history of the world we have seen such increasing number of frail individuals. These people may be suffering from various forms of incapacitation which can limit their ability to ensure proper enjoyment of Human Rights. As the elderly population is increasing rapidly, the rate of problems surrounding elder people are also on rise (Wallace, 1999).

The current global generation is forced to deal with the universal concerns of ageing; hence it is imperative that the Universal Declaration of Rights not be ignored of this growing group. Various countries will have different approaches towards the management of the elderly generation and it is the time to practice the concept of globalization by sharing various strategies that are being used to promote humanitarian treatment of the world's older citizens. It is clearly incumbent upon societies across the globe to utilize the wisdom from the elderly people in promoting the application of Human Rights to this wise sector of global population (United Nations, 1998).

Age is rarely specified as a prohibited ground for discrimination under international Human Rights law. Incorporation of a gender perspective in all policy actions on ageing as well as elimination of discrimination on the basis of age and gender is a great challenge in today's world. The United Nations concern on ageing was first recognized in the First World Assembly on Ageing, in Vienna in 1982, where an International Plan of Action (IPA) on Ageing was adopted, outlining the rights of older persons. In 1991 the United Nations adopted a set of principles for older persons. But these do not have the status of legally enforceable rights. In 1991, the United Nations earmarked 1 October as the International Day for Older Persons, and giving recognition to older persons' contribution to development. The Second World Assembly on Ageing, which took place in Madrid in 2002, adopted the Madrid International Plan of Action on Ageing, with the aim of putting ageing in the mainstream of development processes and promoting and protecting the Human Rights and fundamental freedoms of all older persons, including rights to development, so that they can participate fully in the development process on the basis of equality. Combating discrimination based on age and promoting the dignity of older persons is an important goal of this Plan of Action.

But this plan does not have a binding commitment on governments in respect of implementation or provision of additional resources. It also lacks any mechanism for monitoring implementation, including the incorporation of a gender perspective in all policy actions on ageing. However, the major United Nations Treaty Bodies, conferences and summits have set goals, objectives and commitments which intend to improve the economic and social conditions of all human beings. The Convention on the Rights of Persons with Disabilities (2008) protects the rights of older disabled people, including the right to social protection, and calls for the provision of age sensitive responses throughout. The International Convention on the Protection of the Rights of all Migrant Workers and Members of their families (1990) lists age as one of the grounds on which State Parties must not discriminate against migrant workers or their families. The Committee on Economic, Social and Cultural Rights (General Comment 6) states that states parties should pay particular attention to older women who are often in critical situations with no entitlement to an old age or widow's pension. The protocol to the African Charter on Human and Peoples Rights on the Rights of Women in Africa (2003), Beijing Declaration and

Platform for Action (1995), the Programme of Action of the International Conference on Population and Development (1995), explicitly prohibit discrimination against older women based on age, stating their right to freedom from violence and right to be treated with dignity.

Context of the Present Study

The present micro study is a situational study. It attempts to focus on the situation of the elderly women living in old age homes. The rising life expectancy at birth is one of the major achievements in the 20th century. But instead of rejoicing over the favourable demographic indicates, the world is caught in an 'age-quake'. For the proportion of people aged 60+ is rising and is expected to accelerate in the next 50 years. This 'demographic time bomb' is nearing explosion in developed nations, and Asia, including India, is not far behind.

The last century saw rapid industrialization and urbanization all over the world. In India, these developments brought major changes in the social structure. The centuries old joint family system disintegrated, and with it collapsed the safety of parents and grandparents. Since the welfare of the elderly has been a low priority with the state, they have nowhere to turn, and are left disillusioned, shattered and lonely. No doubt that family has so far been the most effective provider of old age support in India in the absence of institutional support. But with social and economic developments underrunning traditional values, and with the number of the elderly growing rapidly vis-à-vis those expected to provide them support, it is becoming a major problem. The elderly are the major casualties of the breakdown of the joint family system. With the collapse of joint families, it is not just values that have changed but also traditions. It was taken for granted that people will grow old with their children around. But there is no guarantee of that now. It is in this scenario, the concept of old age home is gaining popularity in India like the rest of the world. Migration of young couples in search of better employment and youngsters on their part being sometimes resentful of the attitude of their parents are some of the major causes which forces the elder people to stay in old age homes.

The worst affected by this phenomenon are elderly women. It is the women who suffer most and in greater numbers as they live longer than their spouses. Widows form a large number of the elderly. At the time of marriage, generally Indian women marry men who are 10 to 15 years older than them. As a consequence of this phenomenon, they have to endure longer periods of widowhood. Their conditions very often become worse after the death of their husbands. Many of them are abused severely, verbally, psychologically and physically. Many of them who have only one daughter are unwilling to stay with their old mother. So the old age homes become the last resort to them. These old age homes have been projected as 'Home Away from Home'. Are these old age homes answer to the problems faced by increasing number of windowed elderly women? The facilities provided to them include food, lodging, medical facilities, etc. But are these facilities enough to satisfy their needs? In spite of 'protection of older persons' rights becoming a burning global issue, at every moment they become the victims of Human Rights violations. Keeping these backdrops in mind the present study has been visualized.

Aims and Objectives

In this context, the present study is an attempt to understand the condition of the elderly female inmates and existing institutional support available to them. The study was undertaken with the overall goal of understanding the existing institutional facilities available for the care of elderly women inmates in old age homes of Kolkata and to obtain a perspective of the elderly on various aspects associated with institutional living. The present study has highlighted the following objectives – (a) to understand the functioning of old age homes with regard to service provision, (b) to identify the various problems in ensuring the smooth functioning of the old age homes, (c) to understand the personal and background characteristics of the elderly residing in old age homes, (d) to make a detail study of their daily activities in old age homes and to assess the difference (if any) of lives led by them in old age homes compared to that in their family, (e) to know the various health problems experienced by the elderly inmates and treatment provided to them, (f) to understand the extent of their economic dependency, (g) to know the opinion of the elderly inmates regarding the adequacy of facilities and services, their satisfaction and their views on such institutional living, (h) to understand the extent of human rights violation of the elderly female inmates.

The present micro research is a humble attempt to examine the situations of the elderly female inmates living in three old age homes of Kolkata. In doing so, the attempt has been made from a Human Rights perspective. The problems of ageing are multidimensional. It will be too ambitious to cover all aspects of ageing in a single study. Here ageing is an illuminating lens through which Human Rights perspective of the elderly women inmates of old age home have been examined. From the analysis of the case study it is expected that an overall picture of the elderly women inmates living in three old age homes of Kolkata will come out in a fruitful manner.

Method of Study

The present study has been conducted in the mega city of Kolkata, the capital of the state of West Bengal. For the present study, three old age homes (OAHs) located in three different parts of Kolkata have been purposively selected. Then the total populations of the three old age homes were enumerated. From this enumerated population, 91 elderly female inmates have been selected. All the elderly female inmates have been interviewed directly in their respective old age homes (both in dormitory and also in personal room). Interviews have also been taken from the secretary/superintendents of the respective old age homes to obtain information on various aspects related to services provision and administration. Field work was conducted on all working days with prior appointments fixed through the superintendents of the respective old age homes. In some occasions, recall visits were useful to complete the enquiry.

Data was also collected from the Management of the Old Age Homes. All enquiries for the present study were made by a semi-structured interview schedule where some questions were closed and some were open-ended. Both qualitative and quantitative data were collected and supplemented by interview, direct observation case studies and ethnographic field methods and participant observations. Along with these, focus group discussion (FGD) was an important tool to collect the data on behavioural aspect. Besides in order to understand the general interpersonal behaviour observation was very much useful. This has enabled to take note of the types of respect/neglect extended to the aged inmates by their family members.

About the Old Age Homes

Home I is situated in Sukanta Nagar, Block-N, Sector IV of Salt Lake Kolkata. Home-I took its birth from the initiative taken by Late Fulrenu Guha. Initially it had a hut like structure with ad besters roof. With the passage of time now it is a two storied building accommodating seventeen women inmates. Presently the home is being taken care by the members of Association for Social Health in India. This home is totally a nonprofit organization and funding mainly comes from the members of Association for Social Health, various social organizations, donations and also money received from the borders.

Home II is situated in the Kolkata Municipal Corporation Ward No. 123 of Behala. It was founded by Father P. Thormon. The main objective was to provide shelter to homeless poor, aged people. Mainly emphasis was given to Christians only. But now Hindus are also allowed. This home was founded in the year 1984. Presently the home is being run by the Oxford Mission Cathedral Relief Society. They are the main source of funds for this home. Besides, donations are provided by various organizations and the fees received from the inmates also helps to run this institution for the aged.

Home III is located in the Kolkata Municipal Corporation Ward No. 82 of Chetla. This home was founded in the year 1982 in a rented house only meant for women. The main inspiration came from Rusi B. Gimi and Renuka Ray. Currently this home is run by Women's Coordinating Council. The major source of funding here are done by some eminent political and film personalities. Several social organizations also provide regular donations.

Highlights

Socio-demographic profile of the elderly female inmates are:

Home–I

The total numbers of elderly female inmates are seventeen. As the age increases, the number of elderly female inmates also increase. All the inmates of Home – I are literate. They have completed primary level of education. With the increase in age, number of widow inmates also increase.

Home–II

The total number of female inmates is nineteen. Only one inmate who has continued her education up to post graduation. In Home II number of unmarried inmates are more.

Home–III

The total number of female inmates is 70. Inmates in the lower and middle age group are higher than the highest age group. Majority of the inmates are literate. Only one inmate is separated.

Case Studies

Home–I

Mitra, 86-year-old widow, is a mother of one son and one daughter who are settled with their family. She grew up in the Ramkrishna Mission. The influence of the Mission was very profound on her. So she had a different outlook compared to those who were of her age. After her husband's demise, she started disliking the environment. She felt that her daughter-in-law's mother was too interfering. She felt that her influence was getting stronger over her son. On the other hand, mental mismatch started showing with her daughter-in-law. The gap was widening day by day. It was in this situation that she didn't wish to continue a typical family life, rather to lead an independent life. As a result old age home was the final address for her. This case study reveals that how independence is much necessary for an individual even if the person is almost at the end of his or her life.

Chowdhury is a 65-year-old unmarried woman. In her younger days she worked in various companies including Phillips. Life was fine for her. She earned a lot of money. Our informant also had the habit of spending her own money like anything. Whenever anybody was in need of money, she used to help that person. She has been kind to everybody, but life was not kind to her. Among her relatives, she only had one sister. Her sister and brother-in-law took away all the movable and non movable properties. There was nobody to take care of her. In such circumstances, one of the neighbours gave her the address of present old age home where she resides now. She is very religious and spends most of her time performing puja. From this case, it may not be an overstatement that, to be a good human being is a curse in the present world.

Biswas, a 68-year-old widow, has one son who is unmarried and one daughter who is also married. Our informant for the present case study is a patient of mental depression. At the age of 57, she got some kind of shock after which she cannot talk properly. Her daughter could not take care of her mother because she is also a patient of mental depression. Her son, who is working and unmarried, is not in a position to take care of his mother. She requires special care and attention. Institutional care is the last option for her.

Home–II

Dey is a 66-year-old widow with one daughter. She is a graduate. She was very fond of studies, wanted to pursue higher studies and ultimately took up a job. Marriage was not at all a priority then. But in those days women doing job was not a very popular idea. So her elder brother who was her guardian that time didn't allow. Eventually, she was married. Her husband was conservative. So the question of doing job didn't arise. She became busy in taking care of her daughter. With time, her daughter also got married. After her husband's demise she could not live alone due to health problems. Staying with daughter at her in-laws house was also not possible. As we have seen in many other cases, here also old age home became the last resort for her.

Biswas is a 87-year-old unmarried woman. Her father expired when she was of a tender age. Her mother worked for the Missionaries. When she was in standard VII, her mother also expired. Since then the Christian Missionaries have taken her care. Due to illness she could not continue her studies. She was kept under a very strict environment and was not allowed to interact with anybody. Later, she became a 'Gram Sebika' and worked in villages of Nadia, 24 Parganas. When she was growing old she was sent to this old age home which is under the Missions Trust. Here also she worked as a warden in adjacent schools. She is fond of children and loves spending time with them. She has no regret in her life. Now she is waiting for the final call from the Almighty.

Mullick is a 71-year-old widow with four sons and two daughters. Apart from her elder son, all five of her children are either living in Kolkata or in the adjacent areas. After her husband's death, she used to stay with her third son. But when her granddaughter was born, there were space constraints. Daughters offered help but there also was the same problem of space constraints. Rest of the sons were not at all concerned about their old, feeble mother. In the course of time, her health condition deteriorated. She was in need of special care and attention. In such a circumstance, she was compelled to select old age home as a place to spend her last days of life. So this case study reveals that love, care, affection which should come naturally from children and which are the only resort for the elderly in their twilight years are gradually disappearing from this mundane world. For getting shelter, food, attention, she had to pay money in spite of having six children of her own.

Home–III

Banerjee is a 75-year-old widow having one daughter and two sons, all of them are married and established in their respective fields. Her husband was a civil engineer by profession. She did her MA in Bengali and possessed modern outlook. The reason she came to stay in old age home was that she believed in independence and dignity. Her way of looking at life was that once you are done with your duties at home, you should leave it to the next generation. She thought she should come out of the family. With her kind of family background, she could have very well stayed with her family. But as they were all busy with their work, she also felt lonely. So she preferred to lead a life in old age home where she can live independently with dignity.

Bhattacharya is a 67-year-old woman who is separated from her husband. Life has been very rude to her. Husband left her for reasons unknown. Her son also left home at early age. She had two brothers who made an arrangement for her staying in an old age home. But staying in an institutional care was not her choice. Her financial condition was also not good so that she can take care of herself. Even now, part of her boarding fees is being sponsored by a social organization. Our informant thinks she is deprived, neglected only because of her poor financial condition. However, she was forced to adjust with the home environment. This case study reveals that in today's world how an individual is being treated on the basis of his or her economic condition.

Das is a 80-year-old widow with only one daughter. She was born and brought up in a typical Bengali middle-class family. She never went to school and was married at a young age. Family was the entire universe for her. She devoted her entire time in bringing up her only daughter. After her husband's demise she was left alone. She was staying with her daughter. In the course of time, daughter also got married. After daughter's marriage, some unpleasant incidents hurt her self-respect. She didn't wish to stay with her daughter anymore. The best arrangement available was to stay in an old age home. This case study reveals how a sense of self-respect becomes strong in an individual's life especially during old age.

Human Rights and Elderly

Human Rights refer to the basic rights and freedoms to which all humans are entitled. Examples of rights and freedoms, which are often thought of as human rights, include civil and political rights, such as the right to life and liberty, freedom of expression and equality before the law and social, cultural and economic rights, including the right to participate in culture, the right to food, the right to work and the right to education.

Every human being is entitled to have certain rights by virtue of him or her being a part of the human family. Human Rights are fundamental and inalienable and essential for life as human being. They are possessed by every human being irrespective of nationality, race, religion, gender, caste and creed. Human Rights are fundamental to freedom that allows us to fully develop and use our human qualities intelligence, talents, conscience and to satisfy our physical, spiritual and other needs. Human Rights when written in the Constitution become Fundamental Rights.

'All human beings are born free and equal in dignity and rights. They are endowed with reason and conscience and should act towards one another in a spirit of brotherhood.'

Article 1 of the UDHR

Human Rights are those basic standards without which people cannot live in dignity. To violate somebody's Human Rights is to treat that person as though he/she were not a human being. To advocate Human Right is to demand that the human dignities of all people are respected. The basic rights and freedoms, to which all humans are entitled, often held to include the right to life and liberty, freedom of thought and expression and equality before the law. Human Rights mean the rights relating to life, liberty, equality and dignity of the individual guaranteed by the Constitution or embodied in the International Covenants and enforceable by the courts of India (Human Rights Act of 1993).

Over the past several decades, a massive change has taken place in a key demographic area of the planet's human population. Our current body of scientific knowledge tells us that the history of human kind has always been marked by high birth rates that are accompanied by correspondingly high death rates. Historically, the majority of people on the planet at one time have been aged somewhere in the middle of the then-current age range or have tended to be younger than the median age. However, due to the trend of lower birth rates and lower death rates, according to the United Nations Department of Economic and Social Affairs, one out of every 10 people on the planet is now 60 years of age or older. If the current trend of lowering birth rates and lowering death rates continues, by the year 2050 one out of five people will be aged 60 years or older and by 2150, one out of every three people will be aged 60 years or older. Additionally, the oldest old are the most rapidly expanding segment of the elderly population. Currently, the oldest old make up 11 per cent of the 60+ age group and will grow to 19 per cent by 2050.

Many governments have support systems in place for elderly persons such as social security and free or discounted medical care, for example. However, most of these systems were built on the premise that there will always be significantly fewer older persons than younger or middle-aged individuals living at one time. Because of declining death rates, therefore, these systems are beginning to feel a strain that will only increase over time. Additionally, the older-person support ratio is falling in both more and less developed regions, which could further lessen the ability of societies and governments to care for their ageing populations.

These demographic trends create unique challenges for all people, particularly for the governments of nation-states around the globe. Elderly individuals are often subject to discrimination and abuse because they are perceived as easily taken advantage of. There is also a prevalent belief among many that elderly persons are worthless in today's fast-paced, globalized and increasingly industrialized world. Obviously, with the number of elderly people on earth at any one time rising rapidly, there is an increased urgency to address the rights and roles of elderly persons in our world.

Human Rights at Stake

The rights of aged persons can be broken down into three main categories: protection, participation and image. Protection refers to securing the physical, psychological and emotional safety of elderly persons with regard to their unique vulnerability to abuse and ill treatment. Participation refers to the need to establish a greater and more active role for older persons in society. Image refers to the need to define a more positive, less degrading and discriminatory idea of who elderly persons are and what they are capable of doing. Regional intergovernmental organizations in particular have begun to deal with these categories of rights in some detail in their recommendations and treaties.

Special consideration for the rights of the elderly has been granted relatively recently in recommendations and treaties between international instruments, like the Council of Europe. These more detailed recommendations and agreements on the rights of the elderly, however, are all based upon the fundamental premises established in documents like the Charter of the United Nations and the Universal Declaration of Human Rights. In Article 25, paragraph 1, of the Universal Declaration of Human Rights, it is established that: 'Everyone has the right to standard of living adequate for the health and well-being of himself and of his family, including food, clothing, housing, and medical care and necessary social services, and the right to security in the event of unemployment, sickness, disability, widowhood, old age or other lack of livelihood in circumstances beyond his control.'

Elderly persons' right to security is particularly vulnerable to violation. For example, a component of the right to security is the right to healthcare if one, due to old age, is unable to afford or pursue healthcare on one's own. Although many countries currently have universal healthcare systems, these systems are beginning to deal with the strain of an increasingly aged population, and there is some question about how these systems will be maintained in the future. In other countries, like the United States, where there are only federally and state-subsidized healthcare programmes for those who are indigent, disabled or elderly, rising healthcare costs are threatening the survival of these systems. These rights are related to the right to an adequate standard of living, which is often affected in the case of the elderly, due to lack of an adequate support system for them.

Elderly individuals also have the right to non discrimination. Elderly people should not be thought of as useless to society simply because some of them may need more care than the average person. These stereotypes of the elderly can lead to degrading treatment, inequality and, sometimes, abuse.

Similarly, elderly persons' right to participation is sometimes threatened due to prevailing negative images societies hold of the aged. The aged are often not given the same opportunities as others to be productive members of society. Governments are obliged to aid in creating a more positive image of the abilities and strengths of older populations as well as solid opportunities for elderly people to participate in the ongoing creation of their societies.

The elderly's right to be free from torture or cruelty, inhuman or degrading treatment is also often threatened. People sometimes take advantage of the vulnerability of elderly persons. People in old age, particularly older women, are often victims of neglect and physical and psychological abuse. Additionally, elderly refugees during humanitarian crises often fall victim to the torture and abuse that is sometimes inflicted upon civilian populations.

Who is most at risk for having their rights, as elderly, violated? Elderly women are at the greatest risk of or having their rights violated. In general, women are historically more vulnerable towards violence due to their traditionally subordinate position in most cultures. Coupled with the negative image many cultures hold of elderly people, being a woman can make one particularly susceptible to violence and abuse. Considering that 55 per cent of older persons are women and that, in the oldest category 65 per cent are women, special consideration must the given to the effect of sex on the likelihood of rights violation and abuse.

The General Assembly on 16 December 1991 adopted the United Nations' principles for older persons based on the International Plan of Action on Ageing. These principles are to be incorporated by the government in their national programmes. These principles may be described as follows:

Principles of Independence

Following principles should be observed in order to enable the older persons to maintain their independence:

1. Older persons should have access to adequate food, water, shelter, clothing and healthcare through the provision of income, family and community support and self-help.
2. Older persons should have the opportunity to work or to have access to other income generating opportunities.

3. Older persons should be able to participate in determining when and at what place withdrawal from the labour force takes place.
4. Older persons should have access to appropriate educational and training programmes.
5. Older persons should be able to live in environments that are safe and adaptable to personal preference and changing capacities.
6. Older persons should be able to reside at home as long as possible.

Principles of Participation

Following principles should be observed to enable the participation of older persons:

1. Older persons should remain integrated in society, participate actively in the formulation and implementation of policies that directly affect their well-being and share their knowledge and skills with younger generation.
2. Older persons should be able to see and develop opportunities for service to community and to serve as volunteers in positions appropriate to their interests and capabilities.
3. Older persons should be able to form movements or associations of older persons.

Principles of Care

Following principles provided for the family and community care:

1. Older persons should benefit from family and community care and protection in accordance with each society's system of cultural values.
2. Older persons should have access to healthcare to help them to maintain or regain the optimum level of physical, mental and emotional well being and to prevent or delay the onset of illness.
3. Older persons should have access to social and legal service to enhance their autonomy, protection and care.
4. Older persons should be able to utilize appropriate level of institutional care which provide protection and rehabilitation in a human and secure environment.
5. Older persons should be able to enjoy Human Rights and fundamental freedoms when residing in any shelter care or treatment facility including full respect for their dignity, beliefs, needs and privacy and for the right to make decisions about their care and the quality of their lives.

Principles of Self-Fulfillment

1. Older persons should be able to pursue opportunities for the full development of their potential.
2. Older persons should have access to the educational, cultural, spiritual and recreational resources of society.

Principles of Dignity

1. Older persons should be able to live in dignity and security and be free of exploitation and physical or mental abuse.

2. Older persons should be treated fairly regardless of age, gender, racial or ethnic background, disability or other status and be valued independently of their economic contribution.

These principles are intended to serve as targets and benchmarks to evaluate current policies on ageing. On the issue of care, the principles simply state that older persons should benefit from family and community care and protection in accordance with each society's system of cultural values and expectations, demands on families for providing care, elderly people's perception of loneliness, and the impact these perceptions have on their quality of life and well-being.

The Declaration on the Rights and Responsibilities of Older Persons of the International Federation on Ageing, on which these principles are based, goes one step further by declaring that 'older persons have the right ... to die with dignity by accepting or rejecting treatments designed solely to prolong life'. This concept deserves further consideration. At the same time more serious attention needs to be given to the whole range of implications on the issue of ageing and Human Rights.

Indian Context

Older Persons Maintenance, Care and Protection Bill, 2005

Everyone has a right to a standard of living adequate for the health and well-being of himself and his family, including food, clothing, housing and medical care and necessary social security and the right to security in the event of unemployment, sickness, disability, widowhood, old-age or other lack of livelihood in circumstances beyond his control.

Article 21 of the Constitution of India also echoes the same. It says, 'no person shall be deprived of his life or personal liberty except according to procedure established by law'. Further, Article 39(a) of the Constitution of India says, 'the State shall, in particular, direct its policy towards securing (a) that the citizen, men and women equally, have the right to an adequate means of livelihood'. Article 41 of the Indian Constitution enjoins upon the state to make effective provisions for public assistance, within the limits of its economic capacity and development, in cases of unemployment, old-age, sickness and disablement and in other cases of undeserved want. Both the Central and State Governments are empowered under Entry 23 of List II (Concurrent List) to make provisions with regard to social security and social insurance.

The population of senior citizens aged 60 and above, in India has increased from 42.5 million in 1981 to 55 million in 1991 and is now placed at 70.6 million in the 2001 census. They comprise about 6.9 per cent of the total population. There is greater life expectancy of citizens at birth and the life expectancy at age 60 is also increasing. Family has been the most vital non formal social security for senior citizens in India. Most senior citizens reside with one or more of their children, particularly when independent living is no longer feasible.

The joint family system, prevalent in the country, ensured that the needs of the elderly are taken care of at a stage where they are unable to look after themselves, both financially and otherwise. However, over the years, joint families are gradually disappearing and nuclear families are taking their place.

The traditional Indian value system inculcates respect for elders. Elders are considered an intrinsic part of the family. Children turn to their elders for advice on every aspect of their life. This also results in senior citizens playing an important role in their families and society. In the current scenario, these values are fast eroding. The breaking up of traditional joint families into nuclear families has resulted not only in the separation of families but also in the severance of family ties. Many senior citizens no longer have the same role in their families as was traditionally played. While it is inevitable in the current scenario that the family unit will remain nuclear, this should not result in the breaking of ties and familial responsibilities. Efforts must be made to retain traditional values in this regard despite modernization of society.

A great anxiety in old age relates to financial insecurity. When the issue is seen in the context, one-third of the population (1993–94) is below the poverty line and about one-third is above it but belong to the lower income group, the financial situation of two-third of the population of people aged 60 and above can be said to be fragile. High costs of bringing up and educating children affects the transfer of a share of income for the elderly. Due to the shortage of space in dwellings in urban areas and high rents, persons migrating to urban areas prefer to leave their parents in their native place. These changes have led to a number of senior citizens being left to live alone, with insufficient resources to meet even their most basic requirements of food, clothing, housing and medical care. Lack of social support, breaking down of the joint family system and changing lifestyles aggravate the health and nutritional problems of the elderly.

Thus, there is a need for making provisions to ensure that the basic requirements of senior citizens are met and that they can enjoy their right to live with dignity as is envisaged by Article 21. Across the globe, steps have been taken by various countries such as the United States, Canada, the United Kingdom, New Zealand and Germany to provide social security systems for the elderly and other disadvantaged groups. Such systems ensure that senior citizens are not deprived of their most basic needs when they lack the resources to fulfil them.

In India, provisions have been made under legislations such as the Code of Criminal Procedure, 1973 and the Hindu Adoption and Maintenance Act, 1956 to enable aged parents, with insufficient resources to meet their needs. However, the process under these legislations is cumbersome and time consuming. Some states like the State of Himachal Pradesh have enacted legislations enabling the elderly and other dependants to claim maintenance. However, there is no such uniform legislation at the central level, hence the need for the proposed Bill.

Women and Human Rights

Every woman and girl is entitled to the realization of all Human Rights – civil, political, economic, social and cultural – on equal terms with men, free from discrimination. Women and girls also enjoy certain Human Rights specifically linked to their status as women.

The world has recognized that the Human Rights of women are 'an inalienable, integral and indivisible part of universal human rights' (Vienna Declaration and Programme of Action, para. 18). Women are guaranteed equal treatment and freedom from discrimination in the most basic Human Rights treaties, and women's Human Rights are the subject of a specific treaty, the Convention on the Elimination of All Forms of Discrimination against Women. Far-reaching government commitments to ensure the Human Rights of women have been made at each of the recent world conferences, and women's Human Rights are central to the unanimously approved Beijing Declaration and Platform for Action.

The Beijing Declaration and Platform for Action, organized into Critical Areas of Concern, raises issues involving fundamental Human Rights of women. Human Rights are what each human being is entitled to allow her/his freedom to live a dignified and secured life of choice. We can understand the importance of Human Rights only when we are confronted with violations of our own rights. Human Rights include rights related to the safety of the person, the right to be free from coercion by other individuals, groups or governments, the right to social benefits, rest and leisure, and the right to a good basic education.

Equality is important for effective enforcement of Human Rights. All the citizens should be treated a sequels, that all should get equal protection of law without any discrimination of caste and creed and all should get equal opportunity.

Women Rights are Human Rights

Human Rights should apply to all people – men, women and children – irrespective of caste, creed, religion and region. However, women very often or deprived of their basic rights such as freedom of movement, access to education and participation in decision making process. There are many barriers to equality between the genders. Important factors include gender stereotyping, violence against women, social and cultural attitudes and discriminating laws and practices.

Women throughout the world live in constant fear and conditions of deprivation very often for the simple reason that they are women. Especially elder women are at more risk because of their age, they are more subjected to abuse. More so in this age most of them are widow. And because of their age they are mainly unproductive. Being unable to earn for their own living, they are thus dependent on others.

Since ageing is a global issue, we cannot afford to ignore the problems faced by the elderly women. Everybody is entitled to enjoy their Human Rights as being humans and so thus the aged women. So it is the obligation of the governments to see that the Human Rights of women and especially elder women are being taken care of.

Old age, particularly widowhood, is accompanied by a number of changes with which the elderly and widows have to adjust. Actually a crucial transition in older years that leaves the survivor confused, lonely, depressed and vulnerable is widowhood. Widowhood is often considered as a major life event in later years that induces stress, lowers status and affects the quality of life adversely. It is true that losing a spouse is distressing both to men and women at any age, let alone in old age. But why is it that women face several deprivations when she becomes a widow? They are also an integral part of family life and circumstances of older women, particularly the elderly widows, do not come about by chance. Until recently even in the field of social gerontology, elderly widow females occupy a low priority area.

The changing social structure, especially in the context of India where the impact of modernization and globalization, has led to the breakdown of joint family system to nuclear type family. The myth that aged are being taken care of by the family is being destroyed and it is in this situation that a woman suffers the most because she is a woman, she is elderly and she is a widow. Not only elderly widows, single elderly women are also victims of more or less the same situation. In this situation, old age homes are becoming popular as the last resort for these elderly females.

In this context, it should be mentioned that 'Human Rights' are those basic standards without which people cannot live in dignity. To violate someone's Human Rights is to treat that person as though he/she was not a human being. To advocate Human Rights is to demand that human dignity of all people be respected.

If we take into account the above definitions of Human Rights, then we can very clearly understand that how much the Human Rights of the elderly female inmates living in three different old age homes of Kolkata have been violated. The principles of independence, participation, care, self-fulfillment, and dignity are the five main pillars of Human Rights for elderly people.

If we take a look at the cases which we have already discussed previously, each case is an example of Human Rights violation. To live in his or her own house is a fundamental rights of every individual. But we see that majority of inmates was not allowed to live. This is the first major violation of one's Human Rights.

Even if they were allowed to stay, they were not offered a dignified life. Right to live with dignity is another component of Human Rights. Every individual has the right to be cared. And it is mostly applicable for the aged for whom love and care from their children are the last resort in this phase. Case studies show that how the elderly women inmates were being denied love and care. Everybody has the right to live independently. One has got every right to live her life on her own choices and on her own terms. But many of the elderly women were denied an independent living in their own house. Many of them were not given the opportunity of self-fulfillment were neglected and ignored. Some of them were not given a chance of participation. In some cases the next generation is dominating and the elderly were not given a chance to express their views and opinions.

Discussion

The study reveals that major Human Rights violations have taken place with all the elderly women inmates and we can conclude that it is for this reason that all of them have come to stay at the old age home. Some more facts emerged:

1. Majority of women living in the homes for the aged came from small families, most of them having fewer children. Many lived there because either they were widows or had nobody to take care of them or both.
2. If they had children living then either they had migrated to foreign lands or they were daughters and not sons. Traditionally an Indian parent does not live with his/her married daughters.

3. Another class of occupants was that of the women who never married. Instead of living with the brothers, nephew, etc, they generally being pension holders, depended upon their pension to look after their expenses.
4. Some of them being educated and worked in their young age were aware of the existence of such homes.

The aim of this study was to find out the consequence of ageing and Human Rights violation of the elderly women living in old age homes of Kolkata. This micro study reveals that none of them are aware about their fundamental 'Human Rights' being a person, being a woman and being an aged. In this male-dominated society majority of them have to mutely tolerate their situation and finally be admitted into an 'old age home', accepting it as their ultimate destiny. They have no other alternative. No options were left except to silently accept the hard reality.

Conclusion

We are much concerned about Human Rights. In today's world a lot of hue and cry is being noised about Human Right violations and related issues. Seminars, conferences, meetings are being organized. In universities new courses are being introduced, public forums are also very much aware about this. But all these efforts will be of any worth only if every individual is being aware of their rights by virtue of being a human. A lot is being talked about a girl child's right. Today's girl is tomorrow's woman and future's grandmother. But we don't talk about Elderly Women's Rights. They are an ignored silent majority. No importance is given to this category. The last resort in their twilight years becomes old age homes. This micro study will be better understood by the common people if they can know transparently the fundamental Human Rights that the old people are eligible to exert.

Acknowledgement

The present author is indebted to the authorities and the elderly women inmates of the three old age homes of Kolkata. He is also grateful to Prof. Sarah Lamb, Brandeis University, USA, for her valuable discussions. The present author also acknowledges kind support of Ms Moumita Roy, Calcutta Metropolitan Institute of Gerontology (CMIG), Kolkata.

References

Basu, A.M. 2000. *'Women's Roles and the Gender Gap in Health and Survival'*. Geneva: World Labour Organization.

Bhatia, H.S. 1983. *Ageing and Society: A Sociological Study of the Retired Public Servants*. Udaipur: The Arya's Book Centre Publishers.

Bose, Ashish. 2007. *Beyond Demography*. New Delhi: B.R. Publishing Company.

Census of India. 2001. *Life Expectancy at Selected Ages by Sex and Residence Over Time*. Office of the Registrar General of India. New Delhi: Government of India.

Chadha, N.K. and S. Bhatia. 2005. 'Quality of life Among the Aged'. *Indian Journal of Psychology*. 58, pp. 15–21.

D'Souza, Victor S. 1982. 'Changing Social Scene and Its Implications for the Aged'. In K.G. Desai *Aging in India*. Bombay: Tata Institute of Social Sciences.

Jai Prakash, Indira. 1989. 'Psychological Perspectives of the Rural Elderly Women'. In R.N. Pati and B. Jena *Aged in India*. New Delhi: Ashish Publishing House, pp. 192–212.

Mahabal, Kamayani Bali. 2004. *Report on the Case of Human Rights Violation*. Coordination Committee on Disappearance in Punjab, Punjab.

Simmons, Leo. 1945. *Role of the Aged in Primitive Societies*. New York: Yale University Press.

United Nations. 1985. *The World Ageing Situation: Strategies and Policies*. New York: Department of International Economic and Social Affairs.

——. 1988. *World Population Prospects*, New York: Department of International Economic and Social Affairs.

——. 1990. *World Population Prospects*. New York: Department of International Economic and Social Affairs.

——. 2000. *World Population Prospects*. New York: Department of International Economic and Social Affairs.

Wallace, Paul. 1999. *Agequake: Riding the Demographic Rollercoaster Shaking Business, Finance and Our World*. London: Nicholas Brealey Publishing.

14

Human Rights and the Bengali Women in Vrindavan

RAJESH KUMAR SHARMA

The modern age, known for the process of globalization and advancement of information technology, essentially has some of its boons for every individual in the world. The Human Rights, concept of women empowerment and recently passed Bill in Rajya Sabha guaranteeing 33 per cent reservation for women may be said to have brought about a revolutionary change in the destiny of the Indian women. Today, when all over India, the women of the various castes and religions are busy in celebrating the historic event of passing of the Women's Bill in the Rajya Sabha, there are the Bengali women in Vrindavan, District Mathura (Uttar Pradesh), who are still forced by their unbearable circumstances to lead a life which knows no health, hygiene and nutrition. In the name of religion they spend a major part of their life serving others under the miserable conditions. Four hours in the morning and four hours in the evening, hundreds and thousands can be seen enjoying congregational singing at Sri Bhagwan Bhajanashram and having their existence at the mercy of the donors. It is really shocking to observe that they are deprived even of the Human Rights that every individual of the country is believed to have as a human being. Their whole world and desires are confined to the four walls of the Bhajanashram, a little rice they get from here or to the local colonies where they serve the Brajwasis as their maid servants. They make no complaint against their situations, but their eyes reveal the whole mystery of their existence. When the women of the world are conscious of how to avail themselves of the facilities being provided to them under the health standards of the Human Rights, they are bound to live on the mercy of others eating what they get from others as alms. The branches of Bhagwan Bhajanashram where they serve provide them medical facilities, but these facilities fail to help them sufficiently. The result is that many of them fall victims to several curable and incurable diseases. Not only this, some of them also meet untimely death just because of insufficient medical facilities.

Vrindavan: The City of Temples

Vrindavan, around 15 km from Mathura, is a major place of pilgrimage, on the banks of Yamuna. Attracting about 5 lakh pilgrims every year, it is noted for its numerous temples – both old and modern. Vrindavan is synonymous with the innocent mirth and child like playfulness of Shri Krishna. Vrindavan, the dusty little town known for the temples, big and small, famous and remote strewn all over the place. Vrindavana is 135 km south of Delhi and 55 km north of Agra, just off the Delhi-Agra Road. It is 12 km or a 25-minute auto-rickshaw ride from Mathura. It has a small-town type atmosphere with narrow streets and not much motor traffic. There are said to be over 5,000 temples in Vrindavana. Devotion is the driving force in this river town of Vrindavan, India. The chants of the faithful blend with the chiming of bells from 5,000 temples. But the prayers rising from a small alley have an especially soulful tone. They are the devotions of widows – some still in their early 20s – who were cast away from their families and shunned by society after their husbands died.

Location

Vrindavan is situated in the north Indian state of Uttar Pradesh around 151 km south of Delhi. It extends from latitude 27°33´ in the North to longitude 77°44´ in the East. The place is just 10 km off Mathura, the place where Lord Krishna is said to have spent his childhood. Vrindavan is situated on the New Delhi-Chennai and New Delhi-Mumbai main railway line. A meter-gauge line connects Vrindavan to Mathura. There are quite a good number of passenger trains plying between these two places.

History

The name 'Vrindavan' is derived from 'Vrinda', another name for the sacred *tulsi* (basil) plant. A legend has it that the entire place was a *tulsi* grove at one time. According to another tradition, it was named after Vrinda Devi, one of Krishna's playmates. The earliest known shrine in Vrindavan is said to have been built by the local gosains in a large garden called Nidhiban, later named Seva Kunj. According to tradition, Emperor Akbar was taken blindfolded inside the grove where he had some kind of a spiritual experience. As a result, he acknowledged the spot as being a holy ground. The four temples that were built in honour of his visit are Govind Deva, Madan Mohan, Gopinath, and Jugal Kishore. The first is an impressive edifice built in red sandstone. Architecturally this temple is one of the finest in north India. However, apart from its history, what keeps Vrindavan alive in the popular imagination of the people is its rich legend and mythology. Vrindavan is considered the place where Lord Krishna spent his early childhood. It was here that Krishna indulged in adolescent pranks with the *gopis* (milkmaids) in the forests and stealing their clothes while they bathed in the river.

Demography

As of 2001 India Census, Vrindavan had a population of 56,618. Males constitute 56 per cent of the population and females 44 per cent. Vrindavan has an average literacy rate of 65 per cent, higher than the national average of 59.5 per cent: male literacy is 73 per cent, and female literacy is 55 per cent. In Vrindavan, 13 per cent of the population is under 6 years of age. The number of females is 24,200 including 13 per cent who are under 6 years of age. Vrindavan is also known as the City of Widows due to the large number of widows who move into the town and surrounding area after losing their husbands. According to some Hindu traditions, upper-caste widows may not remarry, so many of those abandoned by their families on the death of their husband make their way here. There are an estimated 15,000 to 20,000 widows living on the streets, many of whom have spent over 30 years there. In exchange for singing *bhajan* hymns for 7–8 hours in *bhajanashrams*, women are given a cup of rice and a pittance of money, which they try to supplement by begging on the streets. An organization called Guild of Service was formed to assist these deprived women and children. In 2000 the organization opened Amar Bari (My Home), a refuge for 120 Vrindavan widows, and a second shelter for 500 widows is expected to open.

Interpretation of Human Rights in the Context of Bengali Women at Sri Bhagwan Bhajanashram in Vrindavan

The most conspicuous finding of the paper is that the Bengali women at Sri Bhagwan Bhajanashram are deprived of the Human Right to health, and that they are not provided even the basic and essential medical facilities which they require because of being human beings. Article 39(e) of the Constitution of India exhorts the State to ensure that men, women and children are not, for want of health, compelled to enter into avocations not suited to them. The State is duly bound under Article 47 of the Constitution of India to raise the level of nutrition and standard of living and improve public health. The General Assembly proclaims this Universal Declaration of Human Rights as a common standard of achievement for all peoples and all nations, to the end that every individual and every organ of society, keeping this Declaration constantly in mind, shall strive by teaching and education to promote respect for these rights and freedoms and by progressive measures, national and international, to secure their universal and effective recognition and observance, both among the peoples of Member States themselves and among the peoples of territories under their jurisdiction The WHO has defined 'health' as 'a state of complete physical and mental well being and not merely the absence of disease'. To quote the words mentioned in the WHO Constitution: *'the enjoyment of the highest attainable standard of health is one of the fundamental rights of every human being…'* Every country in the world is now party to at least one human rights treaty that addresses health-related rights. This includes the right to health as well as other rights that relate to conditions necessary for health.

The role of the Health and Human Rights is to:

- Strengthen the capacity of WHO and its Member States to integrate a Human Rights-based approach to health.
- Advance the right to health in international law and international development processes.
- Advocate for health-related Human Rights.

Human Rights are universal legal guarantees protecting individuals and groups against actions that interfere with fundamental freedoms and human dignity. Some of the most important characteristics of Human Rights are that they:

- are guaranteed by international standards;
- are legally protected;

- focus on the dignity of the human being;
- oblige states and state actors;
- cannot be waived or taken away;
- are interdependent and interrelated; and
- are universal.

Every woman, man, youth and child has the Human Right to the highest attainable standard of physical and mental health, without discrimination of any kind. Enjoyment of the Human Right to health is vital to all aspects of a person's life and well-being, and is crucial to the realization of many other fundamental human rights and freedoms.

The Human Rights Issue

Human Rights relating to health are set out in basic Human Rights treaties and include:

- The Human Right to the highest attainable standard of physical and mental health, including reproductive and sexual health.
- The Human Right to equal access to adequate health care and health-related services, regardless of sex, race, or other status.
- The Human Right to equitable distribution of food.
- The Human Right to access to safe drinking water and sanitation.
- The Human Right to an adequate standard of living and adequate housing.
- The Human Right to a safe and healthy environment.
- The Human Right to a safe and healthy workplace, and to adequate protection for pregnant women in work proven to be harmful to them.
- The Human Right to freedom from discrimination and discriminatory social practices, including female genital mutilation, prenatal gender selection, and female infanticide.
- The Human Right to education and access to information relating to health, including reproductive health and family planning to enable couples and individuals to decide freely and responsibly all matters of reproduction and sexuality.
- The Human Right of the child to an environment appropriate for physical and mental development.

US Secretary of State Hillary Clinton said that Human Rights are women's rights, and vice versa. She said 'Women's rights are Human Rights, and Human Rights are women's rights.' Women's right to health must be enforced through access to treatment and prevention programmes that allow them to persevere in their pivotal roles. Differences between and among men, non-pregnant women, and pregnant women can influence exposure and response to workplace toxicants. These differences should be delineated, compared, and used when setting regulatory standards to protect workers from potentially hazardous workplace environments. Anatomical and physiological parameters include: body composition; surface area; blood, organ, and tissue volume; metabolism; and cardiovascular, pulmonary, gastrointestinal, and renal structure and function. Although men differ among themselves, on average, they also differ from women by weighing more, being taller, and having a larger surface area. Total, body water is 40 per cent greater in men than non-pregnant women; however, during pregnancy, body water increases from 29 to 33 litres. Extracellular and intracellular water volumes are smallest in non-pregnant women, increase with pregnancy, but remain smaller than those in men. Pulmonary function differs; pregnant women have the largest minute volume and greatest volume of air exchanged in an 8-hour period. It is, indeed, shocking to see in India that the Human Rights which are acclaimed to be the women's Human Rights are not allowed to the women. The Bengali women in Vrindavan and in the surrounding tourists witness this bitter truth. They are waiting for some angel that can help them avail themselves of them. They have, however, strong hopes that some day it will be possible for them to enjoy all their rights and enjoy their status as gloriously as any other woman.

Facts about Women in India

There are seven major areas of discrimination against women in India:

1. *Malnutrition:* India has exceptionally high rates of child malnutrition, because tradition in India requires that women eat last and least throughout their lives, even when pregnant and lactating. Malnourished women give birth to malnourished children, perpetuating the cycle.
2. *Poor Health:* Females receive less healthcare than males. Many women die in childbirth of easily prevented complications. Working conditions and environmental pollution further impairs women's health.
3. *Lack of education:* Families are far less likely to educate girls than boys, and far more likely to pull them out of school, either to help out at home or from fear of violence.
4. *Overwork:* Women work longer hours and their work is more arduous than men's, yet their work is unrecognized. Men report that 'women, like children, eat and do nothing.' Technological progress in agriculture has had a negative impact on women.
5. *Unskilled:* In women's primary employment sector – agriculture – extension services overlook women.
6. *Mistreatment:* In recent years, there has been an alarming rise in atrocities against women in India, in terms of rapes, assaults and dowry-related murders. Fear of violence suppresses the aspirations of all women. Female infanticide and sex-selective abortions are additional forms of violence that reflect the devaluing of females in Indian society.
7. *Powerlessness:* While women are guaranteed equality under the Constitution, legal protection has little effect in the face of prevailing patriarchal traditions. Women lack power to decide who they will marry, and are often married off as children. Legal loopholes are used to deny women inheritance rights.

Objectives

1. To study the structure of Sri Bhagwan Bhajanashram.
2. To study the sources of income to Sri Bhagwan Bhajanashram.

3. To study the conditions under which the Bengali women from the West Bengal come here and spend their whole life chanting ' Hare Krishna Hare Krishna Hare Rama Hare Rama'.
4. To know about their chanting activities and hours.
5. To observe their hygiene conditions.
6. To explore the medical facilities provided to them by Sri Bhagwan Bhajanashram.
7. To know about the environment in which they live.

Hypotheses

1. The Bengali women in the West Bengal have a passion to spend their old age in Vrindavan chanting the name of Lord Krishna.
2. They are driven to Vrindavan particularly by their widowhood.
3. Sri Bhagwan Bhajanashram provides them security and shelter.
4. They spend a major part of their day in chanting 'Hare Krishna Hare Krishna Hare Rama Hare Rama'.
5. The health and hygienic conditions in Sri Bhagwan Bhajanashram are not good and satisfactory.
6. The Bengali women at Sri Bhagwan Bhajanashram belong to different age groups, but the majority of them belongs to the age group of 50–70 years.
7. They are the victims of physical, economic and social exploitation.

Methodology

The study of the Bengali women at the Patthar Pura branch of Sri Bhagwan Bhajanashram was made recently in March 2010. The study is based on both the primary and the secondary data. For the purpose of the collection of primary data, the women were categorized under various age groups. The random sampling method was adopted and 100 women were chosen as the units of information. In order to get the primary data, interview technique was adopted, and besides the chosen Bengali women at the Patthar Pura branch of Sri Bhagwan Bhajanashram the other people such as, the Pandas, the concerned authorities of the Bhajanashram, such as, the manager of the Patthar Pura branch of Sri Bhagwan Bhajanashram Prem Chand Goyal, the employees of Bhajanashram, the Chairman Pushpa Sharma, former members of Nagar Palika Jayshree Sharma and Pratibha Sharma Advocate, the inhabitants of Patthar Pura like Shambhu Charan Pathak (the director of Pathak Coaching Institute), Sunit Kumar (the owner of Sharma Medical Store, opposite Sri Bhagwan Bhajanashram), Braj Dulal Mohant (the Ayurvedic Vaidya) Kashinath Panda, Mohan Panda, Hariom Sharma (the BJP leader), Ram Guru (the owner of Nand Bhawan at Patthar Pura), Narendra Agrawal, Murari Das, Braj Dulal Mohant, and many others were interviewed. The books, project reports, journals and the news in various newspapers formed the secondary data. However, the investigator has emphasized more on the primary data than the secondary ones.

Findings

1. Sri Bhagwan Bhajanashram is not a centre for the Bengali widows only, as is generally believed.

2. The women at Sri Bhagwan Bhajanashram are grouped as the Bengali widows, the married forsaken Bengali women, the divorcee Bengali women, the Bengali spinsters, the women other than Bengali ones.
3. The Bengali widows form 70 per cent of the total women at Sri Bhagwan Bhajanashram; the married forsaken Bengali women form 9 per cent; the divorcee Bengali women form 7 per cent; the Bengali spinsters form 4 per cent and the non Bengali women form 10 per cent of the total women at the Patthar Pura branch of Sri Bhagwan Bhajanashram in Vrindavan.
4. According to the age groups, the Bengali and non Bengali women at the Patthar Pura branch of Sri Bhagwan Bhajanashram, 9 per cent of them are above 60 years, 83 per cent belong to the age group 40–60 years and 8 per cent of them fall in the age group 20–40 years.
5. Of the 100 women selected randomly for the primary data through interview, only 17 reported to be in perfect health, while all the other 83 women reported to be suffering from one or the other disease.
6. The common diseases that make them their prey on occasions are – headache, stomachache, starch coughing, tuberculosis, dysentery, cholera, food-poisoning, etc.
7. The main branch of Sri Bhagwan Bhajanashram at Patthar Pura, Vrindavan is divisible into two sections. In both of the sections of the branch there is no proper and sufficient arrangement of urinals, lavatories and bathrooms, as a result they often contract malaria and several other diseases.
8. There is only one ayurvedic charitable dispensary with a single vaidya. Of the 100 women, 41 are satisfied with the medical facilities provided to them by the Ayurvedic Aushdhalaya while the other 59 women were bold enough to say that the Ayurvedic Aushdhalaya at the Patthar Pura branch of Sri Bhagwan Bhajanashram fails to supply them the medicines they actually need. Moreover, there are fixed hours when the aushdhalaya is opened. When the women need medical aid after the bhajan hours, they have to depend on private doctors and physicians.
9. There is no allopathic hospital of the Sri Bhagwan Bhajanashram, as a result often the diseases of the women get prolonged.
10. There is no facility of surgery. As a result, sometimes, the women at Sri Bhagwan Bhajanashram die.
11. Of the 100 women interviewed, 81 were victims to malnutrition, and were suffering from starvation. Only 19 were well nutritioned.
12. About 29 per cent of the Bengali women and 6 per cent non Bengali women have families and join the Bhajanashram in order to provide financial support to their jobless husbands.
13. About 78 per cent women at the Patthar Pura Branch of Sri Bhajanashram go for sweeping, cleaning utensils and washing clothes after the bhajan hours, and in this way, earn a little additional income.
14. For their clothing and woollen clothes they depend on the Marwaris who donate sarees, blankets, quilts and many other things.
15. In all, 2 per cent women serve the visitors and guests at the branch.
16. All the women at Sri Bhagwan Bhajanashram have to observe the dress code of white saree and blouse.

17. The houses in which they live are generally too narrow and unhygienic.
18. About 14 per cent of the women at Sri Bhagwan Bhajanashram reported to have contracted skin diseases, and therefore, there should be an appointed dermatologist, and despite the fact of the serious concern of the National Women's Commission, a dermatologist has not been appointed yet.

Suggestions

1. Sri Bhagwan Bhajanashram trust should give priority to the health of all those women who have been serving here for years.
2. They should be provided with all the basic medical facilities which they deserve as human beings, moreover, as women.
3. The Central and the State Governments must allow some special funds to the widows and destitute women of Sri Bhagwan Bhajanashram.
4. The National Women's Commission and the Uttar Pradesh Women's Commission should look into the matter of these women and force the government to protect the health of these women.
5. There must be a proper sanitation in the campus where these women spend about 8 hours every day.
6. Allopathic medicines must be available free of cost to these women.
7. The payment of the women which is now only six rupees alongwith 250 gm rice should be increased.
8. The donors ought to be requested to donate more and more for the betterment of these women.
9. The NGOs should work in the interest of such women.
10. The women themselves should be conscious of their rights and they should demand being organized.
11. The kinsmen of these women should not allow them to lead a miserable life as puppets at the hands of the authorities of Sri Bhagwan Bhajanashram.

Interviews

- Prem Chand Goyal (the Manager of Sri Bhagwan Bhajanashram, Patthar Pura branch, Vrindavan)
- Pushpa Sharma (the Chairperson of Municipality Vrindavan)
- Braj Dulal Mohant (the Ayurved Doctor at Patthar Pura, Vrindavan)
- Ram Guru (the owner of Nand Bhawan)
- Sunit Kumar Sharma (the owner of Sharma Medical Store, opposite Sri Bhagwan Bhajanashram, Patthar Pura)
- Narendra Agrawal, one of the most leading cloth merchants at Loi Bazar, Vrindavan
- Hariom Sharma, Jayshree and Pratibha Sharma Advocate (ex Members of Municipality)

15

Land Alienation and Indigenous Rights

The Toto Context

SUBHANKAR ROY AND PINAK TARAFDAR

The right to live is not restricted to mere animal existence; it means something more than just physical survival. The 'right to live' is not confined to the protection of any faculty or limb through which life is enjoyed or the soul communication with the outside world but it also includes the right to live with human dignity and all those that goes with it. The Human Right actually refers to those elemental rights which any human deserves to have honoured in order to survive, enjoy well-being and flourish or fulfil him or herself simply by virtue of being human.

The Universal Declaration of Human Rights (UDHR) tells about the individual rights and freedom for everyone. The fundamental aspects of Human Rights secure the freedom, well-being and dignity of all people everywhere. It also secures freedom from discrimination by gender, race, ethnicity, national origin or religion; freedom to develop and realise one's human potential; freedom from fear; freedom from injustice and violation of the rule of law; freedom from thought and speech; freedom from decent work. The fundamental pillar of Human Rights constitute by the equal opportunities to all, egalitarian social justice, rights to food, shelter, health, leisure, dignity and development of individual facilities. The basic attributes of Human Rights clarifies that everyone has the right to life, liberty and security of a person, right to nationality, individual dignity, right to culture and religious freedom, right to justice, right to equality, right to respect and privacy, right to earn and employment and right to property.

But, at the present time, there are several factors which severely tell upon the violation of these fundamental Human Rights. The present study reveals, how the issue land alienation directly or indirectly related with the Human Rights violation in the tribal situation.

Studied Area and the People

Totopara is a small village under the Madarihat-Birpara block of Alipurduar district. The area situated in the Indo-Bhutan border of the bank of river Torsha. The hillocks are from 750´ to 1250´ above the sea-level and lie at latitude 89°20´E and longitude 26°50´W. The northern end touches Bhutan, on the east the river Torsha, and on the south and west titi forests of Jaldapara National Park. The village was named after the inhabitation of the people belongs to the

Toto tribal group. There are several economic transactions have been done between India and Bhutan through Totopara. The village Totopara is divided into six sectors viz., Panchayat Gaon, Subba Gaon, Mondol Gaon, Puja Gaon, Mitran Gaon and Dhumchi Gaon. Both the Toto and non-Toto population lived together in these sectors. As the study is done on the tribal land alienation, mainly the Toto population is considered for this work.

Historical Background

The place Totopara was recorded first time by the British administrators during the second half of the 19th century and so far record goes the authors were O'Donnel and Mr Hodgson, the first two official people from the British administration who covered Totopara and estimated the areas as 1,027.36 acres. They were followed by Mr Sunder who had estimated the area of Totopara as 1,116.74 acres. He also recorded about the people and the crops grown by the people in the survey and settlement of Western Duars in 1895. The second survey was conducted by Mr Milligan during 1906–1916. He wrote a short note on the Totos and recorded an area of 2003 acres for Totopara where 235 individual lived in 60 houses. He had also fixed a capitation tax of an amount of ₹ 120 per year on the basis of 60 adults living in 60 separate houses. In this way, Totos of Totopara were brought under the British colonial administration without much interference in the ways of tribal people. During 1921 Census year, their population increased to 271 with 60 houses. It is worth mentioning that during the decades 1911–1951, the population increased but not the houses. The first non-Toto settlement at Totopara started during late 1920s and eventually six non-Toto males were recorded in 1931 Census and by 1952, one-third population of the village were non-Totos.

The British annexations of Totopara as a part of newly formed district, Jalpaiguri, in 1869 did not have perceptible influence on the Totos except imposition of capitation tax. But indirect influence on the lifestyle of the Totos could be traced since the beginning of the settlement of the tea-plantation in this region.

The Totos had a trial of migration from one place to other before they settled down in the present village, Totopara (Sanyal, 1973). It appears from their tradition and conjectural statements that they had their home in the southern part of the district, Jalpaiguri* in the Western Duars area where from they moved to Bhutan in the north and again came down to Totopara. They cannot recall when they came here but do claim that they are the autochthons of the area and Totopara originally belonged to them only.

Methodology

Stratified sampling has been done for the selection of the sectors in Totopara. Among the six sectors (Panchayat Gaon, Subba Gaon, Mondol Gaon, Puja Gaon, Mitran Gaon and Dhumchi Gaon), four sectors (Panchayat Gaon, Subba Gaon, Puja Gaon and Mitran Gaon) were selected under the two broad category viz., Category–1 (Puja Gaon and Mitran Gaon) and Category–2 (Panchayat Gaon and Subba Gaon). The selection was made on the basis of some

---

* Jalpaiguri district was bifurcated on 25 June 2014 to create new district Alipurduar.

characteristic features like land distribution, land transfer, agricultural category, land holding pattern, loan, indebtedness, etc. The data was collected from the sectors of two categories by using preliminary census schedule, questionnaire, etc. Observation, case studies and interview techniques were also very useful to understand the violation of human rights in connection with the tribal land alienation. The secondary data was collected from various Census reports, journals, books and block office.

Present Scenario of Land in the Toto Society

The Toto community settled in the foothills of sub-Himalayan region in Alipurduar district is one of the smallest tribel communities of West Bengal. The Toto society is not just an egalitarian but a rank society having a tradition of heredity headman locally called *Mondol*. Earlier, the whole area of Totopara Mouza (revenue village) was recorded in the name of the then *Mondoal,* Dhanapati Toto, as a community land on behalf of the whole community. But recently the most important problem among the Toto are scarcity of land and in reality they have been evicted from their cultivable lands which they enjoyed under tribal land tenure system.

Before Independence, the permission was not given to the non-Toto people to live in the Totopara permanently. But after 1951, the non-Toto people, mainly the people from Nepal and Bihar, entered the Totopara. By using the simplicity of the Toto people, the outsiders started to capture the land of Totopara. But according to the government rule (Section 14c), Land Reformation Act, 1955(5), it is not possible to acquire the land of Totopara by the non-Toto people. Today, the Totos are the minor population group in the village. They constitute only 43.19 per cent population in the total village (Table 1).

Table 1

Population of Totopara since 1931

Year	*Source*	*Toto Population*	*Non-Toto Population*	*Total Population*
1931	Census of India	334 98.24	06 1.46	340 100.00
1952	Cultural Research Institute	383 66.72	191 33.28	574 100.00
1953	Indian Social Institute, New Delhi	322 58.55	228 41.45	550 100.00
1969	Cultural Research Institute	482 41.70	674 58.30	1156 100.00
1981	Census of India	709 47.36	788 52.64	1497 100.00
1991	Census of India	904 50.17	898 49.83	1802 100.00
1993	Cultural Research Institute	962 44.70	1190 55.30	2152 100.00
2010	Field Study	1171 43.19	1540 56.81	2711 100.00

According to Table 1, it can be easily understood that the Totos are facing tremendous problem regarding land due to the rapid influx of the non-Toto population in the area. In 1931, there was only six non-Toto people in the Totopara. But the number of non-Toto population gradually increased day by day and now 56.81 per cent of the total populations formed by the non-Totos. They grabbed the fertile land of Totopara without the permission of the Totos. One investigation, done on the land of Totopara, pointed out that 138 acres of land from the 347.43 acres has already been grabbed by the non-Totos mainly by the Nepalese who came in Totopara for the first time with 12 families after driven away from Nepal in 1950.

Table 2

Year Wise per Head Land Distribution

Year	*No. of Population*	*Total Amount of Land (in acres)*	*Per head land Distribution (in acres)*
1901	171	1,116.74	6.53
1911	235	2,003	8.52
1921	271	2,003	7.39
1931	334	2,003	6.00
1941	321	2,003	6.23
1951	321	1,996.96	6.22
1961	395	1,996.96	5.06
1971	584	347.43	0.59
1981	709	347.43	0.49
1991	904	347.43	0.38
2001	1,157	347.43	0.30
2010	1,171	347.43	0.29

Source: Census of India (1901–2001) and Field Work (2010).

The British government gave the rights to enjoy the land of Totopara Mouza, an area of 1,996.96 acres, to the Totos in exchange of a capitation tax of ₹ 2 per household. Later, in 1931, the tax was raised to ₹ 142 for 63 households. The *Mondal* was responsible for collecting and depositing it to the appropriate authority. After the introduction of the United Front Government in West Bengal (1969) it was stated to the Totos, that if they registered more land, they should pay more tax for that. Because of that reason the Totos registered less amount of land in their name and in this way the total amount of registered land was 347.43 acres. After that the Totos did not pay any tax up to 26 years. At that time no government official alerted them for paying the arrears of rent. They paid their tax of an amount of ₹ 2–2.5 lakh approximately in the later half of the first decade of 21st century and every household had to pay of an amount of ₹ 10–15 thousand. But the most striking feature is that the Nepalese, Biharis and the other non-Toto population do not pay any tax for the land because they do not have any official land in their names.

Another striking scenario regarding the land of Totopara is that, there is no demarcation of land. The Toto people paid the tax for land, but they do not know the place and the area of their land. The Totos requested to the government for demarcation of lands, but the government turned a deaf ear to the Totos. Now the Totos are thinking about a strong movement to solve their problems of land. Table 2 reveals that up to 1961, per capita land was about 5.06 acres per head and in 1971 per head land distribution came to 0.59 acres, and eventually the figure came down to 0.29 acres in the present study conducted in the 2010. According to Table 3, per household land distribution is 04.47 bigha in case of the sectors of Category–1 and in case of the sectors of Category–2, per household land distribution is 05.05 bigha. The Totos were not very much aware of the land alienation, they could not realize its consequences even in 1969 when the Toto chief of the village, Dhanpati Toto agreed to lease out good cultivated land to a Nepali in exchange of ₹ 700 with certain terms and conditions.

Table 3

Per Household Land Distribution in the Four Studied Sectors of Totopara

Name of the Sectors		*No. of Household*	*Total Amount of Land (in Bighas)*	*Per Household Land Distribution (in Bighas)*
Category–1	Mitran Gaon	029	109.35	03.77
	Puja Gaon	022	118.45	05.38
	Total	051	227.80	04.47
Category–2	Panchayat Gaon	062	376.25	06.06
	Subba Gaon	068	281.00	04.13
	Total	130	657.25	05.05
Total		181	885.05	04.88

Source: Field Work (2010).

Table 4

Land Transfer in the Four Studied Sectors of Totopara

Name of the Sectors		*Number of Families*				*Total*
		Sale	*Purchase*	*Mortgage*	*No*	
Category–1	Mitran Gaon	—	02	—	27	29
			06.90		93.10	100.00
	Puja Gaon	01	01	01	19	22
		04.55	04.55	04.55	86.35	100.00
	Total	01	03	01	46	51
		01.96	05.88	01.96	90.20	100.00
Category–2	Panchayat Gaon	04	08	01	49	62
		06.45	12.90	01.61	79.03	100.00
	Subba gaon	04	06	03	55	68
		05.89	08.82	04.41	80.88	100.00
	Total	08	14	04	104	130
		06.15	10.77	03.07	80.00	100.00
Grand Total		09	17	05	150	181
		04.97	09.39	02.76	82.87	100.00

Source: Field Work (2010).

Historically, Toto's relations with the land and forests have been changing since the inclusion of Totopara by the British Raj. It deserves mention in this context that the political relation between the British Raj and the king of Bhutan was delicate and sensitive. The British administration had adopted lenient policy against the tribes of the bordering region and it is more so in case of the Totos. The British administration had made them to establish a peculiar relationship which has been maintaining a ritual relation with the foresters as well as forest workers whom they call *lotamuni*. In this context, it is worth mentioning that the forest workers are known as *Cung-sa* in their indigenous vocabulary. They also perform the worship of *Pidua*. C.C. Sanyal in 1972 reported that the forest department of Lankapara range particularly the Hallapara beat pays an annual subscription of ₹10 and a piece of white cloth (about one metre in length), which the Totos tied to a long bamboo pole and allowed to flutter high above the tree to ward off the evil spirits, ghosts, demons and gobbling.

During the British Raj, the Totos remained more or less secured and maintained their unchanged traditional way of living. The problem started with the increasing number of intrusion of non-Totos in the Totopara since 1952. Economically well off non-Totos made the Totos inferior in the village. At the beginning, the outsiders offered friendship to the Totos, but gradually the friendship and trust of the Totos was betrayed by them. The rapid infiltration of population is not only altering the land-man ratio but also affecting their socio-cultural beliefs and practices.

Another problem faced by the Totos is land alienation. The major demand of the Totos is to restore the land of their ancestors. The prospect of the land of their ancestor being restored to them is still quite difficult. The shift of subsistence strategies from *jhum* cultivation to cash crop had pauperised households and the emerging distressed economic situation stands in the way for many Toto children to attend the schools. Besides, socio-political subjugation even in their own village leads them to feel socially inferior. The pattern of land distribution among the Totos also indicates their poor economic condition and existing inequality in their society. This primitive tribal society has been stratified on the basis of amount of land. The landless cultivators occupied the lower most stratum and the persons doing white collar jobs and who cultivated their huge amount of land with the landless agriculture labourers occupied the highest stratum in this stratification.

The economic life of the Toto has been transformed into a great extent due to the terrace cultivation. They learnt it from their Nepali neighbours. During the cultivation at first they cleared the forest and then they plough their land after preparing terrace. Only cow-dung was used as good organic manure for increasing the fertility of their land. Inter-cropping is now followed in certain cases with the cultivation of ginger and maize. Maize, *maruwa*, paddy, potato, sweet potato, green vegetables, ginger and betel-nut. are mainly cultivated by the Totos. The Totos are mainly depending on land and forest for their economy and food source. If the amount of the land has not been improved, per head land distribution would be decreased with the increase of population. So, the Totos are compelled to think about the family planning programme to control their population. The Totos are peace loving people and many of them attained family planning programme from the government health institutions of Madarihat and

Birpara by changing their names. Table 4 reveals that many economically poor Toto people sold their land to the money lenders and the non-Tribal people who were economically much stronger. Because of the long and expensive ritualistic performances in various occasions the Totos were compelled to sell their only unit of production, i.e. land.

Table 5 reveals that the percentage of owner cultivator is much higher than the other agricultural occupational category in all the four studied sectors, but the percentage is comparatively larger in the sectors of Category–1 than Category–2. On the other hand the percentage of non-cultivating owner is higher in the sectors of Category–2. So it may be said that the peoples of Category–1 are more associated with the agricultural work directly.

Table 5

Distribution of Household According to Agricultural Category in the Four Studied Sectors of Totopara

Name of the Sectors		*Owner Cultivator*	*Non-cultivating Owner*	*Share Cropper*	*Agricultural Labour*	*Total*
Category–1	Mitran Gaon	26 89.65	01 03.45	02 06.90	—	29 100.00
	Puja Gaon	21 95.45	—	01 04.55	—	22 100.00
	Total	47 92.16	01 01.96	03 05.88	—	51 100.00
Category–2	Panchayat Gaon	49 79.03	08 12.90	03 04.84	02 03.23	62 100.00
	Subba Gaon	57 83.82	06 08.82	04 05.88	01 01.48	68 100.00
	Total	106 81.54	14 10.77	07 05.38	03 02.31	130 100.00
Total		153 84.53	15 08.29	10 05.52	03 01.66	181 100.00

Source: Field Work (2010).

'Toto Kalyan Samity' is a non-governmental welfare association whose members are fighting for the rights of the Totos and it is very much concerned with the development of the Totos. They fight against the rapid land transfer in the Totopara and restricted it up to some extent. They are trying to get the declared benefits and welfare assistance for their community members in order to achieve the desired benefits. They have lodged movements and are protesting the bureaucratic structure at the block and sub-divisional level.

Conclusion

Land is the centre of most conflicts because of its importance in the life of the people particularly the tribal people. For the tribal people land is not only a means of production or a possession, they consider land as a part of the total environment in which they carry on their life. They do not own the land but the land owns them and generates them as sons. For this reason the link with land has such a spiritual value. The land among the tribal is very much related with their culture, health behaviour, social structure, and political power. The various processes of land alienation are responsible for violating the basic indigenous rights among the Toto.

As already mentioned, the Totos have been living in the geographically isolated and culturally secluded area adopting Swedish way of cultivation of millets and maizes, as their main subsistence strategy. Historically, this place of land has become the part of Bengal with British annexation of the area in 1869 as delineated above. Since then Totopara has become a revenue village. Later, for about 40 years or so, they became settled agriculturists but their technological adoption of this economy has not reached up to the mark in spite of the fact that modern education has made some imprint on the filial generation. They are suffering from variegated socio-economic problems due to impact of various socio-economic and cultural changes. They become gradually a minority group in their own lands under the influx of various other communities. A good number of them were swamped by waves of immigrants from overpopulated neighbouring localities of non-Toto, over the last three to four decades which have resulted in disequilibrium condition affecting the ecological setting of Totopara.

The present study concludes two things, one the Totos one of the three Particularly Vulnerable Tribal Group (PVTG) of West Bengal are facing tremendous crisis regarding their land. Because of that they are forced to deviate from their traditional cultural practices, norms, customs, beliefs, social relationship, social structure, health behaviour, political power, etc. which ultimately violated their indigenous rights. The scenario of land in Totopara was changed after the intrusion of the non-Toto people (mainly the Nepalese and Biharis) in the village. Mainly that interference was started after the Independence. Within twenty years of the Independence, rapid land alienation occurred when the total amount of land in Totopara shrinked into 347.43 acres. In the later stage it was found that among the 347.43 acres land 138 acres already been grabbed by the non-Toto population. As a result the land-man ratio of the area largely declined because of the rapid land alienation process and gradually increasing number of the non-Toto population which creates a great impact in the Toto economy.

Insufficiency of the land leads economic constraints among some section of the Toto population which compelled them to convert towards Christianity for achieving comfortable economic condition. The entire process is once again responsible for the violation of cultural rights among the Toto.

Although the Totos were very much dependent on their land, but due to their long and expensive traditional ritualistic practices, the Totos had to mortgage their unit of production to the rich money lenders and take credit from them with a very high amount of interest. If they are not able to return the indebted money in stipulated time, the money lenders captured their lands. In that way, the Totos lost their own land day-by-day, which has created a great economic imbalance among them. The people who have their own land became richer in the society; on the contrary those who lost their land became poor. Economically superior people can afford their children get modern education and because of that they are mostly related with the modern economic system.

From the present study it could say that the sectors of Category–2 (Panchayat Gaon and Subba Gaon) is economically and educationally more rich than the sectors of Category–1 (Puja Gaon and Mitran Gaon). As the people of the Category–1 is educationally and economically much better than the people of Category–2, they hold more political power and can avail the modern facilities also. On the other hand, the peoples of Category–2 are more collective in nature and because of poor economic condition they are not able to perform their traditional cultural practices and can not also avail modern facilities. In addition to these it may be said that they are also not in a good political position. So the tribals from the sectors of Category–2 belong to the higher stratum of newly formed social stratification. To reduce violation of the indigenous rights it is very much required to stop the land alienation process by the other community and restore equal land distribution in the tribal village. Furthermore, their traditional knowledge, beliefs, customs, rituals, etc. should be documented in a proper way.

On the way to get modern education and modern economic practices, the young generation of the Toto society are not able to perform traditional cultural practices, norms, beliefs, customs, ritualistic, etc. which were ornamented by their indigenous characteristic attributes. On the other hand, the Totos who were not economically sound could not afford the expenses of their traditional rituals. So it is clear from the present study that land alienation stratified the Toto society into two socio-economic strata. The economically rich people are in the higher stratum and the economically poor peoples are in the lower one. In addition to that both the strata are the departure from their indigenous characteristic notion which also emerges as a threat for their exclusive cultural entity.

References

Bhattacharya, M. 1998. *Toto at Cross Roads*. Kolkata: Aparna Book Distributor.

Brandis, D. 1897. *Indian Forestry*. Woking, UK: Oriental University Institute.

Chakrobarty, P. and K. Chattopadhyay, 1964. 'Some Aspects of Toto Ethnography'. *Bulletin of the Cultural Research Institute*. Vol. III, No. 2.

Chaudhuri, B. (ed.). 1982. *Tribal Development in India: Problems and Prospects*. New Delhi: Inter-India Publication.

———. (ed.). 1990. *Cultural and Environmental Dimensions on Health*. New Delhi: Inter-India Publications.

———. (ed.). 1986. *Tribal Health: Socio-Cultural Dimensions*. New Delhi: Inter-India Publication.

———. 2003. *Health, Forest and Development: The Tribal Situation*. New Delhi: Inter-India Publication.

———. and A.K. Maiti. 1982. *Fuel Need, Social Forestry and the Forest Dwellers*. CADC Sponsored Project, W.B.

Das, A.K. 1969. *The Totos.* Kolkata, W.B.: Cultural Research Institute

Debnath, S.K. 1982. 'Courtship and Ceremonial Aspect of Marriage among the Totos: A Tribal Isolate of Indo-Bhutan Border'. *Vanyajati*. Vol. XXX, No. 1.

Dhali, Debnath. 1987. *Toto* (In Bengali). Kolkata, W.B.: Cultural Research Institute.

Eckholm, E. 1976. *Losing Ground: Environmental Stress and World Food Prospects.* New York: W.W. Norton.

Eckholm, E. 1976. 'Firewood: The Poor Man's Burden'. *International Wildlife,* May – June.

Fernandes, W. (ed.). 1992. *National Development and Tribal Deprivations.* New Delhi: Indian Social Institute.

Fernandes, W. and G. Menon. 1987. *Tribal Woman and Forest Economy: Deforestation, Exploitation and Status Change.* New Delhi: Indian Social Institute.

Government of India, 1982. Ministry of Home Affairs Report of the Committee on Forest and Tribals in India.

Grierson, G.A. 1909. *Linguistic Survey of India*, Vol. III, Part- I.

Guha, R. 1983. 'Forestry in British and Post British India'. *Economy and Political Weekly,* October 29.

Guha, R. (ed.). 1994. *Social Ecology.* New Delhi: Oxford University Press.

Jain, S.K. 1968. *Medicinal Plants.* New Delhi: National Book Trust.

Joshi, G. 1881. *Forest Policy and Tribal Development: Problems of Implementation, Ecology and Exploitation.* Cyclostyled Paper.

Majumdar, B. 1991. *A Sociological Study of Toto Folk Tales.* Kolkata: National Book Trust, India.

Milligan, J. 1919. *Final Report on Survey Settlement Operation in Jalpaiguri District.* Kolkata: Bengal Secratarist Book Depot.

Mitra, A. 1953. The District Handbook: The Jalpaiguri Census 1951, Appendix VIII, Kolkatta: Superintendent of Census Operations.

Pant, M.M. 1978. 'Social Forestry: It's Role in National Economy'. *Eastern Economists,* November. pp. 1032–37.

Rao, Y.S. 1994. *Asia-Pacific Tropical Forestry: Ecological Disaster or Sustainable Growth,* Bangkok: RAPA Publications.

Roy Burman, B.K. 1957. 'Drama of Two Drums I: Mayu Festival of the Totos'. *Indian Folklore,* Vol. II, No. 1, pp. 16–31.

——. 1957. 'Drama of Two Drums II: Mayu Festval of the Totos'. *Indian Folklore,* Vol. II, October–December, pp. 25–38.

——. 1964. A Note on the Socio-Medical Survey among the Totos, *Bulletin of the Cultural Research Institute,* Vol. III, No. 344, pp. 16–19.

——. 1982. *Report of the Committee of Forest and Tribals.* New Delhi: Government of India.

Sanyal, C.C. 1973. *The Meches and The Totos of North Bengal.* Darjeeling: The University of North Bengal.

Sarkar, A. 1991. *Toto: Society and Change (A Sub-Himalayan Tribe of West Bengal).* Kolkata: F.K. Pvt. Ltd.

Singh, C. 1986. *Common Property and Common Poverty: India's Forest Dwellers and the Law.* New Delhi: Oxford University Press, pp. 10.

Singh, R.(ed.). 2000. *Environmental Policy and Tribal Modernisation.* New Delhi: Anmol Publications Pvt. Ltd.

Sinha, D. and B.C. Paul. 1984. 'A Study of Eco-Sociological Change among an Underdeveloped Tribes: The Totos of North Bengal'. *Bulletin of the Cultural Research Institute,* Vol. XVI, No. 1–4.

Tewari, D.N. 1981. *State Trading in Forest Produce in India.* Dehradun: J.K. and Co.

Vidyarthi, L.P. and B.K. Rai. 1977. *Tribal Culture of India,* Delhi: Concept Publishing Company.

Vyas, N.N. 1986. *Land and Tribals,* Udaipur: Tribal Research Institute.

Other Reading Sources

Census India, 1901–2001. New Delhi: Government of India.

Dainik Basumati, 14 August 1944.

Jalpaiguri District Gazetter, 1911.

16

Right to Education

Status of Tribal Women in India

SWATI CHAKRABORTY

By education I mean an all round drawing out of the best in the child and man – body, mind and spirit.

—Mahatma Gandhi.

Introduction

There is a strong interrelation between education and women empowerment. Realizing the enormity of the problems of Indian women, the Government of India has appointed a separate committee on the Status of Women in India, The social backwardness of Indian women points to the great hiatus between their legal status which is more or less equal to that of men, and their actual position in society, which is still far from the ideal which exists on paper. The educational, economical, political and social backwardness of women makes them the largest group hindering the process of rapid social changes. It is inevitable that when this 'backward' group has the major responsibility of bringing up future generations, the advancement of society cannot be rapid or take any significant form of development. In the report of the committee appointed by the National Council for Women's Education, it was emphatically stated that what was needed to convert the equality of women from de jure to be facto status was widespread education for girls and women and a re-education of men and women to accept new and scientific attitudes towards each other and to themselves. Education's importance has been emphasized by a number of international conventions, including the Universal Declaration of Human Rights and the Programme of Action of the 1994 International Conference on Population and Development. The Fourth World Conference on Women, held in Beijing in 1995, recognized that women's literacy is the key to empowering women's participation in decision making in society and to improving families' well-being. In addition, the United Nations has articulated the Millennium Development Goals (MDGs), which include goals for improved education, gender equality, and women's empowerment. The MDGs emphasize education's essential role in building democratic societies and creating a foundation for sustained economic growth. Education contributes directly to the growth of national income by improving the productive capacities of the labour force. A recent study of 19 developing countries, including Egypt, Jordan, and Tunisia, concluded that a country's long term economic growth increases by 3.7 per cent for every year the adult population's average level of schooling rises. Thus, education is a key strategy for reducing poverty, especially in the First World countries, where poverty is not as deep as in other developing regions. According to the United Nations Population Fund, countries that have made social investments in health, family planning, and education have slower population growth and faster economic growth than countries that have not made such investments. In the increasingly open global economy, countries with high rates of illiteracy and gender gaps in educational attainment tend to be less competitive, because foreign investors seek labour that is skilled as well as inexpensive. Various global trends pose special challenges to women who are illiterate or have limited education. Economies' export orientation and the growing importance of small and medium sized enterprises create opportunities for women, but women need the appropriate education and training to take full advantage of these opportunities. It is still not being realized that there is definite connection between education, good motherhood and efficient house management. The management of millions of household and the upbringing of millions of children, thus, is in the hands of illiterate women. It is here that a change is required if our democratic and socialistic intensions are not to remain a mere pretence. People can be motivated to have their children educated only if educational system is directly linked with economic and social development. As long as our education remains oblivious of the felt needs of people to solve their immediate problems and on the contrary, actually alienates them from their natural, social and cultural surroundings, they will rightly resist sending their children to school. It is the area of primary education, especially in rural areas, which should be given maximum attention. Primary education for both girls and boys is what we should be concerned about while planning our policies and allocation funds. It is this sector of our education structure that gets neglected in favour of all sorts of institutes of 'higher learning' and 'research' of a kind that are neither relevant nor pertinent to our pressing problems. The role of women outside home is becoming an important and even essential feature of our present day reality.

Defining 'Education' in Tribal Context

For us 'education' is an integral part of the empowerment process. Empowerment of the tribal community means capacitating tribal communities to secure access and control of their land, forest and water resources as well as sustains and promotes viable alternatives for security of their livelihoods. Empowerment, thus, is an interactive process whereby tribal communities are enabled to participate actively in local governance (decision making that affects their own life situation). It is in this context that we need to define the role of adult education. For us, educating tribal communities in a more concrete sense means to facilitate processes, which will enable tribal representatives to:

- Develop an analytical capacity for assessing their external and internal environment impacting on their own communities;

- Develop confidence and capacity to articulate their interests and perspective thereby participating in decision making processes leading to better governance;
- Develop skills to initiate local relevant alternatives to improve livelihoods and challenge external pressures;
- Value self and community history with a critical appreciation of traditional knowledge systems.

We do recognize that adult literacy constitutes an important part of adult education and we have made some attempts in this direction.

From 1992–97, tribal youth are being facilitated to take up night schools as a part of the government drive for adult literacy. Several of the trainers were absorbed into the state-run literacy programme initiated in 1998. However, our major involvement has been with young adults who have been dropouts of the school system. School dropouts have very little opportunities for further education. The percentage of enrollment in schools is 79 per cent (89 per cent for male and 68 per cent for female). But the dropout rate among the tribal is as much as 71 per cent while for the general population, it is only 65 per cent. The ambitious ones tend to be frustrated with an alienating education experience and some of them often land up joining extremist groups in the area. Mainstream educational institutions do not 'educate' because the curriculum does not give due consideration to the rich traditional knowledge and value systems prevalent within tribal societies These institutions do not create an opportunity to develop and learn skills which are relevant to the needs, lifestyle and aspirations of tribal communities. We believe that it is important to invest in the youth because it is they who are going to steer the future of tribal societies. Hence 'alternative education' has had been focusing mainly on with tribal youth. Education is particularly important in early age. Success of child's life depends on how seriously you involve him or her in early learning.

The Millennium Development Goals and Women Education

The UN Millennium Summit, held in September 2000, produced a set of eight Millennium Development Goals (MDGs) covering a range of development issues, including reducing child mortality, fighting various infectious diseases, eradicating illiteracy, and empowering women. The MDGs and their associated targets and indicators were designed as benchmarks for monitoring progress in developing countries and to provide a framework for sustaining development and eliminating poverty. The international community recognizes that unless girls' education improves, few of the MDGs wili be achieved. Two of the goals deal specifically with female education and women's empowerment:

- *Goal 2:* Achieve universal primary education. Target: Ensure that, by 2015, all children, boys and girls alike, will have access to a full course of primary education. Indicators for this goal: the net enrollment ratio in primary education; the proportion of pupils starting grade 1 who reach grade 5; and the literacy rate of 15 to 24 year olds.
- *Goal 3:* Promote gender equality and empower women. Target: Eliminate gender disparities in primary and secondary education, preferably by 2005, and at all levels of education no later than 2015. Indicators for this goal: the

ratio of girls to boys in primary, secondary, and tertiary education; the ratio of literate females to males among 15 to 24 year old; the share of women in wage employment in the non agricultural sector; and the proportion of seats in national parliament held by women.

The Indian Scenario

The spread of education among the weaker sections of our society is vital as education is a prime requisite for socio-economic development. The policy to promote educational interests of the weaker sections of the people, especially the Scheduled Castes and Scheduled Tribes, has been enshrined in our Constitution as a Directive Principle of state policy. In the days of yore tribal people had a well-organized system of education. The child learnt at home and at dormitories and this training related to various activities of tribal life. But with the advent of Christian Missionaries, modern schools came up in tribal areas. Lack of social mobility and the problem of intercultural communication are major retarding factors in tribal education. As the teacher and the taught in the tribal areas belong to different cultures, the communication barrier becomes almost insurmountable. The late Humayun Kabir had rightly remarked that even the best system of education is bound to fail without an efficient and resourceful teacher. Most of the teachers appointed in tribal areas are a disinterested lot due to various problems faced by them such as lack of proper residential facility, good salary, communication facility and social distance from the tribal people. Thus, the teacher feels isolated and unhappy and a disgruntled teacher is, certainly, not the best communicator of modern ideas and messages to tribal children. So even though the government has come up in recent times with various plans and programmes to improve the educational lot of the tribal, there is not much result to show as there is lack of sincerity on the part of the officials charged with the implementation of these programmes. In fact, a credibility gap has emerged between such officials and the tribal people. If all these problems are to be tackled successfully, the government has to bring about a change in the basic orientation in tribal education. The government in its zeal to provide facilities to the tribal has constructed hostels for the tribal students, supplied textbooks, provided different types of scholarship, etc. But instead of bridging the gap, it has widened the rift. The tribal students staying in separate hostels, availing themselves of separate scholarships, feel naturally ostracized. This should change and instead there might be some percentage reservation of seats for tribal in a general hostel and tribal students should be encouraged to take an active part in various college as well as hostel activities. As regards appointment of teachers, more and more appointments should be made from among the tribal population so that the teachers become accepted and they deal with the tribal students by using a more permissive and motivational approach. The existing teachers should be provided with adequate facilities and they should be properly oriented. It should be a must for the teachers to learn the tribal language and there can also be attempts at writing text books in tribal languages. Moreover, the education of girl children has little functional importance to them. Even after secondary education there can be no gainful employment. Thus, there is no incentive for education. So the existing curricula should be related to socio-economic and cultural life of the tribal. Emphasis must be on imparting skills and modern information on agriculture, poultry, forestry and carpentry, etc. Only by providing better communication facilities, sanitary programmes, teaching materials and methods, the government can hope to bring about an attitudinal change in the tribal population towards education. Otherwise, with the present state of affairs, the dream of our Constitution makers about tribal education would always remain a dream. In spite of certain outstanding examples of individual achievement of Indian women and a definite improvement in their general condition over the last 100 years, it remains true that our women still constitute a large body of under privileged citizens. Women of course do not form a homogenous group in class or caste terms. Nevertheless, they face distinctive problems that call for special attention. The Backward Classes Commission set up by the Government of India in 1953 classified women of India as a backward group requiring special attention. A changing society and a developing economy cannot make any headway if education, which is one of the important agents affecting the norms of morality and culture, remains in the hand of traditionalists who subscribe to a fragmented view of the country's and the world's heritage. The differences between the positions of men and women in society will not lessen; leave aside disappear, as long as there are differences between the education of men and women. Inadequate education or no education is the most important factor contributing to the backwardness of our masses, especially our womenfolk. It is the low literacy among women which brings national literacy figure so low. This gap which exists between the literacy rates of the two sexes also exists between the enrollment of girls and boys at all levels of education. Right from the primary school to the university, we find that the number of girl students is considerably lower than the number of boy students.

According to Article 45 of the Constitution of India, universal compulsory and free education until the age of 14 was to be achieved by the year 1960. Looking at the present condition of primary education in villages, it seems doubtful that 100 per cent enrollment of girls can be achieved by the end of this century. There is no doubt that we have made great headway in the education of women in the last century. It is unfortunately true of our society that children are sent to school not according to their intelligence or aptitude but according to their sex. Such attitudes need to be changed without further delay if we want to achieve 100 per cent enrollment of the primary school going children. Although the disparity between the enrollment of girls and boys has been lessening in the urban areas, the gap between their enrollment is still very wide specially in rural areas. The reasons for this are both economic and social. The economic structure of rural areas is such that children, especially girls, are required to help in household work and perform their chores. Young girls have to look after their younger brothers and sisters, have to get water from the well, have to carry food to the father in the field, etc. Since there is so much to be done at home, they cannot be spared for the luxury of attending a school. The resources of the poor farmer are so limited that he does not have anything to spare for the education of his children. If there are any resources available, the boy of the family will get the chance first. Parents also do not see the value of educating their children specially daughters who would get married after all and be only housewives. Since they cannot see any direct relationship between education and economic betterment, they have very little motivation to send their children to school.

Importance of Tribal Women Education

Educated women are more politically active and better informed about their legal rights and how to exercise them. There are several compelling benefits associated with girls' education, which include the reduction of child and maternal mortality, improvement of child nutrition and health, lower fertility rates, enhancement of women's domestic role and their political participation, improvement of the economic productivity and growth, and protection of girls from HIV/AIDS, abuse and exploitation. Girls' education yields some of the highest returns of all development investments, yielding both private and social benefits that accrue to individuals, families, and society:

- Reducing women's fertility rates: Women with formal education are much more likely to use reliable family planning methods, delay marriage and childbearing, and have fewer and improved babies than women with no formal education. It is estimated that one year of female schooling reduces fertility by 10 per cent. The effect is particularly pronounced for secondary schooling.
- Lowering infant and child mortality rates: Women with some formal education are more likely to seek medical care, ensure their children are immunized, be better informed about their children's nutritional requirements, and adopt improved sanitation practices. As a result, their infants and children have higher survival rates and tend to be healthier and better nourished.
- Lowering maternal mortality rates: Women with formal education tend to have better knowledge about healthcare practices, are less likely to become pregnant at a very young age, tend to have fewer, better spaced pregnancies, and seek pre and postnatal care. It is estimated that an additional year of schooling for 1,000 women helps prevent two maternal deaths.
- Protecting against HIV/AIDS infection: Women's education ranks among the most powerful tools for reducing women's vulnerability. It slows and reduces the spread of HIV/AIDS by contributing to female economic independence, delayed marriage, family planning, and work outside the home, as well as conveying greater information about the disease and how to prevent it.
- Increasing women's labour force participation rates and earnings: Education has been proven to increase income for wage earners and increase productivity for employers, yielding benefits for the community and society.
- Creating intergenerational education benefits: Mothers' education is a significant variable affecting children's education attainment and

opportunities. A mother with a few years of formal education is considerably more likely to send her children to school. In many countries each additional year of formal education completed by a mother translates into her children remaining in school for an additional one third to one half year. In addition, the benefits of female education for women's empowerment and gender equality are broadly recognized:

- As female education rises, fertility, population growth, and infant and child mortality fall and family health improves.
- Increases in girls' secondary school enrollment are associated with increases in women's participation in the labour force and their contributions to household and national income.
- Women's increased earning capacity, in turn, has a positive effect on child nutrition.
- Children – especially daughters – of educated mothers are more likely to be enrolled in school and to have higher levels of educational attainment. Women education and the promotion of gender equality in education are vital to development, and policies and actions that do not address gender disparities miss critical development opportunity (Table 1 and 2). Though there is a massive difference between the attendance rate of Overall and ST student. Here is the projection in Table 3.

Table 1

Literacy Trends for Scheduled Tribes in India (1961 to 2001) (Figures in %)

Year	*Male*	*Female*	*Total*
1961	13.83	3.16	8.54
1971	17.63	4.85	11.39
1981	24.52	8.05	16.35
1991	40.65	18.19	29.60
2001	59.17	34.76	47.10

Source: National Commission for SCs and STs, Fifth Report.

Table 2

Enrollment of Scheduled Tribe Students in Schools, 2000–01 to 2004–05 (in '000')

Year	*Primary (I-V)*			*Upper Primary/Middle (VI-VIII)*		
	Boys	*Girls*	*Total*	*Boys*	*Girls*	*Total*
2000–01	6,330	4,665	10,995	1,879	1,205	3,084
2001–02	6,691	5,040	11,731	2,054	1,306	3,360
2002–03	6,422	5,408	11,830	1,930	1,320	3,250
2003–04	6,776	5,741	12,517	2,136	1,526	3,662
2004–05	7,367	6,369	13,737	2,395	1,776	4,171

Source: Selected Educational Statistics 2004–05.

Table 3
Student Attendance Rate: Overall and ST

State	Stage	Attendance	
		Overall	ST
Andhra Pradesh	Primary (I–V)	73.88	72.08
	Upper Primary (VI–VII)	78.78	72.46
Assam	Primary	82.2	77.4
	Upper primary	84.5	85.5
Chhattisgarh	Primary	75.3	75
	Upper primary	62.3	72.5
Delhi	Primary	-	-
	Upper primary	76.5	73.1
Gujarat	Primary	80.2	77.5
	Upper primary	95.1	95.06
Himachal Pradesh	Primary	93.59	94.57
	Upper primary	86.32	86.15
Karnataka	Primary	87.5	87.50
	Upper primary	87.5	87.50
Kerala	Primary	91.7	88.2
	Upper primary	92.4	89.8
Madhya Pradesh	Primary	73.33	69.5
	Upper primary	70.76	67.44
Maharashtra	Primary	90	86
	Upper primary	90	90
Orissa	Primary	67.77	62.79
	Upper primary	69.47	64.21
Rajasthan	Primary	66.27	57.84
	Upper primary	81.14	70.81
Tamil Nadu	Primary	89.1	82.9
	Upper primary	88.2	86.2
West Bengal	Primary	75.1	69.2
	Upper primary	69.7	71.0

Source: Selected Educational Statistics 2004–05.

The DISE data shows an increasing trend in school completion rates among scheduled tribe students. At the primary level, the dropout rates have reduced by 10 per cent points both overall and for STs.

Barriers to Education

Educationally the tribal population is at different levels of development but overall the formal education has made very little impact on tribal groups. In earlier days, the government had no direct programme for their education. But in the subsequent years the reservation policy has made some changes. There are many reasons for low level of education among the tribal people: Formal education is not considered necessary to discharge their social obligations.

Superstitions and myths play an important role in rejecting education. Most tribes live in abject poverty. It is not easy for them to send their children to schools, as they are considered extra helping hands. The incidence of poverty by social group unfolds the truth that there is higher concentration of poverty among the tribal population in both the rural as well as urban areas of Orissa. Their weak resource base, their low position in socio-economic and political hierarchy, illiteracy, their relative lack of access to facilities provided by developmental measures; and their inadequate participation in institutions are mainly responsible for their backwardness. It is, indeed, a matter of deep concern that the fruits of development fail to reach the weaker sections of the society despite planned efforts. The present publication contains some papers covering topics like problems of tribal women education, tribal women empowerment, and participation of tribal people in regeneration of forests, rehabilitation due to displacement, child labour and economic empowerment of women through self-help groups. Based on both primary and secondary data, these papers focus on the issues of tribal development, its problems and potential. The formal schools do not hold any special interest for the children. Most of the tribes are located in interior and remote areas where teachers would not like to go from outside. There are several reasons for the low levels of literacy in India, not the least of which is the high level of poverty. Over one third of the population is estimated to be living below the poverty line (The World Bank, 1997). Poor families are also more likely to keep girls at home to care for younger siblings or to work in family enterprises. If a family has to choose between educating a son or a daughter because of financial restrictions, typically the son will be chosen. Negative parental attitudes toward educating daughters can also be a barrier to a girl's education. Many parents view educating sons as an investment because the sons will be responsible for caring for aging parents. On the other hand, parents may see the education of daughters a waste of money because daughters will eventually live with their husbands' families, and the parents will not benefit directly from their education. Also, daughters with higher levels of education will likely have higher dowry expenses as they will want a comparably educated husband. However, education sometimes lowers the dowry for a girl because it is viewed as an asset by the husband's family.

Some of the major insights on issues affecting women included:

- Discrimination of women and work on the basis of sex
- Lack of access to education for girl children
- Violation of rights in relation to marriage, family harmony
- Lack of property rights for women
- Sexual exploitation – at workplace and institutions
- Discrimination in wages based on gender
- Atrocities on women by police during combing operations and investigations
- Lack of access to health services (both at family level and government level)
- Domestic violence
- Cultural and belief systems militating mostly against women
- Alienation of resources like land and forests and how they impact women adversely

- Displacement of women due to development projects militating mostly against women.

Gender Bias in Curriculum Still Exists

As long ago as 1965, the Indian Government agreed to rewrite textbooks so that men and women would not be portrayed in gender stereotyped roles. However, a study of Indian textbooks done in the 1980s found that men were the main characters in the majority of lessons. In these lessons, men held high prestige occupations and were portrayed as strong, adventurous, and intelligent. In contrast, when women were included they were depicted as weak and helpless, often as the victims of abuse and beatings (Kalia, 1988). These depictions are strong barriers for improving women's position in society. In many schools vocational programmes remained segregated with cosmetology and secretarial courses only for women and electrical and automotive courses only for men. During the early 19th century, many cities began establishing separate high schools for girls. Most communities built one high school, but designated separate entrances for the sexes. The classes were on separate floors in single sex areas where girls were taught by women and boys by men. Single sex schools were now born! Following a considerable amount of frustration from attempting to receive an education at male dominated colleges, men and women created bold alternative colleges for women. Gender bias in education is an insidious problem that causes very few people to stand up and take notice. The victims of this bias have been trained through years of schooling to be silent and passive, and are, therefore, unwilling to stand up and make noise about the unfair treatment they are receiving. 'Over the course of years the uneven distribution of teacher time, energy, attention, and talent, with boys getting the lion's share, takes its toll on girls' (Sadker, 1994). Teachers are generally unaware of their own biased teaching behaviours because they are simply teaching how they were taught and the subtle gender inequities found in teaching materials are often overlooked. Girls and boys today are receiving separate and unequal educations due to the gender socialization that takes place in our schools and due to the sexist hidden curriculum students are faced with every day. Unless teachers are made aware of the gender role socialization and the biased messages they are unintentionally imparting to student's everyday, and until teachers are provided with the methods and resources necessary to eliminate gender bias in their classrooms, girls will continue to receive an inequitable education. 'Sitting in the same classroom, reading the same textbook, listening to the same teacher, boys and girls receive very different educations' (Sadker, 1994). In fact, upon entering school, girls perform equal to or better than boys on nearly every measure of achievement, but by the time they graduate high school or college, they have fallen behind (Sadker, 1994).

However, an inconsistency between the performance of girls and the performance of boys in elementary education leads some critics to argue that boys are being neglected within the education system. The dropout rates for both boys and girls increase sharply as their educational level increases. Among the general population, the dropout rate in classes IV during 2002–2003 was 35.85 per cent among boys, while it was 33.72 per cent among girls. Among all tribal groups, the dropout rate in classes IV was 41.13 per cent among boys and 41.91 per cent among girls. At lower levels of education when the children are relatively young, there is no significant gender discrepancy in the dropout rates among all groups. However, as the level of education increases, the gender gap becomes much more pronounced among the tribal groups. The dropout rate among tribal boys in classes VIII is 66.86 per cent, while it is 71.17 per cent among girls. The dropout rate among boys in the general population is 50.82 per cent, while it is 52.10 per cent among girls (Table 4).

Table 4

Illiterate Persons in India, 2000 Census (Millions)

	Total	*Male*	*Female*
Total per cent	47.8	35.8	60.8
Rural per cent	55.5	44.2	69.7
Urban per cent	26.9	19	36.1

Sources: Government of India, Population Division, Census, 1991.

Table 5

Urban and Rural Literacy Rates of Scheduled Tribes by Gender (2001)

States	*Rural*		*Urban*		*Total*	
	Male	*Female*	*Male*	*Female*	*Male*	*Female*
Mizoram	86.11	77.71	87.55	96.01	91.71	86.95
Nagaland	67.09	57.72	91.63	85.60	70.26	61.35
Meghalaya	58.72	53.97	88.95	84.58	63.49	59.20
Bihar	37.57	13.30	74.18	55.28	39.76	15.54
Orissa	50.35	22.07	69.80	45.77	51.48	23.37
West Bengal	56.60	27.88	68.57	48.20	57.38	29.15
Madhya Pradesh	52.51	27.24	67.47	45.89	53.55	28.44
Gujarat	58.06	34.60	71.01	51.78	59.18	36.02
Maharashtra	64.52	39.88	82.98	64.70	67.02	43.08
Rajasthan	61.23	25.22	75.74	42.97	62.10	26.16
Uttar Pradesh	46.71	18.34	60.61	39.54	48.45	20.70
Himachal Pradesh	77.18	52.50	92.03	81.15	77.71	53.32
Andhra Pradesh	46.09	24.48	66.16	45.99	47.66	26.11
Kerala	70.20	57.28	84.96	77.70	70.78	58.11
Tamil Nadu	47.19	29.48	66.56	50.68	50.15	32.78
India	57.39	32.44	77.77	59.87	59.17	34.76

Source: Annual Report. Ministry of Human Resource Development, Government of India.

Implications for Policy Advocacy

The exemplary issues of concern that require policy advocacy in tribal areas today:

- Decreasing access and control over natural resources on which the survival of the tribal communities depend.

- Lack of access to basic services: health, education and infrastructure.
- Violation of their identity rights leading to cultural erosion.
- Encroachment of their right to self-governance.
- Human Rights to education especially in the current context where there is an increasing threat to access and control of natural resources by indigenous communities.
- Development of skills to initiate and sustain relevant micro alternatives that address livelihood issues from a long term perspective.
- Value based education with critical appreciation of traditional knowledge systems and relevant responses to the changing external environment. Need to create special opportunities to respond to the educational needs of women. Consequences of the development processes are not neutral. They militate more against women than men and, hence, tend to result in greater negative effects on women. Loss of access and control of resources in tribal areas tend to push women out of productive activities. This also affects negatively their status in their family and community as their participation in the economy decreases. Lack of basic services, particularly related to health and education makes women especially vulnerable.

Conclusion

The status of woman has undergone a remarkable change during the past five decades, principally due to education and economic prosperity. Thanks to the efforts of government, big strides have been taken in the field of education. At present more than 3,000 educational institutions are functioning in the length and breath of tribal areas with 2,42,862 students on roll. These include 2,13,021 male and 29,841 female students. The spread of education has immensely broadened their outlook. Women are no longer considered inferior and they enjoy the privilege of exerting their healthy and loving influence in domestic spheres. Though Kerala and Mizoram are the only states in India that have achieved universal female literacy rates, the improvement in social and economic status of women is said to be one of the reasons for literacy. In cities, the literacy rate is almost equal between girls and boys in the country. However, the rate in rural areas continues to be less than the boys. Hence, 40 per cent of the centres under NFE, non formal education programmes are set apart for women. According to statistics of women education in India today, 0.3 million NFE centres have provided education to 0.12 million girls out of 7.42 million children. However, in tribal areas there is not much of a gender bias as compared to all other castes, tribal community statistics show lower male ratio in spite of much low income, literacy, education and other facilities. Several efforts are being made towards women education and empowerment. From previous experience it is clear that the recognition of learning in the tribal context are taken place through struggles on this issues of focusing on Human Rights of tribal communities are still persist.

The development of general awareness of multiple stakeholders is crucial for perspective building on tribal reality. More specifically, structured, systematic training initiatives for developing change agents add lasting value on internalizing learning processes. Also, education on alternatives, which challenge the existing processes of development, is crucial from the perspective of sustainable livelihood. Hence as stated before, it is imperative that indigenous 'education' must be an integral part of the empowerment process. For a lasting impact, youth must be the centre of development activity. Therefore, the need to invest in the education of young men and women in tribal areas are coming as a challenge now a day. Governance functions in the future will be played by today's youth so the direction of development of tribal areas depends on them. Within this framework, the following are some specific policy implications:

The government is taking steps to increase the rate of women education and employment of the tribal society by putting so many schemes and policies. Women education in India is reaping high dividends to society and country with the little investment made through the girl child education. It is said that to educate the girl child amounts to educating a family. It is the educated woman who brings up the family by educating her children. One success story of 2010 is that of the toppers of the CBSE Board this year being girls, as per the CBSE results published on 21 May. However though efforts have been made in some areas, the country has still a long way to go until female literacy is on par with male literacy rates in India. At present, the adult literacy rate of females is 71 per cent of male literacy rate. Enrollment and attendance is 96 per cent of the male attendance rate in primary schools. With regard to secondary schools, the women's rate is 83 per cent of the male enrollment rate. Women in the church have been greatly responsible for education of women in India especially in the rural and remote areas of the country as also in the cities. Thousands of diocesan schools in the country have lent a hand in offering education especially in the remote areas as much as in the cities of India.

References

Annamalai, E. 1973. 'A Programme for Bilingual Education in India'. In Ashok Kelkar et al. (eds) *Proceeding of the Fourth All India Conference on Linguistics*. Agra.

——. 1990. Linguistic Dominance and Cultural Dominance: A Study of Tribal Bilingualism in India, in Debi Prasanna Pattanayek (ed.), *Multilingualism in India*, USA: Multilingual Matters.

Aronowitz, Stanley. 2008. *Against Schooling: Toward an Education that Matters*. CO: Paradigm Publishers.

Bailey, S. 1992. *How Schools Shortchange Girls: The AAUW Report*. NY: Marlowe & Company.

Bellew, Rosemary T. and Elizabeth M. King. 1993. 'Educating Women: Lessons from Experience'. In Elizabeth M. King and M. Anne Hill (eds) *Women's Education in Developing Countries*. Washington D.C.: World Bank.

Central Statistical Organization. *Statistical Abstract India*. 1992. New Delhi.

Commissioned by Department of Elementary Education, MHRD, GOI and International Labor Organization, New Delhi.

Report of Educational Resource Unit. 2006. '*Inventory of Innovative Practices to Strengthen the Public Education System with Special Attention to Children at Risk.*'

Gautam, V. 2003. 'Education of Tribal Children in India and the Issue of Medium of Instruction: A Janshala Experience'. New Delhi: UN/Government Janshala Programme.

India Education Report, 2002.

India Registrar General. 1995. 'SRS Based Abridged Life Tables 1988–92'. Occasional Paper No. 4, New Delhi.

Jones, K., C. Evans, R. Byrd, and K. Campbell. 2000. 'Gender Equity Training and Teaching Behavior. *Journal of Instructional Psychology.* 27 (3), pp. 173–178.

Kalia, N. Nath. 1988. 'Women and Sexism: Language of Indian School Textbooks'. In Rehana Ghadially (ed.) *Women in Indian Society*. New Delhi: Sage Publications.

Kanungo, Akshaya K. and Hrushikesh Mahapatra. 2004. *Tribal Education in Rayagada: A Review of Language, Textbook and Medium of Instruction*. New Delhi: Kalpaz Publications.

Klein, S. 1985. *Handbook for Achieving Sex Equity Through Education.* Baltimore, MD: The Johns Hopkins University Press.

Kundu, M. 1994. *Tribal Education*. New Delhi: Gyan Publishing House.

Mishra, M. 2007. *Status of Elementary Education in Tribal Areas of Orissa*. Orissa: Department of Tribal Education.

Report of National Commission for Schedule Tribe, 2008.

Report of UNESCO,2002.

Sadker, David and Karen R. Zittleman. 1994. *Still Failing at Fairness: How Gender Bias Cheats Girls and Boys in School and What We Can Do About It*. NY: Simon and Schuster.

Singh, Bhupinder and Mahanti Neeti (eds). 1995. *Tribal Education in India*. New Delhi: Inter-India Publications.

Yadappanavar, A. 2003. *Tribal Education in India*. Delhi: Discovery Publishing House.

17

Right to Education and Empowerment of Tribal Girls

A Case Study of Binapani Ashram of Mouldanga, Sriniketan

SWAPNA BHATTACHARYA (CHAKRABORTI)

I

Binapani Ashram: What is its Concern?

To many of us Mouldanga is an alien place name. But over the last two decades or so this village has turned into a 'place of pilgrimage' for the Santhal families from the entire Birbhum belt who want to see their daughters equipped with education and training – to become good citizens of India. The slogan *Sarva Siksha Abhiyan* (Education for All) sounds attractive and appealing. One cannot always blame the government for all the failures. One has to admit the fact that India is home to not only the poor people, but it is, unfortunately, home to a large number of illiterate people as well. A major chunk of this group of illiterate people is from the tribal and the Muslim population. Whereas the backward Hindus (Scheduled Castes) are aware of their right and they explore the possibility of empowerment, the tribals hardly know, or even care to know, what the Indian Constitution and the Indian State offer them for their well-being and development.

The reason which has made Mouldanga such an interesting place has to be found in the location of Binapani Ashram within the village of Mouldanga, Sriniketan. Binapani Ashram is a unique institution in the sense that it is, on the one hand, a residential hostel for the tribals (in major part the Santhals) and other backward communities. On the other hand, through its various programmes Binapani Ashram promotes awareness among the tribals and other backward classes. The paper will address the aims and activities of Binapani Ashram, highlighting the achievement of this registered NGO in the field of education among the Santhals and other backward communities living in the area of Sriniketan-Bolpur Santinikean belt. In spite of the presence of an institution like the Visva Bharati, Santiniketan, in the close proximity of the encircling Santhal villages, education among the Santhal communities in this belt does not give a happy picture. This has been proved by all the scholars whose works I have gone through. Rabindranath Tagore's long cherished dream of bringing the *Har* and *Diku* together thus remained an unfulfilled dream. The Constitution of India grants each citizen of India the Right to Education as naturally as anything else. But, the reality says that the economic compulsion existing in the families concerned of the Santhals blocks the way to education, even at the very primary or secondary level. As we will see from the existing literatures, noted by the present writer, girls have a high dropout rate, leading to the near absence of female tribal students in the academic institutions for higher education. For instance, the condition is similar in the Visva Bharati University that has been founded by the great Noble Laureate, thinker and educationist, Rabindranath Tagore.

Binapani Ashram is a relatively new institution that was established in 1990 in the name of late Binapani Devi (Bhattacharya). Binapani Devi was one of the members of the first women led organization of Santiniketan, *Alapani Mahila Samiti*. The organization itself was established by Indiradevi Chaudhurani (known as Bibidi), the wife of Pramatha Choudhury and niece of Gurudev Rabindranath Tagore. Binapani Devi was the major inspiration behind her daughter Manjushree Saren, a former teacher of Art and Crafts at Sikshasatra, Sriniketan, Visva Bharati. Binapani Devi's son-in-law, Barka Saren, former teacher of Santhali language at the Visva Bharati, was deeply impressed by his mother-in law's love for the Santhal community. Shree Barka Saren has, out of a deep sense of respect for his mother-in law, Binapani Devi, dedicated to her the institution in the official deed of the Trust. Besides Binapani Devi, another person who inspired the Saren couple was the great anthropologist, late Surajit Sinha, widely known as a leading anthropologist who worked on the tribal belt of middle India (Sinha, 1987), not only blessed the couple during their marriage but in his capacity as the Vice-Chancellor personally took interest in promoting the Santhali language and culture at the university level. Thus, Barka Saren became the first teacher in Santhali language at the University of Visva Bharati, Santiniketan. It is of interest to recall here that for the Saren couple, besides this academic patronage from Professor Surajit Sinha, his involvement in their personal life turned out to be indispensable as the Brahmin local priests, the so-called guardians of Hinduism, refused to do the wedding rituals. The local priests' argument was that a high caste Brahmin girl could not marry an *adivasi* Santhal. Certainly it was owing to Professor Surajit Sinha's active involvement that Manjusree and Barka tied their wedlock in the year 1978 in the background of Tagore's songs (*Rabindra Sangeet*) instead of Sanskrit Mantras. Two well-known exponents of Rabindra Sangeet, late Kanika Bandyopadhyay and late Nilima Sen sang the songs. These two great singers were then professors at Sangeet Bhavan, Visva Bharati, Santiniketan. It is to be noted here that the entire wedding ceremony was filmed by the Anthropological Survey of India and is carefully preserved in the archive of that great institution in Kolkata.

The couple, Manjushree and Barka, widely known among the Santhal girls of the entire region as *Marango* and *Maramba*, soon decided to start the institution, Binapani Ashram, in 1990 and have devoted their lives, savings, energy and indeed everything for the educational development of the Santhal society, as a whole, and the ill-fated Santhal girls, in particular. The official name of the Ashram is Binapani Educational and Welfare Trust. My special interest in the Binapani Ashram lies in the fact that this institution is dedicated to the cause of the hapless girls, mainly from the Santhal community. My mother Binapani Devi's deep love for the Santhal community, especially the Santhali women, has always inspired me (Bhattacharya Chakraborti 2009) to know in depth about the community. This unique conference gave me the opportunity to share with my readers some of my observations on the subject of Rights and Empowerment of the Santhals and other backward groups living in and around Mouldanga village in Sriniketan.

As it is known, Sriniketan is that part of Rabindranath Tagore's Visva Bharati (Dutta and Robinson, 1997) which was meant for empowerment and self-reliance of the people from the rural areas. As the entire world celebrates Rabindranath Tagore's 150 years of birth (Kripalani, 2008), this piece of writing may be considered a humble contribution from me and I believe this is the right time for its publication. After all, according to the Saren couple, the empowerment and integration of the girls of Binapani Ashram can be realized only through the real implementation of Tagore's method of total identification of *har* with *diku* and *diku* with *har*. Thus, the girls sing Tagore's songs, in Bengali as well as in their own language, Santhali. As a great educationist Tagore realized that a child can grow best if he or she is left with nature. Secondly, Tagore considered music (O'Connell, 2010: 62–69) and other creative activities, like literary exercises, fine arts, drama, etc. as the purest form of self-expression which inspire the nascent soul to learn effectively his formal syllabus in schools. Education should be open, limitless and all embracing – not necessarily limited to the school syllabus. As will be shown later, Binapani Ashram, through its various activities follow this Tagorean model of education.

II

Santhals in and around the Santiniketan-Sriniketan-Bolpur Area: The Story of their Lives and Struggles as told by the Scholars

Thanks to my close association with the area right from my childhood, I can only endorse the views of the other scholars (mostly anthropologists) that, in comparison to some other tribal dominated areas of West Bengal, Birbhum (*District Statistical Handbook, Birbhum*) lags behind in considerable degree. Martin Kaempchen (2009: 89–94), a close friend of the Santhal community and an eminent writer based in Santiniketan, however, rightly states that there have been major changes in the life of the Santhals of this area so far as their educational achievement is concerned. According to him, about 50 Santhals holding a University degree live and work in and around Santiniketan area. Some of them, however, hail from Bihar and Jharkhand; they were attracted to Santiniketan mainly for Visva Bharati. The contribution of Kaempchen is immensely significant, as it was by his effort and motivation that education could be promoted among the Santhal communities. He had carried on his work in the neighbouring villages of Ghosaldanga and Bishnubati. Mention has been made by Kaempchen (2009) on *Kulhi dhuri*, an association established around 2005 by the Santhal students of Santiniketan to preserve their cultural identity. The *Kulhi dhuri* collects songs sung in Santhali festivals throughout West Bengal, Jharkhand and Bihar. Such practices serve the purpose of reminding the Santhal students about their cultural roots while at the same time motivate or enthuse them with the new spirit of assimilation with the *Dikus*. While Kaempchen's contribution is limited to certain aspects of the Santhal youth from the area under discussion, the recent most contribution of Sen Chowdhury (2010) is quite significant as it addresses the miserable condition of the educational achievements of the Santhali girls from the area under the purview of our discussion.

In course of the present discussion, I will come back to Sen Chowdhury's work. A few words in general on the Santhals of West Bengal and Birbhum in particular would be beneficial for understanding the core issues discussed here. Out of about 39 tribal groups living in West Bengal, the Santhals make the largest group. From the point of view of racial classification, the Santhals belong to the Austro-Asiatic group of people living in India (Dalton, 1960). Seen from the ethnic origin, they are different from the Sanskritic (so called Aryan people), Dravida people and Sino-Tibetan people (Baske, 2006: 1–6). According to the Census of 1981, the number of Santhals living in West Bengal was 16,66,610. Out of that, 8,42,658 are men and 8,23,952 are women (Baske, 2006: 36–37). The largest concentration of the Santhals is in the district of Santhal Parganas. According to the 1961 Census, the Santhal population in this district was 8,99,515 (Ray, 2009: 17) while the thinnest Santhal population is visible in the district of Howrah (Baske, 2006: 35). According to Dhiren Baske, an eminent scholar, Santhali is the second most widely spoken language in West Bengal, next to Bengali. From the pages of Grierson's *Linguistic Survey of India* we get to understand that the Santhali language makes the largest sub-group under the Munda group of languages. The close interaction between the Santhals and the Hindu Bengalis is much too known from the works of a large number of scholars starting from Nabendu Datta Majumder (1956) to Dhiren Baske (2006) and others.

The Santhals, though basically nature worshippers and believers in the spirit, adopted Hindu Gods and Goddesses in their pantheon. On several occasions I myself have witnessed that they follow various norms which are popular among Hindu Bengalis. But, when it came to formal education, compared to their Hindu co-brethren the Santhals lagged behind much. True that the Christian missionary activities and developmental activities of organizations like the Bharat Sevashrama Sangha or the Ramakrishna Mission contributed a great deal in the spread of education among the Santhals and other backward groups, yet there is no doubt that the Santhals, one of the major groups of tribal population of India, could not come to the forefront of the Indian society. No wonder then that in large number of cases, in spite of the provision in the Indian Constitution for reservation of jobs for the Scheduled Tribes, the posts in various educational institutions remain vacant.

The total tribal population of the state of West Bengal, according to the 1991 Census, is 3,808,760. The names of various tribes living in West Bengal are: *Asur, Baiga, Bhumij, Bhutia, Birhor, Birjia, Chakma, Chero, Chik Baraik,*

Garo, Gond, Gorait, Hajang, Ho, Karmali, Kharwar, Kisan, Kora, Korwa, Lepcha, Lodha, Kharia, Lohara, Magh, Mahali, Mal Pahari, Mech, Mru, Munda, Nagesia, Oraon, Parhaiya, Rabha, Santhal, Sauria Paharia, and *Savar.* The Santhal tribals make up 5.59 per cent of the total population of West Bengal and 5.62 per cent of the Scheduled Tribes population of our country.

As Anuradha Chanda (2005) states, the male–female ratio among the tribal population is equal. Chanda further says that tribal women in West Bengal constitute 6 per cent of the total population of the state. I would next wish to make a detailed review of the situation of the Santhals of Birbhum district. Birbhum district is adjacent to the Santhal Parganas that is supposed to be the original homeland of the Santhals. The Santhals make the major chunk of the tribal population of Birbhum district and constitute about 87.3 per cent of the total tribal population of the area (Sen Chowdhury, 2010: 5). Interestingly however, the Santhal population of Birbhum is a very small part of the total Santhal population in the whole of West Bengal. The other areas in the state where the tribal population is distinctly visible are: Medinipur, Purulia and Bankura. According to Datta Majumder, the movement of the Santhals from the areas of Santhal Parganas to the district of Birbhum started in the end of the 18th century (Datta Majumder, 1956: 66). It had something to do with the enactment of the Permanent Settlement Act 1793. The Santhal migration to this rather remote corner of Bengal was accelerated by various British policies in the domain related to land matters. Quoting Hunter's *Annals of Rural Bengal*, Suchismita Sen Chowdhury states that the 'Permanent Settlement' for land tax in 1790 resulted in the general extension of agriculture. Due to scarcity of population, the Santhals were brought in to the area, given land, and, even granted the 'Right of Occupancy' (Sen Chowdhury, 2010: 4).

As we know, in 1855, there was a major rebellion by the Santhals and their kinsmen against British occupation. It was led by Sido and Kanhu who showed exemplary courage and expertize in mobilizing their people (Datta Majumder, 1956: 28–29) against the British. The upward rise in the number of Santhals in Birbhum from 6,954 in 1872 to 47,221 in 1901 and 64,079 in 1931 is visible in the statistics that Datta Majumder has given.

There are a large number of Santhal villages around the Santiniketan-Sriniketan area. I have been watching the socio-economic life and cultural activities of the Santhal community in this area ever since my childhood. Thanks to Barka Saren's and Manjusree Saren's kind help I could go deeper in the Santhal society. What pains me is the low rate of educated youth from the Santhal community. A table by Sandip Kumar Ghatak (2007) bearing the title 'Educational Attainment of the Santhals of Birbhum' presents a very depressive picture. It shows a sharp declining trend – leading to the total absence of the Santhals in the higher educational sector. However, many things have changed in recent years. Even then, it is certainly true that in spite of all the governmental aids and arrangements, a majority of the Santhals don't feel the urge to go for higher education.

Before going to the next section which exclusively deals with the Binapani Ashram, let me give important information on the state of education among the Santhal girls in the district of Birbhum, especially in the

Bolpur-Santiniketan-Sriniketan area. This information is drawn from Suchismita Sen Chowdhury's work to which I referred to in the beginning. The work is based on field research work done in five villages of the Dinajpur district of Bangladesh and four villages in Birbhum district of West Bengal. In this piece of work the researcher (Sen Chowdhury, 2010) has made a survey of the educational situation among the Santhals, especially among the Santhal girls. It is part of her Ph.D thesis which she completed under the supervision of Professor Buddhadeb Chaudhuri. Her data is based on governmental sources primarily. She reports that higher education is almost absent among the Santhal girls of Birbhum district. The Binapani Ashram has, therefore, pledged itself to provide the needed inspiration and motivation to the Santhal girls to move ahead in life by way of either a proper and recognizable education, or, after undergoing a vocational training at least, so that they could be well-equipped to sustain themselves in future.

III

Binapani Ashram: Methods, Aims, Ideals to Empowerment of Santhal Girls from Mouldanga and Beyond

The description above creates the proper background to introduce a discussion on Binanpani Ashram. Right at the outset it should be stressed that Binapani Ashram is not a recipient of any government grants, coming from the centre or the state government. There are eight members in the Board of Trustees who look after all the administrative and financial matters. It is a registered Public Charitable Trust under the I.T. Act. Donors enjoy Tax Relief under Section 80G (5)(VI) of the I.T. Act, 1961 vide order no. DIT (E) 8E/898/07–08/3358–60 of 03/12/2010. The resident girls, going to various nearby schools, are to a great extent, supported by various donors (sponsors). The number of sponsors is quite large and many of them are based in Kolkata. There are Memorial Funds started by the friends and relatives of Binapani Ashram, named after some dear person who is no more. The organization is housed in a three storied building wherein about 50 girls are staying. The girls come from extremely poor families; they are here as their parents have neither the money nor the social environ at home to keep their daughters with them. A handful of the parents whose economic condition is slightly better, offer a humble amount to show their respect to the Ashram. The Ashram started in the form of a mud house. In the initial years Manjusree Saren lived here with a couple of girls. Only after the completion of the building, thanks to the generous grants from all the friends and well-wishers, could the girls start living there. Being first generation learners, the girls were quite unsure and even a little apprehensive about what kind of a life awaited them. However, it is quite remarkable how they adapted to this new way of life, which is so different from their usual lifestyle and condition! It could be mentioned here that integration and assimilation appeared to be a great challenge to them. As stated in the very beginning, the Saren couple tried to find out an exclusive method for integrating the girls to this new world. The only possible method they could think of was Tagore's method of identification, where nature, art, music literature, songs in their own language as well as in Bengali would be the most effective instrument.

Tagore believed in universal humanism and brotherhood. The piece of lyrical work *Gitanjali* speaks for Tagore's ideals of humanism. As for his understanding of the tribal society, especially the Santhals, he never saw them as separated from the mainstream. Indeed, his concept of India was a composite idea of peaceful fusion of various races. Thus, the method followed by the Binapani Ashram aimed at the proper learning of the composite Indian culture. The resident girls are taught to be good citizens of India. They are taught the message of sacrifice and non-violence, as followed by Gandhiji, in matters concerning their private life. At the same time, they are given constant impetus to remain in their own cultural orbit, to respect their own language, i.e. Santhali. Each and every girl is proud of being a Santhal in core and an Indian in general. They are taught by their tutors to be tolerant to every religion. Indeed, the Ashram has girls who are Santhals, Christians, Muslims as well as from the backward Hindu communities.

The girls of Binapani Ashram are enrolled in nearby schools that do not teach Santhali, which implies that they have to be good in Bengali. The girls attend the schools around Santiniketan-Sriniketan-Bolpur area, as well as some Santhal villages like Balipara, Bagan Para, Pearson Palli and Kaligunge. In Badhgora, near Bolpur, there is a high school named Badhgara Kalikrishna Vidyalaya, which also has the necessary infrastructure for the education of Santhal girls. There are quite a few primary schools as well around Santiniketan. Tanayendra Vidyalaya in Goalpara is one of those schools. The girls from Binapani Ashram, however, prefer to go to Surul Primary School (*Surul Nimna Buniadi Vidyalaya*). As many as six (6) girls from Binapani Ashram have passed the Higher Secondary Examination from the West Bengal Board of Secondary Education. One of the girls has already completed her MA in music (Rabindra Sangeet) from Sangeet Bhavan, Visva Bharati University. She has passed the School Service Examination and has started her professional life as a music teacher in West Bengal. Two are admitted in the same Bhavan (Music and Dance Department under Visva Bharati University) with the target to complete their Masters in Indian Classical Dance. Two have completed their BA from Calcutta University. Out of the two, one even completed her MA in Home Science from Biharilal College of the University of Calcutta. Subarna Saren is continuing her higher education at Calcutta University.

To my knowledge, another girl passed her BA from Bolpur College. The next batch of girls have passed their Middle School (Madhyamika), and are now heading for Higher Secondary Examination. Among those going to Higher Secondary School, most of the girls are going to a nearby village, called Benuria. The school is called *Benuria Sumitra Balika Vidyalaya*. The primary school goers are attending the *Surul Buniadi Prathamik Vidyalaya*. The village Surul is just around Mouldanga. Five private tutors are employed by Binapani Ashram to give special hours to the girls in various subjects. The spread of education among Santhal girls of this particular tribal belt now want to cross the boundary of Birbhum district. They want to utilize the opportunity for higher education existing in Kolkata, for example in Calcutta University. Another remarkable case is of Sukla Mondal, a resident of Binapani Ashram, who comes from an economically backward and deprived family. She did excellent in her BA (Bachelor of

Arts) with Japanese Honours at Visva Bharati University. At present, she is working in Bengaluru. To encourage the girls to go to higher school, a merit scholarship scheme has been introduced. A donor organization from Kolkata called Baneswar Shiva Charitable Trust has awarded 10 Merit Scholarship to the first 10 students of class VI standard of Benuria Sumitra Balika Vidyalaya (Binapani Ashram Annual Report 2010, 19). In spite of all these, at every step, it is felt that only routine learning will not bring overall integration of the girls in the main stream of the Indian society. Constant companion should be music and dance, as music and dance constitute an integral part of the Santhal life.

Having all this in their minds, Barka and Manjusree Saren started singing Rabindra Sangeet and the former also took up the most difficult task of translating Rabindra Sangeet (Tagore's songs) into Santhali. Secondly, the Tagorean method of education was introduced in the learning process and lifestyle. Until now, as many as five CDs on Rabindra Sangeet along with the Santhal translations have been released by Music World, Kolkata. All these songs and their Santhali translations have been compiled and edited by Satyabrata Bhattacharya, the Chairman of the Binapani Educational and Welfare Trust (Bhattacharya, 2010). The renderings carry the message of Tagore to the Santhal population of the older generation who do not understand what Tagore wrote about them. This step made it possible that the girl children could start learning *Rabindra Sangeet* in their own language as well as in Bengali. Besides, they also started learning Indian classical dances, Yoga, gardening, methods of food processing, knitting, tailoring, etc.

In the year 2004 when they staged Tagore's *Chandalika*, the girls of Binapani Ashram had the privilege of displaying their artistic talents before an august gathering in the famous Kalamandir auditorium. His Excellency, the former Governor of West Bengal, Shree Viren J. Shah, was very pleased to watch the performers in the act, and blessed them. A large number of distinguished people from various walks of life assembled and enjoyed this well-known dance drama of Tagore. The Santhal girls had literally mesmerised the entire audience by their beautiful performance based on a story that had been, in reality, trying to voice a protest against the prevailing custom of untouchability.

A number of festivals that have become an integral part of Santiniketan life are also celebrated in the Binapani Ashram. For example, Briksharapan (the planting of trees) is observed on the day (22nd day of the Bengali month of *Sravana*) of Tagore's passing away. On the occasion of the Foundation Day of Visva Bharati, *Paush Utsav*, in December, there is always a programme called *Santhalder Kheladhula* (Games and Plays of the Santhals). The girls of Binapani Ashrama are, to this day, invited to take part in this programme that is organized by the Visva Bharati University. Their *Marango*, Manjusree Saren, even after her formal retirement from the Visva Bharati University, takes the major responsibility for organizing this particular event during *Paush Utsav*. Such opportunities along with a number of cultural activities which take place in the Ashram premises bring them closer to a larger world. Over and above, in order to infuse the spirit of nationalism and inspire the girls on the ideals of our nation builders, occasions such as Gandhi Birthday and Rabindra Jayanti are also celebrated. On such patriotic events, the Indian flag is hoisted in the premises of the Ashram. Buddha Jayanti has also been introduced in the list of celebrations from last year.

As has been made clear, the method followed towards promoting education and its concept is in the lines of the Tagorean method which implies 'going beyond the walls'. As envisaged by Tagore, it is more important for the children to express and share their thought on their surrounding nature than to just read books. Tagore always shared the view that a critical understanding of man and nature is more important than bookish knowledge. Thus, the *Sahitya Sabha* (Literary Assembly) has become an essential part of Ashram life. This monthly literary meetings (*Sahitya Sabha*) are held in the evening, when the girls are little relaxed. The resident girls read what they have seen and experienced in their closest proximity. This kind of a literary exercise is very spontaneous and is visible as a lucid expression of their otherwise dormant feelings. This kind of an outpour from the depth of the heart and mind is exactly the method that Gurudev Tagore followed when he started his school *Brahmacharyasrama* in the early years of the 20th century (Dasgupta, 2009). I had once been given the honour to act as the Chairperson in one such monthly *Sahitya Sabha*. They write their articles mostly in Bengali and occasionally in English. The programme has in its agenda a blend of Santhali songs and *Rabindra Sangeet*. This programme thus contributes greatly towards the development of the writing skills of the girls. Besides, this gives them a happy respite from the stress of learning only school books, which however they cannot ignore. Several eminent persons from various parts of the world adorned the chair of *Sabhapati* (Chairperson) in the *Sahitya Sabha*, thereby contributing immensely to the widening of the intellectual horizon of the girls of the Binapani Ashram.

The journal *Baha* (in Santhali language *Baha* means flower) has become a regular mouthpiece of their ideas. *Baha* is unique in the sense that it offers an open platform for intellectual encounters between the Santhal girls and very high profile intellectuals from not only West Bengal but various parts of India, and indeed, world at large. Until now six volumes have been published. One of the volumes is a *Rabindra Sankha* (issue on Rabindranath Tagore) dedicated to Rabindranath Tagore, their Gurudev. The resident girls write poems, short stories, etc. in Bengali as well as in Santhali.

The subjects chosen by the girls cover a very wide canvas that starts from nature, moves on to Children's Day and Jawaharlal Nehru, Gurudev Tagore, Guru Nanak, Sister Nivedita, Lakshmi Puja, deviates to the strange habits of crows and continues on to describe the beauty of the rainy season in Bengal, and so on. One can read between the lines how their inner soul constantly tries to adjust with the outer world, while their play with words on their own imagination continues to blossom unhindered. All this is appreciable more so because this is exactly the method suggested by Tagore and all the other great educationists for the development of the underprivileged. The journal *Baha* is tri-lingual and write-ups in three languages – Bengali, English and Santhali – find a place in its pages. I may mention in this connection that the Binapani Ashram has recently been honoured by 'The Telegraph' School Awards for Excellence (2010) with The Patton Award for 'A School that Cares'.

The sole aim of the Binapani Ashram is to make good citizens out of the girls by educating and equipping them with the necessary learning, so that they could be self-dependent one day. It is quite understandable that the beneficiary group cannot go in for higher education with hundred per cent success and hence they are being introduced to vocational training courses in computer applications and handicraft work that includes knitting, embroidery, dress-making, homestead gardening, fruit and vegetable preservation, pickle making, etc. There are as many as five computers in the centre for the use of the girls of the Ashram.

It is interesting to note that vegetables are regularly being cultivated in the backyard of the Binapani Ashram building all through the year since the last three years for the daily consumption of the Ashram residents. The project was undertaken under the guidance and supervision of Indrabrata Bhattacharya, Professor, Department of Plant Pathology, Bidhan Chandra Krishi Viswavidyalaya (BCKV), Kalyani, Dist. Nadia. Ivy Chakravorty, Reader, Department of Post-harvest Technology, Faculty of Horticulture, BCKV, Mohanpur, Nadia (district) has given training to the students of Binapani Ashram regarding post-harvest processing of tomato and sweet potato. Like Ivy Chakravorty, Arup Chattopadhyaya, Reader, AICRP on vegetable crops, BCKV was also involved in the project as co-investigators. The resident girls are engaged in transplanting, weeding, watering and harvesting of winter vegetables like brinjal, chili and tomato and also summer vegetables like okra, sweet potato, elephant foot yam, cowpea and cucurbits, including pumpkin, bottle gourd, ridge gourd and cucumbers. Parents of the students rendered free services towards land preparation by ploughing, levelling of plot, spading up for vegetable production, etc. All these are hard and strenuous work. The project was granted by the Rastriya Krishi Vikas Yojana and was sponsored by the Department of Food Processing Industry and Horticulture, Government of West Bengal, Mayukh Bhavan, Salt Lake. The project targeted girl students from classes VII and VIII as they are more equipped to learn better, as also to pass on all the knowledge gathered to their family members. The above mentioned project has been the only case (project) where the Binapani Ashram took money from the government.

There is one Binapani Sishu Vikash Kendra that is attached to the Binapani Ashram. While the resident girls of the Binapani Ashram come from various parts of the districts of Birbhum, Burdwan and Santhal Parganas, the children of the Binapani Sishu Vikash Kendra are all from the Mouldanga village itself. A considerable number of them are Muslims, but there are girls from among the Santhals and the Scheduled Castes as well. There are three categories of children in the Binapani Sishu Vikash Kendra. The senior most category among them use this premises as a take-off ground for admission into class I in a primary school. The junior group of children are groomed for two-three years in the nursery section which, it is believed, would facilitate their placement in the local primary school. The children are taught how to write Bengali and they learn to write their parents names, addresses, etc. They are also taught to recite rhymes and short poems. It should be mentioned that all the children are provided with a set of new school uniform, a bag for carrying books and slate pencils. Mid-day meals are also given to the children. The Binapani Sishu Vikash Kendra makes it possible that the working mothers can go to their work without much headache.

Binapani Ashram receives valuable help and cooperation from Bharat Sevashram of Muluk, near Bolpur. As many of us know, the Bharat Sevashram Sangha is a unique institution, established by a monk named Pranabananda Maharaj with a noble aim of bringing about social consciousness among the Hindus of India. The organization has, in its mission, laid the major thrust on the social sector, especially in the education of the backward classes. Though the Bharat Sevashram is a much more established institution as compared to the nascent Binapani Ashram; yet, a parallel could be drawn between the Santhal residential hostel for boys run by the former's local unit in Muluk and the resident girls' hostel run by Binapani Ashram in Mouldanga. Shanti Maharaj who is widely respected for his dedication towards the social causes of this backward community is the Head monk of Bharat Sevasrama, Muluk. This impressive project also has Santhal boys going to schools nearby and participating in some vocational training courses along with few local youth from various sections. Interestingly the land on which the Bharat Sevashram, Muluk, stands had been donated by Barka Saren, who has his origin in the same area Muluk-Kalitala. The Bharat Sevashram, Muluk extends some assistance in training the girls of Binanpani Ashram in tailoring and knitting which could open up self-entrepreneurship opportunities in future for the trainees. Besides, Bharat Sevashram, Muluk, is paying the trainers for their services. It also provides medical help and consultation for the resident girls by having a medical van with a doctor to visit Binapani Ashram for a routine check up of the resident girls every week. Moreover, the Bharat Sevashram, Muluk, also supplies good milk from its own diary. When the trained girls make the effort to launch their income generation activities, on its part, the Binapani Trust undertakes the initiatives to market the hand stitched products and handicraft items through its large number of friends and well-wishers scattered country-wide. There is, in fact, a major plan to establish a training-cum-production centre for the village girls at the premises of the Binapani Ashram in the near future. It is relevant to note here that the Ashram at present has five sewing machines and five knitting machines, all of which are donations from individual or institutions. Thus, through all these activities, the two institutions, working with a similar aim to help the Santhals and the other backward communities, are coming together.

Conclusion

The article here is an attempt to lay out before the reader the objectives and activities of the Binapani Ashram, Mouldanga. The main part, precisely the second part of essay, has been preceded by a presentation of the general survey of the Santhals in Birbhum district and in the particular belt, i.e. the Sriniketan-Santiniketan-Bolpur area. Started off with very limited resources in the form of money as well as manpower, this institution has made its name across the country and beyond. Deeply impressed by the selfless sacrifices and noble mission of Barka Saren and Manjusree Saren, a large number of public and private institutions and individuals have been coming forward all along to offer their help for the cause of the education of the Santhal girls. As has been mentioned, Binapani Ashram does not receive any governmental grant for its regular functioning. It is dependent on the resources that the Saren couple has donated. Besides, a large number of family members, relatives, friends, eminent figures from public life, as well as private and public institutions take the responsibility of sponsoring the girls and also bearing the economic expenses towards the various events organized in the Binapani Ashram. As has been stated already, the small assistance extended by the parents of the girls is also accepted, mainly for showing due respect to them for their noble gesture even in the face of their own hardships and constraints. In the face of all this, therefore, the change in attitude and approach among the beneficiary girls as well as their families is appreciable and significant. It may appear relevant in this context, that the State Bank of India (SBI), impressed by the performance of the girls of the Binapani Ashram, has very recently donated a school bus to this institution. This makes the regular journey from the Binapani Ashram to the schools and vice-versa less strenuous for the girls.

Further, the discussion has also thrown light on the methods of Tagore's vision of national integration and the spirit of internationalism through education that have been implemented in the Binapani Ashram. We have a grasp of how besides their formal education in the schools nearby, the Santhal girls are breaking all geographical boundaries and cultural barriers through their poems, music and dance. In this way the division between *har* and *diku* that Tagore and other great souls rejected, is increasingly narrowing. To do justice to the young talents, it has been decided to bring two separate issues of *Baha*: the one remained for the established writers and thinkers who are in one way or the other associated with the Binapani Ashram. The newly introduced separate *Baha*, of which one issue has already appeared, will be kept reserved for the young Santhal girls and boys, though any one from communities can also write in this *Baha*.

As the number of seats for resident girls is limited, admission tests are held to make the final screening. During admission, a large number of families from far away places (including Rampurhat and Dumka areas) come with their daughters. In fact, this institution has contributed a lot towards bringing about a major change in the educational demography of the Santiniketan-Sriniketan- Bolpur area. As many as six girls have passed the Higher Secondary School examination and are continuing their education in various fields in various universities, including in the Central University of Visva Bharati (Tagore's University at Santiniketan) and Calcutta University. Their achievement in cultural and literary activities has also shown that they could achieve anything and everything, if they are only treated as equal with the other members of the society. The word 'empowerment' is a very valuable word. Empowerment is not necessarily guaranteed only through formal ways, rules, regulations, constitutional provisions, etc. It should come from within the individual when he or she is educationally equipped. On the other hand, in any society, where-so-ever, it is the duty of the privileged group to extend their cooperation so that the underprivileged feel secure to be empowered. This cooperation is nothing but to treat the underprivileged as equal. Otherwise there will always be a clash, openly or secretly.

References

Baske, Dhiren. 2006. *Paschimbanger Adivasi.* Kolkata: Anita Baske.

Bhattacharya (Chakraborti), Swapna. 2009. 'Reminiscences of my Interactions with the Santhal Community of Santiniketan'. *Baha,* 3(1), pp. 97–100.

Bhattacharya, Satyabrata (ed.) 2010. *Aji Jharo Jharo Mukharo Badaro Dine: Tehen Jhipir Jhipir Japut Mahare.* Kolkata: Binapani Educational & Welfare Trust.

Binapani Ashram: Annual Report. 2010. Published by Satyabrata Bhatttacharya.

Chanda, Anuradha. 2005. 'Tribal Women', In Jasodhara Bagchi (ed.) *The Changing Status of Women in West Bengal, 1970–2000: The Challenge Ahead.* New Delhi: Sage Publications, pp. 130–141.

Dalton, Edward Tuite. 1960. *Descriptive Ethnology of Bengal. Indian Studies Past & Present.* Calcutta: Office of the Superintendent of Government Printing (first published in 1872).

Dasgupta, Uma. 2009. *Rabindranath Tagore: A Biography.* New Delhi: Oxford University Press (first published in 2004).

Datta-Majumder, Nabendu. 2009 (reprint of 1956 edition). *The Santal: A Study in Culture-Change.* Kolkata: Department of Anthropology, Government of India. Memoir No. 2 (1955).

District Statistical Handbook. Birbhum. 2003. West Bengal: Bureau of Applied Economics and Statistics.

Dutta, Krishna and Andrew Robinson (eds). 1997. *Rabindranath Tagore: The Myriad-minded Man.* Calcutta: Rupa & Co.

Ghatak, Sandip Kumar. 2007. 'Education among the Santhals of Birbhum'. In Prabodh Kumar Bhowmik and Manish Kumar Raha (eds) *The Tribal People of India: Society, Culture & Development.* Kolkata: Institute of Social Research & Applied Anthropology.

Kaempchen, Martin. 2009. 'The Other Santiniketan I: An Alternative Way of Life' & II: Santhals as Part of the Pure Tradition'. *Baha* 3(1), pp. 89–91.

Kaempchen, Martin. 2009. 'The Other Santiniketan II: Santhals as Part of the Pure Tradition', *Baha* 3(1), pp. 92–96.

Kripalini, Krishna. 2008. *Rabindranath Tagore: A Biography,* New Delhi: UBSPD.

O'Connell, Kathleen M. 2010. Arts Now: 'Rabindranath's Enduring Contribution to Integral Arts Education'. *Tagore beyond Frontiers.* In proceedings of a seminar organised by the Tagore Centre ICCR during a Three Day Festival, 4–6 December 2009, pp. 62–69.

Ray, P.C. 2009. *Socio-cultural Process and Psychological Adaptation of the Santal.* Calcutta: Anthropological Survey of India.

Sen Chowdhury, Suchismita. 2010. 'The Santal Women in India and Bangladesh: A Brief Study on their Education and health Situation'. Occasional Paper, Department of South & Southeast Asian Studies, University of Calcutta.

Sinha, Surajit. 1987. *Tribal Politics and State Systems in Pre-colonial Eastern and North eastern India.* Calcutta: K.P Bagchi & Co.

Tagore, Rabindranath. 2009 (Reprint). *Gitanjali: Song of Offerings.* Kolkata: UBS Publishers in association with Visva Bharati, Santiniketan.

18

Citizenship and Human Rights

Challenges for the Recognition of Indigenous Rights in Latin American Cities

MILKA CASTRO LUCIC

Indigenous in the Cities: Towards De-indigenization

From the last decades of the 20th century there begins in Latin America a movement of diverse indigenous peoples demanding recognition of their rights, in the context of a new legal context – International Convention 169 of ILO (1989) and the Declaration on the Rights of Indigenous Peoples (2007). This new political scene has featured a process of *indigenization* of descendant indigenous people living in the cities. These people have begun to identify themselves as indigenous and they request for state recognition. The paper analyzes the characteristics of this process.

Five Centuries of Subordination and De-indigenization

Five centuries of subordination and de-indigenization, the discovery of America meant that millions of people remain subject to the European domination. The pressure on natural resources in their territories was a constant for more than 500 years, along with various legal actions as strategies of appropriation. Despite this, indigenous peoples have, in the last 30 years, came to occupy an outstanding place in the political fight to demand recognition of their rights. Among the factors that lie behind the indigenous mobilization, we highlight the critique of modern law, strengthening indigenous organizations, the action of international organizations and the globalization of capitalism.

Towards the end of the 15th and early 16th centuries, with the invasion of indigenous people's territory and cultures, Europe became the new epicentre in the global economy. An economic system that was greater than any legally defined political unity, was born. At the same time, it rose the 'world-economy' whose basic link between parts of the system is economic (Dussel, 2001; Wallerstein, 1989). 'Northern Europe (Spain, Portugal, Holland, England, France, etc.) nor the United States began their relationship on peripheral cultures (in Latin America in the 15th century, and since the 18th century in Asia and Africa), with a peaceful proposal of rational arguments.' They always used the violence with weapons. Their armies occupied territorially strategic locations, by means of military technology reducing them to his domain without conditions. 'This is the other side of the modern...' (Dussel, 2001: 371). The primary interest was in discovering new sources of precious metals – gold and silver for Castile and Portugal first, then other European powers were added – Britain, France and the Netherlands. When gold was not enough, agriculture was exploited on usurped indigenous lands. These people's rights over land and territory were raped systematically during the processes of conquest and colonization, laying the foundations of the large property and what was more effective also laid the foundations for the legitimation of the forms of dispossession of their lands that remain till the present. The history of indigenous peoples has copious account of writings from the history, economics, anthropology, philosophy on the tragedy that meant the 'discovery'. From this stage in history, where today indigenous raised their voices by defence and/or recovery from their ancestral territories, their rights and their culture as reflected in the words of Rigoberta Menchú, a Guatemalan indigenous Nobel Peace Prize winner. They are an echo of thousands of speeches of indigenous leaders from around the world: 'in spite of histo worldwide':

> In spite of the history of colonization, racism and exploitation that we suffered, we have been able to preserve these values, knowledge and resources.' 'And by that same story, the struggle for the recognition of our rights continues... (Menchu, 2004).

During a speech at a session of the Permanent Forum on Indigenous Issues, Menchu (2004) stated that if there is anything that indigenous peoples share really is a terrible story of injustice.

> Indigenous peoples have been decimated, tortured and enslaved'. They have been deprived of their political rights, such as the right to vote. Their land they have been seized by the conquest and colonization, or have been declared terra nullius and claimed the 'national' development. Even today her children often grow in poverty and die of malnutrition and disease. Some countries does not allow indigenous peoples study their own language at school. Sacred objects have been stolen and publicly exhibited, in violation of their beliefs. Facing discrimination and the exploitation....[1]

Additionally, allegations studies, rapporteurs and complaints that reveal the existence of a growing loss and environmental damage in indigenous lands and forests, as a result of various processes of looting suffered in colonial and post-colonial periods (Stavenhagen, 2008; Clavero, 2010). In a recent report in the Chilean case of the Special Rapporteur on the situation of Human Rights and fundamental freedoms of indigenous people, James Anaya, said: 'worrying is that apparently there was a mechanism within the Chilean internal order clearly to recognize, restore and protect land and indigenous resources of ancestral occupation rights without had rights listed above' (Anaya, 2009).

The power structure colonial past based on the concept of a nation-state is another point of indigenous complaints. During the conquest and the colonization, the rights of indigenous peoples were undermined but both were recognized in the Indian laws. 'The 'Indian republics' separated from the Spanish, offered a refuge where preserved part of the specificity of the old cultures.' 'It even spoke of 'Nations' to refer to native peoples' (Villoro, 1999: 40). Protective measures emanated from the Spanish Crown and therefore they disappeared with the creation of the nation-state, spurring the rights of indigenous peoples. Under this new conception that is, connecting one nation with the emerging State, the existence of indigenous nations, culture, language, religion and every single right should be ignored. With the recognition of citizenship multiculturalism was refused and hidden. A new organizational system started where violations of their rights continued, this time under the protection of the law. Indigenous community economy was subordinated to the economy of the new owners of the land (landowners, miners, traders). Indians were forced to join violent forms of life and very different work itself, and an economy that was based on the foundations of capitalism, primarily by submitting them as labourers, dispossessed of their lands. They survived as subsistence farmers and relegated at the periphery of the centres of power, semi-desert mountainous, forested areas and regions of soils with low productive value. In general, areas which shared the uniqueness of being remote and hostile conditions of life, but very attractive for private investment. From this socio-economic and geographical periphery, they emerged to demand respect for their rights as nations, as part of a new State which is multicultural and multinational, as has repeatedly been noted in various meetings, forums, etc. The following extract is a sample:

> The plurinational State concept is a viable political proposition for our countries, which part of the recognition of the diversity of nationalities, peoples and cultures, assess them and promote them is a proposal that reach unity in diversity, generating intercultural relations that allow us to build a common future for all. We defend the plurinational State proposal because it is more democratic way of solving the problems that our countries drag historically, it's a new form of political organization, economic, territorial, cultural, legal and administrative, within a cross-cultural and direct democracy equity and economic justice.[2]
>
> The international gathering of indigenous peoples Declaration 'Plurinational State and right to water'. (Quito, 2008)

The Re-indigenization

This 'identity for himself,' is revealing not only the difference compared to other Western countries, but would be making aware the inequality and subordination. Ascribing of the indigenous identity in Chile, has been slow and cautious process; some areas are still reserved.

One of the factors that has strengthened the struggle for the rights of indigenous peoples has been mobilizing, achieving efficiency through strengthening their leadership and the proliferation of local and regional, organizational initiatives in every ancestral land, or what is left of them. These organizations and other associations – national organizations, conferences, forums and summits – coordinators have achieved a remarkable degree of articulation and unification intercontinentaly, moving increasingly towards the progressive consolidation of the indigenous movement. These actions have played a very significant role of mixed Indian on Latin America that has started on the path to re-indigenization, refuting the designs as many times announced the disappearance of the indigenous peoples in the figure of the *mestizo.* As I shall explain below, within a new legal framework, Sambo has the right to recover their identity indigenous; and the field recognizes the figure of the indigenous peasant against all prayer descampesinista – the end of the peasantry to the invasion of capitalism in the agro – claims the right to their land and ancestral territories that increasingly more indigenous medicine and traditional expertise are valued in the new international paradigms.[3] It thus issues the required traditional road to modernity; indigenous movements have fiercely challenged all orthodoxies (Ballón, 2003).

The beginning of the re-indigenization has been product of partly legal recognition from 1989. Chile was in a period of military rule, under the dictatorship of Augusto Pinochet, between the years 1973–1989. That period together with the installation a neoliberal economy with a total openness to the market, institutionalizes the nation as unique and ethnically homogeneous. This meant ignoring the existence of indigenous peoples and therefore they did not have any recognition or special right. In 1989, when Chile returned to democracy, one of the commitments that made presidential candidate win the election (Patricio Aylwin), was enacting a law for indigenous peoples. This law produced an impact among the indigenous people themselves, because they thought that there were only three indigenous peoples: Aymara and Mapuche in the South and North respectively and Rapa Nui in Easter Island. For indigenous people who had migrated to cities, and had joined the assimilationist policies, there was a special recognition as well.

According to the Act, indigenous people of Chilean nationality are those:

(a) who are children of any indigenous father or mother including the adoptive;
(b) indigenous ethnic groups that inhabit the national territory, provided that they possess at least an indigenous surname; and
(c) those who maintain cultural traits of any ethnic group in a usual way or whose spouse is indigenous.

The law makes a distinction among *urban indigenous*, those Chileans, who identify themselves as indigenous and whose domicile in an urban area of the national territory and *migrant indigenous,* those who also have permanent residence in a rural area that is not indigenous territory recognized by law. They are granted the right to form associations as a form of social organization, cultural development, support and mutual protection and aid among the indigenous urban or migrant, respectively. The National Corporation for Indigenous Development supports programmes that are aimed at achieving higher levels of well-being and ensure the maintenance and development of their cultures and own identities and ensure non-discrimination (Law 19.253). As a result there has been a remarkable proliferation of associations primarily motivated by having the possibility of accessing subsidies offered by the State through design contests.

In Chile, migration to cities started in the 20th century, driven directly or indirectly, by the loss of lands and natural resources, the high rate of education as a means of integration into mainstream society, and the need to proletarize as a strategy to incorporate the circuit of money. These factors play both ways of expulsion from their territory to cities by stimulating the migration process. Once in the city, they suffer violations of their human rights – poor access to health, work, housing, education – turning to be a part of the most impoverished sectors of cities. While the indigenous peoples in the city suffer a double violation of their rights as indigenous peoples and rural areas and has especially territorial demands otherwise and collective rights.

Indigenous policy installed in Chile, along with the neo-liberal economic model, began in 1973 with the dictatorship of Augusto Pinochet. It did not recognize ethnic heterogeneity and therefore encouraged indigenous, peasant property division delivering individual titles which would facilitate their inclusion in the land market. While the neo-liberal economic model of market was continued by democratic governments post dictatorship (1989–2010), there were some changes in indigenous policies that favoured the recognition of their rights: enactment of a law and ratification of the ILO Convention 169, in 2009, a legal tool which defends the right to the indigenous territory. In 2010 the government again enacted the political right that channels the policies toward the model imposed during the dictatorship. The fear of leaders is that this would promote 'assimilation, land division, the individual property and unimpeded sale' and they will have to 'by collective territorial and political rights (autonomy, self-governance, territoriality and self-determination) ...and the problem of migration and of residence in urban of the vast majority of our people could transform into the gold mine of public policies with and ideological purposes').[4] Thus divert the State interest in resolving claims of lands, territories and rights to natural resources they use, to give priority to the *indigenous urban.*

Urban Indigenous

The last population Census year 2002 showed most Indians are in the city, as shown in Table 1.

Table 1

Ethnicity by Gender and Area Geographic Area

Indigenous People	*Urban*		*Total Urban %*	*Rural*		*Total Rural %*	*Total*
	Man	*Woman*		*Man*	*Woman*		
Alacalufe	1.214	1.079	87.00	209	120	13.00	2.622
Atacameño	8.925	8.484	83.00	1.927	1.679	17.00	21.015
Aymara	18.529	19.543	78.00	5.659	4.770	22.00	48.501
Colla	1.432	1.311	86.00	255	200	14.00	3.198
Mapuche	184.515	192.618	62.00	120.065	107.151	38.00	604.349
Quechua	2.375	2.608	81.00	662	530	1.192	6.175
Rapa Nui	2.047	2.240	92.00	216	144	19.00	4.647
Yagan	753	709	87.00	123	100	13.00	1.685
Total	219.790	228.592	65.00%	129.116	114.694	35.00%	692.192

Three years later, the 2006 survey by the State showed that the population that is self-identified as belonging to an indigenous people in the country had climbed to 10,60,786 people, raising the number of urban indigenous to the 69.4 per cent. Another feature highlighted is that the indigenous population is still poorer than non-indigenous population and the frequency is higher in rural areas. Poverty distinguishes two types: poor, people who have necessary minimum income per person to fulfill the basic needs, food and non food; while homeless people identify those households that do not have sufficient income as to meet minimum requirements.

Table 2

Poverty and Indigenous Peoples

	Rural Sector		*Urban Sector*	
	Non-Indigenous %	*Indigenous %*	*Non-Indigenous %*	*Indigenous %*
Indigent	5.1	8.7	7.5	14.6
Poor	14.6	21.3	14,7	21.4
Non-Poor	80.3	70.0	77.8	64.0
Total	100.0	100.0	100.0	100.0

Final Considerations

The Chilean State has opened a legal setting for the emergence of new identities, unsuspected by social scientists. The effects of this legal recognition show sectors attracted by government policies that offers a way to overcome poverty in the recovery of their indigenous identity. The role of the state and its relationship with indigenous peoples is in debate. One sector criticizes the idea of citizenship associated with a welfare state, centred on the assessment of the State and the collective[5], because their institutions promote a passive citizen, dependent on the State, at the time that 'in favour of a privatizing withdrawal of citizenship and a special 'clientelism' of the role of citizen' (Habermas, 1992: 10–11). Indigenous peoples among their demands 'have included the suspension of the clearing of the welfare State and of the loss of the social function of the State, and its choice in favor of investment policies rampant'.[6]

Chile Government's multiculturalism is rooted in the transition period towards a democracy that has continued with unconditional loyalty to the inherited neoliberal economic model of dictatorship of 1973–1989. Multiculturalism is thus forged in the process of political transformation of the State.

The current government of President Sebastian Piñera (2010–2014), has rightly chosen to deepen and strengthen the integrationist policies with priority in the urban indigenous above the demands of the rural sector: territory, resources, autonomy.

In the 1980s the indigenization phenomenon emerged in Latin America. Indigenous peoples began to move from the dis-indigenization to the indigenization, in a process with contradictions and inequalities, adhering to cultural roots to validate their actions. The characteristics of each country's history provided a scenario of theoretical and political complexity of proportions.

Many questions arise from the analysis of this phenomenon, for example: Who is the indigenous? This phenomenon is an instrument for profit or constitutes a political proposal? What direction has political action of these groups taken? Another issue that I want to discuss is whether, from the perspective of the action, institutions would be promoting and simultaneously controlling the multiculturalism. Is indigenization a new source of power held by external agents such as the State, NGOs, entrepreneurs, among others? Does it constitute one side of the indigenization factionalism? What is the political leadership of indigenous people in different countries and within the same country?

On the one hand, native peoples were conquered, lost their rights and they were subordinated to the new order. Assimilationistic and integrationistic policies justified were, giving indigenous peoples 'backwardness' and poverty. The dichotomous paradigms between the traditional and the modern, reported this. The indigenous should disappear in modernity and *mestizaje* or miscegenation.

As a result, a departure from the stigma of being indigenous was miscegenation, biological and cultural, which promised a clear path towards uniformity (whitening) of Latin American societies.

The invasion of America brought the concepts to identify and qualify persons of indigenous ancestry as lower, sloths, beings reluctant to change, and so many other derogatory terms. One of the strategies to escape stigma has been voluntary change of surname to avoid the moral prejudice, teasing, and be the subject of insults. As seen in the Chilean case: between 1970 and 1990 there were 31,597 cases of requests for change of name to national level, of which 2,365 belonged to indigenous peoples including Rapa Nui 31 cases, Aymará 279 cases and Mapuche 2,056 cases.[7]

To survive and be included in the Chilean society, one had to be deserting the indigenous culture – not to mention the language choice, conceal the name and/or surname or migrate to the cities to being a mestizo, the national culture. They saw a life strategy in education for their children and forbade them speak their language. These and other actions such as leaving the field work, leave or disguise religiosity indigenous, sell their lands were part of an unbridled race to stop being 'Indian'.

Eurocentric thought penetrated into the social and human sciences, and the reality of the researchers could not get rid of the ideological, social and cultural context. The rationale for this new order, based on the divine power, hegemony that is religious, cultural, political and legal, and racial supremacy, allowed, since the beginning of the conquest, slavery and later, other forms of submission.

Non-recognition and appreciation of cultural differences by states which were born with independence, and hostile attitude on the part of some indigenous peoples towards the State – as the Mapuche people in Chile – not only did not allow a cultural fusion but also installed a racial opposition of unfathomable segregation with implications in the economic, social and cultural fields, between Indians and Whites. Policies and practices to strengthen the new society needed the *de-indigenization*, linguistic and cultural requirements to consolidate the monolingual, nation-states and on the other hand install racism as ideology of the ruling class that explains differences based on race, being in the process of structuring of power, excluding from the political arena of indigenous people, the Métis.

Re-indigenization

Re-indigenization is a process by which a social group, a faction, a movement or a very broad society sector assume that identification with their cultural root is valid for its action-oriented approach. In other words, the indigenization is a tool which uses elites or broad sectors of society, or ethnic groups or population, minority or indigenous peoples or non-indigenous, when they take their own cultural identity as a positive value.

Indigenization as an exclusive quality of the indigenous but as an attribute of any group – big or small – should not be considered when it reaffirms culturally. This is a complex, unequal and contradictory process. Sometimes, the condition for political decolonization processes make it happen, in other cases it occurs as an isolated, marginal and secondary phenomenon. The indigenization and its counterpart the dis-indigenization are a global process linked to culture and faced with globalization. In fact, they are the political faces of every culture and in the end of a civilization.

Turning Indigenous, Wanting to be Indigenous

Without any doubt, indigenous can be perceived as the result of the legal changes, a new political era beginning and the economic and political changes have taken place since the last decades of the 20th century. Understanding this new reality is a pending task, and it is necessary to take into account some elements that are part of the current political context. What moves to the indigenous political action and violent political action? From where comes this force? Is it due to more than five centuries of domination and exclusion? The results are:

1. Participate in the benefits of the State (scholarships, buying land, projects micro, etc.).
2. Validate their historical mobilizations to regain the territories usurped.
3. Organize and strengthen new movements in defense of their territories and natural resources with the arrival of tourism, pollution of waters, forests destruction extractive, businesses, etc.

Strong historical background of subjugation has unique indigenous rebellions which were a constant during the colony and the Republican period. And those who fought to defend their rights are heroes and are paid tribute today – as it happened in the II Continental Summit of peoples and nationalities where indigenous peoples of Abya Yala offered an act of homage to the historical heroes of the indigenous peoples of the continent.

The truth is that they have begun to appreciate the value of the political potential to be indigenous, but the scenario is of enormous complexity in an indigenous world that extends between two extremes: those who have opted for miscegenation, life in the cities, acculturation, social, political, religious, economic transformations and at the other extreme, a peasant sector which has continued stressing their right and their culture in their ancestral territories. So, there is a scenario where the reindigenisation generates between people who today have huge differences and different interests. There are many groups and organizational structures, some people call tyranny, the term which we better think explains is factionalism.

The emergence of identities has installed a powerful multicultural scenario. What is behind multiculturalism? Multiculturalism would represent, in the words of Slovenian philosopher Slavoj Žižek (2008)[8], 'ideally' globalized, capitalism is an ideology Eurocentric serves capitalism and globalization, in the same way of global capitalism there is the paradox of the settlement without a colonizing metropolis of the nation-State. It expresses the 'auto colonization capitalist global' (Žižek, 2004). The interesting thing is that it does not seek to destroy cultures, rather encourages them; and as said Díaz Polanco, it attracts, seduces, transforms them, to integrate them. Here, acting State occurs as guarantor to the rights of indigenous peoples to mitigate shocks of the system, performs a legal court streak, encourages the 'voluntary' participation of the largest possible number of individuals, which promotes the formation of various organizations and associations with their respective leaders, and also of new identities, all this in order to promote networks created by the State to access benefits offered by the State; and thus it neutralizes accession to movements or groups of intellectuals – contrary to this ideology of multiculturalism – whose speeches make the State uncomfortable. It directly attacks the foundation of the communal cohesion fighting for the defense of natural resources and recovery of land and territory, keeping the due reverence to multicultural (Díaz-Polanco, 1997).

Notes

1. Vicesecretaria General de Naciones Unidas. Nueva York, 13 de mayo de 2002. http://www.un.org/spanish/indigenas/2002/dsgindig.htm
2. The Declaration is signed by the following indigenous organizations:Andean indigenous organizations Coordinator CONAIE ECUARUNARI, CONAICE, CONFENIAE, ONIC (Colombia), CONACAMI (Peru), CONAMAQ, CSTUSB (Bolivia), FNCMCIBS (Bolivia), identity Lafkenche (Chile), ONPIA (Argentina), CONAVIGUA (Guatemala), Latin American Observatory of Geopolitics (Mexico). </www.nacionmulticultural.UNAM.MX/declaraciones/Tema/tema13.html>
3. Indigenous and local knowledge and world vision are one of the many treasures of mankind to care for and preserve. See UNESCO, WHO, Convention Biological Diversity (CBD), World Intellectual Property Organization (WIPO), UNCCD, RAMSAR, United Nations Permanent Forum on Indigenous Issues (UNPFII).
4. Henry Antileo, anthropologist, member of Meli Witran Mapu. www.mapuexpress.net.
5. 'The welfare state corresponds to all State institutions providing social policies aimed at improving the conditions of life, to facilitate the integration of classes and social groups, levelling and matching – although not taken – material resources.' The equal rights of citizens, and especially those directly involving the basic well-being of people, made affordable wealth inequalities generated by capitalist systems and has mitigated the social conflicts that inherently carries. Moreno (op.cit)

6. Declaration of Lima of the Peoples Indigenous and Afro, 2006. http://www.nacionmulticultural.unam.mx/declaraciones/docs/decl_012.pdf
7. (Jaivas and Llanquileo, 1990)
8. Žižek. S. Título Original: 'Or, the Cultural Logic of Multinational Capitalism Multiculturalism'. Posted in *new left review,* No. 225, September–October 1997. http://newleftreview.org/?page=article & view = 1919Gustavo Macri translation. Jameson, Fredric and Žižek, Slavoj: *Cultural Studies. Reflections on Multiculturalism*. Buenos Aires, Paidos, 1998, pp. 137–188

References

Anaya, James. 2009. 'The situation of indigenous peoples in Chile: Follow-up to the recommendations made by the Special Reporter above'. Electronic document www.politicaspublicas.NET/docs/2009_relator_anaya_informe_chile_unedited_version.PDF

Ballon, Francisco. 2003. 'Indigenization versus Factionalism'. In *Magazine Contributions Andean*. March, 2003.

Clavero, Bartolomé. 2010. 'Colombia: Responsible Government, International and Military in Indigenous Dispossession and Mortality'. Electronic document <http://Clavero. derechosindigenas.org/?p=6279>.

Díaz-Polanco, H. 1997. *The Zapatista Eebellion and Autonomy*. Siglo XXI Editores, Mexico.

Dussel, E. 2001.*Towards a Critical Political Philosophy*. Toronto: University of Toronto Press.

Habermas, 1992, In: Kymlicka, W. *Multicultural Citizenship: A Liberal Theory of Minority Rights,* Oxford: Clarendon Press.

Menchu, Rigoberta. 2004. 'Meeting on the role of the Indian peoples in the struggle for the unity of our America'. *Magazine Regional Unit – Images of our America.* N°16 (January-April). Electronic document www. aunamexico.org/Publicaciones/Revista/N16/rev16ene04-Menchu-Stavenhagen.htm>

Stavenhagen, Rodolfo. 2008. Rapporteur UN Rodolfo Stavenhagen on indigenous issues to close to the declaration on the rights of IP, Ex speech'. Electronic document www.unep.org/indigenous/pdfs/StavenhagenEnglish. pdf.

Villoro, Luis. 1999. *Plural State, Plurality of Cultures*. Mexico: Paidos.

Wallerstein, I. 1989. *Historical Capitalism*, London: Verso.

Žižek, S. 2004. The Ongoing Soft Resolution. *Critical Inquiry*, 30(2): pp. 292–323.

19

Second Class Citizens?

Human Rights for Indigenous People in Mexico City

LAURA R. VALLADARES DE LA CRUZ

Through this article I wish to speak about the concerns of the indigenous population in Mexico City in respect of their citizenship and Human Rights, as also to discuss the difficulties and challenges in legislating the collective rights of both the native indigenous populations and the other indigenous peoples who reside in Mexico City. I will also attempt to show that although the Mexican Government has adopted multicultural policies since the decade of the 1990s, there are great obstacles that actually show up in the way of building up a nation which respects the ethnic diversity of the country. All this is in the backdrop of an indigenous population that is of pre-Hispanic descent and which has come to be a part of the self-defining Mexican narrative.

A Multiethnic City: The Multicultural Mosaic of Mexico City

At the very outset of this article I will begin by pointing out that Mexico City and its surrounding metropolitan area is the third most populated urban area on the planet.[1] More than 650 thousand of the over 22 million inhabitants that live here belong to an indigenous or ethnic group (which represents approximately 3 per cent of the total metropolitan area population).[2] When considering such a large population, we must remember that Mexico City is the smallest entity in the country in terms of territory, as it has an area of only 1,484 square kilometres, which represents just 0.1 per cent of the whole national territory (of a total of 2 million square kilometres); 20 per cent of the total population lives within this area.[3] This data alone allows us to imagine the complexity, not to mention the social, political and economic density of this cosmopolitan megacity.

I am interested in highlighting some characteristics of the city, such as its diverse landscapes, economic, political and cultural activities and the variety of educational options. It would be just as significant to mention the problems that have showed up due to the entangled settlement in a small valley submersed in a national context of profound inequality. On the one hand, even though Mexico is considered to be an emerging economy, more than 54 per cent of its population lives in poverty. In Mexico, the Ministry of Social Development admitted that 54 per cent of the Mexicans are in poverty, which indicates that they make a living on less that 4 dollars a day. While 32 per cent of this poor people live on less than $2.50 dollars a day, 24 per cent exist on less than $2 dollars daily. Chiapas, Guerrero, Oaxaca, Tabasco and Durango, where the highest percentages of indigenous population are concentrated, are the poorest states in the country. Poverty is directly related to the capacity to generate employment, and is potential for all kinds of development on the basis of education, university graduation degree, skilled workers and research. All this gives the region the means for the creation of marketable products and services as well as for the development of an infrastructure which allows the region to have an economic and labour relationship with other sectors.[4]

However, in Mexico, the unequal distribution of wealth has paved the way for a concentrated income from commerce in certain sectors, such as those which are specifically devoted to exporting goods and services to the disadvantage of the other areas, like agriculture, which greatly depend on the pace of development of the just-mentioned states. The indigenous areas also suffer due to marginalization in terms of the number of schools and the distance between one educational centre and another. This is mainly since, in the rural areas, schools are populated by students from distant areas which, due to difficulty in accessibility, leads to a lack of attendance. Secondary schools are scarce and there are even fewer high schools (technical education) and universities. Health services are concentrated in the most populated areas, such as capital cities, making transportation difficult since there is nearly no means of transporting patients to healthcare centres or regional hospitals. These indicators refer mainly to the indigenous population among whom there are greater levels of malnutrition, illiteracy and mono-lingualism and which results in the highest rates of unemployment and practically no participation within the structures of power and representation in the country (Yanes, 2004; Yanes et al., 2006).

On the other hand, it is important to point out that despite great cultural diversity, not all ethnic groups or cultures have the same socio-economic conditions. Also they neither possess the same ways and skills of adjusting to society nor the same opportunities to express, reproduce and take on their cultures and identities. It is worthwhile to mention that historically Mexico City has grown by receiving various migration waves originating from different states, especially the Nahua peoples who come from the central areas of the country. There are other populations living in Mexico that have diverse ethnic, religious and cultural backgrounds, to name some of the most relevant – the North Americans, Germans, Jewish, Japanese, Chinese, Argentinians, Spanish, Italians and the Lebanese. Their presence is due to diverse factors, yet on the whole, international immigrants, with the exception of those from Central America, are linked to the highest economic and cultural sectors of the country and therefore have access to schools, cultural centres, restaurants and clubs and live in residential areas of the city. Such a position has allowed these populations to find Mexico a place for financial growth and well-being and for the reproduction of their culture.

Paradoxically, the diversity among the indigenous population in Mexico City is neither welcome nor accepted. Seeing that the nation was constructed emulating a liberal European model, ethnic diversity was considered to be a foundational defect needing to be fixed. That is the reason why throughout its history, several programmes and projects that aimed to 'incorporate' these populations have been implemented with the ultimate goal of building a homogenous nation in terms of race and culture (Díaz-Polanco, 2000; Valladares, 2009; Sánchez, 2008). However, diversity has not disappeared and, on the contrary, for the last 25 years, the indigenous peoples have been claiming their right to autonomy and demand respect for their ways of political organization, their lands, their culture and their justice systems. At the same time they have also been trying to establish their right to participate in the decision making process of the entire country. Such demands have been echoed and expressed in the metropolitan area of Mexico City, not only by its native indigenous population but also by the thousands of migrants and residents that populate the city. I must point out that *Residents* is a term that has been ascribed to the indigenous peoples and it is also a term which is used by government agencies in Mexico City (Banda, 2006; Sánchez, 2004; Valladares, 2009).

Indigenous migration to Mexico City goes back to more than five decades. Thousands of indigenous people began to migrate continuously towards Mexico City since the 1960s, owing to an agrarian crisis which battered the country, especially the agricultural sector. At times, this emigration was due to the search for better paid jobs as well as for access to secondary and higher education and, in more recent years, we can say that this is about a population that has been driven from their native lands or displaced from their territory due to violent conditions, whether those be economic, political or related to drug trafficking. Without a doubt, Mexico City has not received migration waves as in the earlier decades; yet the city continues to be a magnet for migrants or a place of passing for migrants who wish to reach the northern US border. Nowadays, there are more than half a million indigenous people from nearly every ethnic group in the country. These people combined with the native Nahua people and made Mexico City the most culturally diverse entity in the country. This is reflected by the fact that nearly every indigenous language in the country is spoken here; in other words, around 62 of the 68 known languages are spoken (Yanes et al., 2006).

Regarding Citizen and Collective Rights of the Indigenous Population

In the context of ethnic and cultural plurality, the exercise of indigenous rights and the respect of those are quite problematic due to several reasons. The first is related to the subservient incorporation of these rights into the economy since generally indigenous men and women become under-employed and work in the informal economy as street vendors, construction workers and, for the majority of women, as domestic servants. Generally these are jobs in which the workers are completely unprotected in terms of labour rights (Oehmichen, 1999, 2003).

Secondly, they find themselves in a city where racism is expressed on a daily basis, making them a vulnerable sector facing an infinite amount of open and well known discriminatory practices (Ortíz, 2006). In the third place, although there is a widespread debate in Mexico regarding the collective rights of indigenous peoples and till date there have been legislations in terms of indigenous rights in 23 of the 32 states, (López, 2005; Valladares, 2009), there is yet to be a legislation which protects the indigenous residents of this great megapolis, since the instruments of defense and protection for the collective rights of indigenous peoples allude initially to the original territories as a requirement and the setting where the rights of these minorities are recognized and protected (Gómez, 2004; Kimlycka, 1996; Rouland et al., 1996). In this way, there is no existent legislation which protects the rights of indigenous residents or temporary workers although it can be affirmed that this issue is being considered from various perspectives.

Two outstanding proposals have been considered for establishing the position of the indigenous people. One of these is related to the introduction of distinct government programmes which seek to attend to the main issues and demands of this sector of city dwellers, while the other involves the debate concerning the need to legislate in favour of the indigenous peoples in Mexico City, which centred on matters such as: whether indigenous migrants should be taken into consideration in an Urban Indigenous Rights Law and whether they should be recognized as migrants or as residents. Taking this into account, what kind of rights could they have, if this is not their ancestral land? Such a question itself explains why it is thought that indigenous residents and/or migrants in the city are like foreigners and subordinates in their own country besides being second class citizens (Díaz-Polanco, 1991; Sánchez, 2004). This is due to the fact that many indigenous people do not have any kind of official documents that allow them to exercise any rights such as to vote, or to be voted for, to receive governmental support, or to have access to a formal job and expedite justice (ONU, 2003; CDH-DF, 2008; Valladares et al., 2010).

When facing this impasse in the recognition and incorporation thereafter of the rights of the indigenous peoples in the Mexico City Constitution, the government in Mexico City opted to begin various programmes which aim to take care of the needs of this sector of the population.[5] The following lines will be devoted to this topic.

State Policies towards the Indigenous Population

The needs and demands of indigenous peoples and those of indigenous migrants are different in that these groups take part in city life in a different manner. On the one hand, indigenous people who migrate to the city suffer from both prejudice and the stigma of being indigenous, meaning they are stereotyped as being ignorant, lazy, and dirty (Castellanos, 2003). They are discriminated against because of their class and ethnic status; in the case of the women, gender status adds to this situation. As a result, many indigenous people deny their cultural identity or, on the contrary, stick together living with other families or community members where they find mutual support.

In contrast to the migrant or resident population, the native indigenous population that is located in the southern areas of the city faces the loss of land and natural resources due to the rapid growth of the urban sprawl. In fact, they face the loss of their cultural practices as new generations, in their new environment, no longer form cultural bonds, distancing themselves from their own cultural practices in order to be a part of the 'modern city life'.[6]

In this respect, the Mexico City government has found it necessary to create programmes which are directed specifically towards these sectors. In the case of the native indigenous population, organized groups constituted by the *Indigenous Peoples Support Programme* (PAPO as abbreviated in Spanish) have been granted support in order to promote social and cultural rights, which respect their social and cultural identity, habits and customs and their own ways of community organization as well as foster activities which promote equality, social well-being and the respect of diversity by way of support to community projects.[7]

Under this framework, various agencies and partnerships have been created in order to serve the indigenous population, including the Ministry of Rural Development and Equality for Communities (SEDEREC as abbreviated in Spanish), created in 2006, whose primary responsibility is to establish and carry out public policies and programmes on rural development, serve indigenous peoples and ethnic communities, in addition to the migrants and their families (López, 2006).

Another way the government attempted to meet the demands of the indigenous population in Mexico City has been through the creation of the Mexico City Council for Native Peoples and Local Communities as the coordinating body of the Mexico City Public Services and Citizen Participation which focuses on fomenting, conserving and transmitting the original culture and traditions of the peoples and local communities that are originally from Mexico City.[8] This organization, for instance, offered its opinion on the *Proposed Law for Indigenous and Native Peoples* which was presented by the Indigenous Affairs Commission of the Mexico City Legislative Assembly. The proposal was that any initiative which recognizes rights should be proceeded by a consultation among the inhabitants of the indigenous peoples so as to guarantee that their needs are included and a law could be created which truly satisfies their needs.[9] In the last few months, a consultation model and various forums have been undertaken; however, there is yet to be any law initiative which is applicable to the demands and needs of indigenous peoples.

In addition, the Mexico City Council for Indigenous Consultation and Participation was constituted as an organization for advising, consulting, consensus building and coordination of the Mexico City Public Services towards the planning, promotion, development and evaluation of the policies and programmes which serve the indigenous peoples and the resident indigenous communities in Mexico City.[10] The Interdependent Commission for the Equality of Indigenous Peoples and Ethnic Communities in Mexico City was created in the year 2007; it was constituted with 11 Ministers and another 16 heads of municipalities.[11]

In as far as progress – on the lines of services to indigenous peoples and residents – is concerned, the emphasis was on the access to justice where legislation marks the right that all indigenous peoples who have been implicated in a legal process need to have a translator and an expert on culture throughout the whole legal process. This explains why the public prosecutor's offices are obliged to request the services offered by the Translators and Interpreters and Promoters of the Indigenous Languages Organization, AC.[12]

Other areas like health, education, housing and productive projects already have programmes which are specifically designed for the indigenous population. For instance, under this heading, there is a programme called *Equality for Rural,*

Indigenous, Guest and Migrant Women in Mexico City, which is a productive project that implies the gender perspective. Such programme have had moderate success although it is important to recognize the willingness of the city government to work with the dozens of indigenous organizations located in the entity. There is still a long way to go towards building a government which recognizes the Rights and does not focus on programmes which mitigate poverty (Bonfil, 2004; Valladares, 2009).

The Dispute for Indigenous Rights in the Metropolitan Area

Currently the indigenous people remain invisible for the majority of the city's inhabitants and their rights and freedoms are dismissed. They are still not given any recognition as legal law-abiding citizens as a result of which their corresponding collective rights are also still rejected. This lack of recognition has been the main reason behind a long list of grievances, often put forward by the representatives of these people, like agricultural lags, delay in the legalization of their lands, expropriation and privatization of their lands and resources, the negligence of the authorities towards their own people and communities, the imposition of projects, the meddling of municipal authorities and of Mexico City institutions in community affairs, the lack of opportunities for indigenous people to represent and participate in administrative bodies in the city government as well as in the Mexico City legislative Assembly and the Federal Congress and, as a result, their exclusion from the formulation of legislative and administrative proposals has been proclaimed (Sánchez, 2004).

Despite such adverse conditions or because of them, for more than two decades, the indigenous peoples and residents of the city have organized themselves into committees, associations, organizations, networks, co-fraternities, or NGOs, among many other associative bodies, in order to resolve the problems they face (Sánchez, 2004).[13]

Certainly, the exercise of citizens' rights is still on the 'to do' list in this megacity and the exercised extended rights referring to multicultural citizenship are processes under construction (Kymilcka, 1996; Rouland, 1996; Valladares, 2003, 2009). In order to exercise these rights, it is necessary to reverse the effects of this mindless model of capitalism, which in place of cultural recognition has actually perpetuated inequality.

Without a doubt then, the rights of indigenous migrants in urban spaces are enormously complex. To start with, it must be recognized that this is a current reality, to exemplify, according to the data available, 50 per cent of the indigenous population in the country do not live in their towns of origin but have lived for generations in the city and are 'city people'. In terms of a conceptual approach, we cannot continue considering indigenous rights to be linked only to ancestral lands. Nowadays, indigenous territories have extended, communities have become transnational, the reproduction of their identity has extended past their place of origin to large cities and beyond national borders, (Poutignat and Streiff-Fenart, 2006; Giménez, 2009) they are citizens of the city who construct together with the rest of the citizens of the contemporary megalopolis and should be considered likewise in terms of the law and daily life.

Notes

1. Only the population in Tokyo, Japan is larger; 31 million inhabitants and of New York, 30 million http://www.top10.com.mx/las_10_ciudades_mas_pobladas_del_mundo_y_mexico.htm
2. Basic information documents, 2005, Municipal Database. National Commission for the Development of Indigenous Peoples, 2006.
3. The total population of the country is 100 million inhabitants.
4. See: http://www.explorandomexico.com.mx/about-mexico/6/107/, consulted on December 6, 2011
5. See Valladares, Laura, Angeles Uriega and Alejandra Toriz, *Report on the Situation of the Rights of Indigenous Women in the Metropolitan Area of Mexico City*, CDI, Mexico, 2010.
6. See: (Report on the Consultation with Indigenous Women, 2010).
7. Electronic document, link http://www.transparencia2008.df.gob.mx/wb/Transparencia/programa_de_apoyo_a_pueblos_originarios_del_distri
8. The Official Federal District Gazette, March 21, 2007. Agreement under which the *Mexico City Council for Native Peoples and Local Communities* was created.
9. http://www.dfinitivo.com/archivos/2008/07/21/iniciativa-de-ley-para-reconocer-los-derechos-de-los-pueblos-originarios-del-df/
10. The Council is made up of the following institutions: Ministry of the Interior, Ministry of the Environment, Ministry of Economic Development, the office of the Mexico City Attorney General, Ministry of Social Development, The Institute of Housing of Mexico City, Municipal Representatives, Academic representatives, social organizations, Members of native indigenous peoples.
11. In addition, heads of the Mexico City Attorney General Office are invited on an ongoing basis from the Metropolitan Delegation of the National Commission for the Development of Indigenous Peoples and the Native Peoples and Neighborhoods Council in Mexico City.
12. Special report on the rights of resident indigenous communities in Mexico City, 2006–2007.
13. The Organization for Indigenous Migrants in the City is particularly active as well as two organizations of domestic services headed by indigenous young people who for several years have demanded their work be reglamented obliging employers to offer them the minimum legal benefits established for all workers.

References

Banda, Oscar e Issac Martínez. 2006. 'Residentes indígenas y espacio territorial', In Yanes, Pablo, Virginia Molina y Óscar González, *El Triple Desafío. Derechos, instituciones y políticas para la ciudad de México*, Gob-DF-UACM-Secretaría de Desarrollo Social, México, pp. 285–291.

Bonfil Sánchez, Paloma. 2004. 'Lo público es ancho y ajeno. Obstáculos y desafíos para la construcción de una agenda de mujeres indígenas', In Hernández, Aída, Sarela Paz y Teresa Sierra, *El Estado y los indígenas en tiempos del PAN: neoindigenismo, legalidad e identidad,* CIESAS-Cámara de Diputados-Porrúa, México. pp. 53–80.

Castellano, Alicia (Coordinadora). 2003. *Imágenes del racismo en México,* UAM-I-Plaza y Valdés, México.

Comisión de Derechos Humanos del Distrito Federal (CDH-DF). 2008. *Informe sobre los Derechos Humanos de los indígenas en la ciudad de México,* México.

Díaz-Polanco, Héctor. 1991. *Autonomía regional. La autodeterminación de los pueblos indígenas.* Siglo XXI, México.

Giménez, Gilberto. 2009. 'El debate contemporáneo en torno al concepto de etnicidad', *In*: Valladares, Laura, Maya Lorena Pérez y M. Zárate, (Eds), *Estados Plurales. Los retos de la diversidad y la diferencia.* Edit. Plaza y Valdés – UAM-I, México, pp. 35–49.

Gómez, Magdalena. 2004. 'La constitucionalidad pendiente: la hora indígena en la corte', *In*: Hernández, Aída, Sarela Paz y Teresa Sierra (coord.) *El Estado y los indígenas en tiempos del PAN: neoindigenismo, legalidad e identidad.* Cámara de Diputados-CIESAS-Porrúa, México. pp. 175–205.

Kymlicka, Will. 1996. *Ciudadanía Multicultural. Una teoría liberal de los derechos de las minorías.* Paidós, Barcelona, España.

López Bárcenas, Francisco. 2005. *Los movimientos indígenas en México. Rostros y caminos,* Centro de Orientación y Asesoría a Pueblos Indios, México.

López Mercado, Alejandro. 2006. 'Políticas públicas en materia indígena del Gobierno del Distrito Federal', *In:* Yanes, Pablo, Virginia Molina and Óscar González (eds), *El Triple Desafío. Derechos, instituciones y políticas para la ciudad de Méxic*o, Gob-DF-UACM-Secretaría de Desarrollo Social, México, pp. 341- 369.

Oehmichen, Cristina. 1999. 'Las mujeres en la comunidad extraterritorial. Las mujeres indígenas migrantes en la comunidad extraterritorial', *In*: Barrera Bassols, Dalia and Cristina Oehmichen, (Eds), *Migración y relaciones de género en México,* GIMTRAP-IIA/UNAM, México. pp. 319–320.

Ohemichen, Cristina. 2003. 'Relaciones interétnicas en la ciudad de México', *In:* Cartellanos Alicia (Ed), *Imágenes del Racismo en México,* UAM-Plaza y Valdés, México, pp. 315–360.

ONU. 2003. *Informe del Relator Especial sobre la situación de los derechos humanos y las libertades fundamentales de los indígenas*. Adición Misión México. Naciones Unidas, Consejo Económico Social. Comisión de Derechos Humanos 60° periodo de sesiones, 23 de diciembre. ONU.

Ortíz Quintero, Larissa. 2006. 'Indígenas y Derechos Humanos', *In:* Yanes, Pablo, Virginia Molina and Óscar González (Eds), *El Triple Desafío. Derechos, instituciones y políticas para la ciudad de Méxic*o, Gob-DF-UACM-Secretaría de Desarrollo Social, México, pp. 269–283.

Poutignat, Philippe and Jocelyne Streiff-Fenart. 2006. *Theories de l ethicité,* París, Francia.

Rouland, Norbert, Stpephane Pierré-Caps and Jacques Poumaréde. 1996. *Droit des minorités et des peuples autochtones.* Presses Universitaires de France, París. Francia.

Sánchez, Consuelo. 2004. 'La diversidad cultural en la ciudad de México. Autonomía de los pueblos originarios y los migrantes', *In:* Yanes Pablo, Virginia Molina and Oscar González (eds) *Ciudad, Pueblos Indígenas y Etnicidad. UACM-Dirección General de Equidad y Desarrollo Social*, México, pp. 57–87.

Sánchez Santiago, Patricia C, Maximino Gonzalez Rojas, Benedicto Ayala Cortes, Lorenza Gutierrez Gomez, Katia De La Torre, Bulmaro Ventura and Fortino Hernandez Matias. 2004. 'Sobre la experiencia y el trabajo de las organizaciones indígenas en la Ciudad de México, In Yanes Pablo, Virginia Molina and Oscar González (Eds) *Ciudad, Pueblos Indígenas y Etnicidad. UACM-Dirección General de Equidad y Desarrollo Social*, Mexico, pp. 287–320.

Valladares, Laura. 2003. 'Democracia y derechos indios en México: la ciudadanía multicultural como modelo de paz', *In:* Revista Mexicana de Ciencias Políticas y Sociales. Número 188–189, UNAM, México, pp. 121–146.

Valladares, Laura. 2009. Políticas Multiculturales vs. Movimiento Indígena. La lucha por la autonomía en México, (Unpublished Ph.D. Thesis) ENAH, México.

Valladares, Laura, Angeles Uriega and Alejandra Toriz. 2010. *Report on the Situation of the Rights of Indigenous Women in the Metropolitan Area of Mexico City*, CDI, Mexico.

Yanes, Pablo. 2004. 'Urbanización de los pueblos indígenas y etnicización de las Ciudades. Hacia una agenda de derechos y políticas públicas', *In:* Yanes, Pablo E, Virginia Molina and Oscar González (eds), *Ciudad, Pueblos Indígenas y Etnicidad. UACM-Dirección General de Equidad y Desarrollo Social*, México, 191–223.

Yanes, Pablo, Virginia Molina and Óscar González (eds) 2006. *El triple Desafío. Derechos Instituciones y políticas para la ciudad pluricultural.* Gobierno DF-Secretaría de Desarrollo Social-UACM. México.

20

A Profile of *Bidi* Binder with Special Reference to their Problems and Rights

SAMIK ROY

Bidi binder or workers are among the most exploited workers in India. They are easy prey for unscrupulous contractors. The low pay *bidi* binders receive keep them in poverty; it doesn't help them escape poverty. Minimum wages fixed by the government are between ₹ 40–64 per 1,000 *bidis* rolled, but rollers frequently receive much less. Many *bidi* binders are not aware of the harmful effects of *bidis* on health and have very low literacy rates. The present study gives an account of problems of the *bidi* binder; about existing government policies, their awareness of their rights, and the nature of deprivation and exploitation.

Area and People

The present study was conducted on a sub-urban area, Gopalnagar of the district, North 24 Parganas, West Bengal, India. The district is bounded on the north by Bangladesh and the district of Nadia, on the east by Bangladesh, on the south by district of South 24 Parganas and Bay of Bengal and on the west by Hooghly district. The headquarters of this district is Barasat. Total area of 8,90,156.98 hectares, this district is inhabited by villagers of the district and cultivable area covers 74.07 per cent of the district and agriculture is the main economy.

The district, at present, comprised 33 Police Stations and 22 Community Development Blocks.

North 24 Parganas has emerged as the second most densely populated district in the country with a population of 1,00,82,852 according to the 2011 Census report. Total population of the district according to 2001 Census is 90,25,832 persons (comprising 46,84,860 males and 43,40,972 females). The Scheduled Caste and Scheduled Tribe population of the district as per 2001 Census are 18,56,602 (male 9,57,206 and female 8,99,396) persons and 1,97,628 (male 1,01,064 female 96,564) persons, respectively:

Table 1

Rural, Urban Population and Decennial Growth of the Region

	% of Rural Population		% of Urban Population		Decennial Growth (%)	
	2001	2011	2001	2011	1991–2001	2001–2011
West Bengal	72.03	68.11	27.97	31.89	17.77	13.93
North 24 Parganas	45.70	42.41	54.30	57.59	22.69	12.86

Source: Census of India.

The percentage of the rural population of this district has decreased 3.29 per cent from 2001 to 2011 Census. Again, in case of urban population it has increased 3.29 per cent from 2001 to 2011 census. The decennial growth rate is 12.86 of the district.

The village Gopalnagar is multiethnic in nature. The Hindus form the majority of population, but other ethnic groups also reside there and a large number of the people of Gopalnagar have migrated mainly from Bangladesh or *Purbo* Pakistan, now Bangladesh; and in course of time they have settled here permanently.

Table 2

Migration History

	Born in Locality	Migrated from Present Bangladesh	Migrated from Former East Pakistan	Not Known	Total
No	30	3	45	3	81
%	37.03	3.70	55.57	3.70	100

During my study, they informed that they have migrated from Bangladesh or Pakistan, but could not tell me the exact year of migration.

There are 3.70 per cent of families out of eighty one who have migrated from present Bangladesh and 55.57 per cent migrated from former East Pakistan.

The people of Gopalnagar exchange their views in Bengali language with each other. There is a varna system of this village that is Brahmin, Baisha, Khatrya and Sudra. In my study sample of *bidi* binder, a huge number belonged to the Scheduled Caste community (fifty families out of eighty one families).

Table 3

Caste wise Distribution of the Population

Sex	General Caste (%)	Scheduled Caste (%)	Scheduled Tribe (%)	Other Backward Caste (%)	Total
Male	0	9(11.11%)	0	2(20.0%)	11(13.26%)
Female	20(24.69%)	41(50.61%)	1(1.23%)	8(80.0%)	70(86.74%)
Total	20(24.69)	50(61.72)	1(1.23%)	10(12.34%)	81(100%)

The society mainly depends on agriculture and agricultural related jobs. The most striking point of this society is that both male and female members of the family earn for their livelihood. They migrated here as agriculture labourers and most of them continued their previous job whereas a section of them now have shifted to other occupations due to different causes, one of them is *bidi* binding. The new occupations like government employee, van rickshaw puller, day labourers, etc. are popular among them. Due to scarcity of work in this area, a large part of the younger generation migrated to outside places, even to cities of other states, (Mumbai, Bangalore, etc.) for a new occupation.

Methodology

The study was conducted on the basis of both primary and secondary data. In the context of primary data the villages were selected in *bidi* binder dominated areas. The types of villages were selected considering the scope and objective of the proposed study, the presence and absence of *bidi* binder in the studied areas.

Anthropological methods were followed to collect the information. The basic information of the village and the people were collected with the help of census and interview schedules. The socio-economic and socio-cultural profile of the people was collected using the interview schedules. Data were also collected on implementation of development and welfare programmes among them including different types of loan sanctioned to them. Data was collected on different types of schemes like medical facility, stipends facility, etc. from the officials of Bongaon Block Labour Office, Barasat Labourers.

I also collected genealogical data which helped in gathering a large number of facts concerning social structures and other institutions of the people being studied to know the changes of educational status through different generations, changing pattern of religion, types of the family, etc. Lastly, by using this method, I could draw out the inter-generational educational differences and occupational mobility and changes.

Case studies were also collected to examine the variety of factors within a communal part. Relevant data were collected through review of existing literature, books, journals, government's records, etc. Since major part of the data were collected through case studies, more emphasis was given on qualitative analysis.

Findings

Socio-Economic Life

Bidi binders are the essential part of this cottage industry. It is an industry where all the engaged labourers belong to very poor families. The people of this industry have no separate workshop for making or binding *bidi*; they collect raw materials from the owner's house or office. The people do their binding job in the home. This is helping them to manage their domestic household work side by side. It has been observed that sometime the females bind *bidi* when they enjoy their leisure time with their friends and neighbours. It has been also observed that young girls to old age women, all are engaged in this occupation.

Table 4

Age-Sex Composition of the Population

Age Group (in year)	Sex		Total No (%)
	Male No (%)	Female No (%)	
0–4	13(3.6)	12(3.3)	25(6.8)
5–9	16(4.4)	15(4.1)	31(8.5)
10–14	16(4.4)	16(4.4)	32(8.8)
15–19	27(7.4)	25(6.5)	52(14.2)
20–24	22(6.0)	20(5.5)	42(11.5)
25–29	22(6.0)	16(4.6)	38(10.4)
30–34	15(4.1)	10(2.7)	25(6.8)
35–39	7(1.9)	10(2.7)	17(4.7)
40–44	7(1.9)	15(4.1)	22(6.0)
45–49	13(3.6)	8(2.2)	21(5.8)
50–54	9(2.5)	11(3.0)	20(5.5)
55–59	5(1.4)	10(2.7)	15(4.1)
60–64	9(2.5)	8(2.2)	17(4.7)

Table 4 depicts the age and sex composition of the studied population. It has been found that maximum frequency of male and female in the age group of 15–19 years is 14.2 per cent and 20–24 years is 11.5 per cent.

Educational Status

Education is the fundamental aspect of the socio-economic status as well as the development of a society. Literacy is extremely perfect social indicator which shows the approach of the community towards decision making.

The educational status of the studied population shows that the literacy rate of the studied population was 31.78 per cent among the male while the female education rate is 24.38 per cent.

Table 5

Educational Status of the Studied Population

Education Group	Male	%	Female	%	Total	%
Can not sign	58	15.89	86	23.61	144	39.45
Can sign	11	3.01	5	1.37	16	4.38
Below primary	7	1.91	6	1.64	13	3.56
1–5	53	14.52	45	12.32	98	26.86
6–8	20	5.47	21	5.75	41	11.23
9–10	24	6.57	10	2.73	34	9.31
11–12	1	0.27	2	0.54	3	0.82
Graduate	5	1.37	0	0	5	1.37
Not Applicable	6	1.64	5	1.37	11	3.01
Total	185	50.68	180	49.31	365	100

Regarding their educational status, the guardians were willing to admit their children in primary school but due to lack of time they do not care about their children and as a result the dropout was found to be common due to poor educational and occupational status of the parents.

Economic Condition

The main occupation of the population was *bidi* binding, mainly females are involved in *bidi* bindings, beside that they were also involved in day labour, household work, etc. agricultural labour on seasonal basis but they mainly depended on *bidi* binding to run their family:

Table 6

Monthly Income of the Family

Monthly Income (in Rupees)	*No. of Family (%)*
Upto 1,500	16(19.75%)
1,501–2,000	28(34.56%)
2,001–2,500	32(39.50%)
2,500+	5(6.17%)
Total	81

Regarding the family income, 16 families earned up to ₹ 1,500, 28 families earned up to ₹ 1,501–2,000, 32 families earned up to ₹ 2,001–2,500, and only five families earned above ₹ 2,500. However, it was very hard for them to fulfil the daily livelihood needs of the family members.

Table 7

Occupation wise Distribution of the Population

Categories	*Agriculture (%)*	*Agricultural Labour (%)*	*Day Labour (%)*	*Bidi Binding (%)*	*Service (%)*	*Total (%)*
Male	7(4%)	24(13.71%)	28(16%)	15(8.57%)	2(1.14%)	76(43.42%)
Female	—	—	18(10.28%)	81(46.28%)	—	99(56.57%)
Total	7(%)	24(13.71%)	46(26.28%)	96(54.85%)	2(1.14%)	175(100%)

Again, 28 female workers out of 81 were involved in *bidi* binding for 8 hours which is the highest hours vs. person involved ratio, 31.28 per cent of total number involved in *bidi* binding for 8 hours a day, thereafter 7 and 6 hours of engagement of *bidi* binding has been noticed. and only 1.04 per cent of the total number were involved for 3 hours.

Table 8

Distribution of Population on the basis of Working Hours

Working Hour	*Male*	*Female*	*Total Number*
3	1	0	1(1.04%)
4	1	7	8(8.33%)
5	3	1	4(4.16%)

Cont'd...

...Cont'd

6	3	16	19(19.79%)
7	2	19	21(21.87%)
8	2	28	30(31.28%)
9	2	7	9(9.37%)
10+	1	3	4(4.16%)
Total	15	81	96(100%)

Living Situation

To know the overall living situation of a population it is very crucial to observe their daily health practices and knowledge about health and hygiene. In this studied area, the main source of drinking water is general tubewell (67.90%), there are three deep tubewell (40 pipe) which provide non arsenic water, only 32.10 per cent of families have on access to it.

Table 9

Sources of Drinking Water

Source of Drinking Water	*No. of Family*	%
Tube Well	55	67.90
Deep Tube Well	26	32.10
Total	81	100.00

Again, 85.19 per cent of the studied population have used proper sanitation but 14.81 per cent do not have latrine facility and they use open field. Due to lack of knowledge, a number of diseases like fever typhoid, malaria, diarrhoea, spread because of unhygienic and poor living condition.

Table 10

Sanitation Facilities

Sanitation Facility	*No of Family*	%
Absent	12	14.81
Present	69	85.19
Total	81	100.00

Disease and Nature of Treatment Among the Population

Information is collected from primary health centre, local doctors' chambers, anganwadi regarding disease pattern and nature of treatment. The disease pattern reflects the existing healthcare practices, sanitation practices and food habits of the studied population. Asthma, tuberculosis, typhoid is found among the studied population, male and female both are affected by this disease, but percentage of female who are mainly engaged with the industry is high. Diseases like diarrhoea, skin diseases, cough and cold, stomach problem have also been found and are caused by their poor unsanitary condition and drinking water.

Table 11

Diseases Treatment Pattern of the Population

Diseases	*No of effected Persons*	*%*	*Type of Treatment*			
			Allopathic	*Homeopathic*	*Quack*	*No Treatment*
Arthritis	6	3.87	2	–	4	–
Anaemia	3	1.93	–	2	1	–
Asthma	21	13.54	15	2	4	–
Cough and Cold	11	7.09	–	–	3	8
Chicken Pox	1	0.64	1	–	–	–
Hypertension	4	2.58	–	3	1	–
Diarrhoea	8	5.16	–	–	8	–
Eye Problem	9	5.80	7	2	–	–
High Fever	12	7.74	6	–	6	–
Headache	10	6.45	2	–	6	2
Jaundice	2	1.29	–	–	2	–
Malaria	8	5.16	2	–	6	–
Reproductive Diseases	2	1.29	–	–	2	–
Skin Diseases	7	4.51	2	3	2	–
Stomach Problem	7	4.51	1	–	6	–
Tuberculosis	19	12.25	7	–	12	–
Typhoid	12	7.74	3	2	7	–
Ulcer	12	7.74	2	4	6	–
Paralysis	1	0.64	1	–	–	–
Total	155	100	51(32.90%)	18(11.61%)	76(49.3%)	10(6.45%)

Of the affected persons, 49.3 per cent preferred quack treatment, 32.90 per cent of affected persons preferred allopathic treatment and 11.61 per cent preferred homeopathic treatment and 6.45 per cent did not go for any treatment.

Rights of *Bidi* Binder

The area is multiethnic and inhabitants belong to different castes, community, and religion. Though their community or religion was not the same but their economic status was more or less the same; all of them suffered from poverty. The income was not adequate to them in the work. As a result they were not able to fulfil all their needs to run their family properly.

Though government has some schemes and welfare measures to eliminate this problem but no such scheme was implemented here. To improve the public health and sanitation, medical facilities and to work for the prevention of disease, the Government of India set up 12 hospitals and 206 dispensaries including one chest clinic spread all over the country under the nine regions of labour welfare organization to render outdoor and indoor treatment, pathology and radiological test and distribution of medicines, free of cost, to the *bidi*/mines/cine workers, and their family members and dependents. Under the Kolkata region, 15 static-cum-mobile dispensaries for *bidi* worker at Kolkata and one 50 bedded central hospital in West Bengal have been established to render medical/health service to the *bidi* workers and their dependents.

The facility of healthcare for them provided by government in welfare scheme but they could not avail this because some of them were not aware about this facility and a few of them did know but distance of Kolkata is more than hundred km from the studied area and they were not able to go there for minor problems. But this minor problem often became major problem and till that time they did not avail such services.

The major problem was among the studied population. Only 7.29 per cent had some knowledge about labour laws and 92.70 per cent have no knowledge about it and among them 11.45 per cent are male and 81.25 per cent are female.

Table 12

Awareness about Labour Law

Sex	*Yes*	*No*	*Total (%)*
Male	4(4.17%)	11(11.45%)	15(15.63%)
Female	3(3.12%)	78(81.25%)	81(84.37%)
Total	7(7.29%)	89 (92.70%)	96(100%)

Another major and crucial problem is they are not registered in the factory labour attendance book or not treated as employee of the company or factory or factory owner. Under such a situation, they were not entitled to bear an identity of registered labour of this industry. Due to this they have no identity card or any kind of health card. Without health card the facility related to health were not given to them. Their union also knows the fact but they have not taken any step in this matter and have kept silent.

Table 13

Membership of the Labour Union

Sex	*No of member of CITU(Centre of Indian Trade Unions)(%)*	*No of member of INTCU(Indian National Trade Union Congress)(%)*	*No of member of AITUC(All India Trade Union)(%)*	*Total (%)*
Male	8(8.33)	6(6.25)	1(1.04)	15(15.62)
Female	54(56.25)	16(16.66)	11(11.45)	81(84.38)
Total	62(64.58)	22(22.91)	12(12.5)	96(100)

Another most important part is education for development of a community or society. This is the only part where the family of *bidi* binders gets some privilege. The education scheme for development of children of the labour class is promoted by the government. This facility is available to the people of this area especially who were *bidi* binders. Scheme for financial assistance to school going children of *bidi* binders for purchase of dress/slates/notebooks/text books were available.

The other schemes on social security, housing, recreational, etc. and welfare schemes were also offered by the government. But in this studied area no such scheme was working and no facility was provided to the *bidi* binder's family or worker.

Conclusion

This section of our society is deprived by the law makers and the factory owners; due to the simplicity and innocence of the *bidi* binders and as they are largely unaware about their legal rights and governmental provisions, they are often exploited by the factory owners. It has also been noted that if someone from among the *bidi* binder rises to protest on the owner's unethical behaviour, then the owner creates the pressure to deduct his wage. In many cases the unions affiliated to some political are not very helpful; many governmental schemes and facilities are there to promote and protect the *bidi* binders, but the *bidi* binders are unable to benefit from them.

It was also reported that often factory owners, law holders and officials and some members of the political parties have some understanding, the different benefits do not reach the *bidi* binders. In many cases, the workers face health problems associated with this job, but do not get any protection. As a large number of people are associated with this job, which neither demand much investment or qualification, to protect these people, it is urgently necessary to: (1) formulate proper development policy (2) provide proper safety protection (3) provide appropriate medical facilities and lastly (4) proper implementation of the various schemes.

References

Asongothito khetre sromikder jonno kolayan mulok yojona- ekti dristipat, (in Bengali), Kolkata: Office of Labour Welfare Organization.

Bhatt, S.C. 1997. *Encyclopedic District Gazettes of Indian Eastern Zone.* Vol. 12. New Delhi: Gyan Publication House.

Chauhan, Y. 2001. *History and Struggles of Bidi Workers in India.* New Delhi: All India Trade Union Congress.

District Demography of North 24 Parganas access from http://north24parganas.gov.in/n24p/page.php?nm=Demography on 10.10.11, 12.33pm

Genesis Public Relations. *360 Degree Analysis of Beedi Industry.* Mumbai: Genesis Public Relations. undated.

International Labor Organization, 2003. Sectoral Activities Programme, Working Paper. *Making Ends Meet: Bidi Workers in India Today, A Study of Four States.* Geneva: International Labor Office.

Jonathan, M. and Heather Wipfli. 2009. 'Building Tobacco Control Training Capacity in India'. *Current Science.* Vol. 96, No. 10, 25 May.

Kothari, C.R.1985. *Research Methodology: Methods and Techniques.* New Delhi: Wiley Eastern Limited.

Sthayee Samiti, *Khudra Silpo tran O Janakalayan,* Rajjya Panchayat proshikhan Sangstha, First edition July 1995.(in Bengali)

Sunley, Emil. *India:* The Tax Treatment of Bidis. Available from: http://tobacocofree center.org/file/pdfs/reports_articals/sunley-Biditax%20final–5feb08.pdf

Tobacco Institute of India. 1999. *Workers & Redemption of Bidi Workers from Exploitation.* New Delhi TII: The Golden Leaf in Parliament. November 29–December 23.

21

Poverty and Crisis in Daily Life

A Study on Migrant People

BISWANATH GAN AND SAMAR KUMAR BISWAS

Migration is a major demographic process that has been an integral and salient feature of human history since time immemorial. It has been an importance means by which human civilization has spread out, enriching cultures, disseminating ideas and generating social, political and economic changes at the places of origin and of destination (Sekhar, 1997: 13). The movement of population has been and remains an essential component of economic development, social change and political organization (Jackson, 1969: 1). In general migratory movements are caused by economic, social and political conditions prevailing in the areas of immigration and emigration. Most migrations in modern times are motivated by economic factors. Migration especially across countries is viewed as the consequence of individual's decision to accumulate wealth. In case of rural to urban migration, the people mostly move out of their villages due to decreased availability of land, unemployment and underemployment. Changes due to migration can also be observed in the social and occupational mobility of migrants (Sekhar, 1997: 23 and 26). An estimated 214 million people currently live outside their country of origin, many having moved for a variety of reasons in which the search for protection and the search for opportunity are inextricably entwined. Migration affects every region of the world, and many countries are now simultaneously countries of origin, destination and transit. Large numbers of migrants today move between developing countries, and around 40 per cent of the total global migrant population have moved to a neighbouring country within their region of origin (United Nations Human Rights, 2012).

Hence, from the viewpoint of present discussion a study has been done on stone crushing community of the Balasan river basin adjacent to Siliguri town of Darjeeling district, West Bengal, India, with a special focus on their livelihood including the right to live, shelter, food and education. The concept of Human Rights is evolving in nature apace with the evolution of human civilization in the context of a changing social, political and cultural milieu. Everyone has the right to a standard of living adequate for the health and well-being of himself and of his family, including food, clothing, housing and medical care and necessary social services, and the right to security in the event of employment, sickness, disability, widowhood, old age or other lack of livelihood in circumstances beyond his control (Saksena, 1999: 169 and 242).

Methodology

To conduct the present study, data was collected both from primary and secondary sources. The primary data has been collected through intensive field work, whereas secondary data was collected from several books, journals and websites. The several anthropological methods were used to pursue the present study such as census schedule, interview, key informant interview, observation, case study and so on. There were so many settlements at Balasan river basin, but for the convenience of present research study one of the village, namely Purba Rangia was selected where the stone based occupation was the prime source of earning of the people. The preliminary census schedule was used to collect the necessary quantitative as well as qualitative data from 250 stone crushing families in order to fulfil the objectives of present study. Further, interviews were taken from key informants as well as from others of the studied area especially in order to know about the early settlement, their previous socio-cultural practices, information regarding economic life, basic needs as well as their daily livelihood too. Interview was also taken about the formation of the studied village and the factors related with their stone crushing occupation. Thereafter, several case studies were taken on the people regarding their economy, food habit, shelter and education. The data collected from the field was analysed in detail to meet the needs of the present study.

Area and the People

The village namely Purba Rangia was selected for the present study which was located at Balasan River basin adjacent to Siliguri town and lies in the foothill region of the Himalayas. The study was done on 250 families who were engaged in stone based occupation. The studied families had 1,238 populations, with 633 males and 605 females; and the sex ratio was 956. In the studied area, a large number of families (93.86%) belonged to Rajbanshi community.

The Rajbanshis are the chief scheduled caste of north Bengal. They are the early settlers of north Bengal, West Bengal, and Rangpur, Dinajpur and Rajshahi districts of Bangladesh. Agriculture was their prime earning source. They were the village dwellers and their way of life was fully based on folk culture. They were mostly depended upon the locally available natural resources in many respects for living. As the time of Independence of India (1947) and Independence of Bangladesh (1971) and later, many of the people migrated to north Bengal and especially settled in Siliguri town. In 1971, a serious political unrest took place in Bangladesh that seemed to be the most important factor for migration. Due to this fact, a huge number of people had to leave their early settlement, land and property and become migrant, homeless, landless as well as resourceless that put a question mark on their daily existence. Thus, they were in crying need to make a place for settlement but the lack of purchasing capacity forced them to search for a permanent job in the hope of getting a minimum security for their establishment as early as possible. In this regard, Siliguri is the largest urban centre of north Bengal seems to be the most significant place for its position from geographical and socio-economic point of view as well. Many rivers like Mahananda and Balasan come down from top hill regions of Himalayas and pass through the Siliguri town with natural resources like boulder, stone and sand, those that were used as raw materials for urban constructions and it emerged as the prime source of earning for the people residing in the river basin. Indeed, the stone field of Balasan river bed seemed to be the best option for them because such type of working involvement does not need any kind of capital investment except physical labour. However, the Balasan river bed not only provided them the economic opportunity but the land to establish a new residence as well. For the past 25 years, the homeless, landless as well as resourceless migrated people were living at the Balasan river bed, and with the changes of economy and habitat their way of living became changed.

Poverty and Crisis Faced by the People in their Daily Life

Poverty is the prime obstacle factor to meet the basic needs for living. Due to this fact, people face serious crisis in case of economy, food, and shelter in their daily life. Obviously, there must be certain reasons to create poverty.

Case Study 1

Sujit Barman, aged 45 years, belonged to Rajbanshi community. In his family, he had his wife and two children. They migrated here from Bangladesh about nine years ago, i.e. 2003, due to political unrest. After migration, both husband and wife got involved in stone based work as their prime earning source. But they were paid ₹ 1,800 per month and indeed they could hardly run their family with this little remuneration. However, finding no other means, he sent his children to the stone field in the hope of getting a financial aid. Hence, all of the family members had to do this work altogether. He had no other alternative to get rid of utter fiscal hardship. The monthly income of the family including the income of children, was ₹ 2,500. They did both stone crushing and stone collection activities throughout the day without any adequate rest in any climatic condition like biting cold of winter and scorching heat of summer and under heavy shower as well. Thus, indeed they were paid very little remuneration as compared to their hard physical labour.

In the context of present study, all the families of the studied area were migrants as they were forced to leave their house, land and property due to some unavoidable circumstances that resulted in roofless, landless as well as resourceless situation. Indeed, after migration finding no other alternatives they became fully dependent upon the stone based occupation for eking out a living. Earlier they were involved in agriculture related activities mostly. But after migration they got involved in various stone based activities like – stone collection and crushing, sand gathering and truck loading. They had to do hard physical labour in the stone field to earn a living. But they were paid very little remuneration which was not enough for fulfillment of life's basic needs. The data reveals that around 90 per cent families could earn not more than ₹ 3,000 per month. Indeed they had no other means to augment their earnings because all the members of their family including children earned altogether in the same working field throughout the day paying no attention to scorching heat of summer and biting cold of winter. In this connection the data reveals that they spent 7–8 hours in a day in the stone field. Their hard struggle for survival deprived them of all the enjoyments in life rather they felt the pain of living each and every moment of life. It was true that they could not meet to the prime needs adequate for living in a healthy way. Therefore, the people faced several problems in their daily life which are discussed below:

Case Study 2

Prafulla Barman, 37-year-old man, belonged to Rajbanshi community. He was born in Bangladesh. He migrated from Bangladesh in 2002 due to unavoidable circumstances. After migration he got involved in stone based occupation in order to run his family. In his family, he had his mother, wife and two daughters aged 11 and 9 years. But it was simply impossible to run a family with his single earning. As a result, the utter economic hardship pushed the rest family members into the stone field in order to contribute to the family income as he had an urgent need to get a financial aid to augment the family earnings. Thus, all the family members worked together in the stone field. So far reported from him about their daily working schedule was usually like this – they wake up very early in the morning with the first ray of sun and soon after morning fresh-up and breakfast of only tea and pup rice, they go to the stone field. They have their lunch with rice, pulses and very little amount of vegetables directly in the stone field. They work hungry in the stone field because after having little breakfast they have to do work hard until the lunch break. They felt hungry after returning from the stone field in the evening when the work was over for the day. They make brisk preparations for dinner but mostly have the same things in the dinner. Their little earnings are not enough to accumulate a fold of rice thrice a day. Indeed, they are going through a tough condition as if after meat comes mustard.

In their daily diet they could hardly accumulate the proper nutritious food. Even they could hardly afford eating meal thrice a day. Due to utter financial constraints, they could hardly purchase even the least expensive animal protein from the market. Thus, they took their meals with rice, pulses and little amount of vegetables. The data reveals that most of the families could hardly accumulate meat (92%) and fish (42%). Even it was simply beyond their capacity to cater for milk and other health drinks to their children. Thus, due to poor economic condition, they had to face a lot of problems to provide food to all the family members.

Case Study 3

Krishna Barman, aged 48 years, belonged to Rajbanshi community. His family consisted of five members including his wife and their children. They worked all together in the stone field. But their earning was too little to erect a better house. They lived in *kachha* house made of wattle walls, corrugated tin roofs and devoid of proper ventilation and there was no separate kitchen. The house had two small-size rooms and it was not spacious. It was reported from him they had to face lot of problems throughout the year as during summer the inside of the houses was suffocating and in rainy season, the floor became muddy and damp. Their housing condition was seemingly not in favour of the living.

In this connection the data reveals that around 84 per cent families lived in the *kachha* houses and around 57 per cent and 34 per cent of the houses were made of single room and a couple of room respectively. Further, the *kachha* houses were made of one the three small rooms which were not well ventilated while except very few, most of the families had not separate kitchen and due to this fact they were found to cook inside their main room. The fact was that most of the families faced the same problem, i.e. a congested and suffocating situation in the rooms during summer while during the rainy season the muddy floor of their houses became drenched and intricate. Moreover, the condition of their houses was not in favour of living. But the truth can't be ignored that ultimately the river provided the land to them and due to this fact with their little earnings they were able to erect a house made of wattle walls, corrugated tin roofs devoid of proper ventilation.

Case Study 4

Suren Singha, aged 14 years, whose birth place was Bangladesh was unmarried. He and his parents migrated here from Bangladesh about 7 years ago, i.e. 2005. Both of his parents got involved with stone based job as prime earning source. After migration, they settled down at Purba Rangia village. But their earnings could not provide them even the minimum support to run their family smoothly. Thus, finding no other ways, they provoked Suren to get involved in stone based occupation to augment their family earnings a bit. Suren got involved in stone based job when he was 9 years old. He had two brothers who were younger to him. They also provided a financial support by applying physical labour in the stone crushing field. Suren was engaged in stone collection and truck loading activities mainly. He had to work for the whole week without any adequate rest. He had dropped out of school while he was in class IV. His only remorse was that he always used to try to attend the class regularly but it was hardly possible because of his busy working schedule. He was scolded bitterly or even often he was beaten by his parents if he was absent from work or by denying this work if he engaged himself in other play games, etc. His daily working schedule was generally like this – he used to get up at around 8 am. After morning fresh and having tea with pup rice he went to stone field. He generally had lunch of rice with pulses and little amount of vegetables. The work was often continued after evening also. Thus, he generally came back home at the evening when the work was over for the day. Sometimes he went out from the class to join the work in the stone field. However, prolonged working schedule did not let him continue his studies.

The scenario of education in the studied area reveals an unpleasant condition. Indeed all the family members including children worked hard altogether for the whole day in the stone field. The matter of education was not at all important to them. Most of the children in the studied area were first generation learner as their parents either belonged to illiterate category or can sign only. The data regarding the educational standard of parents reveals that around 72 per cent of both the parents were illiterate. Therefore, the children could not hope to get proper guidelines for education from their parents. Besides this, the busy working schedule for the whole day was a great hindrance to pay adequate attention to their studies and due to this fact the dropout and stagnation rate were found high among them. In this regard, the data reveals that 33.51 per cent and 29.57 per cent of female and male working children had dropped out of school and a tendency for the same was found more in primary level rather than secondary. On the contrary, the percentage of stagnation was quite high as compared to dropout rate. They were deprived of their educational right which was a major obstacle factor for their development. The members of present generation were able to see the light of education but it was mostly up to primary level and a large number of them was first generation learner. It is postulated that education is an essential need of the child. It helps them to develop the knowledge, judgment, and social and moral values to play his proper role in society when they become an adult (Mitttal, 1994: 45–46). But in the studied families their little earnings as well as busy working schedule might have resulted in a poor level of educational standard among them. Moreover, they could not come in the light of proper education.

General Observation

The present discussion highlighted their utter fiscal scarcity and its adverse impact on their living as well as the violation of rights in the perspective of livelihood. A drastic change had taken place in their way of livelihood after migration, as with the changing dimension of time and changes of habitat naturally their way of livelihood cannot remain static. These migrant people were forced to leave everything including their land, house, property and they were even deprived of locally available natural resources for livelihood. Indeed, the undeniable fact was that before migration they were not financially strong at all but they seemed quite protected in the lap of nature. But after the resettlement in the Balasan river basin, they faced a lot of problems in many respects inextricably related to their living which pushed them into uncertainty by putting a question mark on their secure future. They were always found in struggle against the pain of poverty in order to accumulate a fold of rice twice a day in the way they started work very early in the morning without having adequate breakfast but tea with pup rice. But often they went to the stone field hungry and usually they were found to return home in the evening when the work was over for the day. After resettlement their prime need was to have a strong economic backbone but the present stone crushing occupation was unable to provide them the concerned security. Thus, their little earning was not of much help in bettering their life chances and they were deprived of minimum necessary livelihood requirements. They could hardly afford to accumulate the rice meals thrice a day and even purchasing the least expensive animal protein was beyond their capacity. Thus, they took rice with pulses and little amount of vegetables. Moreover, their poor housing and living condition indicated their inability to meet the needs for living. Besides these, the daylong working involvement had an adverse impact on their education. Majority of the children in the studied area were first generation learner as most of the parents were illiterate and though few of them were literate but they could hardly cross the threshold of primary level of education. Moreover, the children were forced to get involved in the stone crushing work from the very beginning of life in order to get rid of poverty a bit. But the pressure of familial requirements cannot be ignored in the involvement of children into work and due to which they were deprived of all the facilities like opportunities of education, leisure and recreation, intellectual development, freedom from exploitation and so on essential for their overall development. However, their social relations as well as kinship relationships faded away, rather a strong competition in economic field, struggle for survival and anxiety for future life were found to have developed among them. Even they could not sleep well at night because a thought of work for tomorrow often came into their dreams. Thus, only God knows what is their fate. Thus, the stone crushing people were completely debarred of minimum attributes of fundamental needs and rights for survival especially related with standard of living, security of proper nutritious food and proper shelter.

References

Jackson, J.A. 1969. *Sociological Studies 2-Migration*. London: Cambridge University Press.

Saksena, K.P. 1999. *Human Rights: Fifty Years of India's Independence*, New Delhi: Gyan Publishing House.

Sekhar, T.V. 1997. *Migration and Social Change*, Jaipur: Rawat Publications.

United Nations Human Rights, *Migration and Human Rights,* Office of the High Commissioner for Human Rights; http://www.ohchr.org/EN/Issues/Migration/Pages/MigrationAnd HumanRightsIndex.aspx, retrieved on 5 February 2012 at 4.30 pm.

22

Negotiation of Rights in the Process of Urbanization

A Case of Migrant Construction Workers of Chennai City

ARUNKUMAR, A.S. AND JESURATHNAM DEVARAPALLI

The inputs of modernization have changed the urban set-up in rapid pace. Urban development is firmly supported by the provision of infrastructure and new facilities created by the construction firm. The gigantic buildings, shopping malls, roadways, metro rails, techno parks, and bridges that showcase the urban cities are the contributions of construction industry. Construction industry is the second largest establishment in the country after agriculture (Barnabas, 2009: 122) and is a significant contributor to the national economy, acting as a provider of employment to large number of unskilled workers.

In developing countries like India, which has large labour force in its rural areas, are the hidden men *on par* behind all these infrastructural development in the urban cities. These unskilled construction workers come from the rural areas as temporary migrants to work in the construction industries. Though it is considered that the development of the urban infrastructure is basically for the well-being of the masses there, the migrant construction workers, who actually toil for these developments, are denied of all kinds of basic amenities as a right.

According to Construction Workers Federation of India (CWFI), construction workers are not only just one of the categories of workers in the informal sector, but also one of the largest categories and one of the most exploited categories of workers within the sector. In the industry, these workers contribute the base of the structure. It was the labourers who put their hard work into the project, but at the same time were in a very vulnerable and risky position (Anwar, 2004: 118). As the construction sector is to a large extent labour-intensive, it demands a relatively large proportion of unskilled workers. According to the dual labour market theory, the low social status associated with physical work makes such employment unattractive for the domestic labour force in highly developed countries (Bobek, 2008: 3). In the Marxist tradition, the concept of exploitation plays a predominant role in discussions on capitalism. Probably the discussions of the Marxian concepts can now be well suited in all the industries – which are a by-product of the capitalism including the construction firm.

The violation of rights starts from the point the construction labourer decides to migrate to certain urban centres. In the process of decision making for migration, the influence of labour agent plays a major role, as he motivates them with larger offerings and handy exposure of the cities. As Fahys-Smith (2008) says in his paper that one of the predictable variables of migration among construction workers is the dissatisfaction on the availability of facilities and services, along with the four strongest predictor variables like time in community, job security, age, and lack of house integration. The violation of the basic rights further continues in the construction site as proper dwelling, sanitation, health, security to women, schooling facility for the migrant children, etc. are conspicuously lacking.

Problem and Approach

As it is evident throughout India, the unskilled rural migrants find an employment in the construction sector when they come to urban centres. Though economic respite is found in this industry, the annoying situation of leading a life of frustration, anxiety and humiliation is noticed as the individuals are denied of their self-dignity and honour. The present study is aimed at understanding the living condition of the migrant labour in industry and to explore the violation of basic rights and kind of exploitation they are subjected to at the work site. In order to achieve this dual goal, anthropological field work was conducted at a construction site in Chennai.

Two sets of schedules were administered in the field – one was containing the basic questions pertaining to the family details, education qualification, social belonging and the reason and causes of migration. The other had detailed account of questions enquiring into socio-economic endeavours, problems faced during their travel, remittance to the family and the health aspects in the migrant place in comparison to the native place.

Apart from the schedules, structured and unstructured interviews were added as tools to obtain the information from the officials and the gents apart from conducting case studies. There were nearly 55 questions administered among the respondents. Moreover, the happenings were even observed personally and some of them have been recorded on a voice recorder and in the form of photographs.

Place of Study

The construction site chosen for the study is a building of residential flat in Ernavoor of Chennai, Tamil Nadu. It is spread over 13.4 acre land proposed by the Tamil Nadu Slum Clearance Board (TNSCB) and the National Highways Department (NHD) for the displaced fishermen whose dwellings along the coastal belt of north-Chennai encroached Ennore-Beach road.

The construction work of the site said was started in 2007, under the aegis of TNSCB and the NHD in order to accommodate about 5,440 of the dislocated households. Of them, 3,840 flats are constructed by the TNSCB and the remaining by the NHD.

During the period of the study, the constructions by the NHD were almost completed and the allotment of flats was in the process (few flats were already allotted and started occupying). While the construction works of TNSCB was still on. In overall, the site has 170 blocks, each comprising four floors. Each floor has eight flats in it, making it 5,440 flats all together. The interior design of each unit comprises a hall and a kitchen, making it a 10:12 foot flatting. The project has planned to provide all the basic facilities like provision of electricity, bore-pumps for domestic purpose, and separate tanks in front of every row for drinking water, a centralized septic tank that is linked from every flat.

The construction work of the site is contracted by three construction companies – NR Constructions Limited, Sathyamoorthy Constructions Private Limited and Muthu Construction Private Limited. NR Construction Limited has the highest number of contract, out of the 92 blocks that are under the control of TNSCB, 40 blocks are contracted by them, then 33 by Sathyamoorthy and 19 by the Muthu Constructions.

Migrant Construction Workers

The site inhabits and employs; skilled, semi-skilled, and unskilled labour. Unskilled labours are mostly migrants from other parts of the country like Madhya Pradesh, Orissa, Andhra Pradesh and from other districts in Tamil Nadu. They perform works like plastering, raising the wall, painting, centring and electric works, etc. and have been provided with the provision of residing within the work spot. So, the migrant workers dwell within the huts and sheet dwellings provided by the construction company. These migrant workers either migrate along with their family or leave their family in their home town or village and migrate alone and the lone are mostly men who take up the challenge.

Basic Amenities

It is mandatory for the construction company to provide the migrant workers with basic infrastructural facilities for their stay until the contracted project is over. of the Building and Other Construction Workers (Regulation of Employment and Conditions of Service) Act, 1996 act no. 27 of 1996, the sections 28 to 37 deal with the service of building workers, welfare measures and other conditions of service of building workers. In most of the construction companies the migrant labour are provided with least basic needs including the provision of dwellings, water supply, electricity, etc. The three sites under consideration are also provided with least basic facilities.

Dwellings

There is no specific settlement pattern observed in the dwellings, instead the migrants have a preference of being close to their kin, known ones and villagers belonging to the same district, and language. Accordingly, most of the migrants dwell together on the basis of language and live together. The allotted dwellings are contiguous columns with segmentation arranged in a single row on all the sides of the site. The roof of the dwellings is either a metallic sheet or thatched with coconut fronds. It is a single-room segment with 10:12 square feet. The allocation of houses is not according to any listing or record, rather is occupied by the migrants on their own wish. Each hut has a family comprising three–five members on average. While in case of individual migrants, a group of six–eight members brought by the same agent are lodged together in a single room.

But during the period of the study, most of the building was raised and some of the workers took residence within the building itself. Of the surveyed 55 samples, 25 of them were residing inside the new unfinished buildings. This happened actually during the rainy season, when most of the allotted dwellings are uninhabitable due to heavy rain; the workers take asylum in the buildings to protect themselves from the rain. Rule 34 of the Building and Other Construction Workers (Regulation of Employment and Conditions of Service) Act, 1996, which recommends that accommodation facility has to be provided by the construction firm, had been completely ruled out at this site. Once if the dwellings are constructed, then the firm would not bother to look in to its maintenance. The dwellings are taken care of by the migrant dwellers themselves at their own risk in case of mending the dwelling.

Convergence Facilities

The site is situated in the centre of Ernavoor. From south, the Thiruvottiyur High road connects the site, while in the east a stretch of Ennore road is connected by the Manali highway which runs towards the west, paving entrance southwards for the site.

The site has three entrances – southern side, eastern side and western side. Bharathiyar Street connects the eastern and southern entrances, leading southwards to the Manali high road. On the one side of the Bharathiyar Street, the compound wall of the site extends till the end of the street. While on the other side of the street, there are eight lanes and are packed with the native residences leading eastwards to the Ennore high road. Meanwhile, in case of the western entrance, it is tar road of Balaji nagar, which is a traditional residential area of dalit settlers leading to the Manali high road.

The Chennai Metro Transport Corporation (MTC) buses from Manali to Broadway, Ennore to Broadway, and Manali Newtown to Vallalar Nagar would pass through this way frequently. These buses would lead these construction workers till the main city. Thereby, the migrants have an easy access to the Thiruvottiyur market where they frequently used to go and to Chennai Central Railway Station, in case they had to move to their place of origin. Even shared autos are available till Thiruvottiyur. From there, either bus or suburban unit trains till Chennai Central are available. Mostly these migrants commute only through the MTC buses.

Availability of Provisions

At all the three entrances, petty shops are available and in the eastern entrance, there is a small provisional store and in front of the southern entrance, a shop of fancy products and adjacent to it is a pawn brokers shop. Along the roadside of Manali high road petty hotels, medical shops, nursing home, provisional shops and chicken stalls are available.

For large scale shopping, most migrants use to go to the Thiruvottiyur market to purchase household articles, vegetables, and fruits. These migrants usually prefer to go to markets on Sundays because it is mostly a holiday or half-day work. Generally females are found to go to markets with their co-migrants accompanied by their children. But only in a few families men are also found to go to market. For the migrant families, going to the market is a joyful moment as they consider going to the market is like going out of the site to roam and purchase new things.

Entertainment

After the day's work, all the migrant workers return back to their dwellings. Thereafter, women would be engaged in their household activities and men go to the nearby wine shop to consume liquor. Later in the evenings, women would either chit-chat with her neighbours and the men would sit to play cards. The individual migrants would roam around the site, consume liquor, chit-chat and watch television. On Sundays, the families would go to the nearby places, cinemas, parks, etc. otherwise, play cards and games like snake and ladder.

Water Facility

The process of building construction requires large amount of water. So, all around the site, bore pumps have been dug to pump out water and utilize it for construction work. In the entire site there are about 47 bore pumps available and are fitted with motors to serve the purpose. Among them, eight bore-pumps are dug near the dwelling area and are fitted with the hand pump. Cement base is built around the hand-pump for washing clothes and some dwellings nearby the bore-pump wash the vessels too. Mostly women, after returning from their work, carry water from these bore pumps for both drinking and for household purposes.

Of the Building and Other Construction Workers (Regulation of Employment and Conditions of Service) Act, 1996 Act, Rule 32 insists on and recommends the provision of safe drinking water at the worksite. It also clearly delineates that the drinking water source must be clearly distinguished from the source water for other household purpose and recommends that the drinking water source must at least be six metres away from any washing place, urinal and latrine. But in case of Ernavoor site, the handpumps are situated just nearby the compound wall, where the other side of the wall is used for open-air defecation by the migrants. Also nearby the hand pump, washing activities are done.

Electricity

Commercial electricity is given to the construction company mainly for utilizing it for construction purpose. It is also granted to the migrant workers dwellings. They utilize this facility only for lighting a bulb during night and for a table fan when they are resting in their huts, because they do not have too many household electronic articles except for television and radio that too only in a few households. Thereby, the tariffs for the consumption of the electricity are borne by the construction industry itself.

Sanitation

There is a clear violation of sanitary rights stated in the Building and Other Construction Workers (Regulation of Employment and Conditions of Service)

Act, 1996, Rule 33 as these migrant labourers are subjected to inhabit an area with poor sanitation facilities. The site has a single toilet built for about 10–15 households and is not even properly connected with the septic tank. So, none of the migrants use them and now it is found totally in dilapidated condition. It is found standing only for name sake. So the migrants had to go for open-air defecation just nearby the compound wall of the site. Usually females go for open defecation early in the morning and some time they are misbehaved with and molested by local people by pelting stones on them and harassing them from distance, etc. Women are still hesitant to opt for open defecation because of the behavior of the locals.

Each household has a separate, own built *kaccha* bathroom at the site. These bathrooms are usually made by coconut fronds or sometimes with old cloths and plastic cement covers, fastened to the frame of sticks. Women take bath in it and men usually take bath near the hand pump. The vessels are washed in front of their dwellings and those nearby the hand pump wash under the hand-pump. So, there water stagnates around the hand-pump and in front of the dwellings. All the household wastes are discarded just behind the compound wall plays a breeding ground for many vectors and spread infectious disease.

Health and Safety

Chapter VII of the Building and Other Construction Workers (Regulation of Employment and Conditions of Service) Act, 1996, refers to the safety and health measures to be taken by the construction firm in the work site. As far as the health situation of the site is concerned, the sanitation of the work spot has a crucial role in maintaining hygiene and health. Due to improper sanitation facilities, the water from bathing; washing vessels and clothes remain stagnant in front of the dwellings, making it difficult for the easy movement of the people. Further these conditions encourage the growth of mosquitoes and other vectors. Often, children and adults fell ill with fever, cold and cough. Just two months before the fieldwork was conducted, most of the migrants were affected by chikungunya fever. The fever was widespread in Chennai city and did not spare these migrants either. It is a communicable disease and had rapidly spread among most of the workers. The construction company advised them to go to the nearby government hospital in Thiruvottiyur for treatment, while some of the workers chose to go to the nearby private clinic and some went to the government hospital. Most of them are still suffering pain in the joints, even after the fever ceased. Probably the government had advised those suffering with chikungunya to treat themselves in the government hospitals, but the construction firm advised the migrants to get the treatment even for other kinds of disease and health issues from outside; withdrawing its responsibility from providing medical facilities for the well-being of migrant construction workers.

These construction workers are extremely prone to minor to major accidents; and follow no safety measures like wearing a helmet, gloves and shoes to protect themselves from injuries at the work place. The need for a safety measure is not insisted and regulated by both the contractors and the engineers who are supposedly responsible in procuring safety measures as a norm in the work place or in case of any accident, they prefer to go only to the nearby private clinics. They go to government hospital only if it is a major accident or a disease that needs proper medication, whereby a continuous treatment is needed. When major accidents occur, the labour agent would act to fetch the expenditure of at least the first-aid from the construction industry. But the remaining expenses on treating them have to be incurred by the worker itself.

Interaction with Locals

Ernavoor has a mixed population, and the area near the site also has the same kind of population blend. Towards the east of the site, i.e. on the seashore, traditional fishermen are living and towards the western side of the site are the traditional Schedule Caste – Parayars and Adi-Andhra. The habilitation of Bharathiyar Nagar started about four decades ago and is a multi-caste and multi-religious area.

The migrant workers have no connection or any interaction with these neighbours. The main cause for it is the perception of new land and new place in the minds of migrants which dominate and alienate them from the rest of the local neighbours. Even though some of the migrants are from Tamil Nadu who can speak the local language, the perception of new place alienates them. But for the other migrants, apart from Tamil Nadu, find even language as a barrier in interacting with the locals.

Income and Occupation at Home

The migrant labour leaves their native places in search of a suitable employment to meet their livelihood needs which are scarcely met at home under the prevailing conditions of unemployment and underemployment with inadequate wages.

Table 1

Showing the Nature of Employment in the Native Place

Nature of Employment in the Place of Birth	*Frequency*	*Per cent*
Agriculture	40	72.7
Fishing	8	14.5
Construction Labour	7	12.7
Total	55	100.0

More than 70 per cent of the migrants are agriculture labours at home, while 14.5 per cent were subsisting on fishing. The main reasons for the migration that formulated the push factor among these migrant workers were identified as lack of employment in the place of origin, low wages, crop failure, lack of rain for agriculture, low price for the fish caught, and indebtedness. These reasons can also be called as the push factors for the migration.

Lack of Employment in the Native Place

Mostly the responses from the migrants showed that there was no regular employment in agricultural sector like cultivators or agricultural coolies as there was increase in the price of inputs such as seeds, pesticide and fertilizers and labour, lack of copious irrigation facility as the irrigation or the canals would drain off; and the irregular climatic conditions leading to erratic rainfall also adds to the traumatic condition of the agriculture at home. So, there is no employment for a major portion of the year, thereby in search of an alternative employment opportunity they are forced to move out. About 53 per cent of the respondents responded that they migrated because; they do not have proper employment opportunities to run their family.

Low Wage

One very important cause of migration to the construction industry in urban centres is the low wage given to the workers in their native place whether it is agricultural work or of any other unorganized works. Kaliya, a 24-year-old migrant, says, 'I worked as an agriculture coolie, would go for daily wage works like loading and unloading, etc. but I earned ₹ 100 only per day. Later I went to the nearby construction works where I was given ₹ 130 per day'.

Another person named Shanthi, aged 33, said, 'I was working as an agricultural coolie in my native place engaged in weeding, sowing and other agricultural related works and earn ₹ 60 only per day'. The less amount of demand for the agricultural labour in the rural area and the age old traditional practice of land based institution of caste system has created no space for bargaining in the wage determination.

Crop Failure

Most migrants in the site were marginal cultivators with small landholdings. Migrants from Madhya Pradesh had cultivated paddy, maize, etc. while the cultivators from Orissa and Andhra Pradesh cultivated vegetables and leguminous varieties. The improper irrigation facilities and the lack of seasonal rainfall caused the crop failure in the native place.

Decline of Price Value of Fishing

The migration to the construction industry also includes the fishermen from Madhya Pradesh and Orissa. One among them is the Marar caste of Madhya Pradesh, which traditionally follow the fishing in the backwater and rivers. But men from these communities have also migrated because their traditional occupation is no longer remunerative and there was heavy competition in the inland fishing.

Debt

In their native place, the migrants are forced to take loans in order to run their family during the periods of unemployment and even during any emergency crisis. All the above mentioned reasons ordinate to some extent and pressurize the individual to be indebted in some way or the other. So they take loan from either the labour agent or from the neighbours in hometown eventually ending up as a migrant construction work to clear the debts.

Wage

There is a standard wage fixed by the company and the government, but the labour agent who acts as the mason decides the wage and accordingly the wage is given. The average wage of male per day is ₹ 200 and for the female it is ₹ 130 per day. The wage is given on the weekends. There are different wage rates for different kinds of unskilled job profile. The *periyal* whose main work is raising the wall and plastering the wall is given ₹ 250, while the helper is given ₹ 200. Mostly every woman working on this site are helpers in worker profile, so they are given ₹ 100 to ₹ 150 per day.

Although the wage they earn through the construction industry is comparatively high, there are violations of the basic recommendations in the wage of the worker. The discussion with the building incharge revealed that the *periyal* was given ₹ 450 and for both male and female helpers ₹ 300 were given. But the disparity in wage is conceived in the mind of the workers and the benefit is gained by both the labour agent and the construction industry.

Role of Agent in the Construction Industry

The labour agents are the first persons to locate the site. He maintains a contact with a number of construction firms in order to seek contract of the work. The network of labour market is established first from the relatives, neighbours and then it extends through the contacts of earlier worked network. The agents make use of the pull factors prevailing in the rural villages and attract them by a comparatively high packages of wages they are getting in the urban centres or by providing loans to the people who are in need. A mutual verbal agreement is contracted between the lender and the receiver of the loan. So, as per the agreement, these workers had to work for the labour agent until the debt is repaid.

But at certain instances, if the migrant shifts loyalty then the labour agent would threaten their family with goondas and illegally intrude the police for the compromise of the issue. As one of the labour agent Bhakyaraj, 46 years old, from the Tamil Nadu claims that 'the work to deal with the labour needs a good deal of relations and contacts of many persons like local policemen, *goondas* and other labour agents and local politicians. Because I pay the advance to them by getting loan from someone else, and I have encountered the problem of loss by some of the migrants running off the site. That's why I mostly prefer to get more number of workers from my own place and community'. This shows community and caste plays a role in the selection of the workers to be roped in and, however, individual loyalty and sincerity matters much.

There is no compulsion to work under the same agent until the migrant repays the loan. It is the migrants wish to continue with the agent or move on to the another agent in search of construction job. But still, he would prefer to be under any one of the labour agents as he provides employment opportunity or else if a worker keeps on changing the labour agent, he would not be given job. The nexus of contract agents are such widespread that every agent maintains the contact with each other and constantly rotate these migrant labours according to the demand in their respective sites. So if the migrant takes up a loan and leaves to his hometown, he has no other option to come back to any of the work site again. The poor migrant workers are extremely vulnerable and often resort to employment through exploitive contractors and middle men rather than taking up individual contracts directly with their employers. This greatly increases the dependency of the group on these middle men and accentuates risks and uncertainty (Sengupta, 2008: 97). Most of these labour agents must have worked in the construction industry as an unskilled worker earlier. With that contact, they return back to their hometown and call up on for the labour.

The construction companies usually allocate these labour agents in order to reduce the spending on permanent workers by avoiding the local workers. In practice, many risks and costs have been transferred from contractors to labour agent as subcontractors. Contractors avoid all cost related to labour recruitment and hiring. Almost all the uncertainities are transferred to the labour agent, then in turn those 'costs' are passed on to the labourers (Anwar, 2004: 118). This chain of process in the recruitment of the unskilled worker, obviously involves many mal-practices in it like the regression in the actual wage of the worker. For instance, the cost of all the expenses in getting the worker to the work site will be ultimately extracted out from the workers wage. The labourer does not have any contact or link with the construction company. All the dealings including the distribution of wage is also decentralized to the labour agent. So the unskilled worker has to completely rely upon the labour agent for his or her employment.

Migrants During Travel

Migrants have travelled to this work site through buses and train from different places across India. Migrants from Andhra Pradesh, Orissa, and Madhya Pradesh have come here by train, while the migrants from other districts of Tamil Nadu have travelled through buses. For a new construction site, a migrant will be accompanied by the labour agent of the site, where he introduces the construction site. Later on they would travel alone to their home town whenever they wished to leave.

Migrants travelling from Orissa, Andhra Pradesh and Madhya Pradesh would be usually commuting through train regularly in an unreserved bogie. Every time they have to face the abuse of the co-commuters. It becomes worse during nights, as the small kids and children would tend to sleep on the floor of the train and commuters passing through would abuse them, asking them to move their children out of the way. Or else, taking the advantage of their innocence, some would threaten to confine them in a constricted space in the train. The major part of their problem deals with occupation of the space during the travel. Apart from that, in the unreserved compartment, the water for the sanitary purpose gets exhausted within a day and the toilet gives a foul smell, making the situation worse. There would be no water even to wash the face or even clean the hands. Even the food brought in the train is unhygienic and highly expensive. So these passengers have to pay high price, even for a low quality food, as there is no other go.

During every festival the migrants get back to their hometown to celebrate. Within the site, Vishvakarma puja or Aayudha puja is celebrated. Individual workers go to their home very frequently or else at least once in two months.

Women at the Site

Women play a crucial role in the social construct in any community. The involvement of women in the migration has contributed to the economic and social construct of the family. Women in spite of hardships put their effort in maintaining the family by accompanying their husbands for economic endeavours. At the site, most of the women work as construction workers to earn for their family. Usually, in the process of migration, it must be noted here that women belonging to the poor and depressed sections are pushed into construction jobs for making their livelihood (Barnabas, 2009).

The working condition of the women construction workers is pitiable. They face instability and insecurity of employment, low wages, non-observance of labour laws and bondages to the middleman who employ them. Further, women construction workers are almost always totally unskilled without any rational explanation of why this should be so (Sudhir, 2002: 35). The most vulnerable problem faced by the women is the physical harassment and the health problems.

Mostly the construction workers are prone to diseases like cancer, lung infection, asthma, etc. as they are constantly prone to dust from cement, sand and other dust particles. There is a high possibility of skin disease in the construction work spot as the workers are in constant touch with building materials like cement, lime, etc. Pregnant women who are carrying heavy loads run the risk of abortion. While interviewing Ranjitha, aged 28, from Orissa, she revealed that her friend who worked along with her was aborted because of the tireless work she had to perform in the work spot. Shivani was 26 years of age got married six years back and had a four-year-old kid. Last November (2009), she was three-months pregnant, but still she was working along with her man at the site. While she was carrying water in a plastic pot to the second floor, she slipped and got severe stomach pain. Later, she was rushed to the nearby clinic and she got aborted there and sustained minor injuries in the hands.

Because of mobility, the sexual behaviour of migrants takes specific forms with increased vulnerability to STIs and HIV (Wolffers, 2002: 259). Many studies suggest that the separation of migrant workers from their families, the transient nature of their employment and their temporary residence releases migrants from both normative and formal social control. According to Fernandes and Paul (2008), migrant workers are more anonymous in their new surroundings and free of the pressures of social conditioning. No longer controlled by social norms and values of their home villages, they have liberty in environments conducive to sexual encounters and drug use. Men in these circumstances tend to be less responsible than women and it is more accepted when men spend their earnings frivolously. Even in this context, women suffer the cultural and status quo in the society, labelling the women as illegal traitor.

At the site, there were very limited responses from migrant women approving that there was ill-treatment on them among the co-migrants and with the mason or the labour agent. It was observed that most of the women were hesitant to reveal whether they were molested or ill-treated because of the cultural milieu. But still, a middle-aged woman said that they would be abused by the mason, if they were even a little bit late in providing the mortar or water or other materials. Even some young mothers would get to hear, 'why should you be coming to work if you cannot hold your little ones at home'. And the mother would them immediately run back to work, leaving her child crying. Sometimes these masons even molest women orally both during work and off work.

The oppressing perception of the society on women is clearly exposed at the site where they had to go for open defecation in the bushy hidings just near the

Figure 2

Responses on the Kinds of Problems Faced by Women

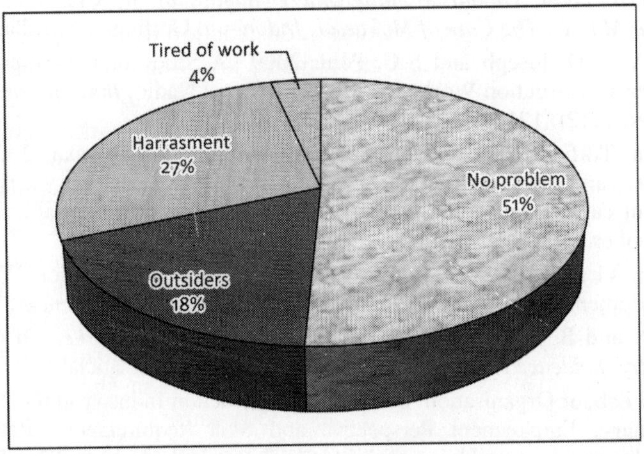

compound wall of the site. They had to wake up early at dawn so to protect themselves in the darkness of the early hours. Otherwise there were reports of stone-pelting on the women during the process by the outsiders and some anti-social elements would sexually harass the women from the far-off hidings.

Altogether, because of the constant work both in the work spot and back in the home, she gets very limited time to rest herself. So, some of the migrant women have responded as they were tired of all these routine works.

Apart from physical difficulties, she has to bear the family most of the time. Most of the males an the site are alcoholic and most of their earnings are spent on alcohol, meanwhile women take up the responsibility of bringing up the children and taking care of the family.

Conclusion

Although many efforts have been made to map out the Human Rights responsibility of corporations through legal and non-legal means, there are still questions regarding the responsibility of corporations in weakly governed, resource rich and often conflict ridden states. In the present study, there are violations in providing the proper infrastructure facility in the dwelling for the residence of the construction migrant workers. The migration of these workers has been at the cost of their children's education for those children migrated along with their parents.

However, there are efforts taken up by many voluntary organizations to defend the workers' right, the vigil eye of the labour agent and construction industry is always there on the migrant workers to corner them away from such kind of organizations. Although there are many provisions and laws to protect the construction workers like the 1996 Construction Workers Act, more effective steps need to be taken to safeguard the future of the children and save the unskilled construction workers from the exploitation by the industry and the labour agent.

References

Anwar, Chairil. 2009. *Labour Mobility and Dynamics of the Construction Industry Labour Market: The Case of Makassar, Indonesia.* Gottingen: Cuvillier Verlag.

Barnabass, A., A.D. Joseph and S.C. Paul. 2009. 'A Study of the Empowerment of Women Construction Worker as Mason in Tamil Nadu'. *India Journal of Women Studies*. 11(2): 121–141.

Bobek, Alicja, Torben Krings, Elaine Moriarty and Jutyna Salmonka. 2008. 'Migrant Workers and the Construction Sector in Ireland', A preliminary report from the migrant careers and apiratins research project, Trinity Immigration Initiative, 3 September.

Fahys-Smith, Virginia. 1982. 'Migration of Boom-town Construction Workers: The Development of an Analytic Framework. *Minerals and Environment*. Vol. 5.

Fernades, D. and B. Paul. 2008. *Social Network of Migrant Workers in Construction Industry: Evidence From Goa*. Mumbai: Tata Institute of Social Sciences.

International Labour Organisation. 2001. The Construction Industry in the 21st Century: Its Image, Employment Perspective and Skill Requirements. Retrieved from http://www.ilo.org/public/english/standards/relm/gb/docs/gb283/pdf/ tmcitr.pdf on 29 March 2010.

Madhok, Sujatha. 2005. *Report on the Status of Women Workers in the Construction Industry*. New Delhi: National Commission for Women.

Sengupta, K. Arjun. 2008. *Report on Condition of Work and Promotion of Livelihood in Unorganized Sector*. National Commission for Enterprises in the Unorganized Sector, Government of India. New Delhi: Academic Foundation.

Verma, Vidhu. 1998. Exploitation and Justice; Should we be interested in a theory of exploitation. *Economic and Political Weekly*. 33(3): 115–121.

23

Issues of Conflict among Working and Non-Working Mothers in an Urban Set-Up

BINITA BASU

Motherhood is considered as the best gift of nature to the woman. Moreover, the women are considered as the natural homemaker and a family builder whereas the children are considered as the future of the nation. So under the parental care, a child not only attains its physical maturity but also becomes humanized and socialized. Socialization is the process by which a child learns to become the future member of a society where the growing infant has to learn the ways of the culture into which it is born and gradually becomes a 'self-aware, knowledgeable' person, a social being (Mayer, 1970). During the first year, this very important process of primary socialization takes place in a child's life in which a child develops language, individual identity, the learning of self-control and cognitive skills. Within this period, a child also learns the internalization of moral standards, appropriate attitudes, motivations and a basic understanding of social roles (Hagedorn, 1983). The intra family relationship plays a very vital role to a human child in its socialization process where mother has to play the crucial role. So in order to secure the socialization process, children need special care and proper attention from their mothers for the sake of survival of the whole society.

Traditionally, women were confined within the four walls of the home to perform their duties as dutiful wives and loving mothers. They neither showed nor were expected to show any interest in the outer world. But in the present day context, due to the change in socio-economic conditions of our society, women – both the unmarried and the married with children – are forced to work outside the home to give their children and family a better life and sometime also to earn the bread which is a very common phenomenon in an urban setting. Thus, one may find a large number of working mothers engaged in the labour force. Women's role and position, at present in this new situation are, therefore, ambivalent which is typical in a state of transition. Neither the working mother, their husband and other relatives, nor the society in general are clear and definite about their roles in this particular situation. So far as the status and role of women in our society are concerned, the question is no longer one of capability but has become one of social expediency (Chakraborty, 1978).

For working mothers, job responsibility is very demanding not only in terms of time, but also of energy coupled with the stress factor of the job. In such a situation, it is not easy to cope with the pressure of a high-stress job and the demands of a baby as well as family. Due to the job responsibilities of the working mothers, they can't even spend enough time with their children. As a result they suffer from a kind of conflicting situation, both covert and overt coupled with conscience of irresponsibility, anxiety and overstrain. Out of this inner conflict, the working mothers used to replenish her long absence and lack of due responsibilities by giving various types of inducements to their children for their self-satisfaction. In contrast, the non-working mothers are more focused on their family and children rather than self. These are all very common problems and scenarios in an urban set-up which have been discussed many a time but still it is a big problem and requires further attention.

The research done over the last 40 years shows that the mother's employment status is separately not that much an important variable whereas the study on the children of working and non-working mothers in addition to the previous one reveal meaningful differences. Relationships have to be examined with attention to other variables that have moderated effects, such as social class, the mother's marital status, whether the employment was full or part-time, the parents' attitudes, and the child's gender. (Effects are different in the middle class than in the lower class and different for boys than for girls).

Although very few works have been carried out directly in this topic in India, it has been seen that many research works have been done abroad. The scholars who have worked abroad studying the conflicting situation of women includes the works of Levine's *Mother vs. Mother* (1985), Engel's *Urban Women: Balancing Work and Child Care* (2000), Hillebrand's *The Woes of the Working Mother* (2003), Hoffman's *The Effects of the Mother's Employment on the Family and the Child* (1989), etc. Whereas in India, work has been done dealing with a related important aspect of this paper-child rearing practices. The work includes the contribution of Philip Mayer (1970) on the 'Socialization: The Approach from Social Anthropology', Aphale (1976) in the publication of 'Growing up in an Urban Complex', Bhogly (1978) on child rearing practices among three groups (Hindus, Backward Hindus and Muslims) of Hyderabad city; Kar (1995) on some basic fact of child rearing practices among the Tea Labour of Assam, and so on.

Area of Study

The present study has been conducted in Ward No. 25 under the jurisdiction of Howrah Municipal Corporation that falls under the purview of Shibpur Police Station. The area is inhabited by the Bengali people with Mahisya caste, followed by the Brahmins and Kayastha. The urban setting of the studied area is very interesting for such a study as it includes mothers engaged in two sectors on the basis of nature of job-formal (encompasses all jobs with normal hours and regular wages, and are recognized as income sources on which income taxes must be paid and informal sector with reverse features (as maid servant, care work, tea stall, labour, etc.) living in both slum and non-slum areas.

Objectives of the Study

The present study intends to see the problems of the working mothers, including their children:

1. Whether the mothers' employment affects their children's socialization process or not.
2. Whether this impact is different from that of a non working or home stay mothers.

Method

This is mainly a qualitative study. The data for the present purpose has been collected from the working and non working mothers by using open ended questionnaires, interview, and observation method. Census records (covering age, sex, ethnicity, income, education, occupation, etc.) have been taken into consideration. Case studies have also been taken into account to understand the problems of the working mothers and their children as well as from the non-working mothers and their children. Purposive stratified sampling has been done for this.

Studied Population

Table 1 shows that the numbers of male child are slightly greater than the female. The highest percentage (34.29%) in case of male can be found in the age group 5–9 years. The sex ratio is not balanced and for the children it appears to be 880 female per 1,000 male. Probably, the child preference of a boy is evident among the working mother.

Table 1

Age and Sex-Wise Distribution of Issues of Working Mothers

Age Group (in Years)	*Male*		*Female*		*Total*	*%*
	No.	*%*	*No.*	*%*		
0–4	6	17.14	4	18.18	10	17.54
5–9	7	20.00	9	40.91	16	28.07
10–14	12	34.29	4	18.18	16	28.07
Total	25	71.43	17	77.27	42	73.68

On the other hand, a sample of 31 families with working mothers and 29 families with non-working mothers have been selected out of total 173 families for the study. Moreover, out of these total 173 families, the nuclear family type contributes the bulk of 93 per cent followed by 19 per cent extended and only 3 per cent joint family both in slum and non-slum areas. The mothers working in formal sector have small families (48.39%) whereas medium (32.25%) to large (19.36%) family size with more than two issues is common among the mothers working in informal sector.

Most of the working mothers from Brahmin (43.75%) and Kayastha (33.05%) are engaged in formal sector and only about 23 per cent in informal type of job. Most of the working mothers from Mahisya caste (73.34%) are involved in informal sector and the remaining 26 per cent of the same caste in formal one.

The age group of working mothers from 21–45 years has been taken into consideration, working in both sectors. Mothers working in formal sector include teachers in government and non government sectors, lawyers, working in private firms, etc. with educational qualification from Higher Secondary to Post-Graduate; whereas mothers from informal sector include maid servant, cook, care worker, working at a tea stall, etc. They are mostly non-literate with a few exceptions (22%).

The fathers living in slum area are mainly rickshaw pullers. Besides this, a few (29%) are broker, vegetable seller, owner of a tea stall and most of them are educated upto class III (63%), followed by class V to VIII (15%) passed and the remaining part include those who are non-literate or and can sign their name only; whereas fathers of non slum area are engaged in research work, schools, private companies, multi national companies, having educational qualification of Graduate and Post-Graduate, including various professional courses.

The path between the mother's employment and child outcomes is a long process covering many steps in between. To understand how maternal employment affects a child, one has to understand how it affects the family because it is through the family that the effects take place. Previous research works, as well as the present study, indicate that the various aspects of the family are hence affected by the mother's employment and, in turn, affect the child. The various aspects includes the father's role, the mother's sense of well-being, the qualitative time spent by the working mothers with their children and the parents' parenting styles that is how they interact with their children and the goals they hold for them, etc. Before entering into the findings and discussion part, a few case studies have been mentioned in the following paras:

Case Study–I

Father's Name: Gurupada Samanta (39)
Education: M.Sc., Doing research works
Occupation: Lecturer
Married: 11 years

Mother's Name: Nandini Samanta(34)
Education: Graduate (B.A., B.Ed.)
Occupation: School teacher
Children: A daughter (9) and a son (3)

The four live in a flat separately. No elder person is there to look after the children. They have two part-time paid maids – one for household works and other to look after the children during the parents absence. But Nandini can not rely on her fully. Hence, she has to make alternative arrangement whereby her own sister and mother came to stay to look after the children till from school in the evening. Though her elder daughter is quite responsible to take care of her little brother, mainly after school hours. Nandini feels that she is neglecting her children even in their education as they are not getting their mother's time and involvement in studies and in other aspects too as much they want study. In this case, though Samanta does not express any opinion or objection to his wife's job but still he believes that it hampers the home, especially the rearing of their children. But still he tries to help her wife and family by extending his co-operation.

Case Study–II

Father's Name: Gouranga Dutta (40)
Education: Graduate (B.Com)
Occupation: Business
Married: 16 years

Mother's Name: Dola Dutta (39)
Education: Graduate (B.A.)
Occupation: Employee in a private firm
Children: A son (13+ years)

They three live in the same household along with Gouranga's two elder brother's family, but separately. Mr Dutta is busy with his business throughout the day and hence is unable to perform his duty for his family and son. So, Dola has to manage the entire job responsibilities at home and working place, too. They don't have any paid servant. Managing all these three spheres of home, business and hers on Dola becomes so tired and tempted especially when she goes for teaching her son at night. In absence of Dola, her son has to serve his own food at afternoon; he even has to arrange his tiffin. That is why, considering her son's future, Dola and her husband had admitted their only son in a boarding school before he was four years. But within few weeks, the boy comes back to his home. Dola still can't give much time and attention to his son and son's study. She feels that her son is becoming disobedient, self-centred, demanding and not only is he in bad company with some senior boys of their locality but he has also started smoking. Presently, to fulfil his monetary and outside needs, he sometimes steals money from his parents purse and things from other family members. Dola feels that it happens due to their (father and mother) long absence from home coupled with time and physical constraints.

Case Study–III

Father's Name: Kabol Chandra Ghorui (35)
Education: Can sign only
Occupation: Business
Married: 13 years

Mother's Name: Lakshmi Ghorui (29)
Education: Class II passed
Occupation: Maid servant, business
Children: A son; Biswajit (12), two daughters; Chaitali (9), and Mamoni (5)

Ghoruis have their own tea and snacks (*tele bhaja*) stall. They all live in a slum area. The shop is situated in a popular market place near to their home. In requirement of helping hands during morning, evening and night time (as peak hours) in this shop, Lakshmi used to help her husband in their shop from evening to night because at morning she works as a maid servant and serves three different families. His elder son Biswajit helps his father from 8 am to 10 am. Sometimes even in the evening, he has to extend his help either to his father or his mother in absence of the other. He is only class III passed and he has discontinued his study. Moreover, for the last 5 months he has joined the labour force and is working as a child labourer in an iron factory and there he works from 11 am to 5:30 pm everyday except Sunday. On the other hand, in absence of these three family members, Chaitali takes care of her little sister and the neighbourers also take care of these two. Lakshmi realizes that it is her luck and the economic necessity that his son had to sacrifice his study and childhood. Moreover, she is sad as she can't take proper care and can't provide proper facilities to her children for their future and growth. But still she wants to provide a better life and bright future to her son and daughters.

Findings

Though most of the working mothers feel that they are in much more advantageous position than the non-working mothers as they really can provide more facilities to their children due to their job and financial freedom and for this they feel a sense of pride and accomplishment but still the working mothers suffer from multidimensional problems and face conflicting situations which are as follows:

Findings–I

Problems of the Working Mothers

The working mothers mainly suffer from two types of conflict – inter-role and intra-role conflict.

The working mothers feel that it is not easy in the family for them to work outside without proper arrangement and management. Many adjustments are required for that, and even then also it cannot be done successfully. Most of the time the family members though accept the idea that their housewives will work outside, they are not willing to excuse or co-operate with them and help them to fulfil duties as career mothers, creating a lag between action and attitude and this in turn gives rise to intra-conflict situation within a family.

Sometimes even a comment from their children or family members make them feel the conscience or guilty of their ways.

Another type of problem as experienced by the working mothers arises from the inner conflict of feelings of guilt, anxiety and tension since they fail to give full attention to their children due to their job responsibilities. They feel guilty of neglecting their children and their families because of their career. This further takes an emotional toll on them. Gradually this covert guilt feeling and anxiety of the working mothers are transmitted not only to their children but they also make everybody anxious and a kind of neurotic tendencies may develop out of this in the whole family.

Above 90 per cent working mothers from formal sector try to make up this lacuna of their part by giving various inducements (as money, sweets, chocolates and expensive presents) to their children and thus spoil them.

Again the conflict of the working mothers may be of two types – physical and psychological. One is due to the practical difficulty of combining simultaneously two diverse types of commitments and two contradictory role expectations. Here the problems arise from the physical strain which the working mothers have to face while distributing their limited time, energy and physical capability between two full time roles which continuously put their demands on the incumbent. While performing their duties at home and at work place, they hardly find any leisure. The multiple role performance of a woman as wife, mother and career woman saps all her energy and the psychological and emotional price she has to pay is excessive.

As the working mothers face a triple burden of home, children and job, in the evening after returning from office when the working mothers sit with their children for their study, they soon become angry, insensitive and irritable and their role conflict spontaneously expresses overtly.

Today with the break down of the joint family system, elderly family members are no longer at hand to look after the children, and with the maids being both unreliable and difficult to procure. Moreover, the mothers are aware about the fact that the servants though look after a child's basic needs in their absence, they still cannot be responsible for the child's intellectual, social and emotional development. During this crucial time of a child's life and development, the working mothers just can't give their baby to a complete stranger to mould but they have to. They know that these are the years that can either make or break the child for the rest of his/her life. So this in turn creates another mental and emotional toll on the working mothers.

The problem is more serious among the working mothers with newly born children (within one year) because this time period is considered as very crucial for proper growth (changing of nappies, feeding time to time, etc.) and development of language, individual identity, the learning of self-control and cognitive skills which further demands intensive parental care. So another problem arises in this part related to leave. Those who work in formal sector avail 180 days of maternity leaves whereas mothers working in informal sector have a risk of losing their income and job too.

The problems of the working mothers are different in case of pre-school care and school-going kids (to keep them occupied in after-school hours).

In addition to this, the working mothers, mainly working in an informal sector is more vulnerable to violence and harassment at the workplace (about 33%).

Findings–II

Problems of the Children of the Working Mothers

The little children of the working mothers cannot understand the mental complications and conflicts of their mothers, what they find is that their mothers are very insensitive which in turn threatens or breaks parent-child relationship.

In case of a single child, the problem is more acute. As an effect of their mothers' job and long absence from home, the children get habituated to various inducements and gifts from their mothers as compensation and as a consequence the children become more demanding, arrogant, stubborn, selfish, self-centred and with a lessened sense of responsibility to their family and society.

The long absence of the mothers also has a negative impact on their children's academic and social performances.

Those children who let themselves into a cold and empty house after school hours, and are left to amuse them are becoming increasingly common today. Children of working mothers may feel neglected and seek stimulation outside the house. There is always a danger of such children becoming delinquents and sullen. Sometimes their personality becomes distorted and they may start taking drugs, alcohol, etc. or often may get into bad company as the last resort. Though these are the rare findings (above 12 years boys) but still a very few children in non-slum area are prone to make social crimes (stealing money from the parents) to meet their outside needs.

Moreover, many a time little children suffer from various physical problems like malnutrition due to long gap in feeding, unhygienic, etc.

Findings–III

Problems of the Non-Working Mothers

The connection of children with their mothers at a young age creates a close bond. The attention and moral values that a child receives from his/her mother and family help and guide that child in a positive direction as he gets older. The non-working mothers are satisfied in this respect as they can spend their whole time with their children. But somehow most of them at any time feel that their life is becoming meaningless, disheartening due to the burden of monotonous household routine which they are performing everyday since they have chosen to be a non-working mother.

Though the home stay mothers are working round the clock even if they don't go to office but still their service and devotion to their family demand a great value. But this value of a housewife as mother, her love and care for the children and spouse at home is not appreciated at all. As a result, full-time non-working mothers are angered and shaken by this low esteem with which many career women regard them.

While a working mother has a wide range of social and professional contacts, the non-working mothers at a certain time become isolated to her immediate surroundings. This lack of adult support can lead into depression and the feeling of being overwhelmed by what lies before them.

While the non-working mothers are staying at home for the betterment of their children academically and emotionally, the amount of actual quality time is not always as sufficient as that of a working mother. The time spent at home is usually utilized for completing household chores that does not include spending time with the child.

Findings–IV

Problems of the Children of Non-Working Mothers

The children of non-working mothers always compare themselves with the children of working mothers as those children get their desired things and expensive gifts from their working mothers, whereas the non-working mothers fail to do it.

While comparing with the children of working mothers, sometime the children (10–14 years) of non-working mothers feel that they don't have that much space or axis so that they can lead their personal lives according to their wish as their mothers are staying with them for the whole day watching their children in every activity.

Analysis

The conflicts and findings are not in general sense but only related to the concerned field area. From the above findings it can be inferred that this new feature of mothers' employment in an urban setting has a far reaching impact affecting them, their children as well as the whole society. It has been seen that most of the time the working mothers are dissatisfied with their working place and the family as they can't give their best in any of the two and often caught in between with a kind of covert quilt or conscience of irresponsibility and mental toll. Thus, it creates a conflicting situation in their mind itself as they are not able to find any satisfactory or balancing way. Not only this, the overstrain, triple burden and anxiety gives rise to an inner conflict among the working mothers which further manifests overtly in their behaviour by making them insensitive, short tempered while interacting with their children and other family members. This conflicting situation of the working mothers has a direct relation with intra-family relationships (relation between husband and wife, among siblings, parent-sibling and among others). The co-operative and adjusting relation between husband and wife lessens the burden of a working mother at home and thus minimize her inner conflict and mental strain. Again the relationship between two or more children in a single family is more friendly, sociable, sharing and adjustable, decreasing mother's tensions and worries whereas in case of a single child they become more self-oriented with less sense of responsibility in them which further increases psychological strain of the mothers. Moreover, a relative or governess or maid plays a significant role by helping the mothers. Especially if this agent is a female member then she plays a vital role being a representative of his/her mother in any crisis of a child during the mother's working hours. On the other hand, the children of the working mothers are becoming much more demanding, emotional, self-centred, delinquents and sullen with less adjustable power in the family. They found their mothers' insensitive and impatient attitude towards their children and this gradually creates a distance between the working mothers and their children thus loosening the traditional strong and close bonding between them. The other side of the coin shows that the non-working mothers are also dissatisfied frustrated due to their monotonous, rewardless job and life. It has been revealed from their version that most of the non-working mothers lament for not having that kind of qualification, education, and financial freedom like the working mothers and even to some extent they are devoid from this less known outer world with loose social network. Side by side their children feel that they have no choice to do things independently as their mothers forced them based on their personal liking and disliking. Not only that they think they don't have any privacy as their home stay mothers always stay with them watching their all activities.

Conclusion

Working mothers, as a level, refers to women who are mothers and who work outside the home for income in addition to the work they perform at home in raising their children. Their attitudes toward their jobs and their decisions about child care are shaped by a range of social and economic factors: (i) marital status and family structure, (ii) type of job, (iii) income level, (iv) number and ages of their children including their special care, so on and so forth. Again the problems of working mothers and their children are prone towards dissatisfaction which in a way disrupts the whole socialization process. Out of the guilty conscience and call of irresponsibility, most of the working mothers from formal sector practice providing various types of inducements to their children. The children of the working mothers get habituated to this type of inducements and gifts which further makes them more insistent and gradually a tenacity to make social crime arises among them (resulting impaired socialization). Again, in informal sector the working mothers are practicing child labour by taking their children to join the labour force snatching their childhood only for the sake of economic benefit. As a result this neglecting attitude of working mothers due to their job responsibility, economic need and moreover their conflict between economic and social responsibility though different in forms in two sectors but are affecting their responsibility towards their family and children and giving rise to impaired socialization. As a consequence, a working mother often fails miserably but unintentionally to perform her due responsibilities in the socialization process of her children. So, it is the high time for all of us to reshape the changes in women's roles in this changed social perspective by reconsidering the factors as household responsibilities and job sharing by implementing alternative day care arrangement, flex-time or part-time job, shifting duty, strategies for childcare, means of obtaining food security and even to promote community awareness and education considering the crucial factors for the healthy development of a child and a happy family life as the foundation for the child's security and well being. Moreover, the society and state should take proper steps to play their responsibility by applying proper devise to solve this conflicting situation of the working mothers and also concentrate to solve this kind of impaired situation in socialization.

References

Bandyopadhyay, Asit Kumar. 1995. *Howrah Saharer Itivritta*. Vol. II, Shibpur: Lions Press.

Chakraborty, Krishna. 1978. *The Conflicting Worlds of Working Mothers*. Calcutta: Progressive Publishers.

Hagedorn, Robert et al. (ed.). 1983. *Sociology*. Dubuque: Brown Company Publishers.

Jena, Sanjoy Ketan. 1993. *Working Women and Modernization*. New Delhi: Efficient Offset Printers.

Maitra-Sinha, Anjana. 1993. *Women in a Changing Society*. New Delhi: Ashish Publishing House.

Mayer, Philip (ed.). 1970. *Socialization: The Approach from Social Anthropology,* New York, London: Tavistock.

24

Legal Horizons

The Legal Hopes and Realities Regarding Mass Migration in America

SARAH ROGERS

Mass migration has a tremendous impact on laws on local, national and international levels. Universally, the rights of migrants are often overlooked or completely ignored. Because countries have sovereign power over who they decide allow to become citizens, many migrants are forced to stay in countries that do not provide them with a humane way of life. Many migrants are simply denied the right of freedom of movement. The right to freedom of passage is considered a progressive entitlement of nondiscrimination and gives individuals the right to freedom of choice. Although there are many laws meant to aid migrants, these laws are often not enforced. On a global level, Marchetti suggests that a new form of global citizenship be introduced thus making the issue of original residency less significant (Marchetti, 2008). This paper will discuss migration on a global level, laws and acts passed in the US concerning migration and migrant health, Presidents Bush and Obama's migration policies, and the effects immigration laws have on families.

The United States is an example of one of the countries in the world that has faced mass immigration issues. For example, the US Citizenship and Immigration Services has enacted laws enabling non-US citizens to be eligible for citizen status for a longer period of time than originally intended (National Immigration Law Center, 2005). Also, many laws have been passed relating to migrant health. Many of the laws, however, need more co-operation from healthcare providers (Youdelman, 2008). Like former President Bush, President Obama advocates tightening the reigns on border control and policies meant to help migrants. Both presidents believe that migrants should be allowed to the United States to work because of the country's history of being comprised of immigrants (Organizing for America, 2013). Finally, one of immigration's laws biggest shortcomings is that family policy tends to be overlooked. Unfortunately, immigration law focuses on border control and employment opportunities instead of keeping families united (Holland, 2008).

Global citizenship will provide a way for migrants to be free to move and join different societies. It provides an alternative to global migratory management and open border policies. Multilayered citizenship and political membership developed under a universal membership regime will ensure the social, civil, and political rights of all migrants (Marchetti, 2008). The aspiration to promote the ideal of a world community coincides with universal rights (Carter, 1997). For social welfare to be increased, freedom of movement needs to be arranged within a multilayered scheme of political rights. If a global, single principle of justice were created, a system would be generated that is internally differentiated and thoroughly consistent. The manner in which migrants are treated will become a test of the soundness of the political system (Marchetti, 2008).

A focus on global citizenship is likely to require rejection of loyalty to a particular state. However, nationalism conflicts with the idea of worldwide Human Rights and the idea of a global community (Carter, 1997). Migrants will benefit from the idea that individuals, not tribes, communities, or nations make up the main 'units of concern.' Individuals should give each other the same amount of concern, even if they do not share the same nationality, religion, or characteristics (Pogge, 1992). It is important not only that immigrants appreciate the opportunity for global acceptance or citizenship but also that the people accepting immigrants into their countries willingly extend the gift of citizenship. Unfortunately, hostility to foreign immigrants is prevalent in countries such as France, Britain and the United States. One reason that hostility is tolerated by governments of the world is to maintain a cohesive national identity. Therefore, xenophobia is encouraged by some governments, thus causing an erosion of the most basic form of global citizenship: the right to live safely elsewhere (Carter, 1997).

Around the world the accepted, traditional stance on migration gives each state the sovereign power to accept or reject immigrants. When a country exercises its right to reject a foreigner into its territory, it contributes to an atmosphere of international exclusionism – each country strives to accept only the 'best' immigrants or no immigrants at all. Therefore, this sovereign power becomes part of the problem, not part of the solution (Marchetti, 2008). Dauvergne says that failures of policy, imagination, and law are due to state sovereignty. Therefore, sovereignty is often an obstacle to exercising the opportunity to extend rights and protections to immigrants. Thus, the state itself often encourages illegal immigration. States desire to maintain control of migration even though some of the efforts toward control are not reasonable. For example, sealing borders denying immigrants the right to travel to other parts of the world is counterproductive and will not address the core of the problem (Dauvergne, 2008). Maintaining the idea that immigration laws are aimed first at protecting the state is logical. However, this nationalistic concept limits the rights of people to be citizens in parts of the world where they were not born. According to some theorists then, deterring nations the sovereignty to refuse immigrants is the only way forward (Dauvergne, 2008).

In order to follow this line of thinking then, it becomes clear that creating legal global citizenship will require some form of supranational government. The way this can be achieved is to place some limits on state governments and to make it possible for citizens around the globe to have a voice. A good option is to introduce reforms to the United Nations starting with a more representative group of members of the Security Council. Another option is to have a second

UN Assembly that is elected by the peoples of the world (Archibugi and Held, 2011). More and more states are realizing the possibility of people having multiple allegiances. An international organization that is dedicated to the global deliberation on managing migration would be beneficial. The different stakeholders have the chance to present and weigh their claims from an equal standing. If the world were to develop a global migratory regime, states would lose their privilege of being the sovereign power on the admission of foreigners. Some of the injustices that are occurring under the current nation-led system could be erased if there were a world migratory regime (Marchetti, 2008).

Another option to aid the establishment of global citizenship would be to have a World Migration Agency. If such an agency were formed, it could possibly operate under the umbrella of the United Nations. This would provide for a place to have negotiations, implement policies, or address conflicting claims. It should have supranational power that has the authority to override national decisions. This agency should be characterized by all-inclusiveness (Marchetti, 2008).

The United States has been one of those countries in the world that has dealt with the issue of mass migration. There have been many Acts to alleviate the strains on migrants presented to the US Congress. The Dream Act was proposed for the development, relief, and education for alien minors. It addresses young people who grew up in the United States and graduated from high school, but whose future is compromised by current immigration laws denying them the right to continue their education (National Immigration Law Centre, 2010). Under the present law, if these young people have parents who are not documented they have no way to obtain legal residency. The Dream Act would permit individuals who have grown up in the US to apply for *conditional non-immigrant status*. Individuals qualify if they display good moral character since entry and if they came to the US at 15 years of age or younger. Furthermore, students will receive *conditional non-immigrant status* upon acceptance to college, graduation from a US high school, or being awarded a GED Individual will not qualify if they have committed crimes or are a security risk. Under this bill, individuals will have to prove that during a ten year period of *conditional non-immigrant status* that they had upheld good moral character, not committed certain crimes, refrained from violating travel restrictions, and paid back-taxes. After three years in legal permanent resident status, individuals would be able to apply for citizenship (NILC, 2010). While this bill would have proven to be valuable for migrants, it was not passed by the US Congress, and young people in this position still face problems when attempting to become citizens. It is imperative that Congress find a satisfactory way to pass this legislation.

The Safe, Orderly, Legal Visas and Enforcement (SOLVE) Act is a bill that would strengthen employment and labour protections for workers in the US. This bill would include immigrant workers and workers who would be employed under a temporary worker program that would be created by the act. The act would establish an *earned adjustment program* where most undocumented workers in the US could apply for lawful permanent resident status. It would also provide *family reunification* designed to address the problem of the huge backlog of family-based visa applications and other issues that keep families apart for years. The act would also strengthen worker protection provisions. It would provide for a transitional status for workers who are present in the US but cannot meet all earned adjustment requirements. The Solve act would also recognize that workers are not to be denied any monetary relief funds for unlawful employment practices, even if the employee was hired in violation of immigration laws (NILC, 2004).

While the Dream and Solve acts would have proven valuable to immigrants, they were not passed by the United States Congress (NILC, 2010). In spite of the well-intentioned efforts of some lawmakers, migrants still have to deal with education and employment issues. In the United States, it is imperative that Congress finds a satisfactory way to pass bills to legalize the basic rights of these migrants. The same issues of migration will continue to be world-wide problems until remedies are not only proposed but actually put into action. Until then, the future is extremely grim for migrants. Moreover, the United States and other countries with immigration issues will have to realize that educating and employing their immigrants is more beneficial to the country than excluding them.

Another problem facing migrants is their healthcare. The International Organization for Migration aims to reduce and prevent the repercussions of both infectious and non-infectious migration-related diseases. Medical screening and evaluation practices need to be under constant supervision because of the evolution of diseases and ill health in migrant populations (International Organization for Migration, 2003). Using the United States as a universal example, it is common that immigrants in the US do not speak English 'very well' and receive less access and lower quality of health care. About one in 12 Americans are not able to receive adequate healthcare because they have limited English proficiency (Youdelman, 2008). Encountering language barriers leads to inadequate health literacy, which is associated with higher mortality. The International Organization for Migration (IOM) provides assistance to formulating policies on migration-related health topics including health education, publications, and supporting the well-being of migrant populations. It also seeks to ensure quality care of physicians (IOM). A major part of the care migrants need to receive is help in alleviating the problem of the language barrier. Non-English speaking patients are less likely to use preventative care and public services. Instead, they use emergency and receive fewer services than patients who speak English (Youdelman, 2008).

The IOM and healthcare system can aid migrants facing language barriers by realizing that capable language services are a necessity. Again, in the United States, essentially every healthcare provider must abide by Title VI of the Civil Rights Act of 1964, which states that federal money will not support providers who discriminate on the basis of colour, race, or national origin (Youdelman, 2008). The US Department of Health and Human Services and the Supreme Court have interpreted Title VI to protect minorities who do not speak English well. Therefore, if an American healthcare provider accepts federal funding, then he/she must provide assistance to patients who have limited English proficiency. In 2000, President Clinton issued Executive Order 13177, 'Improving Access to Persons with Limited English Proficiency', which brought renewed attention to title VI. It was reinstated by President Bush in 2001 and called for each federal agency to draft guidance tailored to its federal fund recipients (Youdelman, 2008). Despite these federal laws, however, lack of enforcement and education leaves millions of people unable to receive the same quality of care obtained by English speakers (Youdelman, 2008).

Though former President Bush reinstated Executive Order 13177, many of his other attempts at migration reform were met with conflict (Kirkpatrick, 2005). Bush proposed a guest worker programme and called it a priority, but Republicans did not put it on their list of top goals. Bush wanted a programme that would allow migrants to come to the US and work for a period of time. He stated that he wanted to deal with the issue compassionately and humanely. Conservatives, however, opposed Bush's guest worker plan and said it provided amnesty to illegal immigrants (Kirkpatrick, 2005). President Bush and his advisors always sensitively addressed immigration issues because they wanted to strengthen his appeal to the fast-growing Hispanic population (Stevenson, 2005). Bush tried to satisfy both groups by toughening border enforcement coupled with his proposal of a guest-worker programme (Bumiller, 2006). His programme would allow some of the estimated 11 million immigrants into the US to register for legal status. The immigrants could remain in the US for up to six years. The former president asserted that the US benefits from the immigration of hardworking people and that the country is a land of immigrants (Bumiller, 2006). It is important to note that President Bush grew up in an American state with a shared border. As a Texan, Bush was accustomed to Americans and Hispanics crossing each other's borders to live and work. Therefore, his stance on immigration was actually more liberal than that of the Republican Party. It becomes apparent that those who fear immigration could benefit from the experiences of those who have grown up on borders and have learned to expect immigration. The whole world could benefit from 'living on the border' as President Bush did.

President Obama, like Bush, is trying to appease everyone with his immigration policy. He is pushing for tough border control while reaffirming our heritage as a nation of immigrants. The Obama administration has used unprecedented resources in securing US borders and weakening the flow of illegal traffic. While the administration has tightened border control, it has also attempted to aid immigrants. A website has been launched that permits legal immigrants to check the status of their applications online and via text messages. This website is unprecedented, and three million people registered for its services in its first month alone (OFA). President Obama also supports a system that allows undocumented immigrants who are in good standing to pay a fine, learn English, and go to the back of the line to become US citizens. To alleviate the economic desperation that leads to illegal immigration, President Obama will back economic growth in Mexico. Finally, the Obama administration wants to facilitate legal immigration so that families can stay together.

The mass migration of individuals inevitably affects families. The modern immigration debate is usually focused on border control and employment opportunities. Family policy is often overlooked (Holland, 2008). Because of this omission, immigration law has a limited vision of the family unit. The US Supreme Court has held that having different sets of rules for mothers and fathers wanting to apply for citizenship is not in violation of the Equal Protection Clause. Immigration law also requires an unmarried father, but not an unmarried mother, to verify a legitimate relationship with his child in order to petition for that child's immigrant visa (Holland, 2008). There can be no advantage either to the United States or globally to separating parents and children.

While there are different standards for men and women that negatively affect families during the immigration process, there have also been laws passed in the United States that are designed to assist families. Other countries might do well to consider adopting the V Visa procedure which was established as part of the Legal Immigration Family Equity Act of 2000. It permits spouses and children of legal permanent residents to have a lawful status while waiting to become legal permanent residents (NILC, 2005). The prior Immigration and Naturalization Service provided that non-citizens would lose their V–2 or V–3 once they turned 21 years old. Luckily, this policy has been reversed and a 'no age-out' policy has been adopted (NILC, 2005). It is imperative that immigration law's implicit regulation of the family is recognized. Lawmakers must be encouraged to better understand and calibrate immigration law's effects on families (Holland, 2008). If immigration law does not receive some adjustments, the goal of family unification will only unite some families while other contemporary families will be kept apart. One of the primary goals of immigration law should be family unification (Holland, 2008).

Immigration is a global issue that will need global resolution. It is idealistic to hope that we will all become 'citizens of the world.' However, the effects of mass immigration will cause world-wide problems without world-wide help. Therefore, the experiences of countries like the United States should be studied for positive and negative examples of ways to deal with the immigration problems. Finding solutions to these problems will be a global benefit.

References

Archibugi, Daniele and David Held. (eds.). 2011. From the United Nations to Cosmopolitan Democracy. *Cosmopolitan Democracy*. Cambridge: Polity Press. pp. 121–162. (January).

Bumiller, Elisabeth. 2006. 'Bush is Facing a Difficult Path on Immigration.' *The New York Times*, March 24. Electronic document <http://www.nytimes.com/2006/03/24/politics/24bush.html> (January 7th, 2010).

Carter, A. 1997. Nationalism and Global Citizenship. *The Australian Journal of Politics and History*. Vol. 43(1), pp. 67–81.

Dauvergne, Catherine. 2008. *Making People Illegal: What Globalization Means for Migration and Law*. Cambridge: Cambridge University Press.

Holland, Aubry. 2008. The Modern Family Unit: Toward a More Inclusive Vision of the Family in Immigration Law. *California Law Review*. Vol. 96(4), (August).

International Organization for Migration 2003. 'Project Areas.' Electronic document <http://iom.ramdisk.net/iom/artikel.php?menu_id=2#labou> (6 January 2010).

Kirkpatrick, David D. 2005. 'Republicans Squaring Off Over Bush Plan on Immigration.' *The New York Times*, January 27. Electronic document <http://www.nytimes.com/2005/01/27/politics/27.immig.html> (January 6th, 2010).

Marchetti, Raffeale. 2008. Toward a World Migratory Regime. *Indiana Journal of Global Legal Studies.* Vol. 15(2), pp. 471–487.

National Immigration Law Center. 2005, 'CIS to end Age-Out Policy for V–2 and V–3 Visa. *Immigrants' Rights Update. (*February). Electronic document <http://www.nilc.org/immlaw/Policy/obtainlpr/oblpr106.htm>

National Immigration Law Center. 2010. 'Dream Act: Summary.' Electronic document http://www.nilc.org/im/Mlawpolicy/dream/dream-bills-summary–2010–09–20.pdf

National Immigration Law Center. 2004. 'Solve Act: Democrats Introduce Comprehensive Immigration Reform Proposal.' *Immigrants' Rights Update. Electronic document* http://www.nilc.org/immlawpolicy/obtainlpr/oblpr101.htm

Organizing for America, 2013. 'Comprehensive Immigration Reform.' Electronic document http://www.Barackobama.com/issues/immigrationre form/ index.php

Pogge, T.W. 1992. 'Cosmopolitan and Sovereignty'. *Ethics.* 103: 48–49.

Stevenson, Richard W. 2005. 'Bush Renews Push to Overhaul Immigration.' *The New York Times.* November 29. Electronic document <http://www.nytimes.com/2005/11/29/politics/29/bush.html> (11 January 2010).

Youdelman, Mara K. 2008. 'The Medical Tongue: U.S. Laws and Policies on Language Access.' *Health Affairs.* 424 *(*March). Vol. 27(2), pp. 242–433.

25

Migration, Legality and Rights

The Case of Undocumented Mexican Youth in the State of Oklahoma (USA)

VICTORIA CHENAUT

Having lived for a few months in Oklahoma City (USA), I would like to speak from my own experiences to reflect upon the circumstances of undocumented Mexican young people who arrive in the country as children along with their immigrant parents, grow up in the United States and have no aspirations to return to their parents' country of birth as they desire to become a part of the American society. Since they do not possess legal papers, it is not possible for them to exercise any rights as citizens; their access to a higher education is limited just as they lack the scopes of finding a job due to their limited education. I would like to talk about some aspects which affect their daily lives and their futures, taking into account their lack of legal documents which lead them to be considered illegal in the country where they have grown up since a young age. This legal status is neither voluntary nor sought out or desired, yet it marks their lives in a contradictory manner. They cannot fully become a part of a country where they live, even though they have on the most part assimilated to the American lifestyle, having gone to elementary and junior high school and having close friends and family. They associate the country with their expectations in life and have no plans to return to their parents' country of origin, to which most are actually unfamiliar with.

These young people could at any moment face a deportation process unexpectedly which could radically change their lives. The words of a young man recently deported to Mexico, begging his Mexican friend living in the United States; 'Help me, I don't know how to get by living in Mexico', sums up the cultural and identity conflict experienced in these types of situations. In the first part of this discussion, I have tried to project the undocumented Mexican youth in the context of a Hispanic youth in the United States and the debate surrounding the Dream Act which, if approved, could grant the former the opportunity to become legal. In the second part, I will comment on the case of the undocumented Hispanic youth in Oklahoma City.

The Vulnerability of Migrants

I will begin with the assumption that laws affect and make an impact on people's lives producing roles, identities and subjectivities which in this case is by means of the definition of legality which has to do with having legal documentation allowing residence in a foreign country. Laws (migratory or any other type) are situated within the historical context and are a product of various processes in which both relationships of power and macro structural conditions are expressed. Currently, this is under a neo-liberal political framework. Although I do not intend to go into the complex history of migratory legislation in the United States, I would like to point out that according to Varsanyi (2009: 882), in the neo-liberal context, this policy implied that the Federal government return partial and incomplete decision-making power to the state authorities to implement federal legislation on migration which, I believe, is relevant in order to discuss the case of Oklahoma's 1804 Law passed in 2007, as described further on.

In 1996, the IIRIRA Act (Illegal Immigration Reform and Immigrant Responsibility Act) was passed at the federal level in the United States limiting the rights of undocumented Mexican migrants (in relation to access to services such as healthcare, state welfare and protection during criminal proceedings and an increase in deportation cases). According to Varsanyi (2099: 892), these laws create a category of people who are beyond the reach of constitutional protection and public welfare programs. Therefore, the number of such laws has grown what Bustamante (2001) calls the 'vulnerability of migrants as subjects of human rights' and I ask myself: How does this affect the situation of the undocumented Mexican youth?[1]

Immigration laws result in individuals who not only live with the awareness that their rights are limited but also with the ongoing fear that either they or their loved ones could be deported. The implications of being or not being legal go beyond the individual level becoming a determining factor affecting families who, as a group of people, are joined by ties of blood and a sense of belonging. Mexican youth who find themselves having an illegal migratory status often are a part of a family whose legal status is mixed, their younger brothers or sisters are perhaps American citizens since they were born in the country. According to the data from the 2005 Census (CONAPO), Marroni (2009: 177–179) demonstrates that 75 per cent of the children of Mexican immigrant heads of families were born in the United States and only 25 per cent of their children migrated from Mexico. There are diverse types of combinations which can be found in terms of the legal and illegal status of members within a family, which is why there are members with different rights which can generate divisions among them (Marroni, ibid.). A plurality of legal status is manifested within families which are dynamically interwoven into daily life, creating tension, conflict, negotiation and accommodation among family members while the fear of being deported, separated and uprooted, is always present and experienced by all, which is the case of deportations in Oklahoma which I am aware of.

The importance the total Hispanic population represents, in terms of numbers, has been pointed out, constituting the largest and youngest minority (in terms of average age) of the US population. Among the Hispanic population, there are high levels of school dropouts and young people who do not continue with a university education which is attributed to various reasons. Young people interviewed by the Pew Hispanic Center mention the need to financially support their families as the most important reason. Twenty-two per cent of the Hispanic youth between the ages of 16 and 25 are undocumented immigrants (Pew Hispanic Center, 2009; Foxen, 2010).

What kind of outlook do they have to become a part of American society? Their expectations are greatly based on the congressional approval of the Dream Act,[2] which would allow undocumented young people to obtain their legal permanent residence and later their citizenship, if they fulfil certain requirements such as completing a minimum of two years of university level education or military service (Martin, 2009). The law would allow them to pay state resident tuition fees and receive financial aid in order to finish their studies. If this legislation gets passed, it will abolish Section 505 of the Law enacted in 1996 (IIRIRA), which prohibited the states to grant any kind of support for university studies to undocumented foreigners, as long as American citizens were eligible for this benefit. However, because this law was unclear about the granting of resident tuition rates for undocumented students, several states, among them, Oklahoma, took measures starting in 2001 to favour such students, allowing them to obtain this benefit of paying state resident tuition rates if they fulfilled certain requirements (Russell, 2007: 2).

Yet the dreams of the undocumented young people were once again crushed due to the outcome of the vote of the Senate in December of 2010, despite their mobilization, hopes of approval and the subsequent disappointment that they felt. Although it is without a doubt that many benefits could have been brought about by the approval of this law for not only these young people but for the entire nation, this lack of approval contributes to the creation of a marginalized class which is poorly educated and therefore has a low work profile (Gonzáles, 2009).[3] The wishes of these young people is reflected in the messages we can see on their signs at Dream Act protests saying 'We are the future of America', 'I have a dream', 'This nation needs an educated (work) force'; we can imagine the chanting as they march towards the capital building[4] demanding the approval of the Dream Act: 'We are dreamers... Powerful, powerful dreamers who will not abandon our struggle for legalization!' This reflects their dream of being legal citizens and rightful active members of the American society.

However, if the Dream Act would be approved, not all of the Hispanic youth would fulfill the requirements for the law as demonstrated by a statistical analysis. Of a total of 2.1 million potential beneficiaries (56% males) and taking into account the educational requirements that the candidates must fulfil, only 38 per cent of them (8,25,000) could obtain legal status through the Dream Act (Batalova and Mc Hugh, 2010).

Migrants in the State of Oklahoma

In 2007, the Oklahoma Tax Payer and Citizen Protection Act was enacted. At the time, it was considered to be one of the most severe laws acting against illegal immigration in the United States since it prohibits obtaining an employment and criminalizes sheltering or transporting undocumented individuals as well as rent housing among other measures.[5] This law has created fear and confusion among migrants and has resulted in 25,000 people leaving the state in order to seek a better future or return to their country. Out of fear of being detained, those who stayed on took measures to avoid any kind of situation which could lead to a sanction or deportation, for instance, not taking a sick child to the hospital, quitting their job, closing bank accounts, not denouncing their spouse in case of domestic violence, and limiting the amount of time spent outside the home or for purchases to an absolute minimum.[6]

Since 2007 and the passing of this Act, other measures have also been taken, one of them being the revision of documents before hiring workers. As a counter measure, there is a large market for false documents, which is not spoken about publicly, as there is an eerie silence around the matter of not having papers, due to the fear of being denounced. According to some talks I have had, this Act is not fully applied as there are citizens who are not willing to denounce the workers who do not have papers. In fact, they show solidarity in many cases; for example, a few have reportedly been kind enough to take an undocumented migrant to the hospital to receive care although they could be sanctioned for such an action.

In spite of the fact that thousands of Hispanics left the state due to this law, the Hispanic population in Oklahoma county grew by 67 per cent between 2000 and 2009, surely due to a new flow of migrants and the adjustment of those who stayed and learned to deal with the limitations imposed by the law.[7] Likewise, the state population of the Hispanic students rose, making up 11 per cent of the total students in public schools in 2009 in comparison to 3 per cent in 1990.[8]

The undocumented youth visualize a future in which their life is unrestricted and they could fully exercise their rights. 'What is it like to be legal?' a young undocumented Mexican girl asked during her presentation at an event on this topic.[9] 'What would it be like to not have to hide and lie in order to move about freely?' What would she feel like if she were legal when she never has been before? Undocumented status radically marks and defines a person's life and restricts the enjoyment of many rights. For those who make a conscious decision to migrate (first generation), the mark is different from that of their children who arrived in the US from a young age (the so called 1.5 generation) (Gonzáles, 2009: 7). The first group can live in the United States for years without speaking English or only understanding the language at an elemental level and carry out their lives living in neighbourhoods among a large Hispanic population (like in the southern part of Oklahoma City), where businesses and services operate in Spanish, they are near their close relatives or related families, their social networks including relatives, friends and 'compadres' reproducing cultural traditions which are anchored by their country of origin.

On the other hand, their children, although they hold on to their Hispanic identity and were partially or fully schooled in the United States, desire to assimilate to the American culture as well as have work opportunities and social mobility just like their friends. Yet they cannot fully enjoy such rights, because they do not have a social security number, finding themselves limited in furthering their education at the university level since they lack financial resources and there are few options for their scholarships. An undocumented Mexican young man described himself as 'fully adapted to the culture but can't enjoy (the culture)'. He says that the dilemma which pervades his life is: (Where do I belong)…'here or there?'[10]

Upon approving Oklahoma's Law of 1804 in 2007, the state legislature halted financial aid that was being granted to those students who were paying state resident tuition rates.[11] Instead, the Oklahoma State Regents for Higher Education was allowed to make decisions concerning the granting of state resident tuition rates to those students who qualified (Adams, 2010).[12] What seems to be a fact is that some state universities give scholarships to students who do not have legal papers, although this does not take place at all state institutions of higher education. The difficulty in continuing with a higher education is certain and makes graduating from high school an especially important event at the end of a school year. It is celebrated with huge graduation parties which are not only important social events but also represent, most likely, their last educational opportunity. According to a psychologist who works with Hispanic migrants, of the few Hispanic young people who graduate from university 'only those who have a great imagination are going to find work within their field.'

An undocumented Mexican student commented that it is difficult to get a job when you don't have papers, even if you have studied, but really 'it's not the end of the world'. For him, the jobs that are easier to get are limited to the service area where the possibilities of upward mobility are quite difficult. However, the words of this young man suggest that his agency is expressed through the way he lives out and faces challenges in his daily life, within the limited status of being both an undocumented individual and a Hispanic.

Finally, I would like to express that the conception of legality/illegality (documented/undocumented) is a product of laws which can be contested by the mobilization of undocumented migrants (Gómez, 2007), the exercise of the right to not vote for legislators who have opposed reforms which benefit migrants and, finally, the use of the state justice system itself through the filing of a lawsuit, as in the case of Oklahoma's 1804 Law. The fact that laws are products of historical processes and changes within the society provides for the imagination of a future where a comprehensive migratory reform can be achieved and all who lack legal papers can hope for a life free of fears and the full enjoyment of their human rights.

Notes

1. Amnesty International defines an 'undocumented migrant' as 'any person who lacks documents which authorize them to legally enter or stay in a country', and due to their legal condition, their human rights are limited (2006: 15).
2. The DREAM Act (Development, Relief and Education for Alien Minors Act) was approved in the year 2010 in the House of Representatives, but in December of the same year, the Senate voted against the project being discussed in this legal body.
3. 'We Cannot Afford not to Pass the DREAM Act: A Plea from American Scholars'. This letter was signed by nearly 400 scholars from 38 states in the country. (Internet)

4. El Universal, Daily Newspaper, December 16, 2010.
5. 'Oklahoma's Law caused an Exodus of Immigrants', January 26, 2008; http://www.diariolibre.com/noticias
6. This law has been challenged before the court which has suspended part of the law.
7. According to information from the year 2008, 90,077 people of Hispanic descent reside in Oklahoma county (13% of the country's population) ('Demographic Profile of Hispanics in Oklahoma', Pew Hispanic Center. http://pewhispanic.org/states/)
8. 'The President renews the national initiative to support Hispanic students', November 14, 2010, http://www.newsok.com
9. Event titled 'The Undocumented Immigrant… in Pursuit of the American Dream', taking place in Oklahoma City University, April 15, 2010.
10. An intervention made at an event titled 'The Undocumented Immigrant…in Pursuit of the American Dream', Oklahoma City University, 15 de abril 2010.
11. 'In-State Tuition and Unauthorized Immigrant Students', National Conference of the State Legislature, Revised January 28, 2010.
12. Besides federal level grant, in Oklahoma there are two grant programs at the state level, one is the Oklahoma Tuition Aid Grant (OTAG), which establishes the eligibility requirements for undocumented immigrants: to have graduated from a public or private High School in the state of Oklahoma, to have resided in the state with a parent or legal guardian for at least 2 years prior to the date of graduation and have a valid temporary visa or have requested the legalization of immigrant status. (http://www.okcollegestart.org/Finantial_Aid). The last requirement is the most difficult to comply with on the part of undocumented youth.

References

Adams, Terrance. 2010. 'In-State Tuition for Illegal Inmigrants'. USA, OLR Research Report. Electronic document, http://www.cga.ct.gov/2010/rpt/2010-R–0497.htm

Amnistía Internacional. 2006. *Vivir en las sombras. Una introducción a los derechos humanos de las personas migrantes*. Madrid, Editorial de Amnistía Internacional.

Batalova, Jeanne and Margie Mc Hugh. 2010. 'Dream vs Reality: An Analysis of Potential Dream Act Beneficiaries'. USA, Migration Policy Institute, National Center on Inmigrant Integration Policy. Electronic document, www.migrationpolicy.org

Bustamante, Jorge A. 2001. 'Un marco conceptual de referencia acerca de la vulnerabilidad de los migrantes como sujetos de los derechos humanos'. En *Los rostros de la violencia*, El Colegio de la Frontera Norte, Tijuana, pp. 19–53.

Foxen, Patricia. 2010. *Speaking Out: Latino Youth on Discrimination in the United States*. USA, National Council of La Raza.

Gonzales, Roberto. 2009. 'Vidas jóvenes en espera: los sueños universitarios de estudiantes indocumentados'. USA, College Board Advocacy. Electronic document, http://professionals.collegeboard.com

Marroni, María da Gloria. 2009. *Frontera perversa, familias fracturadas. Los indocumentados mexicanos y el sueño americano*. Puebla/México D.F., BUAP/Gimtrap.

Martin, Susan F. 2009. 'La política de la reforma de la inmigración en Estados Unidos'. En Agustín Escobar y Susan F. Martin (Coords), *La gestión de la migración*

México-Estados Unidos: un enfoque binacional. México D.F., SEGOB/Instituto Nacional de Migración/CIESAS, pp. 175–203.

Pew Research Center. 2009. *Between Two Worlds. How Young Latinos Come of Age in America*. USA, Pew Hispanic Center. Electronic document, www.pewresearch.org/millennials

Russell, Alene. 2007. 'In-State Tuition for Undocumented Inmigrants: State's Rights and Educational Oportunity'. USA, American Association of State Colleges and Universities, A Higher Education Policy Brief.

Santamaría Gómez, Arturo. 2007. 'El movimiento de los inmigrantes indocumentados en Estados Unidos'. *En Política y Cultura*, No. 27, pp. 99–120.

Varsanyi, Monica W. 2009. *'Rescaling the 'Alien', Recaling Personhood: Neoliberalism, Inmigration and the State'*. USA, University of California, San Diego, The Center for Comparative Immigration Studies, Working Paper 173.

Index